WALES AND THE ARTHURIAN LEGEND

WALES AND THE ARTHURIAN LEGEND

BY

ROGER SHERMAN LOOMIS

M.A. (*Harvard*); B.LITT. (*Oxon.*); HON. D.LITT. (*Wales*)
Docteur Honoris Causa de l'Université de Rennes
Professor of English, Columbia University

THE FOLCROFT PRESS, INC.
FOLCROFT, PA.

First Published 1956

Reprinted 1969

WALES AND THE ARTHURIAN LEGEND

BY

ROGER SHERMAN LOOMIS

M.A. (*Harvard*); B.LITT. (*Oxon.*); HON. D.LITT. (*Wales*)
Docteur Honoris Causa de l'Université de Rennes
Professor of English, Columbia University

CARDIFF
UNIVERSITY OF WALES PRESS
1956

Upsala College
Library
East Orange, N. J. 07019

PRINTED IN GREAT BRITAIN

Preface

It is a matter of great satisfaction and pride to me that the University of Wales Press Board has graciously seen fit to include among its scholarly publications the present group of articles which have appeared separately since 1932. In the order of their appearance and under their original titles the articles were: '"Chastiel Bran", "Dinas Bran", and the Grail Castle', *Miscellany of Studies in Romance Languages and Literatures in Honour of L. E. Kastner* (Cambridge, Heffer and Sons, 1932), pp. 342–50; 'The Irish Origin of the Grail Legend', *Speculum*, viii (1933), 415–31; 'The Arthurian Legend before 1139', *Romanic Review*, xxxii (1941), 3–38; 'King Arthur and the Antipodes', *Modern Philology*, xxxviii (1941), 289–304; 'The Spoils of Annwn', *Publications of the Modern Language Association*, lvi (1941), 887–936; 'More Celtic Elements in *Gawain and the Green Knight*', *Journal of English and Germanic Philology*, xlii (1942), 149–84; 'Morgain la Fée and the Celtic Goddesses', *Speculum*, xx (1945), 183–203; 'The Combat at the Ford in the *Didot Perceval*', *Modern Philology*, xliii (1945), 183–203; 'From Segontium to Sinadon', *Speculum*, xxii (1947), 520–33. I am greatly indebted to the editors of these journals and to Messrs. Heffer and Sons, publisher of the Kastner Miscellany, for permission to reprint these articles in modified form. Most of the articles I have reproduced with little change except for harmonizing the typographical style and bringing up to date the source-references. But I have omitted sections of the articles on 'More Celtic Elements in *Gawain and the Green Knight*' and on 'The Spoils of Annwn', and have made considerable revisions of 'Chastiel Bran'. I have also profited by the corrections and suggestions of Professor Thomas Jones. Finally I have added an article, hitherto unpublished, 'Brân the Blessed and *Sone de Nausay*'.

Readers will understand that the articles were written as separate treatments of various topics and, though there may be some overlapping, there has been no attempt to fit them into a general scheme. Nevertheless, I trust that a consistent interpretation of the complex phenomena of Arthurian tradition, a unifying theory of the origins and development of the Matter of Britain will emerge from these scattered papers. Those whose curiosity may prompt them to explore the subject more fully may find similar views elaborated in Professor Helaine Newstead's *Bran the Blessed in Arthurian Romance* and in my *Arthurian Tradition and Chrétien de Troyes*, both books published by the Columbia University Press.

In dedicating this collection of articles to the late W. J. Gruffydd I wish to acknowledge, however inadequately, the great debt which I have incurred to him since he first permitted me to attend his lectures on the *Mabinogion* at Cardiff in the spring of 1927. These served to elucidate many puzzling features of Welsh literature related to the Arthurian legend so convincingly that, supplemented by his detailed analysis of *Math Vab Mathonwy*, published in 1928, they have guided my thinking ever since, not only about the Welsh texts but also about the vast cycle of stories in many languages which had their roots in Wales.

ROGER SHERMAN LOOMIS

3 December 1955

Contents

I.	*Segontium, Caer Seint, and Sinadon*	1
II.	*The Irish Origin and the Welsh Development of the Grail Legend*	19
III.	*Chastiel Bran, Dinas Brân, and the Grail Castle*	42
IV.	*Brân the Blessed and* Sone de Nausay	53
V.	*King Arthur and the Antipodes*	61
VI.	*Welsh Elements in* Gawain and the Green Knight	77
VII.	*The Combat at the Ford in the* Didot Perceval	91
VIII.	*Morgain la Fée and the Celtic Goddesses*	105
IX.	The Spoils of Annwn: *an Early Welsh Poem*	131
X.	*The Arthurian Legend before 1139*	179
	General Index	221
	Index of Subjects	230

CHAPTER I

Segontium, Caer Seint, and Sinadon

THE majestic architectural remains of Roman civilization have inspired divers works in divers ages. Suffice it to name but a few from the literature of Britain. An Anglo-Saxon poet in the eighth century was moved by the colonnades and courts of Bath to wonder at this work of giants, broken by Wyrd, where once warriors, flushed with wine, gazed on treasure.[1] Giraldus Cambrensis in the twelfth century noted with awe the palaces, temples, theatres, and aqueducts of Caerleon on Usk, vestiges of its former splendour.[2] Spenser published in 1591 a lament of the personified city of Verulamium for the stately buildings, overgrown by black oblivion's rust and haunted by grisly shades.[3] 'It was at Rome, on the 15th of October 1764', wrote Gibbon, 'as I sat musing amid the ruins of the Capitol, while the bare-footed friars were singing vespers in the Temple of Juppiter, that the idea of writing the Decline and Fall of the city first started in my mind.' Byron in 1817 wrote the famous apostrophe to the Niobe of Nations and a long dithyramb on the monuments of her glorious past.

All this, of course, is familiar, but it is not generally recognized how much of medieval legend and romance was twined about those awe-inspiring but crumbling walls which survived for centuries the fall of the imperial city. Bédier, to be sure, bore witness regarding the *chansons de geste* that 'les abris préférés de nos légendes furent les ruines romaines', and noted a score of scenes laid in or near amphitheatres, arches, aqueducts, and cemeteries.[4] And Professor Gruffydd has reached a similar conclusion for the Matter of Britain.[5]

Archaeologists still hope to find Arthur's Round Table at Caerlleon on Usk; they have not yet realised that the old caers of the Romans

---

[1] Text in *Exeter Book*, ed. G. P. Krapp, E. V. K. Dobbie (New York, 1936), pp. 227–9. Trans. and comment in C. W. Kennedy, *Old English Elegies* (Princeton, 1939), pp. 18–22, 67–69.
[2] Giraldus Cambrensis, *Opera*, vi, ed. J. F. Dimock (London, 1868), p. 55.
[3] E. Spenser, *The Ruines of Time*.
[4] J. Bédier, *Les Légendes Épiques*, ed. 3 (Paris, 1913), iv. 413 f.
[5] W. J. Gruffydd, *Math Vab Mathonwy* (Cardiff, 1928), p. 346. Cf. H. M. and N. K. Chadwick, *Growth of Literature* (Cambridge, 1932), i. 297–9.

were to the Britons, in whose minds these legends grew, the symbols of a great past in which they had no part, and that it was the wistful memory of ancient greatness which made them connect their Arthur, born in evil times of good old Roman blood, with the relics of that greatness which they saw about them; so Caer Vyrddin [Carmarthen, where the old brick walls were standing in Giraldus' time], Caer Llion, Caer Seint [Segontium, near Caernarvon] and many another Caer were inevitably made the scenes of Arthur's splendour and great exploits.

Despite these pronouncements of two distinguished scholars, the importance of these memorials of a past civilization in the formation of medieval legends has not been widely realized. The following pages will be devoted to bringing out, more fully than has been done hitherto, how Caer Seint, just mentioned, one of the remotest of the imperial outposts, located at the base of Snowdon, where the River Seint flows into the Menai Strait, persistently served as a focus for the myth-making fancy and called forth a series of legends.

It was probably under the governorship of Agricola that a fort was built on a hill-top above the modern town of Caernarvon, occupying an area of about $5\frac{1}{2}$ acres.[6] The site was excavated some thirty-five years ago, and it was shown that from about A.D. 80 to about 380 Segontium was garrisoned by Roman troops, except for two long intervals. Under Constantius (292–304) a smaller fort, of which some walls are still standing, was erected about 500 yards away on a cliff above the River Seint.[7] Up to 1923 over a thousand coins, known to have been discovered in or near these sites, have been catalogued, including twelve of Helena (wife of Constantius), seventy-four of her son, Constantine the Great, forty-three of his son, Constantine II.[8] From Segontium Roman roads led through the mountains, eastward to Chester and southward to Carmarthen and Caerleon, portions of which are known to this day as Sarn Elen, 'Elen's Causeway'.[9] By one of these routes the last Roman garrison must have withdrawn, perhaps in 383 when Maximus drained the

[6] R. E. M. Wheeler, 'Segontium and the Roman Occupation of Wales', *Y Cymmrodor*, xxxiii (1923), 15–20. See also Wheeler, 'The Segontium Excavations', *Archaeologia Cambrensis*, lxxvii (1922), 258–326.

[7] *Cymmrodor*, xxxiii. 12, 95–98. *Archaeologia Cambrensis*, lxxvii. 304.

[8] *Cymmrodor*, xxxiii. 123. *Archaeologia Cambrensis*, lxxvii. 314 f.

[9] *Cymmrodor*, xxxiii, map opp. p. 176. On Sarn Elen cf. J. E. Lloyd, *History of Wales*, ed. 3 (London, New York, 1939), i. 67, 74, 78; W. J. Gruffydd, op. cit., p. 346; S. Baring-Gould, J. Fisher, *Lives of the British Saints* (London, 1911), iii. 258; *Breuddwyd Maxen*, ed. I. Williams (Bangor, 1908), p. 27.

province of its troops, vanquished the emperor Gratian, and slew him.[10] The region about Segontium was left in the possession of its native Goidelic inhabitants. But not for long. About the year 400 a British chief, Cunedda, led his war-bands down from the Firth of Forth and subjugated North Wales.[11] To the new-comers, as well as to the natives, the silent, empty courts, the roofless towers, the scattered coins, the Latin inscriptions, the hard-surfaced roads must have been objects of curiosity and puzzled wonderment.

About the year 800 a priest of South Wales, known as Nennius, gathered up what fragmentary information he could about the history of the Britons, and included some scraps of history and tradition about the Roman occupation. He (or a later compiler) gave a list of the twenty-eight cities of Britain.[12] The 'cities', so far as they can be identified, were Roman settlements or forts; the forms of the names are Welsh. Only three of the towns, however, were located in Wales, and they are mentioned together: Cair Segeint, Cair Legeion guar Uisc, Cair Guent,[13] i.e. the old Segontium, Caerleon on Usk, and Caerwent. Evidently the ruins of Segontium must have been impressive, else they would hardly have been chosen for mention in preference to the remains of Cardiff and Carmarthen.

It is to Nennius that we owe the first legend attaching to the site. Speaking of the Romans who ruled in Britain, he wrote:[14]

> The fifth was Constantinus, son of Constantinus the Great, and he died there, and his tomb is shown outside the city which is called Cair Segeint, as letters which are on the stone of the grave witness. He sowed three seeds, that is, of gold, silver, and brass, on the pavement of the said city, so that no poor man should ever dwell there.

Apparently native antiquaries had been led to believe by some inscription in the Roman cemetery outside the fort that here was the burial-place of a Constantine,[15] and, since Constantine the Great was known to have died in the East, the tomb was adjudged to be that of his son. 'Matthew of Westminster' recorded long after that

---

[10] *Cymmrodor*, xxxiii. 90 f. [11] Lloyd, op. cit. i. 116–19.
[12] *Antiquity*, xii (1938), 44–55.
[13] F. Lot, *Nennius et l'Historia Brittonum*, Bibl. de l'Éc. des Hautes Études, cclxxiii (Paris, 1934), 210. Cf. pp. 103–6, 131–4.
[14] Ibid., p. 166; chap. 25. Prof. J. J. Parry has a good discussion of the legends about the Constantines, Helena, and Maximus in *Speculum*, xiii (1938), 272–5, but I find no dependable authority for the existence of a 'Constantine of Caernarvon', son of Maximus. [15] Lot, op. cit., p. 59.

Edward I in 1283 caused the body of Constantine's father to be deposited in the church of that place, presumably Llanbeblig church, which stands close to the Roman cemetery.[16]

The story of the seeds of gold, silver, and brass sowed by Constantine was no doubt devised by antiquaries to explain the large number of coins inscribed with the name. As already remarked, at least 117 coins of the two Constantines have been dug up at or near Segontium in modern times. By the end of the eighth century, then, imaginative archaeologists had created about these monuments and relics an aura of association with the Caesars.

A manuscript of Nennius (Harley 3859) contains some Welsh genealogies of the tenth century which, though not alluding directly to Cair Segeint, mention personages destined to be linked to it in legend. Two pedigrees mention Maxim Guletic,[17] the second adding, 'qui occidit Gratianum, regem Romanorum'. This is, of course, the historic Maximus, who may have been responsible for the final evacuation of Segontium. The first pedigree, moreover, ends with Constantine the Great, son of Constantius and Helen Luitdauc, 'que de Britannia exivit ad crucem Cristi querendam usque ad Ierusalem . . .'. Thus in these pedigrees, tracing the descent of Welsh princes from Roman emperors, we discover the same urge to link the history of Britain to that of Rome. And here is the beginning of that strange legend which derived St. Helena, mother of Constantine, who was actually a native of Asia Minor, from Wales.[18] Is it not possible that coins inscribed with her name may have led patriotic Welshmen to make this claim? Her sobriquet Luitdauc, meaning 'of the host', seems based on the statement that Constantine 'misit suam matrem, Helenam, cum magno exercitu, ut exquireret sanctum lignum crucis Domini'.[19]

In the eleventh century legend was still busy with the decaying fortress above the mouth of the River Seint. According to the mabinogi of *Branwen*, which Sir Ifor Williams dates about 1060,[20] it was here at Caer Seint that Brân, King of the Island of the Mighty,

---

[16] *Cymmrodor*, xxxiii. 185. *Flores Historiarum*, ed. Luard (Rolls Series), iii. 59. In the 12th and 13th centuries the fort was called Caer Custennin. *Breuddwyd Maxen*, pp. xviii f. *Speculum*, xiii. 274.

[17] J. Loth, *Mabinogion*, ed. 2 (Paris, 1913), ii. 331 f.

[18] Ibid. i. 224, n. 2. Baring-Gould and Fisher, op. cit. iii. 255-60. On p. 256 it is mistakenly stated that Geoffrey of Monmouth called the daughter of Octavius Helen.

[19] A. Holder, *Inventio Sanctae Crucis* (Leipzig, 1889), p. 4.

[20] I. Williams, *Pedeir Keinc y Mabinogi* (Cardiff, 1930); pp. xl f.

was holding an assembly when the starling brought him the letter from his sister Branwen, hidden under its wing.

Geoffrey of Monmouth in the *Vita Merlini*, composed about 1150, makes two allusions to *urbs Sigeni*, which Lot and Professor Parry identify with the Cair Segeint of Nennius.[21] When Rodarchus, King of Cumbria, sought to lure Merlin from the forest of Calidon, he offered many gifts, and among them 'pocula que sculpsit Guielandus in urbe Sigeni'.[22] We know that the reputation of the Germanic Wayland as an artificer was very great in the French-speaking world at this time.[23] A sword forged by him was sent by Henry I from the royal English treasury to Geoffrey of Anjou on the latter's marriage to Matilda.[24] Geoffrey of Monmouth's allusion suggests that he had learned of some marvellously wrought cups discovered among the ruins of Segontium. Later in the poem Merlin prophesies that the *urbs Sigeni* and its towers and mighty palaces shall lament in ruins until the Welsh return to their former domains.[25] The *Vita Merlini* proves that reports of these imposing survivals of Roman grandeur had reached the ever-hospitable ears of the Oxford *magister*.

His earlier and more famous work, the *Historia Regum Britanniae*, completed about 1136, makes no reference to *urbs Sigeni*, but it contains a story fabricated from various sources—Nennius, Bede, Gildas, and Welsh genealogies—which was destined to influence indirectly the growing legend.[26] The *Historia* was rendered freely into Welsh at different times, and the earliest version preserved is that of the early thirteenth-century manuscript, the *Dingestow Brut*. The story in question, as given in this manuscript, may be summarized as follows:[27]

On the death of Coel, King of Britain, Constans [Constantius] took the crown, married Coel's daughter, Helen Luydauc, and begat on her a

[21] *Annales de Bretagne*, xv (1899–1900), 327, n. 1. *Vita Merlini*, ed. J. J. Parry, *Univ. of Illinois Studies in Lang. and Lit.* x, no. 3 (1925), p. 119.

[22] *Vita Merlini*, p. 44, vs. 235.

[23] P. Maurus, *Wielandsage in der Literatur* (Erlangen, 1902), pp. 31–43.

[24] *Comptes Rendus de l'Académie des Inscriptions*, 1923, p. 123. P. Marchegay, A. Salmon, *Chroniques des Comtes d'Anjou* (1856–71), p. 530. A. Schultz, *Höfische Leben zur Zeit der Minnesinger*, ed. 2 (Leipzig, 1889), ii. 6 f.

[25] *Vita Merlini*, pp. 66 f., vss. 614 f.

[26] Geoffrey of Monmouth, *Historia Regum Britanniae*, ed. A. Griscom (New York, 1929), pp. 338–50. E. Faral, *Légende Arthurienne* (Paris, 1929), ii. 183–203.

[27] *Brut Dingestow*, ed. Henry Lewis (Cardiff, 1942), pp. 69–78. On the Bruts cf. *Brut y Brenhinedd*, ed. J. J. Parry (Cambridge, Mass., 1937), pp. ix–xviii.

son named Custennyn [Constantine]. Custennyn in turn succeeded his father, but departed from Britain for Rome and seized the empire from a tyrant, Maxen. In his absence, Eudaf, earl of Ergyg and Yeuas [the districts of Erging and Ewias in Herefordshire], grasped the sceptre of Britain. As old age approached, Eudaf sent a messenger to Rome, inviting another Maxen, styled Maxen Wledic, a cousin of Helen Luydauc, to marry his daughter and become his heir. Maxen Wledic set out for Britain with a large fleet, found Eudaf at London, wedded his daughter, also named Helen, and received the crown. Eudaf's nephew, Kynan Meiriadauc, disappointed in his hope of succeeding his uncle, rebelled, but after several battles was reconciled. Five years later Maxen Wledic invaded Brittany, conquered it, and granted it to Kynan to rule. He slew the Roman emperor Gracian.

In the main this narrative follows Geoffrey's *Historia*. But his text distinguishes the tyrant Maxentius, crushed by Constantine, from Maximianus, a Roman senator, who came to Britain and married the daughter of Octavius (who corresponds to Eudaf). Moreover, Geoffrey has at this point but one Helena, namely, the daughter of Coel. It is not hard to perceive how the Welsh redactor managed to produce two Maxens and two Helens. Having rendered the name Maxentius naturally as Maxen, he concluded that Maximianus was only a scribal variation and rendered it also as Maxen, and recognizing the similarity of this Maxen to the Maxim Guletic of the genealogies, both having slain the emperor Gratian, he added the title. Thus we have two Maxens, the second called Maxen Wledic. Moreover, the author of the *Brut* seems to have thought that the daughter of Octavius (Eudaf) ought to have a name, and since she resembled Helena, the daughter of Coel, in being the daughter of a British king and in wedding his successor, it seemed right to give her also the name Helen. It is only by reference to Geoffrey's *Historia* that we can understand the duplication of the Maxens and Helens, and the substitution of Maxen Wledic for the more authentic Maxim Guletic.[28]

Some such volume as the *Dingestow Brut* must have come into the hands of a Welsh author and affected the exquisitely imaginative *Dream of Maxen*, apparently late in the twelfth century.[29] The

[28] If the *Dream of Maxen* was altogether independent of Geoffrey, as Sir Ifor Williams asserted in his edition of the former, p. xxi, it is hard to explain how Maximus came to be called Maxen, how Maxen, instead of the historic Constantius, came to be the husband of Helen Luydauc, and how she came to be the daughter of Eudaf. All is explained by the *Dingestow Brut*.

[29] Loth, *Mabinogion*², i. 30.

influence of the *Brut* is indicated plainly by the fact that Geoffrey's Maximianus is introduced as Maxen Wledic, and Eudaf's daughter as Elen. New confusions have been added: Elen has acquired the epithet of Helena, daughter of Coel, and is called Elen Luydauc; Kynan is her brother, not her cousin. But the prosaic narrative of the chronicle has been freely handled and suffused with a Celtic glamour. No sordid lust for a kingdom moved Maxen to seek a British bride, but the dream of a beautiful maiden filled him with a burning passion. He finds her dwelling with her father, not in London, but beyond the mountains of Snowdon in a radiant palace on the banks of the Seint. Thus a new legend of Segontium came into being. *The Dream of Maxen* tells, in brief, the following story.[30]

Maxen Wledic, Emperor of Rome, after hunting one morning in the valley of the Tiber, went to sleep and dreamed that he set out on a long journey. He walked up the valley, over the highest mountain in the world, and down across plains to the sea. Crossing the sea in a splendid ship, he traversed a great island, came to a mountainous region, and saw beyond it at a river-mouth the fairest fortress he had ever seen. Entering, he found the hall roofed with gold,[31] vaulted with sparkling gems, equipped with golden doors and couches. There he saw two richly dressed youths playing chess, a venerable man carving chessmen, and a maiden of radiant beauty seated on a golden throne. As Maxen embraced her, he awoke. Thereafter she appeared to him as often as he slept, and he was filled with love for her. On the advice of his wise men, he sent messengers to seek her, but though they travelled about for a year, it was in vain. A new search was undertaken. The messengers followed the route Maxen had taken in his dream and came to the mouth of the River Seint. Entering the *caer*, they discovered the youths, the grey-haired man, and the maiden, and hailed her as Empress of Rome. When Maxen received their report, he set sail with a great fleet, came to Caer Aber Seint (the fortress at the mouth of the Seint), and saw there the grey-haired man, named Eudaf, his sons, Kynan and Adeon, and his daughter, the lovely Elen. That night Maxen was united with her in marriage.

The remainder of the tale consists of aetiological details and garbled history. We learn how Caerleon and Carmarthen came to be built, and why roads, connecting the fortresses, were called

[30] Ibid. i. 211-29. *Breuddwyd Maxen*, ed. I. Williams. Both books contain valuable notes.
[31] Geoffrey of Monmouth in his imaginative description of Caerleon in Arthur's time (ed. Griscom, p. 452) says that it imitated Rome with its *aureis tectorum fastigiis*.

Ffyrdd Elen Luydauc, 'the roads of Elen of the Host'. We learn, also, how Maxen after seven years set out to recover Rome from a usurper, was unable to do so until he received aid from a small band of Britons commanded by Kynan and Adeon,[32] and, in gratitude to the brothers of Elen, sent them forth with a great host to make conquests. We learn finally how Kynan and a portion of the Britons settled in Brittany and how that land came to be called Llydaw.[33] Except for the aetiological details, which are derived probably from native tradition, the *Dream* is clearly a romantic and free reconstruction of materials provided by the *Brut*. The romantic element is clearly due, as Rhys has shown,[34] to the influence of a Celtic theme, the search for a dream-maiden, of which an example is provided by the Irish *Dream of Oengus*, dated by linguistic criteria as a composition of the eighth century.[35]

Oengus, son of the Dagda and Boann, dreamt one night of a maiden, the most beautiful in Ireland, but as he was about to draw her to him she vanished. The vision recurred nightly for a year, and Oengus wasted away with the violence of his passion. When the physicians of Ireland were consulted, one of them divined the cause of his suffering. A year was spent in vain searching for the maiden. A new search was undertaken by Bodb, king of the fays of Munster, and the maiden was discovered with one hundred and fifty others beside a lake. Her name was Caer and she was the daughter of Ethal, lord of a faery mound in Connaught. Eventually, Oengus, learning that she assumed the form of a swan every other year, sought her out, mated with her in her bird shape, and brought her back with him to his home under the famous tumulus, the Brugh of the Boyne, where she remained with him thenceforth.

The similarities between the two tales are too obvious to be itemized. Be it noted that the personages in the *Dream of Oengus* are all supernatural beings, gods of the old pagan pantheon,[36] and

[32] A Gadeon, son of Cynan, son of Eudaf, appears in certain Welsh genealogies. H. M. and N. K. Chadwick, *Growth of Literature*, i. 275. The form Adeon seems due to the wrong division of *a gadeon*.

[33] On this legend cf. Loth, op. cit. i. 212, n.; 228 n.; *Breuddwyd Maxen*, p. 29.

[34] J. Rhys, *Lectures on the Origin and Growth of Religion as Illustrated by Celtic Heathendom*, ed. 2 (London, 1892), pp. 169–73. Cf. also *Breuddwyd Maxen*, p. xvi.

[35] *Dream of Oengus (Aislinge Oenguso)*, ed. F. Shaw (Dublin, 1934), p. 37. A summary in German is given in R. Thurneysen, *Irische Helden- und Königsage* (Halle, 1921), pp. 301–3. English translations have appeared in *Revue Celtique*, iii (1877), 342–50, and in K. H. Jackson, *Celtic Miscellany* (London, 1951), pp. 99–103.

[36] Thurneysen, op. cit., pp. 62 f. H. M. and N. K. Chadwick, op. cit., pp. 255 f.

though the geography is precise, an elfin glamour hangs over the landscape, as over the Vale of Tempe and the field of Enna. And this mythological atmosphere has been transferred, either from the *Dream of Oengus* or from some tale closely resembling it, to the *Dream of Maxen*. The *caer* at the mouth of the Seint is not, obviously, what the Welsh author had observed on the spot or even what he fancied might have stood there in a remote antiquity, but the description of the hall with its profusion of gold and glittering stones suggests rather a faery dwelling like the palace of Gwynn, King of Annwn, in the *Life of St Collen*.[37] Elen herself, though playing her part in an ostensibly historic narrative, has absorbed something of the magic quality of the swan-maiden Caer.

What led the author to transport her and her father from London, where the *Dingestow Brut* placed them, to the ancient Segontium? I believe that he found ready to his hand a Welsh legend of a princess Elen who had been seen in a dream by a royal huntsman and had been sought out and won by him, and that this legend followed the strong native tradition in associating her with the Roman ruins above the Seint. It is a curious fact, which I have set forth in my *Arthurian Tradition and Chrétien de Troyes*, pp. 445-7, 458 f., that the *Conte del Graal* not only mirrors in distorted form the picture of Elen's father, sitting in a magnificent castle on a throne adorned with eagles, carving chessmen, but also contains the motif of a huntsman who sends a love-message to a beautiful maiden whom he has never seen and who dwells in the same resplendent castle above a river. Here palpably are two correspondences with the *Dream of Maxen* which cannot be due to mere chance. Yet it is not likely that the text of the *Dream* was in circulation early enough to influence, through several intermediaries, Chrétien's French source for the *Conte del Graal*; and moreover, there is no trace in Chrétien's poem of the pseudo-historic setting of the *Dingestow Brut* such as we might expect to find if he was indebted to the *Dream of Maxen* for the Welsh parallels. We may reasonably conclude, then, that there existed a legend of the dream-maiden Elen and her wooing by a huntsman king, containing many features preserved in the *Dream of Maxen*, including the localization at Caer Aber Seint, and that this legend was the common source of the *Dream* and of certain elements in that fictional medley, the *Conte del Graal*.

[37] Baring-Gould and Fisher, op. cit. ii (1908), 158-60. *Rhyddiaith Gymraeg* (Cardiff, 1954), 36-41. Cf. *Beihefte zur Zts. f. rom. Phil.* lxx (1921), 235.

Though the *Dream of Maxen* did not apparently infiltrate French romance, it had a vogue in its native land. It was referred to by Welsh poets and was summarized in a triad.[38] St Peblig, to whom the church near Caer Seint was dedicated, was said to be the son of Maxen and Elen in a text of the twelfth century, and other sons of Maxen are mentioned in later and even more unreliable texts.[39] The *Dream* influenced a fourteenth-century version of the *Brut*, represented by Cleopatra B v and the Book of Basingwerk,[40] for here the beauty of Elen is emphasized, Maxen is filled with love for her after hearing a description, and it is at Caernarvon (not London) that he meets her and her father Eudav.

Up to and through a part of the thirteenth century, as we have seen, the Welsh called the old Roman station Cair Segeint, Caer Seint, or Caer Aber Seint. But in the middle of the twelfth century, though Geoffrey of Monmouth reflects the Welsh practice in his *urbs Sigeni*, the Anglo-Normans knew the place by another name. Gaimar declared in his *Estorie des Engles*:[41]

> En Wales ot plusur citez
> Ke mult furent renomez;
> Cum Karrewein e Karliun
> E la cité de Snauedun.

First, let it be noted that two of these once famous towns are precisely the two Roman settlements, Caerwent and Caerleon, which are named together with Cair Segeint in the Nennian list of the twenty-eight cities of Britain. Secondly, let it be noted that as early as 1095 the Anglo-Saxons called the Snowdonian range Snawdune,[42] and later records show that the whole district was referred to by their descendants and the Anglo-Normans by some variant of this name, such as Snaudune and Snaudon.[43] Since there was no other *cité* so conspicuous or renowned in the region, it is clear that Gaimar was referring to Caer Segeint, the fortress at the foot of the slopes of Snowdon, as *la cité de Snauedun*.

[38] Loth, op. cit. i. 30, 213 n., 224, n. 2.
[39] *Vitae Sanctorum Britanniae et Genealogiae*, ed. A. W. Wade-Evans (Cardiff, 1944), p. 323. For date cf. ibid., p. xvii. *Speculum*, xiii. 274.
[40] *Brut y Brenhinedd*, ed. J. J. Parry, pp. 98–100.
[41] Gaimar, *Estorie des Engles*, ed. T. D. Hardy, C. T. Martin (London, 1888), i. 285.   [42] *Anglo-Saxon Chronicle*, anno 1095.
[43] *Historia Meriadoci* and *De Ortu Walwanii*, ed. J. D. Bruce (Göttingen, Baltimore, 1913), pp. xxv, 1, 15. *Vitae Sanctorum Britanniae*, pp. 232, 246. *Littere Wallie*, ed. J. Goronwy Edwards (Cardiff, 1940), pp. 39, 41 f., 103.

Segontium, Caer Seint, and Sinadon

Under this name the Breton *conteurs*, who were the great propagators and fabricators of Arthurian romance and who circulated widely over the domains of their British ancestors, from the Firth of Forth to Mount's Bay,[44] came to know of the imposing though ruinous town in the far corner of Wales, and some of them must have visited it. They proceeded to make use of their knowledge by referring to it or making it the scene of traditional adventures, just as they did with Caerleon and Caerwent. And from the Breton *contes* the name of Snauedun, in one form or another, passed into the Anglo-Norman and French romances. Biket's *Lai du Cor*, contemporary with Gaimar's *Estorie*, introduces us to a *roi de Sinadoune*.[45] In a version of the second continuation of the *Conte del Graal*, edited by Rochat, Perceval declares, 'A Sinadon la fu jo nes'[46]—a statement which harmonizes with the evidence that Perceval's father was king of North Wales.[47] Particularly impressive is Béroul's evidence, since he reveals an unusual knowledge of British geography, at least that of Cornwall, with his references to Lancien, St. Michael's Mount, &c.[48] Béroul represents Yseut's squire, Perinis, as departing from Tintagel in Cornwall, coming to Cuerlion (Caerleon) in South Wales, and, after inquiry there, pursuing his journey to Isneldone, where he beholds Arthur seated at the Round Table.[49] Though this itinerary, which takes the traveller from Tintagel through Caerleon to the city of Snowdon, may be correct by accident, yet it is correct.

Renaud de Beaujeu, writing his *Bel Inconnu* about 1200, affords decisive proof that, by some channel or other, knowledge had reached him of the general situation and the condition of the *cité de Sinadon*. Let me summarize the essential portions of his poem.[50]

Arthur was holding his coronation feast at Charlion (Caerleon) on the sea, when a beautiful maiden, clad in samite, rode into the court on her palfrey. Her name was Helie, and she asked the king to send a doughty

---

[44] Marie de France, *Lais*, ed. K. Warnke, ed. 3 (Halle, 1925), pp. xxv f. Thomas, *Tristan*, ed. J. Bédier, ii (Paris, 1905), pp. 126–9. I have treated this matter in *Arthurian Tradition*, pp. 15–23, 27–32. See also *infra*, pp. 183–8, 195–7.

[45] Vs. 415.

[46] A. Rochat, *Ueber einen Unbekannten Percheval li Gallois* (Zürich, 1885), p. 91.

[47] H. Newstead in *Romanic Review*, xxxvi (1945), 3–31, especially pp. 5, 20 f.

[48] I cannot accept, however, many of the identifications made by J. Loth in *Contributions a l'Étude des Romans de la Table Ronde*, such as the Blanche Lande, Morois, &c.

[49] Béroul, *Tristran*, vss. 3368–84.

[50] Renaut de Beaujeu, *Le Bel Inconnu*, ed. G. P. Williams (Paris, 1929).

knight to succour her mistress, daughter of the King of Wales. Arthur assigned the mission to an unknown youth who had just arrived. The damsel in disgust left the court, but the youth overtook her and insisted on accompanying her. In a series of adventures he demonstrated his valour. Finally Helie and her escort arrived at their destination, 'la Cité Gaste'. 'No man ever saw a town so fair in appearance as it had formerly been; now it is waste, it seems. The city, which was very large, lay between two roaring streams. They gazed on the towers, houses, belfries, keeps, the good resplendent palaces, and the glittering images of eagles.' The youth learned that he would find the buildings destroyed and would see neither man nor woman in the streets, but that in the midst of the city there was an ancient marble palace, where at a thousand windows jongleurs sat playing their instruments. Donning his arms, the hero crossed a bridge into the deserted and ruinous town. In the hall, brilliantly lighted with candles, he found the minstrels, who prayed God to save him. A knight, riding in from a dark chamber, attacked him, but was forced to flee. A second adversary, in black armour, mounted on a fire-breathing steed, spurred against the youth, but after a prolonged fight was killed. The minstrels rushed away; the candles went out. As the hero waited alone and exhausted, a hideous wyvern, shedding a bright radiance, entered, approached him humbly, kissed him on the mouth, and retired. A voice informed him that he was the son of Gavain by a fay and that his name was Guinglain. After slumbering a while, he woke to find that it was full day. A woman, lovelier than words could describe, stood beside him and told him that she was the daughter of King Gringras. Her city had been cast down and she herself had been transformed into a wyvern by the enchantments of two brothers, Mabon and Evrain.[51] The waste town was properly called Senaudon, and was the capital of the realm of Gales. After the news of the queen's deliverance was spread abroad, the enchanted city was restored by the sprinkling of holy water and exorcisms. Finally, after an episode which does little credit to Guinglain, he was wedded to the Queen of Gales at 'la cité de Sinaudon'.

It is evident that, though Renaud lived and wrote in France, he had some authentic information about the far-off fortress at the base of Snowdon. He knew that it was one of the chief cities of Wales. He knew that it was ruinous and deserted. Possibly, though by no means certainly, the statement that it lay between two streams may be based on knowledge of the actual situation of the town between the Seint and the rivulet Cadnant.[52]

[51] On the motif of the *Fier Baiser* cf. *Studi Medievali*, xvii (1951), 104–13.
[52] *Cymmrodor*, xxxiii. 15.

Moreover, it is worth noting that in the cognate Middle English romance, *Libeaus Desconus* (*c.* 1340),[53] the beautiful maiden messenger and guide is called, not Elie, but Elene, and the itinerary which would take her from Caerleon to the site of Segontium, through Abergavenny, Y Gaer, Llandovery, and Tomen-y-Mur, was one of those roads connecting Roman stations which the *Dream of Maxen* called Ffyrdd Elen and portions of which are known to this day as Sarn Elen, 'the causeway of Elen'.[54] It might seem that the coinciding of the route of Elene and the causeway of Elen might be merely fortuitous, since the roles of the two ladies show little resemblance. But that both *Le Bel Inconnu* and *Libeaus Desconus* owed something to remote Welsh sources is proved by the names of the two brother enchanters, Mabon-Maboun and Evrain-Irain,[55] for in Welsh literature both Mabon and Owain are said to be sons of Modron, the mistress of Urien, and Owain son of Urien appears in French literature as Ivain fils Urien.[56] Though the identity of Ivain with Irain may be doubted, since nowhere does Ivain appear as a cruel wizard, yet he might well have been assigned such a role by assimilation to his brother Mabon, who can be identified not only with the black knight slain by Guinglain but also with four similar figures of Arthurian story—Mabonagrain in Chrétien's *Erec*, Mabuz in *Lanzelet*, Maduc le Noir in *La Vengeance Raguidel*, and Mabon le Noir or Nabon le Noir in the *Prose Tristan*.[57] None of these four sinister knights resembles the Mabon of *Le Bel Inconnu*, it must be granted, in having any association with the Waste City or the dragon-maiden. Thus we are obliged to conclude that Renaud de Beaujeu's poem incorporated two Welsh traditions, originally

[53] For analysis of *Le Bel Inconnu, Libeaus Desconus,* and other cognates cf. W. H. Schofield, *Studies on the Libeaus Desconus, Studies and Notes in Philology and Literature,* iv (Boston, 1895).

[54] Cf. *supra*, p. 2, n. 9. Of course, neither of the 'Fair Unknown' romances follows this route, *Libeaus* taking the hero to Carlisle and Ireland.

[55] The form Evrain was taken over from Chrétien's *Erec*, like many other names in *Le Bel Inconnu*, Cf. Schofield, op. cit., pp. 59 f., 126. The form Irain in *Libeaus* is therefore more authentic.

[56] *Cymmrodor*, xxviii (1918), 198 f. Loth, *Mabinogion*, i. 312; ii. 1, n.; 284.

[57] *Erec*, vss. 5768–6353. Ulrich von Zatzikhoven, *Lanzelet*, ed. K. A. Hahn (Frankfurt, 1845), vss. 3536–830; trans. K. G. T. Webster (New York, 1951), pp. 192 f. Raoul de Houdenc, *Vengeance Raguidel*, ed. M. Friedwagner (Halle, 1909), vss. 570 ff., 2750. E. Löseth, *Tristan en Prose* (Paris, 1890), pp. 47–50, 215. Cf. also *Romania*, xxv (1896), 285 ff., and *PMLA*, xx (1905), 696, n. 1. Mabon was the name of a giant in Carmarthenshire. Baring-Gould and Fisher, op. cit. iii. 391, n. 1.

separate: the legend of Mabon and his brother; the legend developed by Breton *conteurs* about the city of Sinadon and the road of Elene which led to it.

It was a natural and felicitous decision which led to the fusion of these two legends, to the placing of the evil enchanter Mabon and his victim, the dragon-maiden, in the haunted ruins of Sinadon. This blend had been worked into an elaborate series of adventures which formed the basis not only of *Le Bel Inconnu* but also of its cognates, *Libeaus Desconus* and *Carduino*.[58] Renaud de Beaujeu deserves no credit, therefore, for creating the adventures of Guinglain at the Waste City. But he deserves high praise for the atmosphere of gramarye which pervades the action and the setting: the fallen splendour of towers and pillars, the deserted streets, the brilliantly lighted hall, the mysterious minstrels with their ominous welcome, the darkness, the enchanter knights, whose steeds strike sparks from the stone pavement, the wyvern with her red mouth and supplicating behaviour. Indeed, I recall no Arthurian romance, except *Gawain and the Green Knight*, which evokes the thrill of wonder, the 'Gothic' shiver, so rightly and potently. And to this effect the Waste City at the base of Snowdon made a large contribution.

In 1469–70 Sir Thomas Malory completed his *Morte d'Arthur*, and included in it a spirited redaction of a lost romance of Gareth, nicknamed Beaumayns.[59] Dr. Brugger is of the opinion, for which I have offered some evidence elsewhere,[60] that the lost work must belong to the twelfth century.[61] To a considerable extent Malory's narrative parallels that of Renaud de Beaujeu. It is particularly significant that both conclude with a tournament designed to bring the hero out of retirement, his display of overwhelming prowess, and his wedding the heroine, whom he had earlier delivered from an unwelcome suitor. Moreover, whereas we have seen that in *Le Bel Inconnu* the nuptials were celebrated at 'la cité de Sinadon (variant Senadon)', according to Malory they occurred at Kynkenadon 'by the see syde' or 'by the sandys'—a place also referred to as 'a cyte and a Castel the whiche in tho dayes was called kynke kenadonne upon the sondes that marched nyghe walys'.[62] Can there be any doubt that in the romance followed by Malory the

---

[58] Cf. *supra*, p. 13, n. 53.
[59] Malory, *Morte d'Arthur*, ed. H. O. Sommer (London, 1889), Book VII.
[60] *PMLA*, liv (1939), 664.   [61] *Zts. f. Roman. Philologie*, lxiii (1943), 291.
[62] Malory, op. cit. i. 213, 269 f.

name of the city was written Cincenadon or some similar corruption of Senadon, and that the site was described in some such phrases as *pres des araines, sur la mer de Gales*? In fact, at low tide the sandy flats in the Menai Strait are conspicuous. Evidently, the author of Malory's source had no direct knowledge of the place, neither did he gain such acquaintance as he had from *Le Bel Inconnu*, but he and Renaud were indebted to a more or less remote common source, which preserved the tradition of 'la cité de Snauedun' as one of the renowned cities of Wales.

Though Snaudune as a name for the whole district about the mountain was in common use during the thirteenth century, the old Roman station apparently ceased to be called by that name or any form of it. (The reference in the version edited by Rochat probably goes back to an earlier source.) In 1283 Edward I not only removed the supposititious body of Constantine's father from its tomb to the church near by, as we know, but he also began the building of his magnificent castle on the shore below,[63] which, with the town about it, came to be called Caer yn Arvon, whence the modern name Caernarvon. Ashlar from the old Roman fort on the hill was carried down for use in the new structure, and little was left behind but heaps of rubble and grassy mounds.[64] Nothing remained to impress the imagination, and the magic departed. Except for the vague indications in the romances, the site of Sinadon was unknown. Though more than one scholar has proposed that the name was connected with Snowdon,[65] it remained for the present writer to identify the Waste City with ruined Segontium.[66]

Meanwhile Scotland had been making larger and larger claims to the topography of Arthurian romance. Twelfth-century tradition fixed Tristan's homeland as Loenois, that is, Lothian,[67] which then extended from the Firth of Forth to the Cheviot Hills. The forest

---

[63] A. Hamilton Thompson, *Military Architecture in England during the Middle Ages* (London, New York, 1912), p. 252.   [64] *Cymmrodor*, xxxiii. 94.

[65] J. Rhys, *Celtic Folklore, Welsh and Manx* (Oxford, 1901), ii. 562. J. D. Bruce, *Evolution of Arthurian Romance* (Baltimore, 1923), ii. 196. W. H. Schofield, op. cit., p. 138. *Histoire Littéraire de la France*, xxx (1888), 174 n.

[66] There is a *Gaste Cité* in *Perlesvaus*, ed. W. A. Nitze and others (Chicago, 1932–7), i. 136–8, 283–6. There is nothing in the description, however, to identify it with Sinadon, and instead of the brother enchanters and the dragon-kiss we have the motifs of the Waste Land and Disenchantment by Decapitation. Cf. ibid. ii. 165–7, 281–3.

[67] *Mod. Phil.* xxii (1924), 159–91. *Comptes Rendus de l'Académie des Inscriptions*, 1924, p. 128.

of Morois, to which Tristan was exiled, can be confidently equated with the wild region of Moray.[68] Geoffrey of Monmouth arbitrarily made Lot, Gawain's father, the eponymous king of Lothian. In 1142 King David I, who may well have met Geoffrey the previous year at Oxford,[69] began to use Castellum Puellarum in his charters as an official designation of Edinburgh castle,[70] and this romantic title, translated into French, was employed by the authors of the Breton lai of *Doon* and the romance of *Fergus*.[71] The latter author, Guillaume le Clerc, who knew southern Scotland well,[72] also equated the Arthurian Mont Dolerous with the 'montaingne de Maros (Melrose)' and described it as overhanging 'un gort, grant et marvilous et parfont', and as the site of a great, strong castle.[73] My friend Mr Angus Graham, of the Royal Commission on Ancient and Historical Monuments for Scotland, points out to me that this must refer to the ruins of Trimontium, an extensive Roman fort in the parish of Melrose, strategically situated on a broad ridge which rises abruptly a hundred feet above the gorge of the River Tweed.[74] Needless to say, here is another excellent example of the trend to romanticize the awesome relics of Roman grandeur, an example to set beside that of Segontium. Moreover, Guillaume used for the

[68] J. D. Bruce, op. cit. i. 179 f. Bruce is mistaken in asserting that Lothian was inhabited by Picts. Mr. Angus Graham, of the Royal Commission on Ancient and Historical Monuments for Scotland, wrote me (5 March 1940): 'I know of no evidence that what I call "Picts" ever "controlled" any country south of the Forth.... The Angles were in Midlothian by about 630.... Therefore, I hardly think any Pictish king would have had much of a say there in 780 unless as a temporary result of a raid.'

[69] A. O. Anderson, *Early Sources of Scottish History* (Edinburgh, 1922), ii. 202. R. Howlett, *Chronicles of the Reigns of Stephen, Henry II, and Richard I* (Rolls Series), iii. 75–83. Faral, op. cit. ii. 2.

[70] A. C. Laurie, *Early Scottish Charters prior to A.D. 1153* (Glasgow, 1905), pp. 112, 123, 146. An article in *Speculum*, xvii (1942), 250–4, contains serious errors. Geoffrey did not identify the Castellum Puellarum with 'Montem Dolorosum', as he uses the former in the nominative and the latter in the accusative case. There is no evidence whatever that Mons Agned was really Edinburgh or that there was ever a nunnery there. On the Castle of Maidens and the reason for identifying it with Edinburgh cf. chap. xv of my *Arthurian Tradition*.

[71] *Romania*, viii (1879), 61. Guillaume le Clerc, *Fergus*, ed. E. Martin (Halle, 1872), p. 106.

[72] *PMLA*, xliv (1929), 263 f. *Miscellany of Studies in Romance Languages and Literatures in Honour of L. E. Kastner*, pp. 94–107.

[73] *Fergus*, p. 121; Brugger, in *Zts. f. Franz. Spr. u. Lit.* xliv², 96–98, suggested that Mont Dolerous might be one of the Eildon Hills.

[74] An excellent and fully illustrated monograph on the site of Trimontium and its excavation is J. Curle's *A Roman Frontier Post and Its People, the Fort of Newstead in the Parish of Melrose* (Glasgow, 1911). See especially pls. v, xii, and plan opp. p. 14 for the situation.

main plot of *Fergus* what must have been an established *conteur* tradition about a Lady or Queen of Lothian, which contributed also to Chrétien's romance of Laudine and to Malory's account of Dame Lyones.[75] In 1367 Dumbarton was referred to in a parliamentary record as 'Castrum Arthuri'.[76] It was to be expected, therefore, that sooner or later a Scottish claim would be laid to the mysterious city of Sinadon.

In fact, Froissart, when he visited the great fortress of Stirling in 1365, was informed that 'fu chils castiaux anchiennement, dou temps le roy Artus, nommés Smandon [read Sinaudon], et là revenoient à le fois li chevalier de le Ronde Table'.[77] This, of course, was a patriotic fiction and finds no confirmation in earlier records, but it was long-lived. William of Worcester in the fifteenth century asserted: 'Rex Arturus custodiebat le round table in Castro de Styrlyng, aliter Snowden West Castell.'[78] Sir David Lindsay, in the *Complaynt of the Papingo* (after 1530), carried on the pleasant illusion:[79]

> Adew, fair Snawdoun, with thy towris hie,
> Thy Chapell-royall, park, and Tabyll Round.

There is still a chapel royal (though not the building mentioned by Lindsay) at Stirling, and below the castle is a flat-topped mound, enclosed by banks, called the King's Knot, which may be the 'Tabyll Round'. Scott recalled in the *Lady of the Lake* that 'Stirling's tower of yore the name of Snowdoun claims'. And to this very day the title of Snowdon Herald is customarily bestowed on the Lyon King of Arms, head of the Scottish office of arms, on his retirement. The title, first mentioned in 1448, is doubtless derived from the romantic but spurious name for Stirling castle.[80]

This little study will have served its purpose if it has drawn attention to several matters of significance: the fascination of Roman ruins and relics for amateur antiquaries and professional

---

[75] *Fergus*, pp. 180, 186. Cf. chaps. xv and li of my *Arthurian Tradition*.

[76] W. F. Skene, *Four Ancient Books of Wales* (Edinburgh, 1869), i. 55 f.

[77] Froissart, *Œuvres*, ed. Kervyn de Lettenhove (Brussels, 1867), ii. 313. According to Barbour's *Bruce*, Bk. IV, vs. 181, Kildrummy Castle near Aberdeen was also called Snawdoune.

[78] *Merlin*, ed. H. B. Wheatley (E.E.T.S.), iii (London, 1869), p. lvii.

[79] Ibid., p. lviii.

[80] I am indebted for this information about the Snowdon Herald, first to Sir Thomas Innes, Lyon King of Arms, who generously supplied it, and secondly to Mr. Angus Graham, who at my request procured and passed it on to me and whose help I once more gratefully acknowledge.

story-tellers from the ninth to the twelfth century; the fumbling efforts of the Welsh to fit these archaeological remains into a historical framework and to associate them with some of the great names of Roman history, the Constantines, Helena, Maximus; the indirect contribution of Geoffrey of Monmouth to the *Dream of Maxen*; the creation of new legends about the Waste City of Snowdonia and the Road of Elen by Breton *conteurs* of the twelfth century; the fanciful claims of the Scots, or of others on their behalf, to Arthurian localities. These phenomena are important in themselves; they have an added importance in that they suggest answers to other problems of medieval literature, and especially of the Matter of Britain.

CHAPTER II

The Irish Origin and the Welsh Development of the Grail Legend

It may seem something of an Irish bull to speak of the Irish origin of the Grail legend. What does Irish literature or folk-tale know of Joseph of Arimathea, of his receiving the dish or cup of the Last Supper from Pilate, his catching therein the blood of Christ as He hung on the cross, his imprisonment by the Jews, his miraculous feeding by the same vessel during forty years in a dungeon, his release and his wanderings, the coming of Joseph or of Bron to Britain, the conversion of the land to Christianity, the preservation of the holy vessel in the mysterious castle of Corbenic by a succession of guardian kings, the quest of that vessel by Arthur's knights, their adventures and visions, their voyages over perilous seas in faery lands forlorn, the ultimate arrival of Perceval at a rich and lofty castle, his reception by a maimed king, the entrance of a youth holding a bleeding spear and a damsel with a shining Grail, the miraculous appearance of delicious food at each place as the Grail passes, the hero's momentous question: 'Whom does one serve with the Grail?', the sudden healing of the maimed king, the succession of the youthful hero to the kingship of the Grail? What, one may well ask, does Ireland know of this legend? The answer is: Nothing, save for three fragmentary late texts manifestly translated from the French.[1]

Yet no other theory explains so much of the Grail legend as that of Irish origin and Welsh development; no other theory accords so well with antecedent probability regarding the Arthurian cycle of romance.

Every student of medieval history and literature knows the great gift which Ireland made to European culture when between A.D. 500 and 850 she transfused into the veins of a Continent bled white by the savage strokes of pagan hordes the reviving blood of her own sanctity and learning. From Bobbio in the Apennines to Iceland,

[1] *Zts. für Celt. Philologie*, iv (1903), 381.

Irishmen stood out pre-eminent as the representatives of Christian scholarship, for Ireland was the one country in Christendom which had not felt the shattering onslaughts of the Goth, the Vandal, the Hun, or as yet the Norseman. During these centuries Ireland deservedly won its title as the Island of Saints and Scholars. With this great contribution of Ireland to medieval civilization the scholarly world is familiar.

But few are familiar with a later and perhaps equally momentous gift of Ireland to literature. As Professor Kittredge once put it:

> Something produced a great change in the literature of France in the twelfth century,—that is to say, in the literature of the western world, for at no assignable time could French literature have been charged with more momentous consequences to the course of European literary history. That *something* professes to be the emptying into French literature of a large body of Celtic material,—not a little leaven but a huge mass, operating with extraordinary rapidity and with an effect still traceable not only in subtle ways, but even in such obvious phenomena as the externals of plot and dramatis personae.... The specific results of our study are to emphasize once more the importance of Irish material (and even of 'modern Irish' folklore) in settling these questions.[2]

Such was the matured judgement of one of the most eminent students of medieval literature, a judgement borne out still further by his studies in *Sir Orfeo* and *Gawain and the Green Knight*.[3] This new current which he derives from Ireland and which poured into French literature in the twelfth century was mainly concerned with Arthur and the knights of the Round Table. As we examine this cycle more closely we see how it is possible to claim that much of it is Irish in origin.

Arthur himself was a Celt, a Briton, a Welshman; and Welsh literature, including the story of *Kulhwch and Olwen*, in which Arthur appears, is full of Irish elements. On this point Irish scholars like Douglas Hyde and Welsh scholars like Professor Gruffydd agree. Moreover, the most famous of medieval English romances of the Arthurian cycle, *Gawain and the Green Knight*, has long been recognized as derived through French from an Irish tale of a head-cutting test, which goes back to the ninth century. It is not only possible but also probable that any authentic tradition of the Round Table should be derived from Wales and should contain Irish elements.

[2] *Harvard Studies and Notes*, viii (1903), 265 f.
[3] *Am. Journ. of Philology*, vii. 176; G. L. Kittredge, *Study of Gawain and the Green Knight* (Cambridge, Mass., 1916).

When we study the nature of this second impact of Irish tradition upon European culture through the medium of the Welsh, we soon realize that it was totally unlike the first. It was Ireland, the fervent missionary of a vigorous Christianity, which had cast its light over the earlier ages. It was Ireland, the preserver of Celtic heathendom, which shed an elfin glamour over the twelfth century. St. Patrick only half converted the Irish people, and the zealots who went forth to convert Iceland and Germany and to reinvigorate the faith among the Alps and the Apennines must have left a good many devotees of Lugh and Manannán behind, just as American missionaries to China and India leave a good many worshippers of Lucifer and Mammon at home. As Plummer has said: 'Heathenism [in Ireland] was absorbed without any violent conflict. It disappears in order to reappear, proportionately strong, in the Church.... Where the chief was converted, the clan in most cases would follow; and conversion in masses involves almost necessarily the retention of a large measure of heathenism.'[4]

This survival of a vigorous paganism in Ireland alongside a more vigorous Christianity explains the fact that today one finds holy wells decked with rags, which were once, of course, offerings to the divinity of the spring; and that in the nineteenth century fishermen of the Isle of Man used actually to pray to Manannán son of Ler to give them a good catch.[5] It explains the survival into the late Middle Ages of many Irish sagas in which the old gods figure; it explains how the Irish stories, passing into Wales, amalgamating with similar Welsh stories, and attaching themselves to the person of Arthur, were in large measure remnants of Irish mythology which had survived the victory of the Cross. It is strange but true that, some centuries after Irish missionaries had confirmed Europe in the Christian faith, Irish story-tellers through the agency of the Welsh and Bretons gave to Europe a diluted but still fascinating mythology; and the Irish god Lugh Loinnbhéimionach, though yielding at home to the pale Galilean, enjoyed a second triumph, more extensive than the first, as Lancelot du Lac.[6]

When, however, we turn to the Grail legend, the hypothesis that it originated in Celtic paganism does not at first sight seem

[4] C. Plummer, *Vitae Sanctorum Hiberniae* (Oxford, 1910), I, p. cxxx.
[5] W. Y. E. Wentz, *Fairy-Faith in Celtic Countries* (Oxford, 1911), p. 118.
[6] Ulrich von Zatzikhoven, *Lanzelet*, trans. K. G. T. Webster (New York, 1951), pp. 12-19, 201 f. Cf. *infra*, pp. 161-4.

so plausible. For it is the popular impression, with which certain eminent scholars coincide, that the Grail was from the first conceived as the cup of the Last Supper or at least as a eucharistic dish. This impression is confirmed by the association with Joseph of Arimathea and by the name Galaad, which is found in the Vulgate Bible, corresponding to the more familiar Gilead.[7] But it is difficult to see how such an impression can survive a close examination of the facts. Professor Remy's article in the *Catholic Encyclopedia* points out that the Church has never recognized as authentic the romances connected with the Grail and has displayed a shrewd sense of their unorthodox background.[8] Furthermore, when we first meet the legend in the *Conte del Graal* of Chrétien de Troyes, written about 1180, the atmosphere is, if not actually pagan, markedly unChristian. The hero, Perceval, spends several nights of amorous dalliance with the lady Blancheflor, whom he does not find time to marry. He comes directly from his initiation into love's unhallowed pleasures to the Grail castle. The Grail, as it appears to him, is no chalice; it is not carried by a priest; it is not preserved in a chapel. On the contrary, it is a jewel-decked platter borne by a beautiful maiden from one castle chamber to another. Certainly this first author to introduce us to the Grail either had no conception of the proprieties of Christian ethics and ritual, or he did not conceive of the Grail as a Christian object. The latter seems far the more plausible theory and permits us to respect Chrétien's intelligence. When later he speaks of the Grail as containing the Host, it is clearly an afterthought on his part or on that of his source. Likewise the identification by other authors of the Grail with the dish used by Christ at the Last Supper or with the chalice containing His blood, the grafting of the apocryphal legend of Joseph of Arimathea—all these were no part of the original tradition. In reading so fascinating a Grail romance as the *Perlesvaus*, beautifully edited by Professors Nitze and Jenkins, one feels that he is constantly passing back and forth between the land of faerye and a monastic cloister; at one moment he is listening to the warbling of enchanted birds; at the next he hears the intoning of the mass and the chanting of angelic choirs. This feeling will be quite correct. The fairyland is the realm of Celtic mythology; the cloister is the structure of Christian

[7] A. Pauphilet, *Études sur la Queste del Saint Graal* (Paris, 1921), pp. 135-7.
[8] *Catholic Encyclopedia*, vi. 721; J. A. Robinson, *Two Glastonbury Legends* (Cambridge, 1926), pp. 38 ff.

Irish Origin and Welsh Development of the Grail Legend 23

traditions built as a result of curious misunderstandings in the midst of that magic realm.

Such assertions must, of course, be substantiated by detailed evidence, and it is perhaps proper that they should be met with scepticism. It is necessary for one thing to admit that the case for Celtic origins has not always been presented with much cogency; that La Villemarqué and Rhys and Nutt overlooked much of the best evidence and offered much that produced doubt rather than conviction. My own *Celtic Myth and Arthurian Romance*, I confess, contained chapters on the Grail which I would now withdraw and others that were confused and confusing. Nevertheless, the evidence for the Celtic origin of the Grail continues to pile up. It is possible on the Celtic hypothesis to account for the precise form of the vessel, namely a deep platter; its properties of miraculous feeding, of selecting those whom it will feed, of prolongation of youth and life; the bleeding spear and adventures connected with it; the broken sword miraculously mended; the magic ship in which Galahad, Perceval, and Bors voyaged; Perceval's sister; the Loathly Damsel; the Siege Perilous; the Maimed King; the visits of Gawain and Perceval to his castle; the question test; Gawain's waking in the open; the names of the Grail kings and Grail heroes; the introduction of Joseph of Arimathea; and many other details. No other hypothesis can explain anything like so much. It is due to the perversity of chance, however, that practically all the intermediate stages between the old Irish and Welsh traditions on the one hand and the French romances on the other are lost. Of the Cornish and Breton stages not a syllable is left. Of Welsh material connected with the Grail we have only a score of sentences in the *Mabinogion*, a dozen lines of Welsh poetry, and the list of the Thirteen Treasures of the Isle of Britain. And this material does not stand to the French romances in the relation of direct ancestors but rather of tenth cousins. Luckily the Irish material is more copious, but it is even farther removed. Thus we have no immediate Celtic parent of a Grail romance, but rather the remote relatives. It is this accident of literary history which has given superficial investigators the impression that there is no evidence for the Celtic origin of the legend, and to those impatient of complex evidence drawn from many quarters a chance to object to what is in the nature of the circumstances to be expected.

The complexity and confusion is not altogether in the minds of the proponents of the Celtic hypothesis; it is in the legend itself. Every Grail romance (except those of course which are mere translations) contradicts every other in many and vital points, and not infrequently contradicts itself. The romancers themselves were not unaware of this eccentricity of the tradition they were following, and the author of *Perlesvaus* offers an amusing explanation of his inconsistencies:[9] 'The quest of adventures would not have pleased the knights so well an they had not found them so different. For when they had entered into a forest or an island where they had found any adventure, and they came there another time, they found holds and castles and adventures of another kind, so that their toils and travels might not weary them.' The real reason for all this tantalizing sense of confusion is precisely this: the Grail legend is a composite of scores of Celtic tales and motifs, often quite independent of each other, and woven into a lovely and mysterious, but quite inharmonious tapestry. Arnold's famous analysis of the *Mabinogion* applies here: 'The mediaeval story-teller is pillaging an antiquity of which he does not fully possess the secret; he is like a peasant building on the site of Halicarnassus or Ephesus.' It is astonishing to find as much harmony as we do between the various sculptured fragments which have gone into the Temple of the Grail. The purpose of this chapter is to take up one by one those evidences of Celtic origin which can be most readily apprehended and to present them without resort to hypothetical reconstructions or any other prestidigitation. There are many more arguments besides; these that follow are the simplest, but I believe they suffice.

Let us begin our quest for the origins of the Grail legend by recalling the solemn scene which Malory presents in his Book XIII and which he condensed from the French *Queste del Saint Graal*:

So when the king and all the knights were come from service, the barons espied in the sieges of the Round Table all about, written with golden letters: Here ought to sit he, and he ought to sit here. And thus they went so long till that they came to the Siege Perilous, where they found letters newly written of gold which said: Four hundred winters and four and fifty accomplished after the passion of our Lord Jesu Christ ought this siege to be fulfilled. . . . In the meanwhile came in a good old man and an ancient. . . . And with him he brought a young knight, both on foot, in red arms. . . . Then the old man said unto Arthur: Sir,

[9] S. Evans, *High History of the Holy Grail*, Everyman's Lib., p. 244. *Perlesvaus*, ed. Nitze and Jenkins (Chicago, 1932–7), i, l. 6617.

I bring here a young knight, the which is of ... the kindred of Joseph of Arimathea, whereby the marvels of this court and of strange realms shall be fully accomplished. The king was right glad of his words, and said unto the good man: Sir, ye be right welcome and the young knight with you. Then the old man made the young man to unarm him, and he was in a coat of red sendal.... And anon he led him unto the Siege Perilous.... Sir, said the old knight, wit ye well that place is yours. And then he set him down surely in that siege.... Then all the knights of the Table Round marvelled greatly of Sir Galahad, ... and said: This is he by whom the Sangreal shall be achieved.... Then the King took him by the hand, and went down from the palace to show Galahad the adventures of the stone.... Sir, said the King unto Sir Galahad, here is a great marvel as ever I saw, and right good knights have essayed and failed. Sir, said Galahad, that is no marvel, for this adventure is not theirs but mine.... And in honour of the highness of Galahad he was led into King Arthur's chamber and there rested in his own bed.

Later the French text continues:[10]

The day was fair and clear and the sun had already dispersed the dew, and the palace began to fill with barons of the realm.... The King called Sir Gawain and said to him: Ye first did move this quest; come forth and make ye first the oath.... Then was Galahad called, and he came forth, knelt before the hallows, and swore as a loyal knight that he would follow the quest a year and a day.... Afterwards Lancelot swore likewise as he had done. And then swore Gawain, Perceval, Bors, Lionel, and Helain the White. Then swore all the companions of the Round Table, one after the other.

Some readers will recall the coming of the Irish sun-god Lugh to the court of the god Nuada, as recounted in the *Second Battle of Moytura*.[11]

Nuada prepared a great feast at Tara, and summoned to it the Tuathan nobles to take counsel together. When all were assembled in the hall, the doorkeeper at the gate saw a company approaching, at their head a youthful warrior of handsome form and equipped like a king. ... Then Nuada bade him be admitted. And Lugh entered the hall and took his place in the midst of the Tuathan chiefs, in the seat of the Sage, which was set apart for the wisest.... Then the champion Ogma, wishful to try the stranger's strength, lifted up a huge stone which

[10] *Queste del Saint Graal*, ed. A. Pauphilet (Paris, 1923), pp. 22 f.
[11] I quote from the summary in Maud Joynt, *Golden Legends of the Gael* (Dublin, n.d.), pp. 14–17. For full translation cf. *Rev. Celt.* xii (1891), 79 ff.

lay on the floor of the hall and was beyond the power of ordinary man to move, and he hurled it through the roof-window out over the ramparts of the fort. But Lugh went out and flung it back to the spot where it had lain. . . . When Nuada and the Tuathan chiefs beheld Lugh's powers and saw that he was in truth the Samildanach, they felt they had at last found the hero who could lead their hosts and free them from bondage; and Nuada gave up his place to Lugh for the space of the war, so that henceforth Lugh sat in the king's seat. The next day Lugh called together the great warriors and wise men of the Tuatha, . . . and he asked of each man what he could do. First spoke the druids Mathgen and Figol. . . . 'I will make rivets for the spears and hilts for the swords and rims and bosses for the shields,' said Credne. 'And I,' said Luchta the wright, 'will fashion shields and spear-staves out of wood.'

And the roll-call of the Tuatha Dé Danann follows, like that of the knights of the Round Table. If we remember that the king's seat which Lugh occupied was doubtless an *imda* or couch,[12] and that Lugh was said to have 'a red colour on him from sunset to morning',[13] the parallel between the coming of Lugh and the coming of Galahad speaks for itself. Though the two stories have followed divergent paths for centuries, they retain in common the assembled court, the empty seat awaiting a worthy occupant, the coming of a youth 'with a red colour on him', his taking the seat, the demonstration of his superior strength by means of a stone, the recognition by the warriors that this is their destined leader, the king's relinquishing his couch to the stranger, the assembly on the morrow, the demand that each warrior should undertake a feat, the list of warriors who did so.

Another Grail book, the *Didot Perceval*, gives quite a different version of the Siege Perilous adventure, but this too has its Irish counterpart.[14]

There was an empty seat of stone at the Round Table and Arthur told the young Perceval that it was reserved for the best knight in the world. Perceval nevertheless sat upon it. 'As soon as he was seated, the stone split beneath him and cried with such anguish that it seemed to all those who were there that the world would fall into the abyss, and from the cry which the earth uttered there issued a great darkness.' A mysterious voice announced that the enchantments of Britain had

---

[12] *Studies in Honor of A. M. Elliott* (Baltimore, 1911), i. 34 f.
[13] *Rev. Celt.* xii. 127.
[14] *Didot-Perceval*, ed. W. Roach (Philadelphia, 1941), pp. 149-51, 205-9, 238-42.

Irish Origin and Welsh Development of the Grail Legend

begun and would last until some knight should ask at the palace of the Fisher King: 'Whom does one serve with this Grail?' Perceval, after many wanderings, met Bron, the Fisher King, who invited the youth to his abode. When Perceval found it, it was a magnificent castle and the king had mysteriously arrived before him. Presently a damsel entered bearing two platters (*tailleors*), and was followed by two youths bearing a bleeding spear and a vessel containing the blood of Christ. On this occasion Perceval failed to ask whom one served with these, but on a later visit he did so. Thereupon the enchantments were removed from Britain; Perceval received the vessel from Bron and became king in his stead.

Let us now examine an Irish story, at least as old as the tenth century, *The Prophetic Ecstasy of the Phantom*.[15] Like the previous Irish tale, it opens at Tara, and it deals with a sort of honorific seat, the famous stone, the Lia Fáil; 'on it all the Kings of Ireland were crowned, and it always cried out under the rightful king.'[16] This and other descriptions of Irish coronation stones indicate that they were flat slabs, quite unlike the upright pillar at Tara which now is popularly called the Lia Fáil.

When King Conn of the Hundred Battles was standing on the rampart at Tara with his druids, he happened to step upon a stone, which shrieked many times under him. [Another text says that its heart burst out of it.] After many days the druids told him that Fál was the name of the stone, and that the shrieks signified the number of rightful kings who should descend from him. A thick mist arose and enveloped them. The god Lugh then approached on horseback and invited Conn to his abode, a royal rath. Like the Fisher King, Lugh seems to have preceded his guest, for Conn found him seated in his palace and a golden-crowned damsel also, 'the Sovereignty of Erin', doubtless the goddess Ériu, the personification of Ireland.[17] She gave Conn huge portions of meat, and then asked of Lugh: 'For whom shall this cup be poured?' alluding to a golden cup which was filled from a silver vat, a divine vessel of inexhaustible ale. 'Pour it,' said Lugh, 'for Conn.' The damsel did so, and then repeating the question, she was instructed by the prophetic Lugh to pour it for each of Conn's royal descendants by name. Lugh and his house vanished, but Conn retained the vat and the cup.

[15] M. Dillon, *Cycles of the Kings* (Oxford, 1946), pp. 12 f. E. O'Curry, *Lectures on the Manuscript Materials of Ancient Irish History* (Dublin, 1861), p. 388.
[16] M. Joynt, op. cit., p. 5. T. P. Cross, C. N. Slover, *Ancient Irish Tales* (New York, 1936), p. 11.
[17] *Ériu*, xiv (1943), 11-21.

Despite the differences in motivation and detail, there is here a marked likeness to the adventure of Perceval. The stone which breaks and cries out when the hero sits or stands on it; the darkness or mist which rises; the supernatural figure who invites the hero to his abode and mysteriously arrives before his guest; the provision of food; the damsel with a vessel; the question, 'Who shall be served with the vessel?', the hero's receipt of the vessel—this series of common features can hardly be due to coincidence.

Coincidence becomes even less plausible as an explanation when we discover that in another romance a damsel who bears the platter in the Grail castle appears later in hideous form and is described in almost the same terms as the Sovereignty of Erin, who served Conn with her cup in Lugh's palace and who likewise appears elsewhere in hideous form. In *Peredur*, a Welsh romance based on a lost French original, one of the bearers of the platter or grail comes later to Arthur's court in loathly shape:[18]

> Blacker were her face and her two hands than the blackest iron covered with pitch.... One eye was of a piercing mottled grey, and the other was as black as jet.... Her teeth were long and yellow.... Her figure was very thin and spare, except her feet and legs, which were of huge size.

Compare with this the description of the Sovereignty of Erin as she appeared to the sons of Eochaid Mugmedon:[19]

> Every joint and limb of her, from the top of her head to the earth, was as black as coal.... The green branch of an oak in bearing would be severed by the sickle of green teeth that lay in her head and reached to her ears. Dark smoky eyes she had.... Her ankles were thick, her shoulder-blades were broad, her knees were big.

The Loathly Damsel, Wagner's Kundry, is no other than the Sovereignty of Erin.[20]

Coincidence becomes impossible as an explanation of these parallels when we see that not only has the Grail Bearer her counterpart in the damsel in Lugh's palace; but the bleeding spear also has its Irish counterpart in Lugh's spear. The first continuator of Chrétien's unfinished poem describes the spear of the Grail castle

---

[18] C. Guest, *Mabinogion*, Everyman's Lib!, pp. 209 f.
[19] *Rev. Celt.* xxiv (1903), 197.
[20] R. S. Loomis, *Arthurian Tradition and Chrétien de Troyes* (New York, 1949), pp. 374-9, 415 f.

as fixed in some kind of rack over a silver cup, into which a copious stream of blood flowed from the iron head.[21] Likewise, the spear which was found at the battle of the gods at Moytura and may be identified with the spear which Lugh wielded at the battle is twice described as plunged into a cauldron filled with blood.[22] And before it came into Lugh's possession it had a history strikingly like an episode in the history of the Grail spear. It belonged to a King Pisear of Persia, and was found and carried off under the following circumstances, as told in the *Fate of the Children of Turenn*:[23]

The three sons of Turenn were compelled by Lugh to fetch for him, among other talismans, the spear of Pisear. They came to the king's palace and Brian demanded the famous weapon. When attacked by the king, Brian killed him, and put the courtiers to flight. Then he went with his brothers 'to a room where the spear was kept; they found it with its head down deep in a great cauldron of water, which hissed and bubbled round it. Brian seizing it boldly in his hand drew it forth', and departed. The weapon was delivered to Lugh to use in the Battle of Moytura.

In the romance of Balin from the *Huth Merlin*, retold by Malory, we have this story:[24]

Balin came to the castle of King Pellam, was attacked by the king, and when his sword was broken, fled weaponless through the palace. He entered a rich chamber full of fragrance, and saw a table, 'and upon this table was a great basin of gold, and within this basin stood a lance, perpendicularly, point downward. And anyone looking at it would have marvelled because it was not inserted nor supported nor fastened anywhere'. Balin seized the lance and drove it through King Pellam's thighs. Straightway the castle fell in ruins, killing the King, and Balin was able to depart only through Merlin's aid. He found the land devastated.

The analogy is obvious, and since King Pellam's spear is unquestionably the bleeding spear of the Grail castle, and since Pisear's spear was certainly the lightning spear of Lugh, we may with reason

---

[21] W. Roach, *Continuations of the Old French Perceval*, iii (Philadelphia, 1952), pp. 469, 471.
[22] A. C. L. Brown in *PMLA*, xxv (1910), 22.
[23] P. W. Joyce, *Old Celtic Romances* (Dublin, 1920), pp. 59, 73 f. *Atlantis*, iv (1863), 203-5.
[24] *Huth Merlin*, ed. G. Paris, J. Ulrich (Paris, 1886), ii. 27 f. Prof. Vinaver has kindly filled the lacuna in the Huth text from the newly discovered Cambridge University manuscript.

believe that the spear so frequently seen in the Grail castle and interpreted by Christianizers as the Holy Lance which the centurion thrust into the side of Christ upon the Rood, was originally the spear of Lugh. Though A. C. L. Brown's argument to this effect was not conclusive, his instinct was sound.

The Fate of the Children of Turenn has further significance. Besides affording an adventure cognate with the episode of Balin's Dolorous Stroke, it supplies the counterparts of two curious elements in the Galahad quest: the mysterious role of Perceval's sister, and the long voyages of the three heroes in a self-directed ship. In order to begin the quest for the talismans demanded by Lugh, the three Irish heroes obtained permission to use Manannán's coracle, the 'Wave-Sweeper'.[25]

'They then set out for the Brugh of the Boyne, accompanied by their sister Eithne, leaving Turenn lamenting after them. The coracle they found lying in the river.... They then bade their sister farewell, and leaving her weeping on the shore, they rowed swiftly till they had got beyond the beautiful shores and bright harbours of Erin, out on the open sea.... And then he [Brian] spoke to the coracle, "Thou coracle of Manannán, thou sweeper of the waves, we ask thee and command thee that thou sail straightway to the Garden of Hirbeirne!" The coracle was not unmindful of the voice of its master, and obeyed the command without delay, according to its wont. It took the shortest way across the deep sea-chasms, and gliding over the green-sided waves more swiftly than the clear, cold wind of March, it stayed not in its course till it reached the harbour near the land of Hirbeirne.' Having procured the greater part of the talismans, the brothers returned, only to be obliged to set forth again to complete their quest. 'They went to their ship, and Eithne, the daughter of Turenn, went along with them; and the maiden fell to grief-crying and lamentation.... They went forth upon the tempestuous waves of the green sea: and they were a quarter of a year upon that sea.'

In Malory's narrative of the quest, the three knights, Perceval, Bors, and Galahad, three times embark together in a ship which, as soon as they enter, moves off and flies over the sea.[26] Twice they are accompanied on their voyage by Perceval's sister. It would be indeed curious if the association of three heroes bound on the same quest in a ship moving at once to destined ends, accompanied by a

---

[25] P. W. Joyce, op. cit., pp. 62–64; *Atlantis*, iv. 217–19.
[26] Malory, *Morte d'Arthur*, Bk. XVII, chaps. 2, 7, 21.

Irish Origin and Welsh Development of the Grail Legend

devoted sister, had suggested itself independently to the author of the Irish tale and to Malory's French source. It was a very natural suggestion which W. B. Yeats made years ago, that the *Fate of the Children of Turenn*, though it contains no Grail, was an old Grail quest.[27]

Two accounts of the enchantment of the land and the causes thereof—Perceval's sitting on the Siege Perilous and Balin's dealing the Dolorous Stroke—we have seen had a Celtic framework. In *Sone de Nausay* the Grail Keeper, Joseph of Arimathea, weds a Saracen princess and thereby renders the land of Logres [England] barren and its inhabitants sterile.[28] Just so the Irish king Conn by mating with the evil woman Becuma brings a blight upon Ireland; 'there was neither corn nor milk in Ireland during that time.'[29] And lest any should think that this correspondence between Irish and Arthurian tradition was accidental, let us note how Conn's subsequent attempt to remove the enchantment shows striking similarities to one visit to the Grail castle. In the summaries irrelevant matters are omitted.

Conn embarked in a coracle from the Hill of Howth. He 'was a fortnight and a month on the sea, . . . without knowledge or guidance save that of trusting to the course of the stars and the luminaries. . . . Swiftly uprose the waves, and the firmament trembled'. He landed on an island and approached a palace very like that of the sea-god Manannán as described in the *Adventures of Cormac*. Conn entered and saw the divine figures of Daire, his wife Rigru, niece of Manannán, and their son. His feet were washed by unseen agency. He was led to the fire. Food-laden boards rose up automatically before him. 'After a short space he saw a drinking horn there, and he knew not who had fetched the horn.' Conn washed himself in a vat, a cloak was thrown over him, and he sat down to eat. The rest of the story follows an inconsistent pattern, and we are only concerned to know that eventually fertility was restored to Ireland.[30]

Now we have in the first continuation of Chrétien's poem the tale of a visit to the Grail castle similar in motivation and detail but adapted naturally to the conventions of knight errantry.[31]

[27] W. B. Yeats, *Ideas of Good and Evil* (1903), p. 227.
[28] *Sone de Nausay*, ed. M. Goldschmidt (Tübingen, 1899), vss. 4757–854.
[29] Cross and Slover, *Ancient Irish Tales*, p. 493. Loomis, *Arthurian Tradition*, pp. 390 f. *Eriu*, iii (1907), 155.
[30] *Eriu*, iii. 157. Cross and Slover, op. cit., pp. 494 f.
[31] W. Roach, op. cit. iii. 457–77, 491–5.

Gawain did not cross the sea in a boat, but followed a road over which the waves were breaking. He saw ahead of him a great light and his steed brought him at last to a large hall. Here he was welcomed, led to a fire, and clad in a mantle. Canons entered, chanted a service about a bier, and departed. A tall king came in; he and Gawain washed and sat down at a table. A rich Grail entered and served them with wine and several courses; no bearer was visible. Left alone for a while, Gawain noticed the bleeding lance, and when the king returned and led him into a chamber, he asked about the lance and the body (*cors*) on the bier. Falling asleep, he woke the next morning by the seaside, and no dwelling was visible. As he rode away, he found the land, which the night before had been desolate, restored to fertility because he had asked concerning the lance. The rivers flowed again and the woods were green.

The debt of this episode to Ireland should be manifest. Much of it is paralleled by the preceding story of Conn; the spear, as we saw earlier, is the spear of Lugh; and still another feature can be matched in Irish story. We have already observed that the palace of Conn's adventure resembles the palace of Manannán in the *Adventures of Cormac*. And in the latter story Cormac wakes after his entertainment by the sea-god to find himself lying on the green at Tara,[32] just as Gawain does after his entertainment by the Fisher King. In fact, this waking after a night in the enchanted castle, to find the castle vanished and oneself lying in the open, is a motif recurring again and again both in Irish and Arthurian story.[33]

Even the broken sword of the Grail castle has been shown by Pennington to have Irish affinities.[34] According to Chrétien, Perceval is invited by the Fisher King to his magic abode and is presented with a magnificent sword, which has been destined for him. Later he is informed that he must avenge with it the death of his host's brother. According to Chrétien's second continuator, Perceval is asked by his host to put together the two parts of a sword, succeeds in the attempt, and receives congratulations. Another continuator, Manessier, goes on to tell of the prophecy

[32] Cross and Slover, op. cit., p. 507.
[33] *Romanische Forschungen*, xlv (1931), 74, 76, 82; Stokes and Windisch, *Irische Texte*, iii (1891), 323; *Duanaire Finn*, ed. E. Mac Neill, i (London, 1908), p. 148; Gerbert de Montreuil, *Continuation de Perceval*, ed. M. Williams, i (Paris, 1922), 5; Renaut de Beaujeu, *Bel Inconnu*, ed. G. P. Williams (Paris, 1929), p. 165. C. Potvin, *Perceval le Gallois* (Mons, 1866), iv. 27. Heinrich von dem Türlin, *Crône*, ed. G. H. F. Scholl (Stuttgart, 1852), p. 183.
[34] *Mod. Lang. Notes*, xliii (1928), 534–6.

that a knight would come who would re-weld the sword and slay with it the murderer of the Fisher King's brother. Perceval then sets out from the castle with the sword and fulfils the prophecy. In the *Colloquy of the Ancients*, an Irish text dated 1142–67, the famous warrior Caeilte and a companion pass a *síd* or faery mound and are invited in by two of its lords, one of them Fergus, a son of the great god Dagda. Fergus asks Caeilte to repair a broken sword and two other weapons, and Caeilte does so. Each weapon is destined to kill some person, and Caeilte says that he himself is fated to do some deed for which the men of Ireland and Scotland and the Tuatha Dé Danann will be thankful. After three days' stay, the two warriors set out with the weapons to carry out their missions of death. The similarity of this story to that of the broken sword in the *Conte del Graal* does not need labouring.

One crucial element in the Grail romances is the question, the supreme test on which the success of the Grail hero hangs. It was this tantalizing feature which made plausible Miss Weston's theory that we were dealing with the initiation ceremony of a forgotten cult. But can Irish literature offer an analogue to the question test? We have already seen that the form of the question expected from the hero, 'Whom does one serve with this Grail?' is almost identical with the question asked by the Sovereignty of Erin in Lugh's palace, 'For whom shall this cup be poured?' But though we may suspect some influence from this quarter, nevertheless there is no correspondence between the two traditions as to the purpose of the query or the person who makes it. Nor do we know of any question test in Irish literature, ancient or modern. Yet there is a folk-tale containing a very similar test which seems to fill the gap. As reported by Caesar Otway in 1841,[35] there was a belief in Erris, County Mayo, that there lies a magic island to the west, crowned by a lofty castle, and subjected to an enchanted sleep. The king of the island will sometimes appear to a peasant and 'if rightly asked, this hide-and-go-seek potentate will tell the questioner where he can find untold heaps of gold, but the querist must be very particular, for if he ask as he should do, the wealth will be obtained by the one [the peasant] and the enchantment will be removed by the other; but if not, the king vanishes, never to return, amidst wild laughter'. This seems to be essentially the situation in the Grail castle: the king of an Otherworld castle, which is under enchantment; the

[35] C. Otway, *Sketches in Erris and Tyrawley* (Dublin, 1841), pp. 251 ff.

man who through his stupidity fails to ask the right question, or who by asking the question removes the enchantment and wins wealth. The one essential difference is that the folk-tale places the test outside the king's castle; but even this discrepancy vanishes in other Munster variants of the theme, which tell of a drunken peasant who finds himself in a palace of the fairies.[36] He adds a line to their singing and they are delighted and give him whatever he desires. A crabbed fellow who tries to imitate his success fails to add the words and ends ignominiously. In these humble anecdotes we detect the surviving Celtic analogues of those scenes in the Grail castle which Wagner has invested with such glamour and sublimity, where 'der reine Tor' first fails to ask concerning Amfortas' anguish, and later, 'durch Mitleid wissend', asks, ends the enchantment, and becomes lord of the Grail.

Thus in these Irish traditions, most of which must go back ultimately to pagan times, we find an astonishing kinship to the Grail legend. We find here counterparts of the Siege Perilous, Perceval's visit to the Grail castle, the Loathly Damsel, the bleeding spear, the three knights in the magic ship, Perceval's sister, the Grail Keeper's marriage with an evil woman, Gawain's visit to the Grail castle, his waking in the open, the broken sword, the question test. The correspondence is too complete, many of the points of similarity too specific and unusual, to be accounted for as accidents. Space does not permit the development here of the remarkable parallels between the boyhood of Perceval and that of Finn studied by Nutt and Brown; the resemblance between the nocturnal adventures of Gawain and Bors in Castle Corbenic and those of Cúchulainn in Cúroí's fortress; the Irish arrangements of the Grail castle revealed by Nitze; the Irish origin of the love-trance of Perceval proved by Zenker.[37]

Now everything goes to show that this river of mythological story rising in Ireland crossed the sea, like another fountain Arethuse, sprang up again in Wales, there to mingle with a similar British stream. Hyde from the Irish side and Gruffydd from the Welsh have demonstrated with new evidence the already recognized fact that Wales received a powerful influx of tradition from across the Irish

---

[36] P. Kennedy, *Legendary Fictions of the Irish Celts* (London, 1866), pp. 99–104.
[37] *Folklore Record*, iv (1881), 7–21; *Mod. Phil.* xviii (1920), 211–18; R. S. Loomis, *Celtic Myth and Arthurian Romance* (New York, 1927), pp. 159–75; *Studies in Honor of A. M. Elliott*, i. 19–51; *Romanische Forschungen*, xl (1927), 314.

Sea.[38] And the French Arthurian romances, even when they have their roots in Ireland, show ample traces of Welsh development and transmission.

The nomenclature of the Grail cycle is, so far as we can detect, Welsh. The Fisher King Bron must be the Welsh King Brân, a euhemerized sea-god, who seems to have taken the place of Lugh and Manannán in the Welsh stages of Grail tradition.[39] Brân and the Fisher King were both wounded in the leg or foot. Both were famous for their feasts at which their followers seemed to grow no older. Brân's followers banqueted in an island palace for eighty years, 'nor did one of them know of the other that he was older by that time than when they came there'.[40] In the Fisher King's palace Gawain feasted with twelve ancient knights, 'albeit they seemed not to be so old as they were, for each was of an hundred year of age or more, and yet none of them seemed as though he were forty'.[41] Indeed, to bring together all the evidence for the identity of Brân and Bron would be a book in itself. It is scattered all through Arthurian romance.[42]

Now in four romances the Grail king is uncle of the Grail hero, Perceval, whereas Brân's brother is the step-father of Pryderi. Was Pryderi the Welsh original of Perceval? Though a superficial examination of the evidence might prompt a negative answer, yet research suggests several reasons for the affirmative. It was very easy for the mythological name Pryderi to give way to that of an historical Welsh warrior Peredur, and Peredur, we know, was a name which the Welsh equated with Perceval. Moreover, if we accept Pryderi as the original of Perceval, we have an adequate explanation for the names of those other heroes who challenge Perceval's supremacy in the quest of the Grail.[43] There were probably in Welsh tradition two heroes, Pryderi and Gwri, so alike that their stories were amalgamated and they themselves were by some story-tellers identified. At least, the *Mabinogion* tell us explicitly that Pryderi's earlier name was Gwri (pronounced Goory).[44] This name, plus the

[38] *Transactions of the Fourth Celtic Congress* (1923), pp. 39–56; W. J. Gruffydd, *Math Vab Mathonwy* (Cardiff, 1928). Cf. C. O'Rahilly, *Wales and Ireland* (London, 1924).
[39] Loomis, *Arthurian Tradition*, pp. 385–8.
[40] J. Loth, *Mabinogion* (Paris, 1913), i. 148.
[41] *Perlesvaus*, ed. Nitze and Jenkins, i. 118.
[42] H. Newstead, *Bran the Blessed in Arthurian Romance* (New York, 1939).
[43] Loomis, *Arthurian Tradition*, pp. 341–6.
[44] Loth, op. cit. i. 110, 119.

French nominative ending in *-s*, became corrupted into Gohors, and Gohors by a common scribal error[45] became Bohors, the regular French form of Bors. Gwri seems to have been distinguished for his golden hair and to have had an epithet, Gwallt A(d)vwyn, meaning 'Bright Hair'.[46] This epithet in all probability became Galvagin, the first recorded form of Gawain. The Biblical form Galaad is simply an ingenious substitution for some such form of Gawain as Galaain.[47] Thus the identification of Perceval with Pryderi supplies a complete explanation of the names of his rivals. They are all derived from the name of Pryderi's *alter ego* Gwri or from his epithet.

Furthermore, Pryderi brings a desolating enchantment upon the land of Dyfed (south-west Wales) just as Perceval brings about the enchantment of Britain in the *Didot Perceval*, and he does it in the same way, by sitting upon a perilous seat. We have already summarized this adventure of Perceval's and pointed out its similarity in certain respects to the adventure of Conn and the shrieking stone. But Conn's story does not represent the Lia Fáil as a perilous seat nor does Conn's treading on it bring about a desolating enchantment. Pryderi's adventure, therefore, must have been fused with the Irish tradition, since it accounts so neatly for precisely those elements in the *Didot Perceval* episode which are not paralleled in the Irish analogue. Let us see what the *Mabinogion* tell us. There was above the palace of Arberth in Pembrokeshire a mound called the *Gorsedd* or Mound of Arberth. 'Whosoever sits upon it cannot go thence without either receiving wounds or blows, or else seeing a wonder.'[48] It was obviously a Siege Perilous.

Pryderi, his step-father Manawydan, and their wives began a feast at Arberth. After the first meal, all four went and sat on the mound, and lo, there was a peal of thunder and a thick mist. When the mist cleared, they looked and where they had been wont to see flocks, herds, and dwellings they saw nothing, neither house nor beast nor smoke nor fire nor man nor dwelling.[49]

Though the remainder of the mabinogi of *Manawydan* follows a very different outline from the *Didot Perceval*, yet it attributes to Pryderi one other adventure which corresponds in certain details to an

---

[45] F. Lot, *Étude sur le Lancelot en Prose* (Paris, 1918), p. 148 n.; *Mod. Phil.* xvi (1918), 348.
[46] Loomis, *Arthurian Tradition*, pp. 149–51.
[47] Pauphilet, *Études sur la Queste del Saint Graal*, pp. 135–8.
[48] Loth, op. cit. i. 92 f. [49] Ibid. i. 154 f.

Irish Origin and Welsh Development of the Grail Legend

adventure of Perceval's. Pryderi came to an enchanted castle, and 'beheld a fountain with marble work around it, and on the margin of the fountain a golden bowl upon a marble slab, attached to chains hanging from the air, to which he saw no end'.[50] Now the fountain, the golden bowl, and the chains hanging from the air are all found in an enchanted castle which Perceval visits in the beautiful romance of *Perlesvaus*, translated by Sebastian Evans as *The High History of the Holy Graal*. Besides these three features from the *mabinogi*, the French tale contains seven other features from two old Welsh poems describing an abode of the gods. Let us read the account of Perceval's visit to the land of the immortals.[51]

'Perceval is far from land so that he seeth nought but sea only.... The ship ran on by night and by day as it pleased God, until they saw a castle and an island of the sea.... They came nigh the castle, and heard four horns sounded at the four corners of the town, right sweetly.... They issued forth of the ship and went by the side of the sea toward the castle, and therein were the fairest halls and the fairest mansions that any might see ever. He looketh underneath a tree that was tall and broad, and seeth the fairest fountain and the clearest that any may devise, and it was all surrounded of rich pillars, and the gravel thereof seemed to be gold and precious stones. Above this fountain were two men sitting, their beards and hair whiter than driven snow, albeit they seemed young of visage.' Since these men were living before the crucifixion, as they declare, they must have been four hundred years old at the least. 'Perceval looketh beyond the fountain and seeth in a right fair place a cask made as it were all of glass (*un tonel autresi fez come sil fust touz de voirre*), and it was so large that there was a knight within all armed. He looketh thereinto and seeth the knight and speaketh unto him many times, but never the more willeth the knight to answer him. ... Three and thirty men come into the hall all in a company.... As soon as they enter into the hall, they do worship to God Our Lord and beat their breasts, crying, "Mea culpa". Then went they to wash at a great laver of gold, and then went to sit at the tables. The Masters made Perceval sit at the most master-table with themselves. They were served thereat right gloriously.... He seeth a chain of gold come down above him loaded with precious stones, and in the midst thereof was a crown of gold. The chain descended a great length and held on to nought save the will of Our Lord only. As soon as the Masters saw it descending, they opened a great wide pit that was in the midst of the

[50] Ibid. i. 160.
[51] S. Evans, *High History of the Holy Graal*, Everyman's Lib., p. 357; *Perlesvaus*, ed. Nitze and Jenkins, i. 387–9.

hall, so that one could see the hole all openly. As soon as the entrance of this pit was discovered, there issued thence the greatest cry and the most dolorous that any heard ever.'

Here, then, are not only the castle with its richly adorned fountain, the golden bowl or laver, and the chain hanging from the air, such as Pryderi saw, but also seven features of the Welsh conception of the divine abode as described in two poems in the *Book of Taliesin*.[52] It may be remarked that the name of this castle, Kaer Siddi, according to the authority of Rhys, Morris-Jones, and Gruffydd, is the equivalent of Irish *cathair sídh*, or 'faery fortress'.[53]

Perfect was the prison of Gweir in Kaer Siddi. . . .
Before the spoils of Annwn dolefully he chanted. . . .
In the Four-Cornered Fortress, isle of the strong door, . . .
Bright wine was their liquor before their retinue . . .
Beyond the Fortress of Glass they had not seen the prowess of Arthur; . . .
It was difficult to converse with their sentinel.

In another poem the bard conceives himself as having attained happiness in this island of the gods.

> Perfect is my seat in Kaer Siddi.
> Nor plague nor age harms him who dwells therein.
> Manawyd and Pryderi know it. . . .
> Around its corners are ocean's currents
> And above it is the fruitful fountain,
> And sweeter than white wine is the drink therein.

The principal features of this Welsh paradise of the gods are: an island, a four-cornered fortress, a fountain, a wailing prisoner, ageless inhabitants, feasting, and a structure of glass, with a sentry who would not reply. Every one of these seven features is recognizable in the French romance, even though the fortress of glass has become a *tonel* or 'cask' of glass, probably through a misreading of *torele*, 'turret'. In fact, Nennius tells us of a *turrim vitream in medio mare*, and of men upon it who would not answer the mariner's hail.[54] Another surely Celtic feature is the golden crown dangling from the mysterious chain, for not only have we met the chain in the

---

[52] See *infra*, pp. 165–70.
[53] J. Rhys, *Celtic Folklore* (Oxford, 1901), ii. 678; *Cymmrodor*, xxviii (1918), 238; *Enc. Brit.*, 11th ed., v. 642.
[54] E. Faral, *La Légende Arthurienne* (Paris, 1929), iii. 11; J. Rhys, *Lectures on the Origin and Growth of Religion* (London, 1892), pp. 263 f.

mabinogi but we also find the descending headgear of gold in the voyage of the clerics of Columcille as related by Manus O'Donnell.[55]

> For a long time they were without sight of land until at last they beheld an island. And in this wise was that island: a dwelling fair and well adorned in the midst thereof, ... and a man in holy orders in golden apparel consecrating Christ's body afore every altar. And the household of Columcille entered then and a right courteous welcome was given them. And whilst they were there, a beautiful golden cowl was let down upon the floor of that royal hall. ... And they were richly served and had great cheer that night, and they were given well brewed ale, so that they were drunken and merry.

Needless to say, this island betrays itself by these unholy revels as the pagan Land of Promise; it is the island where Maeldúin saw 'a great number of people, beautiful, wearing embroidered garments, feasting with embossed vessels of red gold', and heard their ale-songs; it is the land to which Mider enticed Étaín: 'Intoxicating is the ale of Inisfáil; more intoxicating is the ale of the great country. There rivers run with wine. There old age is unknown.' It is the Welsh Annwn, where Pwyll beheld 'the fairest household and the best arrayed that anyone had ever seen. ... They dispensed meat and drink, with song and carousal. Of all the courts of the earth that he had seen, that was the court with the least stint of food and drink and golden vessels and royal treasures.'[56] The island of the immortal elders described in the French *Perlesvaus* is clearly the land of the Celtic gods. The two elders are probably Manawydan, son of Llŷr, and his brother Brân. Perceval, who is destined to wear the crown and to reign in the Plenteous Island near by, is, of course, Pryderi.

Finally, Welsh tradition supplies a list of the Thirteen Royal Treasures of the Isle of Britain,[57] which betray on scrutiny that they are the very 'royal treasures' of Annwn just mentioned, and also that they bear kinship to the talismans which we find in the Fisher King's castle in *Perlesvaus*.[58] In this list is the Cauldron of Dyrnog, described in almost exactly the same terms as are elsewhere applied to the Cauldron of the Chief of Annwn: 'If meat were put in it to

---

[55] M. O'Donnell, *Life of Colum Cille*, ed. O'Kelleher and Schoepperle (Chicago, 1918), pp. 399 ff.
[56] I. Williams, *Pedeir Keinc y Mabinogi* (Cardiff, 1930), p. 4.
[57] Edward Jones, *Bardic Museum* (London, 1802), p. 47.
[58] *Romanische Forschungen*, xlv. 68–71.

boil for a coward, it would never be boiled.' Another vessel in the list corresponds closely in form and function to the Grail of the French romances: 'The Platter (*dysgl*) of Rhydderch; whatever food was wished thereon was instantly obtained.' As to function, compare the expression used of the Grail in the *Queste*: 'As soon as it passed before the tables, they were filled at each seat with such food as each one wished.'[59] As to the form of this platter, note that Helinandus defines the word 'grail' as *scutella lata et aliquantulum profunda*, and that Giraldus Cambrensis says that the Welsh were served in *scutellis latis et amplis*.[60] Moreover, it is a *dyscyl* (an earlier form of *dysgl*) which in *Peredur* damsels carry through the hall of Peredur's uncle under circumstances resembling those in the French romances of the Grail.[61] It is the Welsh platter of plenty, manifestly, which has supplanted the various Irish cups of plenty; it was the Welsh word for platter, *dysgl*, which was correctly rendered into French as *graal*.

In this list of the Thirteen Treasures is the Sword of Rhydderch; 'if any man drew it except himself, it burst into flames from the cross to the point'. We have already seen the fiery spear of Lugh converted into a bleeding spear, and should have no hesitation in recognizing the fiery sword of Rhydderch in the sword in *Perlesvaus*, which, when King Gurgalain drew it from the scabbard, came forth all bloody, and which was deposited with the Grail in the Fisher King's castle.[62] Here is the Chess-board of Gwenddolau; 'when the men were placed upon it, they would play of themselves. The chess-board was of gold and the men of silver.' Of course, we discover in the Fisher King's castle, together with Grail and Sword, just such a chess-board: 'with a border of gold, and the pieces were of gold and silver.' 'Messire Gawain sitteth at the game, and they of gold played against him and mated him twice.'[63]

Most interesting of all the Thirteen Treasures is the Horn of Brân; 'the drink and the food that one asked one received in it when one desired.' Here we have a vessel with precisely the property of the Grail, attached to Brân, whom we have had reason to identify with the Fisher King Bron. Though at first sight it may seem as if

---

[59] *Queste del Saint Graal*, ed. Pauphilet, p. 15.
[60] Migne, *Pat. Lat.* ccxii, col. 814. Giraldus Cambrensis, *Opera*, ed. Dimock, vi (London, 1868), 183.
[61] J. G. Evans, *White Book Mabinogion* (Pwllheli, 1907), col. 130.
[62] *Perlesvaus*, ed. Nitze and Jenkins, i. 103-7.
[63] Ibid., pp. 115, 120.

we were on a false scent, since nowhere in French romance does Bron or the Fisher King possess a drinking-horn, yet patient investigation reveals many traces of the tradition; and of these two must suffice. The French were totally unfamiliar with the conception of a sacred drinking-horn and were certain to misunderstand the word *cor*, nominative *cors*, when used in such associations. They explain the name of the Grail castle, Corbenic, as Chaldean for 'most holy vessel', whereas it is of course the easiest kind of corruption of the words *cor benoit*, meaning simply 'blessed horn'. The Grail castle must have contained, besides the divine platter, the *cor benoit*. The nominative *cors* was also the word for 'body'. When, therefore, we find in Castle Corbenic a holy vessel beheld by Galaphes under nearly the same curious circumstances as the *cors* (body) was beheld by Gawain in the Grail castle, the equivalence of vessel and *cors* is strongly implied once more. What explanation is there save that *cors* (body) was a misunderstanding of *cors* (horn)?[64] It may be suggested with considerable assurance that the belief that Joseph of Arimathea was the first keeper of the vessel containing the blood of Christ sprang from the assumption of some unknown early romancer that the *cors benoiz* was the blessed body of the Lord, and that since Joseph of Arimathea was the custodian of that body, he was therefore the first guardian of the *cors benoiz*. Thus in one romance Joseph is actually identified with the Fisher King, who is of course Brân, the keeper of the sacred horn.[65] The consequence of this confusion was a series of more or less bewildering efforts to stitch together the apocryphal legend of Joseph and the Celtic traditions of the wanderings of Brân's followers and the quest of the magic platter and horn by Pryderi and Gwri. And the pagan Celtic elements took on more and more of a pious colouring to harmonize with the sanctity of the newly inferred history of the *cors* and platter.

Thus, it would seem, the tangled skein of the Grail legend is unravelled by drawing out the right threads of old Welsh and Irish tradition. The clues are hard to find in the mazes of the *Mabinogion* and the *Arturi regis ambages pulcerrimae*. But there, in the remains of Celtic heathendom, they are to be found.

[64] *Romanische Forschungen*, xlv. 86-88.
[65] Cf. *infra*, chap. iv.

CHAPTER III

Chastiel Bran, Dinas Brân, and the Grail Castle

IN his edition of *Fouke Fitz Warin*, published in the *Classiques Français du Moyen Age* (No. 63, 1930), Louis Brandin commented on Chastiel Bran as follows: 'peut-être le château de Old Oswestry, et cette ville même', and cited Wright's edition, p. 187, as a reference.[1] Bran Fitz Donwal, who according to the text gave his name to the castle, received from Brandin no comment at all.[2] Both place and person can be identified with certainty. It is well known that the romance of *Fouke* is a prose redaction of a lost original in verse, and that the author of the original version knew the Welsh border and particularly the neighbourhood of Ludlow (Dynan) and Whittington (Blancheville). After speaking of events in Henry the First's time, the romance returns to William the Conqueror:[3]

When King William the Bastard approached the mountains and valleys of Wales, he saw a very large town, aforetime enclosed with high walls, which was now burnt and laid waste, and below the town he had his tents pitched.... Then the king asked a *Bretoun* the name of the town.... 'Sire', said the *Bretoun*, '... the castle was formerly called Chastiel Bran, but now it is called the Old Border (*la Vele Marche*).'

We are told that, on leaving Chastiel Bran later, the king came to a district near by, and 'beside it is a little castle which is called Arbre Oswald but now is called Oswaldestre'.[4] From Oswestry the king went south, crossed the Severn, and distributed to his best knights the lands from Chester to Bristol.

Taking the clues thus provided, we may make the following assertions regarding Chastiel Bran: (1) It was on or near the Welsh border. (2) It was in hilly country and was itself on a height. (3) It was not Oswestry itself but near by. (4) It probably lay to the north of Oswestry, since King William's direction from Oswestry

[1] p. 89.
[2] p. 92. Brandin also failed to notice the identification of Kahuz which I made in *Mod. Lang. Notes*, xliii (1928), 218 f.
[3] p. 3.
[4] p. 7.

Chastiel Bran, Dinas Brân, and the Grail Castle

on was southwards. All these conditions are fulfilled by Castell Dinas Brân on a steep hill near Llangollen, about twelve miles north-north-west of Oswestry. *Dinas*, it may be observed, is Middle Welsh for 'fortress' and is simply a duplication of *Castell*; in fact, the castle is often called simply Dinas Brân. Ruinous walls still stand on this strategic hill overlooking the valley of the Dee.[5] But they are not the remains of the 'ville gastee' mentioned by our author, for the original poem was written about 1260,[6] and the castle whose ruins we see today was built by Gruffudd ap Madog, shortly before his death in 1270.[7] Evidently in the middle of the thirteenth century the hill-top was covered with the shattered walls of an older castle, of which we have no historic record.[8]

As for Bran Fitz Donwal we need have even less hesitancy in making an identification. As the references to Brutus, Coryneus, and Goemagog which the 'Bretoun' introduces into his discourse show, the author was drawing heavily at this point upon Geoffrey of Monmouth. Geoffrey introduces a Brennius, son of Dunuallo Molmutius.[9] In Wace the father's name appears as Donewalmolus and Donvalo Molinus,[10] and in Layamon, following Wace, as Donwallo, Dunwale, and Dunwal.[11] There cannot be the least doubt that the author of *Fouke* had Geoffrey's Brennius son of Dunuallo in mind as the Bran Fitz Donwal of his story. But the immediate source of his form Donwal was probably Wace.

A most interesting point lies in the form Bran, which does not occur in Geoffrey or Wace. But the Welsh redactions of Geoffrey, known as the *Bruts*, regularly use Brân where Geoffrey has Brennius and Wace Brenne.[12] Of course, the author of the original *Fouke* did not consult the Welsh texts. Two alternatives remain: he himself identified Wace's Brenne with the Brân of Dinas Brân, or else the local Welsh tradition had identified the two already, and the Anglo-Norman author learned on the spot that Chastiel Bran was named

---

[5] For description see *Inventory of the Ancient Monuments in Wales and Monmouthshire, County of Denbigh* (London, 1914), pp. 119 ff.

[6] *Romania*, lv (1929), pp. 33, 37, 44.

[7] *Inventory*, &c., *County of Denbigh*, p. 121.

[8] J. E. Lloyd in his authoritative *History of Wales*, 2nd ed. (London, 1912), i. 244 f., describes the place in prehistoric times as 'the hill-fort, named after Brân, a famous figure of Celtic story, which guarded the upper waters of the "wizard stream"'.

[9] Geoffrey of Monmouth, *Historia*, ed. A. Griscom (New York, 1929), pp. 274, 276.   [10] Wace, *Brut*, ed. Leroux de Lincy (Rouen, 1836), i. 105, 108.

[11] Layamon, *Brut*, ed. F. Madden (London, 1847), i. 174, 175, 178.

[12] Geoffrey of Monmouth, op. cit., p. 665; Wace, op. cit., i. 110.

after the famous king of British history, Brenne. The latter supposition seems to me more plausible, since we have noted that other Welshmen, the authors of the *Bruts*, habitually equated Brennius with the Welsh figure Brân.

How much real local tradition is there in the story ascribed to the 'Bretoun'? Of course there is none in the recital of the early history of Britain, a prologue supplied by the author of the original *Fouke* and derived by him from Wace or Geoffrey. But the adventures of Payn Peverel in Chastiel Bran seem compounded of two undoubted Welsh traditions, of which one tells of the Horn of Brân and the other is a tale of hidden treasure still connected with Dinas Brân in the nineteenth century.

At first sight the search for the Horn of Brân in Chastiel Bran may seem futile. The author of *Fouke*,[13] after giving the 'Bretoun's' story, relates how Payn Peverel, entering Chastiel Bran, attacked a devil in the form of a fire-breathing giant, named Goemagog, and overcame him by virtue of the cross on his shield. The devil revealed that there was a great treasure hidden under the castle: there was also a bull (*tor*), which was worshipped by pagan giants as their god, conferred on them this treasure, and foretold coming events. St. Augustine, however, had converted many of them to Christianity. King William kept the giant's huge mace as a curiosity. Those familiar with the romance of *Perlesvaus* may be reminded by this narrative of two consecutive adventures of Perceval's.[14] The hero attacked a fire-breathing devil in the shield of a giant, and overcame him by virtue of the cross on his own shield. He next came to a castle, where there was a bull (*tor*)[15] of copper, which was worshipped by pagans as their god, gave them great abundance of whatever they desired, and answered all questions. Perceval, however, converted thirteen of them to Christianity. The correspondence between the adventures of Perceval in the castle of the sacred *tor* and those of Payn Peverel in the castle of the sacred *tor* is too marked to be due to chance.

What then is the relation between the two stories? Sebastian Evans,

---

[13] pp. 4 ff.

[14] *Perlesvaus*, ed. Nitze and Jenkins, i. 250–6.

[15] The scribes seem to have been puzzled by the word *tor*, MS. O reading *la tor* (tower), MS. Br reading *li cors, le cor* (horn), but since the best MS., P, reads *li tors* (ibid. ii. 21, 316) and Br reads *le torel* (bull calf) in l. 5944, and since the object was mounted on four copper columns and *braoit* (bellowed), as towers are not wont to do, the correct meaning must be 'bull'.

Miss Weston, and Professor Nitze have shown that the author of *Fouke* knew *Perlesvaus*,[16] and those who have a strong antipathy to lost sources will jump to the conclusion that he has borrowed the two incidents from *Perlesvaus*, combined them in one, localized them, and attributed them to his own hero. But so simple a solution does not seem probable. Professor Weinberg has shown that a favourite device of the author of *Perlesvaus* was to divide a borrowed story into two or more parts.[17] This would explain why he gives in the form of two adventures at two places what is told as one adventure at one place in *Fouke*. He must have drawn on a source common to both since he wrote earlier than the author of *Fouke* and since the latter makes no mention of several features prominent in the *Perlesvaus* version, such as the Chevalier au Dragon and the copper men, but makes much of the subterranean treasure, unmentioned in *Perlesvaus*. When the author of *Fouke* in a later passage does borrow from *Perlesvaus*, he not only mentions his source but also follows it accurately.[18] These facts lead to the conclusion that he did not borrow the Chastiel Bran passage from *Perlesvaus*, but that both stories go back to a common source.

This view is confirmed by the evidence that Bran Fitz Donwal, founder of Chastiel Bran, was the traditional possessor of a horn (Old French *cor*) of plenty. In a Welsh version of Geoffrey's *Historia* he is called Brân son of Dyfnwal, and in the division of his father's kingdom he was granted the *Gogledd*, the land north of the Humber; and later in his career he displayed lavish hospitality, giving food and drink to everyone who came.[19] Now a Welsh text describes the Horn of Brân from the *Gogledd*: 'the drink and the food that one asked one received in it when one desired.'[20] We have seen in the preceding chapter that this horn, translated into French as *cors* and mistakenly interpreted as 'body', was responsible for some of the most mysterious features of the Grail legend. Since *c* and *t* are often indistinguishable in manuscripts,[21] *cors* (obl. *cor*) could easily be

---

[16] S. Evans, *High History of the Holy Graal*, Everyman's Lib., pp. xiv f.; *Romania*, xliii (1914), 423 ff.; *Mod. Phil.* xvii (1919), 154.
[17] *PMLA*, l (1935), 26, 34. [18] *Perlesvaus*, ii. 82.
[19] Geoffrey of Monmouth, op. cit., pp. 276, 284.
[20] MS. Peniarth 77, p. 214. 'Corn Bran galed or gogledd; y ddiod ar bwyd a ofynid a gaid ynddo pan i damunid.' On the meaning of *galed* and how Brân was turned from a grudging into a generous man cf. Prof. T. Jones in *Mod. Lang. Rev.* xxxv (1940), 403 f.
[21] The scribe of *Perlesvaus* MS. Br regularly wrote *cor, cors*, instead of *tor, tors*. *Perlesvaus*, ii. 316.

read as *tors* (obl. *tor*) and interpreted as 'bull'. Now the sacred bull in *Perlesvaus* not only resembles the bull in the castle named after Bran Fitz Donwal but it also resembles the Horn of Brân son of Dyfnwal: it provided 'such abundance of every thing they desired that there was nothing in the world that they lacked'.

Of course objections will be raised. It can be urged that bulls were familiar to the imagination of the Middle Ages as objects of pagan worship, whereas horns were not. *Queen Mary's Psalter* depicts nearly every *faus deus* or *maumeth* as a bovine beast.[22] Therefore, *Fouke* and *Perlesvaus* preserve the original tradition in the word *tor*. I admit the fact but not the inference. It is precisely the unfamiliarity of the medieval French imagination with a horn as the object of pagan or Christian veneration which has led to confusions on a grand scale, confusions which no student of Grail romance can afford to disregard. Faced with the word *cor* or its nominative *cors* in sacred associations, a French romancer inevitably sought for any other meaning than 'horn'. Now it is obvious that one of the most natural interpretations would be to substitute *tor* for *cor*, and to see in the object of worship a bull.

Another possible objection to the theory lies in the fact that the earliest mention of the Horn of Brân occurs in a manuscript of about the year 1460.[23] This objection will carry no great weight with Celtists, who know how much ancient literature has been preserved only in manuscripts of comparatively modern date. It is, moreover, offset by the fact that Brân's Horn occurs in a list of magic objects, the Thirteen Treasures of the Isle of Britain,[24] some of which are mentioned in *Kulhwch and Olwen*, which dates roughly from the end of the eleventh century, and were doubtless famous before that time. Three talismans in the list, I have tried to show elsewhere, appear in *Perlesvaus*; two of them, the Sword and the Platter of Rhydderch, could not have been derived from the French romance.[25] There is reason, therefore, to believe not only in the

---

[22] G. F. Warner, *Queen Mary's Psalter* (London, 1912), pls. 13, 14, 57, 67. See H. Newstead, *Bran the Blessed in Arthurian Romance* (New York, 1939), pp. 87 f.

[23] MS. Peniarth 51, of which the late Sir William Ll. Davies, Librarian of the National Library of Wales, kindly wrote me that it dates 'c. 1460'.

[24] Quite a few versions of this list are extant in MS., but the variations are mainly verbal. Two versions have been published respectively by Ed. Jones in his *Bardic Museum* (London, 1802), p. 47, and by Lady Guest in her notes on *Kulhwch and Olwen* (found in most editions of her *Mabinogion*).

[25] *Romanische Forschungen*, xlv (1931), 69 f.

antiquity of the talismans in the list, but also in their influence upon the very literature we are considering.

Not only are the objections to the theory of little weight, but there remain two positive arguments in its favour. It has been contended by a notable line of scholars—Heinrich, Nutt, Martin, Rhys, Anwyl, Brown, Miss Kempe, Professor Nitze—that the Welsh Brân is the original of the Fisher King of the Grail romances;[26] Professor Newstead and I have added other arguments.[27] It now seems fairly certain that the name of the Grail castle, Corbenic, with its variant forms Corlenot and Cambenoyt,[28] represents a misreading of Chastiaus del Cor Benoit, the castle of the Blessed Horn. It will be conceded that if the same story is told of the castle of the Blessed *Cor* as is told of the two castles of the sacred *tor* in *Perlesvaus* and *Fouke*, this group of hypotheses will be confirmed. And we do find just such confirmation.

In the Vulgate cycle of Arthurian romance we find three accounts of heroes who, like Payn, spend a night in the *palais* of a perilous castle. In the *Estoire del Saint Graal* Galaphes, lying in the *palais* of Corbenic, is attacked by a man who seems all in flames and who denounces his audacity and plunges a spear into him.[29] 'Thereafter came many a knight who wished to tarry there, but without fail none tarried there but was found dead in the morning.' Compare the statement in *Fouke*: 'Many came there to see the marvels but never did any escape.' In the *Vulgate Lancelot* Gawain spends a night in the same *palais*, is pierced by a flaming lance, is warned by a knight to depart, fights with him until both are exhausted.[30] The same romance tells how later Bohors essays the nocturnal adventure of Corbenic, how, as in *Fouke*, a terrible storm breaks, how he is

---

[26] G. A. Heinrich, *Le Parcival de Wolfram von Eschenbach* (Paris, 1855), p. 59; A. Nutt, *Legends of the Holy Grail* (London, 1902), pp. 56–65; E. Martin, *Zur Gralsage* (Strassburg, 1880), p. 37; J. Rhys, *Studies in the Arthurian Legend* (Oxford, 1891), pp. 306–11; Hastings, *Encyclopedia of Religion and Ethics*, ii. 5; *Kittredge Anniversary Papers* (Boston, 1913), p. 244, n. 2; D. Kempe, *Legend of the Holy Grail* (London, 1905), pp. xviii–xxv; *Medieval Studies in Memory of G. Schoepperle Loomis* (New York, 1927), pp. 134 ff.

[27] Newstead, op. cit. Loomis, *Arthurian Tradition and Chrétien de Troyes*, pp. 386–8. Prof. Newstead pointed out (pp. 163–7) that Geoffrey of Monmouth modelled Brennius son of Dunwallo in part on Brân son of Llyr.

[28] C. Potvin, *Perceval le Gallois* (1866–71), vi. 150, n. 2; J. L. Weston, *Legend of Sir Lancelot* (London, 1901), p. 159.

[29] H. O. Sommer, *Vulgate Version of the Arthurian Romances* (Washington, 1909), i. 288 f.

[30] Ibid. iv. 344–7.

pierced by a fiery lance, and immediately after encounters and vanquishes a gigantic knight.[31] A significant but badly garbled feature is the appearance to Bohors of a man suffering great torment who awaits his deliverer. In the morning King Pelles asks Bohors if he has seen the Maimed King, the Fisher King, who was awaiting his deliverer. Though Bohors denies it and the details of the text will not permit identification of the Fisher King with the suffering man who had appeared to him, yet in an earlier form of the story, surely, Pelles's question was not meaningless, the Fisher King did dwell in the Castle of Corbenic, and was in fact seen by Bohors. It is most noteworthy that all three accounts of the night spent in Corbenic agree that the heroes behold a service centred about a holy vessel. Thus, taken together, the three stories correspond in six points to the story in *Fouke*: (1) A hero spends a night in the perilous *palais* of a castle. (2) The adventure is usually fatal. (3) A storm breaks with thunder and lightning. (4) The hero fights with a fiery antagonist. (5) The castle has been or is the dwelling of King Bran or the Fisher King, elsewhere named Bron. (6) In it a *tor* is worshipped, or a *saintismes vaissiaus et beneois* (a most holy and blessed vessel) is venerated, the latter, though confused with the Grail, being originally the *Cor Benoit* after which the castle was named. Such correspondences do not occur by accident. The Welsh tradition of the Horn of Brân is at the root of all these stories.

A final fact clinches the matter. *Fouke* states that the castle of King Bran was called the Old March (*la Vele Marche*) in reference to its position on the border of Wales. In the *Vulgate Lancelot* the castle of King Brangoire is called 'le chastel de la Marche', and he feasted outside it in a pavilion.[32] The name Brangoire may be easily explained as a corruption of Welsh *Brân Gawr*, 'Brân the Giant', and in the mabinogi of *Branwen* we read that King Brân the Blessed feasted in a tent because he was so huge that no house could contain him.[33] Once more, then, we find confirmation for the belief that Welsh stories of Brân centred around Dinas Brân on the march of England and Wales.

But it is evident that the stories we have examined about

---

[31] Sommer, *Vulgate Version*, v. 298–303. The adventures of Gawain and Bohors at Corbenic combine with the themes of the visit to the Grail castle and the nocturnal fight with a fiery antagonist the theme of the Perilous Bed. Cf. Loomis, *Arthurian Tradition*, pp. 204–10.

[32] Sommer, iv. 259, 264.

[33] *Mabinogion*, trans. G. and T. Jones, Everyman's Lib., p. 26.

Chastiel Bran and the Grail Castle could not have been transmitted directly from the Welsh to the original author of *Fouke*, for the *cyvarwyddiaid* could not have been guilty of transforming the Horn of Brân into a bull. It is therefore noteworthy that a *Bretoun*, not a *Galeys*, is credited with reporting to King William, of course in French, the legend of Chastiel Bran. For we know that the Breton *conteurs* flocked over to their ancestral home after the Norman Conquest,[34] and took a great interest in localizing their own sometimes distorted tales of Arthur, Brangoire, and Lancelot in regions which had their own traditions of Arthur, Brân, and Lluch Llauynnauc.[35] Thus it is possible to understand how the story told in *Fouke* is compounded of two main elements: the Breton-French distortions of the Brân legend, found also in *Perlesvaus* and the Vulgate cycle; the setting and the local legends of Dinas Brân.

That story can be analysed as follows: The oldest tradition to be detected is that of Brân the Blessed, son of Llŷr, and his vessels of plenty. He has been identified with Bran Fitz Donwal, whom Geoffrey of Monmouth had created by combining Brân the Blessed with the Gallic chief Brennus.[36] The sacred Horn was translated into French as *cors*; this in written transmission was misread as *tors* (bull) and interpreted as an idol which provided its worshippers with treasure. This interpretation either gave rise to, or was supported by, a local legend of buried treasure which survived into the nineteenth century. In 1790 a smith from Dimbraneth began digging for treasure at Dinas Brân, and in 1898 the winner of the Eisteddfod prize reported that there was a cave beneath the castle, filled with treasure, which would only be disclosed to a boy followed by a white dog with *llygaid arian*, 'silver eyes'.[37] This corresponds to the statement of the devil in *Fouke*, who, when asked where the subterranean treasure was, told Payn that it was destined for others, and exemplifies a widespread belief that hidden treasure awaits a predestined discoverer.[38] The ruinous state of the castle suggested that it was haunted by devils,[39] another common superstition,

[34] Cf. *infra*, p. 185; *Zts. f. franz. Sprache u. Lit.* xx¹ (1898), 93, 110.
[35] Loomis, *Arthurian Tradition*, pp. 15-23, 27-32; *Zts. f. franz. Sprache u. Lit.* xiii (1891), 86 f.; Ulrich von Zatzikhoven, *Lanzelet*, trans. Webster, pp. 13 f.
[36] Newstead, *Bran the Blessed*, pp. 163-7.
[37] *Hamwood Papers*, ed. G. H. Bell (London, 1930), p. 254; J. Rhys, *Celtic Folklore* (Oxford, 1901), i. 148.
[38] Ibid. ii. 470-2; E. S. Hartland, *Science of Fairy Tales* (New York, n.d.), pp. 236-9.
[39] W. H. Jones, *Old Karnarvon* (Carnarvon, n.d.), p. 139.

and they of course could only be overcome by the sign of the cross. To provide a flavour of historicity, the devil of Dinas Brân was said to inhabit the body of Geoffrey's Goemagog. Finally, the statement that King William preserved the giant's huge mace as a curiosity accords with other reports about supernatural mementoes.[40] According to Gervase of Tilbury, Robert earl of Gloucester gave a magical drinking-horn from a faery hillock to Henry I. William of Newburgh says that a similar cup, taken from a barrow in Yorkshire, was presented to Henry I, from whom it passed in succession to King David of Scotland, William the Lion, and Henry II.

We may now be prepared to believe the Burgundian poet, Robert de Boron, who declared about 1200 that Bron, the Good Fisher, was the subject of 'meintes paroles contées ki ne sont pas foles'.[41] We are also prepared to believe that these tales diverged widely, since Robert's account of Bron has little in common with those we have examined about Brân. Now the adventure of Payn Peverel at Chastiel Bran could hardly be more different than it is from Chrétien's account of Perceval's adventure at the castle of the Fisher King,[42] and on a superficial view it might seem absurd to propose that a common tradition underlay them both. Yet both present undeniable parallels to the visits of Gawain and Bohors to the castle of Corbenic described in the *Vulgate Lancelot*, and the greatest differences can be accounted for by the fact that Chrétien was riming a narrative in which Brân's horn of plenty had been metamorphosed into the *cors benoiz*, the miraculously feeding Host, whereas in *Fouke* the horn had been converted into a *tors* which conferred wealth on its worshippers. No wonder that such diverse misconceptions led to such divergent developments. In spite, therefore, of the patent unlikeness of the two narratives, it is still reasonable to hold that Chrétien has not only preserved a legend of Brân and his Horn, as transmitted and elaborated by Breton *conteurs*, but that he has also retained in his story of Perceval's visit to the Fisher King's castle some hints of its localization at Dinas Brân. A *conteur* following down the valley of the Dee, still famous for its trout- and salmon-fishing, could well imagine how Perceval met the royal Fishermen, drifting in a boat down the stream, how he glimpsed from a height the castle before him, how he rode up to the

---

[40] Hartland, op. cit., pp. 145 f.
[41] Vss. 3456–8.
[42] Chrétien, *Perceval*, ed. A. Hilka (Halle, 1932), pp. 133–53.

Chastiel Bran, Dinas Brân, and the Grail Castle

drawbridge and, entering, enjoyed the hospitality for which Brân the Blessed and Brân son of Dyfnwal, originally identical, were both renowned.[43]

The legends clustering about the now ruinous castle are not the only evidences of the former celebrity of Brân in Denbighshire. Though the mabinogi of *Branwen* would lead us to believe that he was associated mainly with western Wales from Anglesey to Grassholm, we learn from allusions in the poetry of the *Gogynfeirdd* that the whole of eastern North Wales was called Bro Frân (*y Vrân vro*).[44] The Book of Aneirin also mentions the fight of Brân at Cynwyd (*ymwan bran yg kynwyt*), and Cynwyd is a village on the upper Dee.[45] Not far is a hill named Cadair Fronwen, named after Brân's sister. Near Nantglyn are Gorsedd Frân and Llyn Brân, the hill and the lake of Brân. Such topographical associations, not only with Brân but with other ancient figures such as Manawyd and Mabon,[46] show that Denbighshire must once have been a land rich in myth and legend.

But of all this almost nothing survived the Renaissance. George Borrow, who has some comments on Dinas Brân in chaps. vi, viii, and lxi of *Wild Wales*, translates an *englyn* by a poet of the seventeenth century, Roger Cyffin, but the Welshman seems to know the site only as the haunt of crows (Welsh *brân*, a crow).

> Gone, gone are thy gates, Dinas Brân on the height!
> Thy wardens are blood-crows and ravens, I trow;
> Now no one will wend from the field of the fight
> To the fortress on high, save the raven and crow.

Another *englyn* by a nineteenth-century poet, Taliesin o Eifion, translated by Professor Jackson, displays a similar unawareness of the old traditions.[47]

> *Englyn* and harp and harp-string and the lordly feasts, all these have passed away; and where the nobility of Gwynedd used to be the birds of night now reign.

---

[43] Newstead, *Bran the Blessed*, pp. 19, 166; Geoffrey of Monmouth, *Historia*, ed. Griscom, p. 284.
[44] Anwyl in *Trans. of Third International Cong. of Religions* (Oxford, 1898), ii. 236 f.
[45] Anwyl in *Celtic Review*, iv (1907), 258.
[46] Ibid.; Loomis, *Arthurian Tradition*, p. 184.
[47] K. H. Jackson, *Celtic Miscellany* (London, 1951), p. 149.

The only supernatural association which seems to have lingered about the place in modern times is a folk-tale of one, Tudur of Llangollen, who joined a fairy dance in a hollow on the slopes of the hill called Nant yr Ellyllon, the Dingle of the Elves, only to find the fairies turned into dogs, foxes, goats, and cats, and the fiddler into a horned devil.[48]

[48] W. Sikes, *British Goblins* (London, 1880), pp. 79–81. For other folk-lore of the neighbourhood cf. Rhys, *Celtic Folklore*, i. 238, and *Journ. of Brit. Archaeological Assoc.*, 1878, pp. 426 f. The latter represents Arthur as living in one of the Eglwyseg Rocks, presumably the one called Craig Arthur.

CHAPTER IV

Brân the Blessed and 'Sone de Nausay'

THE two preceding chapters have suggested that the Welsh legend of Brân the Blessed exercised a very remarkable influence on Arthurian literature. Indeed, Professor Newstead devoted a book to the subject, and I have traced other ramifications of the story in my *Arthurian Tradition and Chrétien de Troyes*. Nevertheless, it has remained possible, even in the face of the mass of evidence, for sceptics to ask: 'If, by general agreement, the Welsh traditions about Brân are most fully represented in the mabinogi of *Branwen*, why is there no Arthurian narrative which presents a recognizable correspondence?' This is a reasonable challenge, and I believe it can be met in the romance of *Sone de Nausay*.[1]

This poem, composed apparently late in the thirteenth century, has already been brought by a number of scholars, including Miss Newstead and Bruce,[2] into relation with the Matter of Britain. Miss Weston rightly stressed the passage which attributed the sterilizing of all forms of life in the kingdom of Lorgres (from Welsh *Lloegr* = England) to the wounding of the Fisher King in the reins and below.[3] For, though her speculations about a primitive vegetation cult, partly Christianized and transmitted from the Orient to Britain, lacked solid foundations, her theory of the Waste Land as illustrating a sympathetic nexus between the vitality of a divine king and the life-forces of his kingdom has the support not only of *Sone* but of other medieval texts.[4] The presence of such a heathenish superstition in a poem as pious as *Sone* justifies overlooking the rather late date of the text. If it contains anything so primitive,

[1] Ed. M. Goldschmidt, *Bibliothek des Literarischen Vereins in Stuttgart*, ccxxi (Tübingen, 1899).
[2] Ibid., p. 556. H. Newstead, *Bran the Blessed in Arthurian Romance*, pp. 93–95, 131, 134, 173, 193, 195. *Historia Meriadoci and De Ortu Walwanii*, ed. J. D. Bruce, *Hesperia, Ergänzungsreihe*, ii (Göttingen and Baltimore, 1913), pp. xxxiv f. S. Singer in *Zts. f. deutsches Altertum*, xliv (1900), 330 ff. J. L. Weston in *Romania*, xliii (1914), 403–20; R. S. Loomis, *Arthurian Tradition*, pp. 174, 221, 243, 362, 389, 391, 393.
[3] J. L. Weston, *From Ritual to Romance* (Cambridge, 1920), pp. 20 f.
[4] Loomis, *Arthurian Tradition*, pp. 389 f., 393.

it may preserve other archaic features; it may reflect elements in the Brân legend which have not survived in other Arthurian romances.

Now, though *Sone* has admittedly incorporated some characteristic figures and motifs from Arthurian romance such as Meleagant's sword-bridge, a loathly damsel, the Grail, and the lance of Longinus,[5] it tells a story which has no connexion with Arthur and his court. It sends no Perceval or Gawain in quest of the sacred vessel, and on several other points it diverges from the more familiar versions of the Grail legend. But it is these divergences—difficult to explain on any other basis—which can be accounted for as reflecting in distorted form the last part of the mabinogi of *Branwen*.

Let me sketch, then, the relevant portions of the poem.[6]

Sone, the titular hero, an Alsatian knight, undertook on behalf of Alain, king of Norway, a single combat against a gigantic champion of the king of Scotland. In order to win the favour of Heaven, he went with King Alain to an island off the Norwegian coast, inhabited by a monastic community, there to pray for victory. Disembarking, Sone and Alain were welcomed by the monks, and were seated at a banquet in a meadow, surrounded by a marble wall and overlooking the sea. They had such an abundance of food that it was an arduous task for those who served them.

The next day the abbot related the story of Joseph of Arimathea, substantially as we have it in the first part of the *Estoire del Saint Graal*:[7] his begging the body of Christ from Pilate, the descent from the Cross, the burial, the imprisonment of Joseph, his receiving from the risen Christ a vessel which preserved him alive for forty years, the conversion of the emperor Vespasian, the deliverance of Joseph from prison, and the elevation of his son Josaphus to be the first bishop of Christendom. (At this point the narrative abandons the *Estoire*.)

The abbot went on to relate that Joseph, in company with Vespasian and Titus, discovered the lance-head with which Longinus had pierced the side of God,[8] and carefully preserved it. Soon after, he left Syria in a boat without mast or sail, and by way of Gaeta arrived in Norway, where he expelled the Saracens, slew their king, wedded his daughter, and was crowned. God, displeased

---

[5] *Sone de Nausay*, pp. 119–27, 403 f., 445.   [6] Ibid., pp. 110–48.
[7] Ibid., vss. 4569–700. *Vulgate Version of the Arthurian Romances*, ed. H. O. Sommer (Washington, 1909–16), i. 13–18, 36 f.
[8] On the Lance of Longinus cf. L. H. Loomis in *Speculum*, xxv (1950), 437–56; in *Romanic Rev.* xli (1950), 241–60; K. Burdach, *Der Graal* (Stuttgart, 1938).

because Joseph had married a woman who remained a heathen at heart, wounded him in the reins and below, so that he occupied himself with fishing and was called 'Rois Peschieres'. So long as he was maimed, all forms of life in the land of Lorgres failed to reproduce. Finally a knight healed him, he resumed his martial exploits, and before his death founded the community of thirteen monks which was playing host to Sone and King Alain.

At the close of his discourse, the abbot showed Sone a piece of the 'true cross', the holy Grail, the lance-head, from which a drop of blood hung, and the reliquaries containing the bodies of Joseph and his second son Adan. The abbot, we learn, was well supplied with (or by) holy bodies and he had served them well. During the showing of the Grail and the holy lance, the monks wept copiously. A long banquet of many viands followed.

Assured of the prayers of the monks on his behalf, Sone returned with Alain to the mainland, and the abbot sent after him the sword with which Joseph had guarded the land. With this weapon Sone overcame the giant and cut off his head. Before Sone departed from Norway, King Alain's daughter gave him the cup from which the Fisher King had been wont to drink, and his sword. We learn that the name of the island castle was Galoche.[9]

First, let us consider the very odd fact that, though the realm of the Fisher King is supposed to be Norway, it is the realm of Lorgres, England, which suffers as the result of his wound; and though the castle he built was supposed to lie on an island off the Norwegian coast, it is called Galoche, which, as Bruce observed,[10] must be a corruption of *galesche*, meaning 'Welsh'. As *galesche* is a feminine form, it must have modified a feminine noun, presumably *isle*. It is manifest that the poet has clumsily transferred to Norway a tradition which properly belonged to Britain. Moreover, it is a tradition which centres about the Fisher King and his possessions—Grail, lance-head, sword, and cup—a tradition which in the Arthurian romances is localized in Britain, and therefore one may not dismiss as mere aberrations of the poet's fancy the association of the Fisher King with England and the situation of his home on a Welsh island.

[9] Vss. 5503, 5779. Later in the poem (vss. 16799–17114) Sone returned to Galoche for his wedding with Odee and their coronation, after which the Grail and the lance-head were again exhibited.

[10] J. D. Bruce, *Evolution of Arthurian Romance* (Göttingen and Baltimore, 1923), i. 350, n. 16.

A second odd and significant fact is that the poet, after giving in abridged form the story of Joseph of Arimathea according to the *Estoire del Saint Graal*, at a certain point abandons this source completely and gives an account of Joseph's adventures and of the Grail castle which flouts the authority of all antecedent Grail romances that have been preserved to us. Why? We may choose between two alternatives: either the author was giving free rein to his fancy, or he had discovered, presumably in written form, a legend of the Grail independent of the surviving texts but dependent on old traditions. The second alternative is favoured, not only by the traces of an older localization, just mentioned, and by the primitive concept of the Waste Land which he gives us, but also by the correspondences with the story of Brân as told in *Branwen*.

Turning to the mabinogi what do we find? Brân was a king of Britain, 'exalted with the crown of London'.[11] He led an expedition to a foreign land and was victorious.[12] Nevertheless, he was wounded in the foot with a poisoned spear, and though no causal nexus is mentioned, the islands of Ireland and Britain were rendered desolate.[13] Brân commanded his followers to cut off his head and to proceed with it first to Harlech and then to the island of Gwales off the coast of Pembrokeshire. Obeying his commands, they spent seven years at Harlech, regaling themselves with meat and drink. Then setting out for Gwales, they found there a fair royal place, a great hall, overlooking the sea. That night they spent there without stint, and we may infer that they continued to feast, as they had at Harlech, for eighty years, in the company of the uncorrupted head of Brân.[14] This was called the Hospitality (*Yspydawt*)[15] of the Wondrous Head.

There are, of course, many differences between this eleventh-century tale[16] and the thirteenth-century romance of *Sone*. But let us note the resemblances between what we learn of Brân and what we learn of Joseph of Arimathea, alias the Fisher King.

1. Brân was king of Britain, crowned in London. The Fisher King's realm was Lorgres, i.e. England.

[11] *Mabinogion*, trans. T. and G. Jones, Everyman's Lib., p. 25.
[12] Ibid., pp. 34-37.   [13] Ibid., p. 37 f.
[14] Ibid., pp. 37-39.
[15] Sir Ifor Williams has a long note on *yspydawt* in his *Pedeir Keinc y Mabinogi* (Cardiff, 1930), p. 221. He shows that the earliest dictionaries translate the word as entertainment or feast (*gwledd*).
[16] On date of the *Four Branches* cf. ibid., p. xli.

2. Brân led an expedition to a foreign land and was victorious. Joseph sailed to a foreign land and conquered it.

3. Brân was wounded in the foot and thereafter Britain was desolate. The Fisher King was wounded in the reins and below and, as a consequence, England was waste.

4. Brân ordained that after his death his followers should dwell for eighty years on an island off the coast of Wales. The Fisher King founded a community which after his death occupied an island castle called Galoche, i.e, Welsh.

5. Brân's followers feasted without stint in a royal hall overlooking the sea. The Fisher King's community feasted sumptuously in a walled meadow overlooking the sea.

6. Brân's followers carefully preserved his head on an island off the coast of Wales. The Fisher King's community preserved his body in the island castle of Galoche.

Thus it becomes clear that, though the greater part of *Branwen* offers little resemblance to the Grail portion of *Sone*, the last part presents a remarkable parallel. When one takes into consideration that the *Didot Perceval* calls the Fisher King not Joseph of Arimathea but Bron,[17] the case for the derivation of the legends of the Fisher King from those of Brân seems definitely clinched.

Even though this relationship is established, one may entertain a strong curiosity as to why there are such differences between *Branwen* and *Sone*. How are these to be accounted for? It should be said, in a general way, that when two versions of a legend are separated so far in time and place of composition, great discrepancies are to be expected. Furthermore, it should be kept in mind that *Branwen* was not a unique and sacred text, containing the one complete and authoritative legend of Brân. As with the Irish sagas,[18] variant and inconsistent versions of the mabinogi existed among the Welsh, and there were tales of Brân which were not included in it at all. Once this state of affairs is recognized, a little detective work will serve to account for the chief differences between *Branwen* and *Sone*.

First, let us inquire why the name Brân, preserved in the *Didot Perceval* as Bron, was replaced by Joseph of Arimathea, with the

---

[17] *Didot-Perceval*, ed. W. R. Roach (Philadelphia, 1941), p. 150 and *passim*.
[18] A. H. Healy, *Heroic Romances of Ireland* (London, 1905), I. xviii; R. Thurneysen, *Irische Helden- und Königsage* (Halle, 1921), pp. 413-15, 598; W. J. Gruffydd, *Rhiannon* (Cardiff, 1953), pp. 24-27.

result that a portion of the *Estoire del Saint Graal* was incorporated in *Sone*. The answer has already been suggested in the previous chapters.[19] Though in *Branwen* no mention is made of Brân's possessing any feeding-vessels, a horn of plenty is assigned to him in the Thirteen Treasures of the Isle of Britain. The word for 'horn' in old French is *cors* in the nominative case, but *cors* also meant 'body', and a *cors* with sacred and miraculous associations was much more likely to be understood as a body than a horn. Hence the author of *Sone*—and probably others before and after him[20]— concluded that the owner of the holy *cors* was the custodian of the body of Christ, namely, Joseph of Arimathea. Once this identification was widely accepted, inevitably the Grail was taken to be the dish of the Last Supper and the lance became the Lance of Longinus. There seems to be a survival of the original function of Brân's horn as a source of plenty in verse 4927 of *Sone*, which reads: 'De sains cors fu l'abbés garnis'; for Professor Newstead has shown[21] that though in its context this certainly means that the abbot of Galoche was well supplied with holy bodies, *de* could mean 'by', and the verse may preserve in its ambiguity the original tradition that Brân's followers were supplied on the isle of Gwales *by* his horn of plenty.

Another odd element in the story of Joseph in *Sone*, which has no counterpart in *Branwen*, is his marriage to the daughter of the king of Norway. This, too, can be shown to have traditional backing. For, so far as I am aware, the fact that Geoffrey of Monmouth

---

[19] I have treated the reason for the choice of Joseph of Arimathea rather more fully in *Colloque du Graal* (Strasbourg, 1955).

[20] Robert de Boron, early in the thirteenth century, anticipated the authors of the *Estoire del Saint Graal* and *Sone* in knowledge of the Joseph story, and I believe that they drew on a common source, since the *Estoire* does not repeat the blunders of Robert, such as confusing the names Bron and Hebron and misconceiving the Grail as a chalice. Moreover, episodes common to Robert's *Joseph* and to the *Estoire* are presented in the latter in forms which are closer to parallel secular traditions, and this seems most unlikely if the author of the *Estoire* were dependent on Robert. Cf. *Romanic Rev.* xxxiii (1942), 170 f.; Newstead, op. cit., pp. 51–55; *Mod. Lang. Rev.* xxiv (1929), 421–3, 428, 434.

[21] Newstead, op. cit., p. 94, n. 32. This interpretation is rendered highly probable by the fact that we have a similar statement about a holy body which acts as a talisman of plenty in the *Estoire del Saint Graal* (*Vulgate Version*, ed. Sommer, i. 285) After the death of Josephes, Joseph's son, the Scots carried off his body (*cors*) into their land because of a great famine that was there. 'Then it was a proven verity— and the Estoire du Saint Graal attests it—that at the coming of the holy body (*cors* so many goods and all manner of things came to the land that people said truly that Our Lord had done this for him as a miracle.'

combined in the story of Brennius elements from the career of the historical Gaulish chief Brennus, who sacked Rome in 390 B.C., with traditions of Brân, goes undisputed by any competent scholar.[22] Indeed, the identity of Brennius with Brân was so patent that Welsh translators of the *Historia Regum Britanniae* uniformly substituted the name Brân. It is, therefore, hardly credible that by mere accident Geoffrey says that Brennius crossed the seas and wedded the daughter of the King of Norway,[23] just as in *Sone* Joseph sailed to Norway and married the king's daughter.

Another point on which *Sone* does not harmonize with *Branwen* is in the number of monks who held their feasts in the island castle of Galoche and the number of Brân's followers who feasted for eighty years on the island of Gwales. There were twelve monks and their abbot; there were only seven followers of Brân. On this point *Sone* is corroborated not only by Geoffrey but by other texts also. Of Brennius the *Historia* says that he visited the princes of Gaul, accompanied by only twelve knights.[24] Again, when in *Perlesvaus* Gauvain visited the castle of the Fisher King, he was led into a hall, where he was seated with twelve other knights at a table and served by a damsel bearing the Grail.[25] It is highly significant that these knights, though they were over a hundred years old, seemed less than forty, for we seem to have echoed here the very tradition which appears in *Branwen* to the effect that none of the followers of Brân after the lapse of eighty years on Gwales perceived that another was older by that time than when they came there.[26] In the *Queste del Saint Graal*, too, twelve knights assembled in the castle of the Maimed King and were served by Christ Himself.[27] Evidently Arthurian romance supports *Sone*, as against *Branwen*, as to the number of Brân's followers who enjoyed perpetual feast, namely twelve. How, then, did the author of *Branwen* come to specify seven? Professor Gruffydd wrote me with characteristic

---

[22] Newstead, op. cit., p. 164.

[23] Geoffrey of Monmouth, *Historia Regum Britanniae*, ed. A. Griscom (New York, 1929), p. 277. Book iii, ch. 1.   [24] Ibid., p. 282. Book iii, ch. 6.

[25] *Perlesvaus*, ed. Nitze and others (Chicago, 1932-7), i, ll. 2414-18. Though MS. O reads '.xxii.' the better MSS. read '.xii.'

[26] J. Loth, *Mabinogion* (Paris, 1913), i. 148: 'aucun d'eux ne s'apercevait que l'autre fût plus vieux de tout ce temps qu'au moment où ils y étaient venus.' This is surely the correct translation. *Perlesvaus*, ll. 897-900, 940-7, also stresses the youthful appearance of those who dwell near the Grail.

[27] *Queste del Saint Graal*, ed. A. Pauphilet (Paris, 1949), pp. 267-71; *Vulgate Version*, ed. Sommer, vi. 188-91.

kindness[28] that there must have been some confusion with the tradition, so emphasized in *The Spoils of Annwn* (*Preiddeu Annwn*), that only seven returned from Arthur's raid on the Other World[29]—a theory supported by the fact that Taliesin was one of these seven and also one of the seven who returned with Brân from his disastrous expedition to Ireland.

One last point. The author of *Sone* shows awareness, as we have seen, of authentic Grail traditions preserved elsewhere, but not in such a form that he could have extracted his version from the earlier texts. Another instance of this phenomenon is the statement that when the abbot revealed the holy Grail, and again when he brought in the lance-head, the monks wept.[30] Nothing of the kind is narrated in Chrétien's *Conte del Graal*, but we do find a scene of lamentation in *Peredur* and Wolfram's *Parzival*. In the former, as in *Sone*, when the bleeding spear was introduced, and again when the salver or Grail was brought in, all shrieked and cried.[31] Likewise in *Parzival*, when a squire bore a bleeding spear into the Maimed King's hall, there was weeping and wailing.[32] Now the author of *Sone*, it goes without saying, did not consult *Peredur* or *Parzival*. One must explain the correspondence between the three romances as due either to mere coincidence or to a common traditional heritage, and the latter explanation seems much the more likely.

To sum up, then, it appears that if we take what the mabinogi tells us of Brân's hospitality, his wounding, and the sojourn of his followers after his death on an island off the coast of Wales, add what Geoffrey of Monmouth tells about the marriage of Brennius and about his twelve companions, and interpolate what the *Estoire del Saint Graal* tells of Joseph of Arimathea in the Holy Land, we have all the essential elements and many details of the story of the Fisher King in *Sone de Nausay*.

[28] Letter of 18 April 1939. 'He [the composer of *Preiddeu Annwn*], in the person of Taliesin, has the best right to know about the Harrying of Annwfn, because he was one of the seven who escaped from that Harrowing. Another version of the same story very much disguised is found in the Account of the Survivors from Ireland, of whom Taliesin was one, in the Mabinogi of *Branwen*.... I have no doubt that the attack on Ireland in *Branwen* is to be traced to an attack on Annwfn for the possession of the *Pair*.'

[29] See *infra*, pp. 134–6.

[30] *Sone*, vss. 4901–20.

[31] *Mabinogion*, trans. T. and G. Jones, Everyman's Library, p. 192.

[32] *Parzival*, 231, 17–232, 4; M. F. Richey, *Story of Parzival and the Graal* (Oxford, 1935), p. 80; Mary R. Williams, *Essai sur la Composition du Roman Gallois de Peredur* (Paris, 1909), pp. 91 f.

CHAPTER V

King Arthur and the Antipodes

THE 'Breton hope'—the belief in Arthur's survival and victorious return—proliferated various legends. He lived on in the form of a raven or a chough;[1] as leader of the Wild Hunt, as Maimed King, as the treasure-guarding warrior chief in a hollow mountain;[2] now in the mysterious isle of Avalon, now in Sicily, now beyond the Red Sea.[3] None of these traditions is more curious than the one known as late as Milton's time but recorded as early as 1167–9 (the period of Chrétien's *Erec*) in the *Draco Normannicus* of Étienne de Rouen,[4] which represents the British hero as lord of the Antipodes and furnishes us with a correspondence between Roland of Dinan, King Arthur, and Henry II of England. Appealed to by the Breton Roland, Arthur threatens Henry with a host of his antipodean subjects. Henry, smiling disdainfully, agrees to hold Brittany as Arthur's vassal.

In an article published over twenty years ago[5] J. S. P. Tatlock interpreted this correspondence as an effort by the Norman author to make the Bretons and their belief in Arthur's survival ridiculous; Henry's concession to Arthur's blustering claims over Brittany were

---

[1] J. D. Bruce, *Evolution of Arthurian Romance* (Baltimore, 1923), i. 34 n. Cf. W. C. Borlase, *Dolmens of Ireland* (London, 1897), ii. 595; J. Villa-Amil y Castro, *Antiquedades Prehistóricas* (Lugo, 1873), p. 75, n. 2.

[2] For the Wild Hunt cf. O. Driesen, *Der Ursprung des Harlekin* (Berlin, 1904), pp. 64, 90 f.; K. Meisen, *Die Sagen vom Wütenden Heer* (Münster, 1935); *Romanic Review*, iii (1912), 191; xii (1921), 286. For Arthur as Maimed King cf. E. Martin, *Zur Gralsage* (Strassburg, 1880), pp. 31 ff.; W. J. Entwistle, *Arthurian Legend in the Literatures of the Spanish Peninsula* (London, 1925), pp. 186–9. For Arthur in cave or hollow mountain cf. below, p. 69, n. 36.

[3] For Avalon cf. L. A. Paton, *Fairy Mythology of Arthurian Romance* (Boston, 1903), pp. 25–47, 250 f.; *Mod. Lang. Notes*, lii (1937), 414–16; *Romanic Review*, xxix (1938), 176 f.; *Vassar Mediaeval Studies* (New Haven, 1923), pp. 10–25; *Perlesvaus*, ed. W. A. Nitze and others, ii (1937), 48–59. For localizations in Mediterranean and Orient cf. E. G. Gardner, *Arthurian Legend in Italian Literature* (London, 1930), pp. 12–15; *Mod. Lang. Notes*, lii. 414–16.

[4] *Chronicles of the Reign of Stephen, Henry II, and Richard I*, ed. R. Howlett, ii (London, 1885), 696–707. *Columbia Milton*, ed. F. A. Patterson, i (New York, 1931), 293.

[5] *Mod. Phil.* xxxi (1933), 1–18, 113–25.

intended ironically. With this general interpretation I agree. The satire is aimed at the 'Breton hope', notorious in twelfth-century Europe.[6] But when Tatlock suggests that Étienne invented Arthur's rule over the Antipodes in accordance with his satiric purpose, that is a different matter. Let us first look at the longest and perhaps most illuminating passage in Étienne's poem, which depicts Arthur as ruler of the nether hemisphere:

> Saucius Arturus petit herbas inde sororis,
> Avallonis eas insula sacra tenet.
> Suscipit hic fratrem Morganis nympha perennis,
> Curat, alit, refovet, perpetuumque facit.
> Traditur antipodum sibi jus; fatatus, inermis,
> Belliger assistit, proelia nulla timet.
> Sic hemispherium regit inferius, nitet armis,
> Altera pars mundi dimidiata sibi . . .
> Antipodes hujus fatalia jura tremiscunt;
> Inferior mundus subditus extat ei.
> Evolat ad superos, quandoque recurrit ad ima.[7]

Five other references to these inhabitants of the lower hemisphere occur: 'Arturum . . . qui tunc apud antipodes degebat'; 'apud antipodes Arturus colloquium habuit'; 'ab antipodum . . . tellure recessi'; 'bellis antipodum pacatis'; 'antipodum sibi jura favent' (vss. 946–7 head, 954–5 head, 1193, 1207, 1241). The 'Antipodes' then are the inhabitants of the 'hemispherium inferius', and Arthur is represented as leading a host of them to the relief of the Bretons by way of the Cyclades, India, Parthia, and Arabia.

To explain this novel association between the British hero and the lower world, Tatlock put forward with some confidence the suggestion that Étienne invented it.[8] According to this hypo-

---

[6] R. H. Fletcher, *Arthurian Material in the Chronicles* (Boston, 1906), pp. 100–2; E. K. Chambers, *Arthur of Britain* (London, 1927), pp. 17, 25, 46, 107–9, 112, 121–4, 217–32; Gardner, op. cit., pp. 7–9; *Speculum*, viii (1933), 455, 465.

[7] *Chronicles of the Reign of Stephen*, ii, vss. 1161 ff., trans.: 'Then the wounded Arthur seeks after the herbs of his sister; them the sacred isle of Avallon contains. Here the immortal nymph Morgan receives her brother, attends, nourishes, restores, and renders him eternal. The lordship of the antipodean folk is given him. Endowed with faery powers, unarmed, he assumes the warrior's role and fears battles not at all. Thus he rules the lower hemisphere, shines in arms, and the other half of the world is allotted to him. . . . The antipodeans tremble at his faery sway; the lower world is subject to him. He speeds forth to the upper folk, and sometimes returns to the lowest regions.'

[8] *Mod. Phil.* xxxi. 16 f.

thesis, the Norman author 'has preferred to stand alone in placing Arthur's domain, with no alluring description [such as those in Geoffrey of Monmouth's *Vita Merlini* and the *Gesta Regum Britanniae*, perhaps by Guillaume de Rennes], in a region blighted by orthodox disapproval, by scepticism, ridicule, and grotesque description, and portraiture; to set him reigning perhaps over Skiapodes, Cynocephali, and Troglodytes, whose anatomy is even more harsh than their names'.[9] 'With the love of the grotesque in which the medieval artist revelled, the map-maker thoroughly enjoyed himself; parts of the earth hard by the Antipodes are covered with Skiapodes resting in the shade of their own feet, with men having four eyes or but one, or men whose heads do grow beneath their shoulders with faces in their bosoms.'[10] 'Who can doubt that in the twelfth century a purely literary writer would adopt them [the Antipodes] only in a light, sceptical, and humorous context?'[11]

Though willing enough to grant that Étienne emphasized Arthur's connexion with this remote and fantastic region from precisely the motives that Tatlock attributes to him, I believe that he neither invented the connexion nor did he emphasize it with intent to call up visions of monsters in the minds of his readers. For, though he referred to the Antipodes seven times, not once did he suggest any grotesque deformity. Tatlock, who has explored with characteristic industry the medieval texts and maps consulted by the learned, has found not one text or map before 1167 which populates the antipodean region with monsters;[12] and I have been able to discover but one. Isidore of Seville says: 'Antipodes in Lybia plantas versas habent post crura et octonos digitos in plantis.'[13] Famous and familiar though the *Etymologiae* was, it does not seem likely that Étienne could count upon his readers to supply this detail from memory without a hint from him, and he gives no hint that his Antipodes were equipped with other than normal 'understanding'.

[9] Ibid., p. 17. [10] Ibid., p. 18. [11] Ibid.
[12] Only two maps, dated 1203 and 1250, show a Skiapod in what is intended to represent the southern Continent, sometimes confused with the Antipodes (cf. C. R. Beazley, *Dawn of Modern Geography* (London, 1901), ii. 595 f., 603). Tatlock omits from his references the classic article of Boffito, 'La Leggenda degli Antipodi', in *Miscellanea di Studi Critici Edita in Onore di Arturo Graf* (Bergamo, 1903), p. 583.
[13] Isidore of Seville, *Etymologiae*, ed. W. M. Lindsay (Oxford, 1911), vol. ii, XI. iii. 24. Trans.: 'The Antipodes in Lybia have feet turned backwards from their legs and eight toes on each foot.' Probably the feet turned backward are due to a mistaken effort to explain the word *antipodes*.

May I suggest that Tatlock missed the clue to Étienne's novel concept because he has confined his attention too exclusively to the heavy literature of the period and has deliberately[14] brushed aside that mass of light lay tradition which we know vastly intrigued some at least among the learned? This was the age of Giraldus Cambrensis, Walter Map, and Gervase of Tilbury, whom today we should call collectors of folk-lore. It was the age when Wace said of 'les aventures . . . Ki d'Artur sunt tant recuntées' that they were 'Ne tut mençunge ne tut veir, Tut folie ne tut saveir',[15] and even went, himself, to verify the faery marvels of the Forest of Broceliande.[16] Surely, we cannot afford to neglect any evidence from the *nugae* of the period in attempting to discover the origin of Arthur's rule over the lower hemisphere.

Two texts indicate that this belief was traditional. The *Gesta Regum Britanniae*, written about 1235 (perhaps by Guillaume de Rennes) for Cadiocus, bishop of Vannes,[17] condemns Modred's rashness in attacking Arthur,'quem totus metuit mundus, quem totus obhorret Antipodum populus'.[18] Though Tatlock knew this reference, he consigned it to a footnote.[19] Conclusive proof of traditional origin lies in the fact that Chrétien mentions the belief in his *Erec*, dated about 1170,[20] therefore just after the composition of the *Draco Normannicus*. We read that at Arthur's court there appeared among those who held their lands of him

Bilis, king of the Antipodes. . . . Of all dwarfs Bilis[21] was the smallest. . . . To display his wealth and power Bilis brought in his company two kings who were dwarfs and held their lands of him. . . . Everyone regarded them as marvels. When they had arrived at court, they were

---

[14] I say 'deliberately' because though Tatlock had consulted J. K. Wright's *Geographical Lore* (cf. *Mod. Phil.*, xxxi. 12, n. 4; 13, n. 10; 14, n. 16), in which Gervase of Tilbury's story of a visit to the Antipodes is given on p. 161, he ignored it. He also ignored Chrétien's reference to the subject in *Erec*, though he knew my *Celtic Myth and Arthurian Romance*, which discusses on p. 197 both the *Draco* and the *Erec* passages.

[15] Wace, *Brut*, ed. I. Arnold, I (Paris, 1938), lxxxv.

[16] Wace, *Roman de Rou*, ed. Andresen (Heilbronn, 1879), ii, vss. 6395-420.

[17] *Romania*, xxviii (1899), 330.

[18] *Gesta Regum Britanniae*, ed. F. Michel (London: Cambrian Archaeological Assoc., 1862), p. 151.

[19] *Mod. Phil.*, xxxi. 16, n. 24.

[20] *Bulletin Bibliographique de la Société Internationale Arthurienne*, No. 2 (1950), pp. 70-74.

[21] Variants: bylis, belins, bilius. On this figure and his connexion with Pelles, 'li rois de la basse gent', in *Perlesvaus* cf. Loomis, *Arthurian Tradition*, pp. 142-5.

held very dear. All three were honoured and served at court like kings, for they were very noble men.[22]

It is surely no coincidence when we discover that Arthur is conceived as overlord of the Antipodes, not only in the imaginary correspondence of the Breton Roland of Dinan and in a poem dedicated to the Breton bishop of Vannes, but also in the earliest surviving romance of Chrétien de Troyes, whose sources were the French narratives of the Breton *conteurs*.[23] We are evidently dealing with a tradition current in Brittany when Étienne wrote, presumably one of those *nugae Britonum* which William of Malmesbury knew in 1125,[24] one of those many fables of the Bretons which Wace mentioned in 1155.[25] Two points are to be noted in Chrétien's account. First, Arthur is represented as overlord of the Antipodes during his lifetime, not after his passing to Avalon. In this respect the reference to the Antipodes in this passage parallels the reference to Avalon in the same list of Arthur's vassals. For among them is Guingomar, lord of Avalon,[26] whom a careful examination of the facts shows to have been a Breton figure, well known not only in the Arthurian but also in the *lai* tradition.[27] Thus in *Erec* Arthur is the supreme sovereign of the Antipodes and of Avalon during his lifetime, while in *Draco Normannicus* he achieves these dominions only after his passing. A second point is that in *Erec* the inhabitants of the lower hemisphere, though described as dwarfs, are highly honoured and much beloved. They are not grotesque or ridiculous.

Further proof of the traditional nature of this concept of the lower world is furnished by Giraldus Cambrensis, who makes it plain that according to Welsh folk-lore the lower hemisphere was peopled by high-minded dwarfs. In his *Itinerarium Cambriae*, composed about 1191, he tells of a certain priest Eliodorus of the neighbourhood of Swansea, who, as an old man, confessed to the bishop, David II

---

[22] Chrétien de Troyes, *Erec*, ed. W. Foerster (Halle, 1890), vss. 1993–2011. Lot discussed this passage in *Romania*, xlvi (1920), 42 ff. He is probably correct in supposing that Chrétien found some of the guests at Erec's wedding somewhat absurd, but he is certainly wrong in imagining (p. 45) that Bilis and his brother originated in Isidore.

[23] *Mod. Phil.*, xxxiii (1936), 232–7.

[24] William of Malmesbury, *Gesta Regum Anglorum*, ed. W. Stubbs, i (1887), 11. *Mod. Phil.*, xxxiii. 234; *Speculum*, ii (1927), 449–55.

[25] Cf. above, p. 64, n. 15.

[26] Chrétien, *Erec*, vs. 1954.

[27] *PMLA*, xlviii (1933), 1023–7; Paton, *Fairy Mythology*, pp. 60–73; *Zts. f. Franz. Spr. u. Lit.*, xlix (1927), 206–16.

(1148–76),[28] a strange adventure of his at the age of twelve. As he was playing truant from school and hiding under a river bank,

apparuerunt ei homunculi duo, staturae quasi pygmeae, dicentes: 'Si nobiscum venire volueris, in terram ludis et deliciis plenam te ducemus.' Annuens ille, surgensque, secutus est praevios, per viam primo subterraneam et tenebrosam, usque in terram pulcherrimam fluviis et pratis, silvis et planis distinctissimam, obscuram tamen et aperto solari lumine non illustratam. . . . Adductus est puer ad regem eique coram regni curia praesentatus. . . . Erant autem homines staturae minimae, sed pro quantitatis captu valde compositae; flavi omnes, et luxuriante capillo, muliebriter per humeros coma demissa.[29] Equos habebant suae competentes modicitati, leporariis in quantitate conformes. . . . Juramenta eis nulla: nihil enim adeo ut mendaciam detestabantur.[30] Quoties de superiori hemisphaerio revertebantur, ambitiones nostras, et inconstantias exspuebant. . . . Solebat autem puer ille ad nostrum hemisphaerium pluries ascendere. . . . Monitus igitur a matre, ut auri, quo abundabat regio, munus ei quandoque referret, pilam auream, qua regis filius ludere consueverat, ab ipso rapiens ludo, per viam solitam ad matrem deproperans cursim asportavit. Et cum ad ostium domus paternae, populi tamen illius non absque sequela, jam pervenisset, intrare festinanti pes haesit in limine; et sic intra tectum cadenti, matre ibidem sedente, pilam manu elapsam duo pygmaei e vestigio sequentes arripuere, exeundo in puerum sputa, contemptus et derisiones emittentes. . . . Cum via redire pararet quam assueverat, ad aquae descensum hypogeumque meatum cum pervenisset, aditus ei jam nullus apparuit.[31]

[28] Giraldus Cambrensis, *Opera*, vi, ed. J. F. Dimock (London, 1868), 104, n. 1.
[29] Certain characteristics of these dwarfs are paralleled in the thirteenth- or fourteenth-century Irish text *Imthechta Tuaithe Luchra* (S. H. O'Grady, *Silva Gadelica*, i. 238; ii. 269). The beauty of the dwarf king is emphasized; cf. T. P. Cross and C. H. Slover, *Ancient Irish Tales* (New York, 1936), pp. 475, 484. The little warriors have long hair (cf. ibid., p. 484); the king's steed is small (cf. ibid., p. 476: 'A russet-clad hare I see').
[30] Cf. the noble dwarfs of modern Welsh folk-lore (J. Rhys, *Celtic Folklore, Welsh and Manx* (Oxford, 1901), i. 158 f.). The Irish tradition also attributes 'truthful utterance' to the dwarf king (Cross and Slover, p. 475). For another faery king of a subterranean land (though not a dwarf) who keeps faith cf. *Sir Orfeo*, vss. 451–69 (W. H. French and C. B. Hale, *Middle English Metrical Romances* (New York, 1930), p. 337). Chaucer seems to have borrowed the idea in the 'Merchant's Tale', vss. 2311–15. Cf. L. H. Loomis, 'Chaucer and the Breton Lays', *Studies in Philology*, xxxviii (1941), 14–33.
[31] Giraldus, vi. 75 f. Trans.: 'Two little men of pygmy stature appeared to him, saying, "If you will come with us, we will lead you into a country full of delights and sports." Assenting and rising up, he followed his guides through a path at first subterraneous and dark into a most beautiful country, adorned with rivers and meadows, woods and plains, but dim and not illuminated with the full light of the

Here, then, is a Welsh tradition concerning the inhabitants of the lower hemisphere notably close to that preserved by Chrétien: they are dwarfs; they are very noble; they have a king. Two other points to which we shall recur later are: they have special mounts adapted to their size; their subterranean country is the scene of a well-known folk-tale plot—the 'Robbery from Fairyland'.

Lest anyone should doubt that Eliodorus, when he ascended into *nostrum hemisphaerium*, was coming up from the Antipodean land, let me cite another folk-tale of a familiar pattern narrated by Gervase of Tilbury in his *Otia Imperialia*. Like Giraldus, the clerical author is careful to furnish a clerical authority for his marvellous story and names as his source that *vir religiosissimus*, Robert, prior of Kenilworth, who held office from about 1160 to about 1180.[32] Thus, though Gervase wrote about 1211, the tale is as old as Étienne's poem. The story is entitled 'De antipodibus et eorum terra'. It relates that a certain negligent swineherd of William Peverell of Peak Castle in Derbyshire lost a pregnant sow.

Cogitavit penes se, si quo fortassis casu sus illa foramen Pech famosum, sed usque ad illa tempora inscrutatum, intrasset. . . . Intrat sun. . . . The boy was brought before the king, and introduced to him in the presence of the court. . . . These men were of the smallest stature, but very well proportioned in their make; they were of fair complexion, with luxuriant hair falling over their shoulders like that of women. They had horses adapted to their small stature, equal in size to greyhounds. . . . They never took an oath; they detested nothing so much as lies. As often as they returned from the upper hemisphere, they reprobated our ambitions and our inconstancies. . . . The boy frequently returned to our hemisphere. . . . Advised by his mother to bring her some time a present of gold, with which that region abounded, he stole, while at play with the king's son, the golden ball with which he used to divert himself, and ran back in haste with it to his mother by the usual path. And when he reached the door of his father's house, but not unpursued by that people, and was entering it in a great hurry, his foot stumbled on the threshold, and he fell down into the room where his mother was sitting; two pygmies who had followed his tracks seized the ball which had dropped from his hand, and departed spitting at the boy with scorn and derision. . . . When he prepared to return by the accustomed way, and when he had reached the waterfall and the underground passage, no entrance whatever was visible.' Miss Paton has already pointed out (pp. 126–30) that this concept of the finely formed, truth-loving dwarf is found in the *Conte del Graal* and *Huon de Bordeaux*. It should be noted, however, that it was not the Petit Chevalier who came from Wales, but, as Miss Weston long since showed, it was Bleheris, invoked as an authority for the description of the Petit Chevalier, who was born and bred in Wales (*Romania*, xxxiv (1905), 100; liii (1927), 84–92). The story of the Petit Chevalier is found in C. Potvin, *Perceval le Gallois*, v (Mons, 1870), 38–78.

[32] Gervasius von Tilbury, *Otia Imperialia*, ed. F. Liebrecht (Hannover, 1856), p. 24. For the date of Prior Robert cf. *Victoria History of County of Warwick*, ed. W. Page, ii (1908), 89.

cavernam tempore tunc ab omni vento tranquillo et cum diutinam in procedendo viam perfecisset, tandem ab opacis in lucidum locum obvenit, solutum in spatiosam camporum planitiem. . . . Inter spicas pendentes scropham, quae multiplicaverat ex se suculos editos, recognovit. Tunc miratus subulcus et de redintegrata jactura congratulatus, facto rerum, prout evenerat, verbo cum praeposito terrae illius, scropham recipit, et cum gaudio dimissus ad gregem porcorum educit. Mira res: a messibus subterraneis veniens, hyemalia frigora videt in nostro hemisphaerio perseverare.[33]

Taken together, these passages from Giraldus and Gervase leave no doubt that in twelfth-century Britain the folk belief in a subterranean fairyland was taken seriously by clerics and adapted to contemporary geographical conceptions as the lower hemisphere—the land of the Antipodes.[34]

It is of primary importance for our study, moreover, to observe that two folk-tale types of the visit to a subterranean fairyland had thus been adapted, as early as the twelfth century, to this semi-scientific localization. For both these folk-tale types are found elsewhere attached to the concept of Arthur as king of a subterranean region; and, though that region is not identified with the lower hemisphere, we have already seen how inevitable that identification would be.

The first fairy-tale type, illustrated by Giraldus's narrative of Eliodorus, is called the 'Robbery from Fairyland' and is the subject of a chapter in E. S. Hartland's *Science of Fairy Tales*.[35] It is connected with Arthur in a Welsh legend of which various nineteenth-century

---

[33] Gervasius von Tilbury, p. 24; cf. also pp. 117–23. Trans.: 'He thought within himself whether the sow by chance had entered that famous hole of the Peak, hitherto unexplored. . . . He entered the cave at a time when it was undisturbed by any wind, and when he had long proceeded on his way, he at length came out of the darkness into a bright place, opening out into a wide plain of fields. . . . Among the drooping ears of grain he recognized the sow, who had littered many pigs. Then the swineherd marvelled and rejoiced that he had made good his loss. He told what had happened to the lord of that land, received the sow, and, dismissed with joy, he led her back to the herd of swine. Wondrous to relate, though he came from the subterranean folk at harvest, he found winter cold prevailing in our hemisphere.' A French translation of this passage in MS. 461 in the Morgan Library renders 'praeposito terrae illius' as 'seigneur de celle terre'.

[34] Both Lambert of St. Omer (*c.* 1120) and the widely known Martianus Capella (fourth or fifth century) speak of the reversal of seasons in the hemispheres. Cf. J. K. Wright, *Geographical Lore of the Time of the Crusades* (New York, 1925), pp. 158, 160; A. P. Newton, *Travel and Travellers of the Middle Ages* (New York, 1930), p. 8.

[35] Chap. vi.

King Arthur and the Antipodes

forms were collected and analysed by Rhys.[36] I give it in the summary of Sir Edmund Chambers.

A Welshman, crossing London Bridge with a hazel staff in his hand, is met by a stranger, who tells him that beneath the tree from which that staff was cut lies a treasure hoard. They return to Wales together and find a cavern under the hazel. In the passage hangs a bell. It must not be touched, says the cunning man; if it is the inmates of the cave will wake and ask, 'Is it day?' and the answer must be given, 'No, sleep thou on.' In the cave are warriors sleeping, and one wears a crown. It is Arthur, waiting until the bell gives the signal to rise and lead the Cymry to victory. Within the circle of warriors lie a heap of gold and a heap of silver; there is a taboo against taking from more than one of them. The Welshman accidentally strikes the bell, but gives the required answer, and escapes with his treasure. When it is exhausted, he pays a second visit. But this time he forgets to give the answer. The warriors take the gold from him, beat him, and send him forth a cripple. The cave can never be found again.[37]

Though this late tradition is a composite of several cave legends,[38] yet its authenticity can hardly be doubted when we note that it preserves characteristic features of Giraldus's twelfth-century tale of Eliodorus: a human visitor is led to a subterranean land; finds there a king and his people; returns on a later occasion; tries to carry off gold; is prevented therefrom and humiliated by the subterranean folk; is never able to find the entrance again. It is highly significant that in the modern variant of this legend Arthur has taken the place of the king of the Antipodes.

Exactly the same substitution has occurred in the other folk-tale type, illustrated by Gervase, of the servant who, after losing an animal, follows it into the underworld and has it restored to him by the ruler of the country. And it is Gervase himself who supplies the

---

[36] *Celtic Folklore*, ii. 458–66, 492–7. For other cave legends of Arthur cf. F. J. Snell, *King Arthur's Country* (London, 1926), pp. 208, 214–17; *Notes and Queries*, xii (9th ser., 1903), 502 f.; J. A. Robinson, *Two Glastonbury Legends* (Cambridge, 1926), p. 52; *Minor Poems of the Vernon MS.*, E.E.T.S., cxvii. 488 f.; P. S. Barto, *Tannhäuser and the Mountain of Venus* (New York, 1916), pp. 11–17, 116–19; T. Parkinson, *Yorkshire Legends and Traditions* (London, 1889), ii. 169 f.; *Monthly Chronicle of North-Country Lore and Legend* (1888), pp. 220–2; (1889), p. 41; (1891), p. 567; M. A. Richardson, *Local Historian's Table Book, Legendary Division* (London, 1844), ii. 42 ff.; *Journal of British Archaeological Association* (1878), p. 426.

[37] E. K. Chambers, *Arthur of Britain* (London, 1927), pp. 222 f. Krappe points out that, though recorded late, these Welsh tales must hark back to the early Middle Ages (*Mitteilungen der schlesischen Gesellschaft für Volkskunde*, xxxv (1935), 90).

[38] Cf. the analysis by Rhys, ii. 492–7.

variant in which Arthur is king of that country. Though the adventure is localized in Sicily, there is general agreement that the tale was a part of the *matière de Bretagne* imported by the Normans and that Gervase picked it up when he visited the island about 1190.

In Sicilia est Mons Aetna. . . . In hujus deserto narrant indigenae Arturum magnum nostris temporibus apparuisse. Cum enim uno aliquo die custos palafredi episcopi Catanensis commissum sibi equum depulveraret, subito impetu lascivae pinguetudinis equus exiliens ac in propriam se recipiens libertatem, fugit. Ab insequente ministro per montis ardua praecipitiaque quaesitus nec inventus, timore pedissequo succrescente, circa montis opaca perquiritur. Quid plura? arctissima semita sed plana est inventa; puer in spatiosissimam planitiem jucundam omnibusque deliciis plenam venit, ibique in palatio miro opere constructo reperit Arturum in strato regii apparatus recubantem. Cumque ab advena et peregrino causam sui adventus percontaretur, agnita causa itineris, statim palafridum episcopi facit adduci, ipsumque praesuli reddendum ministro commendat.[39]

This is obviously the same story as that Gervase told of the swineherd, who through negligence lost his sow, followed her down an underground passage, came at last upon a bright plain, and had the strayed animal graciously restored to him by the *praepositus terrae illius*. Here again Arthur has taken the place of the ruler of the Antipodes. And lest there be any question whether Arthur's abode be conceived by Gervase as under the mountain,[40] let us note that he uses here the phrase *circa montis opaca* and uses in the cognate tale *ab opacis* with reference to the underground passage. Furthermore, Caesarius of Heisterbach in his variant of the same Sicilian tradition, which he records on the authority of Godescalcus, canon

[39] Gervasius von Tilbury, p. 12. On this and similar Sicilian legends cf. Paton, p. 250 ff.; Gardner, pp. 12–15; A. Graf, *Miti, Leggende e Superstizioni del Medio Evo* (Turin, 1892–3), ii. 303 ff. Trans.: 'In Sicily there is Mount Etna. . . . The natives say that in the wilds of this mountain the great Arthur appeared in our time. For when one day a groom of the Bishop of Catania was currying the palfrey in his charge, by a sudden impulse of wanton fatness, the horse darted off and fled away to liberty. The pursuing menial hunted for him in the peaks and precipices but did not find him, and with growing fear the groom sought him in the dark places of the mountain. In short, he found a very narrow but level path; the youth came out on a very wide plain, gay and full of all delights. There in a palace made with marvellous art he found Arthur lying on a bed of royal splendour. When the stranger and wanderer had related the reason of his coming, and made known the cause of his journey, at once Arthur had the bishop's palfrey brought in and gave him to the servant to return to the prelate.'
[40] Barto, *Tannhäuser*, p. 16.

King Arthur and the Antipodes

of Bonn, as a historic fact of the time of the Emperor Henry's conquest of the island (c. 1194), leaves no doubt on the matter.[41] The strayed palfrey is 'in monte Gyber', that is, 'within Etna', and there Arthur dwells. In this British folk-tale which had migrated to Sicily, Arthur as king of the lovely subterranean plain has taken the place of the ruler of the Antipodes in the Derbyshire version.

All this makes it perfectly clear that among the Welsh and the Bretons at least one conception of the Other World was that of a moderately bright region underground, peopled by a race of noble dwarfs; that the immortal Arthur was sometimes imagined as king of that land; and that, when learned geographical notions were applied, he inevitably became king of the Antipodes.

These are not the only conceptions of Arthur as an Otherworld king which were current in the twelfth century. Gervase adds to his account of the adventure of the Sicilian groom that Arthur, after restoring the palfrey, went on to say that he had been lying there ever since the battle with Modred, his wounds annually reopening, *vulneribus quotannis recrudescentibus*.[42] This testimony, taken in conjunction with the witness of a Majorcan poet, writing between 1350 and 1381, that the wounded Arthur dwelt in a Mediterranean island and was kept alive and youthful by a yearly ministration of the Holy Grail,[43] leads to the inference that the British hero was equated with the Maimed King, whose wounds, as Miss Weston showed,[44] were in sympathy with the vital forces of nature and who, according to the French romances, was fed by the Grail.

Gervase further adds a reference to the tradition that Arthur lived on as leader of the Wild Hunt.

Sed in sylvis Britanniae maioris aut minoris consimilia contigisse referuntur, narrantibus nemorum custodibus ... se alternis diebus circa horam meridianam et in primo noctium conticinio, sub plenilunio luna lucente, saepissime videre militum copiam venantium et canum et

[41] Caesarius von Heisterbach, *Dialogus Miraculorum*, ed. J. Strange (1851), xii. 12. This version has been influenced by the clerical tradition that Etna and other volcanoes were pits of hell (cf. J. A. MacCulloch, *Medieval Faith and Fable* (London, 1932), pp. 98 f.).
[42] Gervasius von Tilbury, p. 12.
[43] *Canconer dels Comtes d'Urgell*, ed. D. G. Llabres (Societat Catalana de Bibliofils, 1906), pp. 131 ff.; M. Mila y Fontanals, *Poètes catalans* (Paris, 1876), pp. 9–22; V. M. O. Denk, *Einführung in das Studium der altcatalanischen Literatur* (Munich, 1893), pp. 222–8; Entwistle, *Arthurian Legend*, pp. 81, 186–9.
[44] *Romania*, xliii (1914), 403 ff.

cornuum strepitum, qui sciscitantibus se de societate et familia Arturi esse affirmant.[45]

The evidence we have culled mainly from twelfth- and early thirteenth-century sources establishes the fact that the Welsh and Bretons adapted their concept of the immortal Arthur to already familiar concepts of a supernatural king. He assumed the part of the Maimed King, the faery lord of Avalon, the leader of the Wild Hunt, the sleeping king in the hollow mountain. When he was elevated to the sovereignty over a fair subterranean land peopled by noble dwarfs, as he is in Chrétien's *Erec*, he simply took over the role of another faery monarch. And naturally Arthur acquired some of the attributes and properties of the personages he displaced. From the Maimed King he acquired the Grail with its vitalizing power; from the lord of Avalon he seems to have acquired the ministrations of Morgain la Fée, for there is strong reason to believe that twelfth-century Welsh tradition derived the name of the isle from Avallach, father of Morgain and her sisters;[46] from the leader of the Wild Hunt he took over the clamorous company of riders by moonlight; from the king in the hollow mountain he probably inherited the host of sleeping warriors awaiting the day of victory. When Arthur became lord of a subterranean land peopled by noble dwarfs, did he acquire any attributes or properties of the traditional king of that country?

This question suggests the solution of a problem in iconography posed by a mosaic portrait of 'Rex Arturus' in the cathedral of Otranto in southern Italy.[47] This city in 1165, the date of the mosaic, lay within the same Norman kingdom as Sicily, where we have seen that genuine traditions of Arthur were fixed later in the century. We need have no hesitation, therefore, in looking to genuine British traditions for an explanation of the fact that the mosaic clearly depicts the British hero as riding on a goat.

[45] Gervasius von Tilbury, pp. 12 f. On the Wild Hunt cf. above, p. 61, n. 2. Trans.: 'But in the forests of Great and Little Britain exactly similar things are said to have happened, and the wood-wardens ... relate that on alternate days, about the hour of noon or in the first silence of night, by moonlight in the full of the moon they have very often seen a band of knights hunting and the noise of hounds and horns, who declared to those who asked that they were of the fellowship and household of Arthur.'

[46] *Romanic Review*, xxix (1938), 176 f.

[47] R. S. Loomis and L. H. Loomis, *Arthurian Legends in Medieval Art* (New York, 1938), p. 36, figs. 9, 9a; E. Bertaux, *L'Art dans l'Italie Méridionale* (Rome, 1904), i. 488–90; *Studi Medievali*, ii (1906–7), 506.

King Arthur and the Antipodes

Giraldus's tale of Eliodorus's visit to the dimly lighted subterranean land of the dwarfs has already informed us that the little people had horses of appropriate size, as small as greyhounds. Walter Map, in a chapter of his *De Nugis Curialium*, written about the same time as Giraldus's *Itinerarium*, gives us a portrait of a noble dwarf king of a moderately bright subterranean land, riding on a goat.[48] He appeared once upon a time to Herla,[49] a king of the most ancient Britons. 'Institit homuncio capro maximo secundum fabulam insidens.' He introduced himself as follows: 'Ego rex multorum regum et principum, innumerabilis et infiniti populi, missus ab eis ad te libens venio.' He proposed a covenant that he should attend the wedding of King Herla and that Herla should reciprocate a year later. Then the dwarf vanished. At Herla's nuptials the little king and his diminutive subjects provided an abundance of viands and drinks in precious vessels. A year later Herla was summoned to attend the marriage of the pygmy potentate.

Cauernam igitur altissimae rupis ingrediuntur, et post aliquantas tenebras in lumine quod non uidebatur solis aut lune sed lampadum multarum, ad domos pigmei transeunt, mansionem quidem honestam per omnia qualem Naso regiam describit solis.[50]

After a stay of what seemed to be three days but was in reality 200 years or more, Herla returned to the light of the sun, laden with the gifts of his diminutive host.

In this story the nether world is not identified with the antipodean land, but it is certainly recognizable as the same moderately bright subterranean country, inhabited by high-minded dwarfs and abundant in treasure, which Giraldus in his tale of Eliodorus identifies with the lower hemisphere. Map depicts the supreme king of that land as mounted on a goat, and Chrétien, Étienne de Rouen, and the author of the *Gesta Regum Britanniae* make it appear that Arthur was overlord of that land. Thus it would be a perfectly

[48] Ed. M. R. James (Oxford, 1914), p. 13; trans. Tupper and Ogle (London, 1924), pp. 15–18, 233.

[49] The name of Herla is, of course, due simply to etymologizing the name of the Wild Hunt, Hellequin or Herlething, as Herla-kin or Herla-thing. The real etymology of the word Hellequin is uncertain, but it is certain that Herla is not the name of any British or Welsh king.

[50] Trans.: 'They entered therefore a cave in a very high cliff and after passing through certain regions of darkness they came out into a light which did not seem to be that of the sun or moon but of many lamps to the dwellings of the pygmy, a glorious mansion in all respects like the palace of the sun described by Ovid.'

natural inference that Arthur, in this role, was mounted on a goat. Legends of the immortal Arthur dwelling in a subterranean realm were established in Sicily by 1190; it is therefore not surprising to find Arthur represented astride a goat at Otranto in 1165. Though I put forward this explanation of the mosaic in 1938 as purely conjectural,[51] I now contend that it has strong odds in its favour. The complete disappearance of this grotesque concept of the British king from all later documents certainly requires no reasoned explanation; the causes are too easily imagined.[52]

The foregoing discussion of Arthur in the Other World has wider implications. It is strange that three such eminent medievalists as Lot, M. Faral, and Tatlock should have in their writings resolutely excluded from their interpretation of twelfth-century Arthuriana any influence from Celtic tradition. I quote three typical passages:

> Le nain Bilis, 'roi d'Antipodés', et son frère 'graindre ou demi pié ou plaine paume — Que nus chevalier del reaume', auraient-ils jamais été imaginés si Chrétien n'avait gardé un souvenir, quoique confus, des passages d'Isidore qu'on vient de reproduire?[53]

> Ce que Geoffroy a conté de cette île [Avalon], ce qu'il a conté de cette fée [Morgen] ne saurait d'aucune façon passer pour une tradition galloise qu'il aurait recueillie parmi ses contemporains: c'est en tout et pour tout, la combinaison fantaisiste de notices empruntées à quelques polygraphes anciens, auxquelles il a mêlé tout juste un trait nouveau, tiré de la légende érudite de saint Brendan, qu'avaient inventé des clercs d'Irlande.[54]

> I thoroughly agree with M. Faral's admirable book that the foregoing description of the Insula Pomorum in the *Vita Merlini* is due to early accounts of the Insulae Fortunatae.[55]

These scholars are, of course, right in assuming that men of letters such as Geoffrey, Chrétien, Étienne de Rouen, Gervase, and Giraldus were familiar with their Latin texts; they would not have

---

[51] R. S. and L. H. Loomis, *Arthurian Legends in Medieval Art*, p. 36.

[52] For later association of the goat with lechery cf. *Text of the Canterbury Tales*, ed. J. M. Manly and E. Rickert (Chicago, 1940), i. 594; E. Mâle, *L'Art Religieux de la Fin du Moyen Age* (Paris, 1908), pp. 355-8; A. Katzenellenbogen, *Allegories of the Virtues and Vices in Mediaeval Art* (London, 1939), p. 61.

[53] *Romania*, xlvi (1920), 45.

[54] *Mélanges de Linguistique et de Littérature Offerts à M. Alfred Jeanroy* (Paris, 1928), pp. 252 f.

[55] *Mod. Phil.*, xxxi. 16.

been clerics if they had been ignorant of the books studied in the schools and filling the shelves of monastic libraries; they display evidence of that familiarity on every page. To quote the immortal Mrs. Gamp, 'Who deniges of it, Betsey?'

But to proceed from probable or certain signs of classical influence on a given passage to the conclusion that there is nothing else; to assume that learned men in the twelfth century scorned the *nugae* which entertained the laity; or even to conclude that the references to such *nugae* or *fabulae* were mere excuses for personal invention – surely, these are procedures and positions which require more justification than they have received. What could be more plain than that, in the instances we have been studying, our clerical authors have been treating lay traditions, many of them of Celtic origin, and have given them a learned slant by harmonizing them with the best geographical science available or by references to Naso? And what could be more natural?

Accordingly, I venture to urge that the question of sources is not settled for Geoffrey of Monmouth when it is pointed out that the story of Estrildis resembles that of Elfildis in William of Malmesbury;[56] that the story of Arthur's birth resembles that of Hercules;[57] that the allies of Lucius Hiberus bear names manifestly culled from contemporary history or the classics;[58] that Morgen and her eight sisters of the Insula Pomorum and the longevity of its inhabitants are paralleled in Pomponius Mela and Solinus.[59] For Geoffrey's method was similar to that of his contemporaries, though far bolder and more fraudulent. He, too, generally had some relic of tradition—a mere hair or a complete skeleton—which he proceeded to enclose in a reliquary artfully constructed from the resources of his reading. Precisely those features of the Estrildis story which are not accounted for by the Latin account of Elfildis are accounted for by the French romance of Isolt, a name of which the Welsh form is Esyllt.[60] It is impossible to ignore in the story of Arthur's birth, with its Cornish locale and nomenclature, the Welsh and Irish connexions brought out by Professor Gruffydd.[61] Though the allies

---

[56] *Speculum*, xi (1936), 121.
[57] E. Faral, *La Légende Arthurienne, Première Partie* (Paris, 1929), ii. 252 f.
[58] *Speculum*, vi (1931), 206.   [59] *Mélanges Jeanroy*, 248 f.
[60] *Mod. Lang. Notes*, xlvi (1931), 177, n. 18.
[61] *Transactions of the Honourable Society of Cymmrodorion* (1912–13), pp. 72–80; *University of California Publications in English*, v, no. 1, 60 f.; J. Loth, *Contributions à l'Etude des Romans de la Table Ronde* (Paris, 1912), pp. 63 f.

of Lucius Hiberus may have been named by Geoffrey at his own sweet will, the name of Lucius himself remains unexplained by Tatlock and can be explained most adequately as a corrupt Latinization of Llwch Wyddel (Llwch the Irishman = Lucius Hibernus).[62] Morgen and her sisters, the isle of Avalon, the longevity of the inhabitants—whatever classical phrases and reminiscences may occur in Geoffrey's description—are originally Welsh.[63] The Matter of Britain is not a mere pastiche of reminiscences from Virgil, Ovid, Nennius, Isidore, Solinus, &c. It was fundamentally a Celtic tradition and a lay tradition, transmitted by word of mouth by professional story-tellers. The fact that the first to exploit that tradition in written literature were clerics, as was inevitable in the twelfth century, and that they naturally injected more or less bookish lore into their work should not blind us to the real nature and source of their material.[64]

[62] Loomis, *Arthurian Tradition*, pp. 187–91.
[63] *Romanic Review*, xxix (1938), 176 f.; *Medieval Studies in Memory of Gertrude Schoepperle Loomis* (Paris and New York, 1927), p. 275; S. H. O'Grady, *Silva Gadelica*, ii. 238 ff.
[64] I wish to express my thanks to my friend, the late Jacob Hammer, for reading and criticizing this chapter.

CHAPTER VI

Welsh Elements in 'Gawain and the Green Knight'

SINCE 1888,[1] when Gaston Paris revealed the derivation of the Beheading Test in *Gawain and the Green Knight* from some form of the eighth-century saga of *Bricriu's Feast*, the evidence for Irish influence on the Middle English masterpiece has steadily accumulated. In 1916 Kittredge made an elaborate study of this relationship, and in the same year Professor Hulbert also argued for Irish connexions.[2] In 1932 Miss Alice Buchanan was able to list in *PMLA*, xlvii. 328 f., thirty-one features of the poem which could be derived with fair certainty from the complex of stories about Cúroí, Cúchulainn, and Bláthnat.[3] In 1943 I urged in the *Journal of English and Germanic Philology*, xlii. 149–69, the addition of two more features as probably developed from the same sources: the Green Knight's girdle and Gawain's device of the pentangle.

But there was nothing in these Irish sources which seemed to explain satisfactorily four important elements in the English poem. (1) The host who entertained Gawain in his castle was emphatically a huntsman. Cúroí, who corresponds to Gawain's host and who entertained Cúchulainn in his fortress, displayed no such interest in the chase. The same may be said of Yellow son of Fair, who entertained Cúchulainn on his way to the Beheading Test; there is no evidence that he was a sportsman. (2) Gawain during his host's absence on the chase was solicited by his wife but maintained strict chastity. Though Cúroí left Cúchulainn in his fortress to be looked after by Bláthnat, who had previously been Cúchulainn's mistress, there is no mention of a temptation, and Cúchulainn was surely not the man to resist the overtures of his former mistress if she had made them. (3) It was according to covenant that a year elapsed

[1] *Histoire Littéraire de la France*, xxx. 71–78.
[2] *Study of Gawain and the Green Knight* (Cambridge, Mass.). *Mod. Phil.* xiii. 433–62, 689–730.
[3] From Miss Buchanan's list I would subtract no. 5, since *dos bili mor* can hardly refer to Cúroí's beard. But I would add to her list the protests of Cúchulainn and Gawain against the delays of Cúroí and Bercilak. Cf. Kittredge, p. 38.

between the first and second meetings between Gawain and the Green Knight. There is no such interval between the meetings of Cúchulainn with Cúroí in one version of the Beheading Test, or with Terror son of Great Fear in the other version. (4) The Green Knight tested Gawain at the crossing of a turbulent brook. Cúroí tested Cúchulainn in the royal hall; Terror tested him beside a loch.

Do these four rather prominent divergences from the Irish traditions of Cúroí, Cúchulainn, and Bláthnat belong together and derive from one source, or are they separate elements originating in the poet's imagination? Three of them, at least, must belong together since they are found in cognate Arthurian tales. In *Diu Crône*,[4] written by Heinrich von dem Türlin about 1220, we read of the close of a Christmas festival, held by King Arthur, and of the departure of the guests on 29 December. The king spent the 29th in the chase, and that night met and fought at a ford with Gasozein, who was wearing a protective girdle given him by Arthur's wife. After an indecisive combat, Gasozein proposed another at the end of a year. Here in this poem, which antedates *GGK* by about 150 years, we find, besides other resemblances, a host who engages in the chase in the month of December; who goes to an encounter at a ford; who agrees to an anniversary combat. In Chrétien's *Conte del Graal*,[5] composed about 1180, there is an episode, long recognized as related to *GGK*, where we find again a huntsman host and a proposal for an anniversary combat. In response to the challenge of a stranger knight, Guingambresil, at Arthur's court, Gauvain set out and was entertained in the castle of a noble huntsman. During his host's absence in the chase, Gauvain engaged in a compromising affair with the lady of the castle. Guingambresil appeared on the scene, and agreed to a combat with Gauvain a year later.

I think it will be admitted on the strength of these parallels that among the materials which were wrought into the fabric of *GGK* and which belonged together were the huntsman host, the pledge to an anniversary combat, and the placing of the combat at a river crossing. There was a strong hint also that Gawain's affair with the wife of his huntsman host derived from the same complex. Whence did this group of non-Irish features come?

I was myself not a little surprised when I realized over ten years

---

[4] *Diu Crône*, ed. G. H. F. Scholl (Stuttgart, 1852), vss. 3205–5027.
[5] Chrétien de Troyes, *Percevalroman*, ed. A. Hilka (Halle, 1932), vss. 4747–813, 5703–6215.

ago that the source for all four elements was the first episode of *Pwyll*. Let me summarize that story.[6]

Pwyll, prince of Dyfed (south-western Wales), met in a forest glade a huntsman, clad in dark-grey[7] wool, mounted on a dapple-grey steed. He revealed himself as Arawn, King of Annwn (the Other World), and admitted that he was being oppressed by Hafgan (Summer White),[8] a neighbouring king from Annwn. When Pwyll agreed to fight Hafgan in Arawn's stead at the end of a year at a ford, Arawn sent Pwyll to his faery palace in his own form. There Pwyll dwelt for a year, sharing the same bed with Arawn's most beautiful wife, yet turning his face resolutely to the wall. At the year's end, Pwyll fulfilled his bargain and met 'Summer White' at the ford by night in the presence of all their nobles. It was proclaimed that none should intervene between the two combatants. Pwyll dealt 'Summer White' one fatal blow, and then departed to his own dominion.

Here, then, are the four non-Irish features noted in *GGK*: the noble huntsman who introduces the hero as a guest into his household; the huntsman's wife, whose embraces the hero spurns; the anniversary combat; its localization at a river-crossing.

It is startling to find here the sources of several features in the Gasozein episode in *Diu Crône*.[9] There Arthur, the huntsman, engaged by night in an indecisive combat near a ford with Gasozein, who was wearing a strangely summery costume for December, clad in a white shirt, bearing a white shield and banner, and riding a white horse. Both revealed their names. Gasozein proposed another fight at the end of a year, during which he would not touch the queen. A second encounter took place (though after a shorter interval) in the presence of all Arthur's nobles. It was proclaimed that no one should intervene. In the first onset Gasozein evaded Arthur's charge, and the battle ended.

Are all these parallels between *GGK* and *Diu Crône*, between *GGK* and *Pwyll*, and between *Diu Crône* and *Pwyll*, meaningless?

Differences between the members of this story-group are, of course, to be expected, since each member contains not only the common element but also extraneous elements. *GGK* is mainly dominated by the two Irish versions of the Beheading Test.[10] The

[6] *Mabinogion*, trans. G. and T. Jones, Everyman's Lib., pp. 3–7.
[7] Sir Ifor Williams emends 'lwyt tei' to 'lwyt-lei'. Cf. *Bull. Board Celt. Studies*, xiii. 196 f.
[8] J. Rhys, *Studies in the Arthurian Legend* (Oxford, 1891), p. 281.
[9] *Diu Crône*, ed. Scholl, vss. 3289–5093, 10113–686. [10] *PMLA*, xlvii. 316–25.

Gasozein episode in *Diu Crône*, I have shown elsewhere,[11] has absorbed ten recognizable features from the Irish saga of *The Violent Death of Cúroi*, and the motif of the queen's taunt from *The Violent Death of Fergus Mac Leite*.[12] The *Pwyll* episode, as Nutt and Professor Gruffydd have proved,[13] has been subjected to another Irish influence, *The Birth of Mongán*, which surely supplied the compact between mortal and god, the visit of one in the other's shape to the latter's home, and the intervention of one in the other's battle.

The significant point is that these various Irish influences on *GGK*, the Gasozein story (*C*), and the *Pwyll* episode (*P*) account for most of the differences. If we subtract the Irish elements from these three narratives, we have left a basic plot which we may thus reconstruct.

There was a supernatural king[14] (*GGK, P*), who was clad in grey (*P*, changed to green in *GGK*) and rode a grey (changed to green in *GGK*) horse. He hunted with a pack of hounds (*GGK, P, C*) between Christmas and Twelfth Night (*GGK, C*, Welsh folk-lore).[15] During his absence but with his connivance a guest was entertained in his magnificent home by his beautiful wife, but maintained strict chastity though exposed to temptation (*GGK, P*). The guest went to a rendezvous for an anniversary encounter (*GGK, P*). It took place at night (*P, C*) at a water-crossing (*GGK, P, C*). One of the participants was a horseman called 'Summer White' (*P*), or was lightly clad in white both summer and winter (*C*). This encounter, or a later, was held in the presence of nobles (*P, C*); a warning against interference was proclaimed (*P, C*); and after a single attack the combat ended (*P, C*).

It cannot be a freak of chance that traces of this story are sharply imprinted, though in different ways, on two narratives so interlocked as *GGK* and the Gasozein episode.

What more can one discover about this Welsh tradition? Hafgan, 'Summer White', evidently furnished Gasozein with his white shirt, worn both winter and summer, his white horse, shield, and banner, and determined his habit of fighting by night at a ford. The fourteenth-century poet, Dafydd ap Gwilym, casts more light on the

---

[11] *Journ. of Engl. and Germ. Phil.* xlii. 159 f.

[12] *Diu Crône*, vss. 3356–657; Loomis, *Arthurian Tradition*, pp. 134–8.

[13] K. Meyer, A. Nutt, *Voyage of Bran* (London, 1895), ii. 16; *Trans. Hon. Soc. Cymm.*, 1912–13, pp. 72–80.

[14] Note that the manuscript of *GGK*, vs. 992, calls the Green Knight a king—a reading which Tolkien and Gordon emended to 'lord'.

[15] M. Trevelyan, *Folklore and Folk-stories of Wales* (London, 1909), p. 53.

subject, for he represents Haf, 'Summer', as a person.[16] Summer is a prince (*tywysawg*). He departs to his own land of Annwn to escape the gales of winter. His favoured month of May is personified as a horseman (*marchog*), and is contrasted with the rigours of January. T. Gwynn Jones remarks with penetration:[17] ' The poems attributed to Dafydd, and many others, derive much of their "natural magic" from legends, and what often passes for imagination on the part of the bards is basically the symbol of a nature cult.' We need not hesitate to identify Dafydd's Haf, the personification of Summer, with the Hafgan of Pwyll. This being so, what of his warfare with Arawn, the grey huntsman with his pack of hounds?

Modern Welsh folk-custom and folk-lore give an answer. As late as the nineteenth century in South Wales a ritual conflict between Summer and Winter was enacted yearly.[18] Two companies of young men were formed. The captain of the summer forces rode horseback, wore a white smock, and was crowned with flowers. The captain of the winter forces was mounted, was dressed in furs, and carried a blackthorn stick. A sham battle took place in some common or wasteland, and the softer season gained the victory. This would be the natural outcome of a symbolic struggle fixed, as this was, on the first of May, *Calan Mei*, the great Celtic festival of the beginning of summer. In the impersonator of Summer we recognize a counterpart to Dafydd's rider, Haf, from Annwn; to Hafgan, 'Summer White', a king from Annwn; and to Gasozein, clad only in a white shirt both summer and winter, and riding a white horse.

If Hafgan is Summer, Arawn his antagonist, clad in grey wool, should be Winter. In the same collection of Welsh folk-lore which

[16] For Welsh text and free English trans. cf. Dafydd ap Gwilym, *Fifty Poems*, trans. H. I. and D. Bell (London, 1942), pp. 252–9; T. Gwynn Jones, *Welsh Folklore and Folk-Custom* (London, 1930), p. 154.

[17] Op. cit., p. 154.

[18] Trevelyan, op. cit., p. 53. Similar customs are found in Scandinavian and Germanic lands. Cf. J. G. Frazer, *Golden Bough*, ed. 3, iv. 254 ff.; J. Grimm, *Teutonic Mythology*, trans. Stallybrass (London, 1883), ii. 758–69; W. Hone, *Everyday Book* (London, 1838), i. 358 f. It is remarkable that near Breitenbrunn in Oberpfalz 'Sommer' speaks of his *weißen G'wand*, and speaks twice of his country as *das Sommerland*, which seems to be the equivalent of the *aestiva regio* to which Melvas carries off Guinevere, discussed below. Cf. *Bavaria, Landes- und Volkskunde des Königreichs Bayern* (Munich, 1863), ii. 260. In Lower Austria and Moravia also 'Sommer' is clad in white. Cf. Frazer, op. cit. iv. 257. In Switzerland he wears only a shirt. Cf. Grimm, op. cit. ii. 769. In most of these instances he carries a green bough.

describes the annual combat we read:[19] 'In some part of Wales it was stated that Arawn and his *Cwn Annwn* [Hounds of the Other World] hunted only from Christmas to Twelfth Night, and was always accompanied by a howling wind.' 'In Glamorgan, Brecon, and Radnor Arawn, the master of these hounds, rides a grey horse and is robed in grey.' 'Stories about the Brenin Llwyd, the Grey King, or Monarch of the Mist, were told in most of the mountainous districts. . . . He was represented as sitting among the mountains, robed in grey clouds and mist.' Arawn's grey woollen coat, his association with grey mists and howling winds, his predilection for the midwinter season, mark him out as the perfect antagonist of Hafgan in an annual struggle for mastery. He is the lord of winter and its storms. His baying hounds are the roaring blasts.

Students of folk-lore will perceive in Arawn a familiar figure; this wintry huntsman not only haunts the lonely mountains and valleys of Wales, but has been seen and heard by the peasantry throughout most of Europe.[20] His company is known by many names: *La Chasse Furieuse, Die Wilde Jagd, Nachtjaeger, Odinsjaeger, La Mesnie Hellequin, Familia Arturi*, &c.[21] It is of very great significance that from the Shetlands to the Pyrenees, as Professor Archer Taylor has shown, folk tradition identified Arthur with the leader of the phantom chase.[22] Arthur's playing the part of Arawn in the Gasozein episode is therefore no isolated instance of this equation. Many are the interpretations given to the Wild Hunt by popular fancy or by scholarly mythologists. But Grimm and Mogk recognized that the most persistent features of this phenomenon in German folk-lore indicate that it is a myth of wind and storm.[23] Despite the multitudinous variations in the European traditions of the Wild Hunt, it is surprising to discover even in German territory many parallels to the Welsh legends of Arawn. In German folk-lore, too, we find the

[19] Trevelyan, pp. 48, 53, 69.
[20] H. Plischke, *Sage vom wilden Heere im deutschen Volke* (Eilenburg, 1914), p. 27. 'Bei allen Völkern Europas läßt sich die Erscheinung, die man in Deutschland das wilde Heer nennt, nachweisen, in den Hauptzügen, ja sogar in der Benennung, zumeist übereinstimmend. . . . Es zeigt sich, wenn der Sturm besonders brausend durch das Land fährt und die Nächte am dunkelsten und unheimlichsten sind.'
[21] For bibliography cf. S. Thompson, *Motif-Index of Folk-Literature*, ii. 388–401; Plischke, op. cit., pp. vii–xii; P. Sébillot, *Folklore de France* (Paris, 1904), i. 165–78; *Mod. Phil.*, xxxviii (1941), 289, n. 2; M. Latham, *Elizabethan Fairies* (New York, 1930), pp. 97 f.
[22] *Romanic Review*, xii (1921), 286–8.
[23] Grimm, *Teutonic Mythology*, trans. Stallybrass, iii. 918–48; H. Paul, *Grundriss der Germ. Philol.*, ed. 2, iii (Strassburg, 1900), pp. 333–7.

huntsman riding only in the twelve days between Christmas and Twelfth Night, or whenever the storm-wind howls.[24] He wears a long grey coat, and his horse is grey.[25] He is met in a forest glade or by a stream.[26] He is attended by a pack of baying hounds.[27] He reappears at the same place at the end of a year.[28] Though, both in Welsh and Continental folk-lore, this phantom hunter has been identified with the Devil or with some wicked mortal, and his tumultuous rout has been interpreted as a troop of lost souls, yet these are obviously the Christian interpretations of a widespread pagan myth. The Grey Huntsman was first created by the imagination of our European ancestors as an embodiment of Storm and Winter. The Welsh alone, it would seem, introduced him into the independent tradition of the mythical conflict.

The same antagonism between Winter and Summer which reflected itself in the nature lyrics of Dafydd ap Gwilym and was dramatized in the ritual combats of the Welsh folk evidently lay behind the yearly conflict at the ford between the kings of Annwn, grey Arawn (or his substitute) and 'Summer White'.[29]

We possess what appear to be two other Welsh versions of the annual combat, and in them, significantly enough, it is represented as a struggle for the love of a lady. In *Kulhwch and Olwen* Gwynn ap Nudd, who was, like Arawn, king of Annwn and a huntsman, carried off the virgin Creiddylad to his home, which a later Welsh tradition localized at Glastonbury.[30] Her husband, Gwythyr ap Greidyawl, 'Victor son of Scorching', gathered an army and went in pursuit. Arthur intervened and decreed that Creiddylad should remain inviolate, and that the two rivals should fight for her every *kalan Mei*, first of May, till the Day of Doom. What is evidently a variant of the same tradition occurs in the *Vita Gildae* of Caradoc of

[24] Grimm, iii. 921; Plischke, pp. 53 f.
[25] Grimm, iii. 931.
[26] V. Schweda, *Sagen vom wilden Jäger . . . in der Provinz Posen* (Gnesen, 1915), pp. 11–14.
[27] Plischke, pp. 32 f.
[28] Grimm, iii. 921. Plischke, pp. 73 f.
[29] In Glamorganshire there was a folk tradition of a battle between fairies mounted on white steeds and others mounted on black steeds. The army on white horses won, and the whole scene dissolved in mist. This is probably another reflection of the mythical combat between summer and winter. Cf. W. Sikes, *British Goblins* (London, 1880), p. 107.
[30] Loth, *Mabinogion*, i. 331 f., 314, n. 1; Baring-Gould and Fisher, *Lives of the British Saints* (London, 1913), iv. 377; J. Rhys, *Celtic Folklore, Welsh and Manx* (Oxford, 1901), i. 203, 216.

Lancarvan.[31] Melvas, king of the *aestiva regio*, 'Summer Land',[32] carried off Guinevere to his fortress at Glastonbury, interpreted as *insula vitrea*, and after a year's interval Arthur gathered an army to win back his queen. Gildas intervened and Guinevere was restored.

In the poems of Chrétien de Troyes the same basic myth can be detected. In *Erec* there is mention of Maheloas, lord of the 'isle de voirre', 'isle of glass', where there is never storm or thunder or winter.[33] All scholars agree that this lord of a summer country is identical with the Melvas of Caradoc and with Chrétien's Meleagant, who is prince of the water-girdled land of Goirre, in which name for excellent reasons we may detect a corruption of *isle de voirre* and the equivalent of *insula vitrea*.[34] Meleagant, like Melvas, abducted Arthur's queen. She remained inviolate through the intervention of King Baudemaguz.[35] When her lover Lancelot came to her rescue he fought three indecisive combats with Meleagant.[36] Meleagant appeared at Arthur's court and demanded another duel after the lapse of a year.[37] It took place in a meadow, green and fresh at all seasons, and beside a stream.[38] The kinship of this narrative, despite all accretions, to the Melvas and Gwynn stories is fairly clear. It is possible to discern also traces of the *Pwyll* version. Gauvain offered to take Lancelot's place in his final combat with Meleagant; being refused, he removed his arms, and Lancelot put them on.[39] This seems to be a reminiscence of Pwyll's taking Arawn's place and shape. Moreover, this combat in both the *Charrette* and *Pwyll* takes place before an assembly of nobles.

Noteworthy is the fact that not only in the stories of Gwynn

---

[31] *Cymmrodorion Record Series*, ii (London, 1901), p. 410; E.K. Chambers, *Arthur of Britain*, pp. 263 f. On date cf. Tatlock in *Speculum*, xiii (1938), 139–52.

[32] Already in Caradoc's book a false etymology has led to the identification of this summer land with Somerset (just as a similar false etymology led to the identification of Maheloas's *isle de voirre* with Glastonbury). Today Gwlad yr Hav, 'Land of Summer', is Welsh for Somersetshire, but some recollection of the fabulous country remains. J. Rhys, *Studies in Arthurian Legend*, pp. 241, 346, n. 1.

[33] Ed. Foerster, ed. 3 (Halle, 1934), vss. 1946 ff. On the isle of glass cf. *infra*, pp. 165–7. On Melvas and Meleagant cf. Loomis, *Arthurian Tradition*, pp. 214–18.

[34] For proof of this cf. *infra*, pp. 166 f.

[35] Chrétien de Troyes, *Karrenritter*, ed. W. Foerster (Halle, 1899), vss. 3378–80, 4068–75. Cf. Cross and Nitze, *Lancelot and Guenevere* (Chicago, 1930), p. 51.

[36] Vss. 306–20, 3600–860, 5007–63.

[37] Vss. 6167 ff.

[38] Vss. 7008–19.

[39] Vss. 6221 ff., 6768 ff. Note that in vss. 6931 f. Gauvain *tost se desarme* and *Lanceloz de ses armes s'arme*. Since Lancelot has arrived unarmed, it is clear that he takes Gauvain's war-gear.

and Meleagant was the lady emphatically not violated by her abductor, but the same point is emphasized in *L'Atre Périlleux*.[40] Escanor was not permitted to lie with the damsel he carried off. It is hardly a coincidence, therefore, that Gasozein promised that even if he won Ginover by arms from her husband, he would not lie with her for a year. There must have been a very strong Welsh conviction that the lady involved in the annual combat maintained her chastity thus long. But though the tradition was uniform the explanations varied. Gwynn, Meleagant, and Escanor could not ravish the ladies whom they abducted by reason of outside intervention. But with Gasozein the promise to refrain was voluntary.

In *Pwyll* and *GGK*, though there is no abduction, and no love-rivalry is involved in the annual encounter, yet there can be little doubt that the chaste conduct of the hero, when left alone with the wife of his huntsman host, reflects the same tradition as the inviolate chastity of other ladies involved in the combats of summer kings and their opponents. The inventor of the plot of *Pwyll* adopted friendship as a motive for his hero's noble conduct, and cleverly combined it with his traditional matter. The inventor of the plot of *GGK* naturally motivated Gawain's conduct by presenting him as a paragon of Christian knighthood, much as the pentangle, symbolic of Christian virtues, seems to have taken the place of solar symbols.

The more one scrutinizes the formation of *GGK*, the more one sees that there was reason in it. What reason, then, was there for superimposing the Welsh traditions of the combat at the ford on the Irish sagas of the several encounters of Cúroí and Cúchulainn? Why does this same combination occur in the Gasozein and Guingambresil stories and in the Scottish romance of *Eger and Grime*?[41] The reason may well be that, whereas modern scholars are in most instances averse to recognizing mythical meanings—and considering some of the specimens of mythologizing which one

[40] Ed. B. Woledge, pp. 32 ff., 55 ff. Brun de Morois, the abductor of Guinevere in *Durmart* (ed. E. Stengel, Stuttgart, 1873, vss. 4220 ff.), declares that he will not ravish her before sunset.

[41] *Eger and Grime*, ed. J. R. Caldwell (Cambridge, 1933). The friendship motif; the defeat of one friend by a supernatural champion at a ford; the victory of the other friend, impersonating him; the hospitable lady—all these features (and more) derive from the Welsh ford complex. The solar features of the supernatural champion; the lady who hates him and reveals to her lover the secret of his strength; the magic sword required to slay him—these seem to reflect Cúroí and Bláthnat.

sees in learned journals even today,[42] they may be pardoned a certain prejudice—yet the Welsh and Breton conteurs had no such antipathies. Even their French and German successors had some realization of the mythical nature of their legends, and the Middle English *Sir Orfeo* is a most skilful effort in blending classical and Celtic myths.[43]

The Welsh doubtless perceived a certain basic resemblance in the meanings of the combat at the ford and of the encounters between Cúroí and Cúchulainn. To be sure, as I have maintained and as Professor Nitze, on the basis of the Beheading Test in *Perlesvaus*, has strongly urged, the basic Irish pattern seems to consist of the annual slaying of a solar divinity (or a human representative) and his replacement by another. This is a somewhat different seasonal concept from the Welsh combat of summer sun and winter storm. And yet it was possible to detect analogies. Cúroí was preceded by a heavy dark cloud; he was clad in a dark grey mantle; his axe descended with the noise of a wood tempest-tossed in a night of storm.[44] He was evidently the counterpart of Arawn. Cúchulainn could withdraw his golden hairs into his head, which then became red with blood; he radiated intense heat and melted snow; he was son of the sun-god Lugh.[45] Evidently, he embodied solar forces, was a natural antagonist to Cúroí (even though Cúroí, too, had his solar phases) and was therefore the counterpart of Hafgan. Three times Cúroí came to demand Bláthnat, 'Little Flower', from Cúchulainn, each time at the end of a year. He defeated Cúchulainn and brought away Bláthnat, but at the end of a year Cúchulainn sought him out, slew him, and brought away the flower lady. The battle for her lasted from 1 November, the beginning of winter (as May Day was the beginning of summer), till the middle of spring. Here, obviously, was a seasonal myth, which had its analogues in the Welsh tales of abduction and annual combats. What more natural than that there should be many efforts at fusion? And it is a happy confirmation of this theory that still in *GGK* Bercilak had a glance like lightning and his appearance at

---

[42] With all due deference to the prodigious learning of A. H. Krappe, his articles in *Speculum*, xiii (1938), 206, and in *Études Celtiques*, iii (1938), 27, seem to me to furnish excellent illustrations of those dubious assumptions and fallacies to which the comparative mythologist is peculiarly prone.

[43] Loomis, *Celtic Myth*, pp. 303–8; *Arthurian Tradition*, pp. 166 f.

[44] Loomis, *Celtic Myth*, p. 50.

[45] Ibid., p. 47. *Feast of Bricriu*, ed. G. Henderson, p. 33.

the rendezvous was heralded by a harsh roar as if he had been whetting his axe;[46] that Gawain's solar sympathies became one of the commonplaces of Arthurian romance; that Gasozein, as the defender of the ford, retained the summery whiteness of Hafgan.

That there were also genetic relations between *GGK* and folk ritual has already been suggested by E. K. Chambers and Professor Nitze.[47] Chambers was naturally misled by the greenness of Bercilak into taking him for a 'green man', a vegetation spirit of the Mannhardt school. But since we have deduced his ancestry from Cúroí and Arawn, neither of whom has any vegetable traits or green garments, and both of whom are clad in grey, we must abandon this view. As I pointed out long since,[48] Bercilak's verdant hue is due not to summer verdure, but to the ambiguity of the Welsh word *glas*, which may mean either grey or green. Probably A. B. Cook and Professor Nitze were right, however, in attaching significance to the cluster of holly borne by the Green Knight.[49] Captain Winter in the Welsh ritual combat carried a blackthorn stick, and the blackthorn still blossoms about Christmas time in the British Isles.[50] In Hampshire, according to Gilbert White, the season when the cold north-east winds blow and the blackthorn flowers was called 'blackthorn winter'.[51] In one South Welsh district the king of Winter was crowned with holly for obvious reasons.[52] It was of course equally fitting for Bercilak as the personification of the same season to carry the appropriate holly. These glossy leaves and coral berries may well be a contribution of folk-custom, rather than myth, to romance. There may be other details, such as Gasozein's white shirt[53] and the songs which he sings,[54] which derive from ritual. But in the main, I believe, the case is clear: Cúroí, Cúchulainn, Bláthnat, Arawn, king of Annwn, his wife, and Hafgan were not

---

[46] Vss. 199, 2199-204. Cf. the noise which precedes the approach of Esclados to the perilous fountain in *Ivain*, vss. 481, 813; and the thunder in *Owain*, trans. Loth, *Mabinogion*, ii. 12 f., 17, 29.

[47] E. K. Chambers, *Medieval Stage* (Oxford, 1903), i. 185 f.; *Mod. Phil.*, xxxiii (1936), 361 f.

[48] Loomis, *Celtic Myth*, p. 59. *PMLA*, xlviii. 1004, 1008, 1029 f. Cf. Kittredge, op. cit., p. 197.

[49] *Folklore*, xvii (1906), 339; *Mod. Phil.* xxxiii. 357 f.

[50] Chambers, *Medieval Stage*, i. 252, n. 3.   [51] Cf. *NED*, *sub* blackthorn.

[52] T. Gwynn Jones, *Welsh Folklore and Folk-Custom*, p. 153. Cf. Chambers, *Medieval Stage*, i. 251, 253.

[53] Cf. *supra*, p. 81, n. 18.

[54] *Crône*, vss. 3412-15; Gwynn Jones, op. cit., p. 154. 'Songs called *Carolau Haf*, "Summer Carols", were sung' by Welsh peasants celebrating May Day.

human representatives of the powers of nature, but the divine embodiments of them. The stories which went into the making of *GGK* were myths. Let me quote the great scholar, W. P. Ker.[55]

Whether in the Teutonic countries, which in one of their corners preserved a record of old mythology, or in the Celtic, which allowed mythology, though never forgotten, to fall into a kind of neglect and to lose its original meaning, the value of mythology is equally recognizable, and it is equally clear that mythology is nothing more nor less than Romance.

'Morgne the goddes', the wrinkled, yellow crone who dwelt in Sir Bercilak's castle and who was responsible, so the poet tells us, for sending him to Arthur's court to rob the knights of their wits and to frighten Gaynour (Guinevere), is a part of this mythological machinery. Kittredge, to be sure, thought that she was introduced, somewhat awkwardly, by the poet to supply the activating force behind the Green Knight's conduct, inasmuch as she was already notorious in Arthurian literature as a trouble-maker and as an enemy of Guinevere.[56] Though this concept of Morgain was doubtless present in the poet's mind and led him to ascribe to her the contrivance of a plot to injure Arthur and his queen, yet her place in the household of Sir Bercilak was derived from another tradition which linked Morgain to the Wild Huntsman. In the chapter on the Combat at the Ford it will be demonstrated that the faery mistress of Urbain, Perceval's opponent at the ford, was identifiable as Morgain, daughter of Avalloc. The corresponding anonymous lady in *Pwyll*, Arawn's wife, must therefore be Modron, daughter of Avallach. She dwelt in the palace of the Wild Huntsman. The inference that Morgain, likewise, was sometimes conceived as the wife or mistress of the Wild Huntsman is curiously corroborated by the dramatist, Adam de la Halle, who in the *Jeu de la Feuillée* (1276) told how Morgue la Fée chose as her lover Hellekin, the leader of the *chasse furieuse* and 'le grigneur prinche qui soit en faerie'.[57] The evidence thus fits together to prove that one of Morgain's multifarious roles was that of mate of the Winter king, who specialized in following his spectral hounds between Christmas and Twelfth Night.[58]

[55] *The Dark Ages* (London, 1904), p. 47.
[56] Kittredge, op. cit., pp. 131–3.
[57] *Jeu de la Feuillée*, ed. E. Langlois, ed. 2 (1923), vss. 604–17, 828–31.
[58] O. Driesen, *Ursprung des Harlekin* (1904), pp. 25–62.

Few, I trust, will object that in *GGK* Morgne is not Sir Bercilak's wife, and that it is the latter who so cleverly, though vainly, plays Morgain's customary part of attempting to seduce the knights of the Round Table.[59] Is it not fairly obvious that Morgne and Bercilak's beautiful lady are doublets, and that the duplication was due to the conflating of two versions of the story? *GGK* has preserved from one version the name Morgne and her character as an ugly and malignant enchantress, and from the other a quite different concept of her as a beautiful seductress. One cannot but admire the ingenuity with which both Morgains have been accommodated to the demands of the plot.

Whoever the genius was who worked out the plot of *GGK*, he performed a miracle, for I doubt whether in the whole history of fiction so perfect a narrative structure has been built almost exclusively from such inharmonious and recalcitrant materials. Well might Mr. C. S. Lewis remark apropos of the poem (as well as of Salisbury Cathedral and the *Divine Comedy*) that in these works 'medieval art attains a unity of the highest order, because it embraces the greatest diversity of subordinated detail'.[60] How diverse and divergent were the traditions which went into the making of *GGK* Mr. Lewis probably did not realize; only a comparative study of the themes of Beheading Test, Temptation, Perilous Castle, Magic Girdle, Gawain's Loves, the Ford Perilous, the Huntsman Host, and the Annual Combat can give one any impression of the complexity and contradictoriness of the matter employed to make this singularly harmonious, neatly dovetailed narrative. Here is an instance where source study, far from detracting from the greatness of a masterpiece, is essential to a full understanding of its greatness. Other medieval romancers had attempted to combine elements of the Challenge and the Beheading Test with the theme of Temptation by the huntsman's wife, and had produced the plots of the Gasozein and Guingambresil stories and of the *Carl of Carlisle* and the *Chevalier à l'Espée*. Another similar effort is the Galagandreiz episode in Ulrich von Zatzikhoven's *Lanzelet*.[61] None of these is remarkable for coherence or for plausible motivation. In *GGK*, however, thirty-five or more traditional features have been shaped into an almost

---

[59] For other examples of Morgain in this role cf. Loomis, *Arthurian Tradition*, pp. 122–7, and *infra*, pp. 108 f.
[60] C. S. Lewis, *Allegory of Love* (Oxford, 1936), p. 142.
[61] Trans. K. G. T. Webster (New York, 1951), pp. 35–41, 171, n. 37.

flawless plot. And nothing could be neater than the employment of the one non-Celtic element, the exchange of winnings, detected by Professor Hulbert.[62] It would seem a hopeless task to find any causal connexion between the Welsh tradition of the hero's chaste behaviour toward the huntsman's wife, the Irish tradition of the treacherous wife who bestows her husband's protective girdle on her lover, and the Irish tradition of the Beheading Test. Yet the creator of the plot of *GGK* found in the extraneous motif—the exchange of winnings—a perfect solution. It was a stroke of genius.

For this triumph in narrative architecture we cannot give the credit to the English poet. At least, nothing in his other works suggests any such power of plot construction; *Purity* in fact is rather loosely strung together. Besides, no one in the fourteenth century had access to the many lost *contes* which the creator of the plot must have used if he were to include the thirty-seven or thirty-eight features derived from Celtic tradition. Most of these *contes* must have been lost in that century, since even a royal collector, Charles V, possessed little or nothing that is not extant today. That the *Gawain* poet had eight or ten French tales representing the various forms of the Cúchulainn–Cúroí–Bláthnat complex and the Hafgan–Arawn encounter, is incredible. His contribution lay rather in the brilliance of the descriptions, in the subtlety and naturalness of the characterization, particularly of Gawain, and in the pulsating vitality of the action. These qualities we find in the other poems of the Cotton MS. and in some of the works of the alliterative school. The author of the English poem deserves and has received his meed of glory. But the credit for the narrative framework must go elsewhere. Not altogether to one man, for in the Guingambresil and the Gasozein episodes, in the *Carl of Carlisle* and the *Chevalier à l'Espée*, we can perceive fumbling efforts towards the shaping of our plot. Still, most of the glory for this structural miracle must go to some great unknown. He was in all probability a Frenchman, perhaps a contemporary of the architects of Amiens and Rheims cathedrals. At any rate, he shared with them the power of building diverse materials, adjusting diverse claims, shaping diverse traditions into a superb unity.

[62] *Mod. Phil.* xiii (1916), 699–701.

CHAPTER VII

The Combat at the Ford in the 'Didot Perceval'

THE reader of Arthurian romance is likely to feel after a time as if he were a child turning a kaleidoscope. The patterns are charming and ever changing, but the bits of coloured glass which make the patterns remain the same. What is the explanation of this monotony, this recurrence of the same situations and motifs?

A theory which enjoyed and still enjoys great favour among the scholars of England, France, and the United States is that a sort of paralysis of the imagination overtook the poets and prose-writers of the thirteenth century, and they repeated endlessly the *données* of Chrétien, the continuators of the *Conte del Graal*, and Robert de Boron. Speaking of the Vulgate romances, Ferdinand Lot gave witty expression to this view:

Que de 'mehaignés'! Josephé, frappé à la cuisse, son père, Joseph d'Arimathie, à la jambe; Caleb Alfassam, transpercé d'un 'glaive' en travers des cuisses; de même Pellehan, le père du roi Pellès; Nascien, aveuglé un instant; Mordrain, aveuglé et paralysé pour plusieurs siècles. La vengeance divine est peu variée dans ses manifestations.... Ce procédé de doublets et triplets, si commode pour les auteurs fatigués, a l'inconvénient de donner à une œuvre d'apparence variée une grande monotonie.[1]

According to this view, which also dominates Bruce's *Evolution of Arthurian romance*, the French poets of the twelfth and early thirteenth centuries were the only really creative artists in the Arthurian tradition, inventing nearly all the motifs and plots of the *matière de Bretagne*. After them came only sterile imitators, *auteurs fatigués*, who repeated because they could not think of anything better.

Another hypothesis, however, has its adherents. It detracts from the originality and fertility of the first romancers and points out that Chrétien himself repeated such motifs as the Perilous Bed and

[1] F. Lot, *Étude sur le Lancelot en Prose* (Paris, 1918), pp. 269-71. On the other repetitions characteristic of the Vulgate cycle cf. ibid., pp. 262-71.

the ignominious overthrow of Keu.[2] It interprets these repetitions and those of the later romancers as due, not so much to barrenness of imagination, however, as to reverence for tradition. The romancers, from Chrétien on down, were not incapable of invention, but they shared the respect of all medievals for the heritage of the past. They were limited by this heritage of oral and written legend. Originality they displayed in the combination, motivation, and interpretation of old narrative patterns, not in the modern sense of inventing new ones. The monotony of the Round Table legends is due to the restricted number of Celtic stories which filtered through to the Breton *conteurs* and proved adaptable to French audiences.

Neither of these two views is held in quite the absolute form in which I have presented them. Those who, like Bruce,[3] believe that Arthurian romance was largely the product of the fancy of the first French poets nevertheless concede that certain recurrent motifs, such as the Beheading Test, were not invented but inherited from the Celts. On the other hand, those who believe in the traditional Celtic origin of most of the themes of Arthurian romance would readily concede that in certain instances the poems of Chrétien and Robert de Boron were the direct or indirect sources of later romancers—French, German, English, Italian, and so forth. The question is, therefore, a matter of degree: To what extent were both the earlier and the later romancers indebted to antecedent Celtic tradition? To what extent were the later romancers merely repeating the narrative patterns of their French literary predecessors, and to what extent were they drawing upon cognate versions which came to them orally through the Breton *conteurs*[4] or through manuscripts[5] long since lost?

---

[2] *Chevalier de la Charrette*, vss. 474–538; *Conte del Graal*, ed. Hilka, vss. 7692–848; *Erec*, vss. 3957–4054; *Chevalier de la Charrette*, vss. 259–69; *Conte del Graal*, vss. 4274–319.   [3] J. D. Bruce, *Evolution of Arthurian Romance*, i. 72–94.

[4] On the part of the Breton *conteurs* in the dissemination of Celtic matter cf. *infra*, pp. 181, 183–8.

[5] The names 'Baudemaguz' and 'Ban de Gomeret' are to be explained only as due to scribal corruption (cf. H. Newstead, *Bran the Blessed*, pp. 134, 145 n.; *Romania*, lxiii (1937), 383 ff.). The Welsh Brân the Blessed had his palace at Aberffraw, the ancient royal court of North Wales (Giraldus Cambrensis, *Descriptio Cambriae*, ed. J. F. Dimock, p. 169). The Welsh word for North Wales—*Gwynedd* —would be written by a Frenchman *Goiñet* (cf. *Fouke Fitz Warin*, ed. L. Brandin (Paris, 1930), p. 94, *sub* 'Goynez'). The *-in-* could be mistaken easily for *m*, and the stroke over the *n* mistaken for the sign for *er*. Prof. Roach very kindly pointed out to me that Potvin in his *Perceval le Gallois* (Mons, 1866–71), iii. 88, vs. 8, made the reverse error, reading *Goinnec* for *Gomerec*. Only as a result of some corrupt manu-

A final answer to this basic question can be given, of course, only when all the important stock situations and motifs of the Round Table cycle have been thoroughly and satisfactorily examined, and that lies a long while in the future. Nevertheless, progress has been made. It will be granted by all that the Beheading Test was not the invention of the author of the *Livre de Caradoc*, the Tristan legend was not the invention of Chrétien or some anonymous French predecessor, the abduction of Guenevere in its many forms did not originate with the *Chevalier de la Charrette*. The studies of Kittredge, Gertrude Schoepperle, and Cross have demonstrated Celtic sources for all these famous themes.[6] Professor Newstead's work on *Bran the Blessed in Arthurian romance* and my own researches on the Perilous Bed motif, the Grail cycle, and the legends of Morgain la Fée[7] should add to the body of material which we can safely attribute, not to the creative imagination of the first French poets, but to the influx of Welsh and Irish stories through Breton channels. More and more evidence, therefore, accumulates in favour of the second hypothesis; more and more clearly it appears that the multitude of maimed or languishing kings, the repeated abductions of the unfortunate Guinevere, the singular recurrence of names beginning with Bran, and the other monotonies so characteristic of the *matière de Bretagne* are due not so much to the meagre inventive faculties of the romancers as to the restrictive force of tradition. In the following pages I hope to add one more to the number of narrative patterns of Celtic origin.

It has been noted by several scholars that one of the stock incidents of Arthurian romance is a combat of the hero with one or more redoubtable antagonists at a ford. It occurs first as Erec's encounter with the robber knights;[8] other important examples occur in the *Conte del Graal*, *Diu Crône*, *Le Bel Inconnu*, Malory's Book of Gareth, *Historia Meriadoci*, *De Ortu Walwanii*, and *Lanzelet*.[9]

script reading could Chrétien have written 'Ban de Gomeret' instead of 'Bran de Goinnet'. Note, moreover, that Chrétien acknowledges that a book was the source of his *Conte del Graal* (vs. 67).

[6] G. L. Kittredge, *Study of Gawain and the Green Knight* (Cambridge, Mass., 1916); G. Schoepperle, *Tristan and Isolt*; T. P. Cross and W. A. Nitze, *Lancelot and Guenevere* (Chicago, 1930).

[7] *PMLA*, xlviii (1933), 1005, 1011–18; *infra*, pp. 105–30.

[8] Chrétien de Troyes, *Erec*, vss. 2795–3085, particularly vss. 3030–40. That this was originally a combat at a ford appears by comparing it with the ford combats in Malory's Book of Gareth and *Le Bel Inconnu*, cited in the next note.

[9] Potvin, vol. iv, vss. 24160–421; Heinrich von dem Türlin, *Diu Crône*, ed.

Kindred versions, though not strictly Arthurian, are found in the *Lai de l'Espine* and the Scottish poem, *Eger and Grime*.[10] A thorough study of these stories and their interrelationships would require a monograph. I must confine myself to the version in the *Didot Perceval*, which Professor Roach has recognized as 'obviously more primitive' than that given in the *Conte del Graal*[11] and in which Jessie Weston pointed out some traces of Celtic matter. I hope to establish the fact that in this romance, which must have existed, in verse-form at least, by 1212, the ford episode is made up of Welsh materials,

G. H. F. Scholl (Stuttgart, 1852), vss. 3356–5083, 8843–925; Renaud de Beaujeu, *Le Bel Inconnu*, ed. G. P. Williams (Paris, 1929), vss. 322–588, 965–1226; Malory, *Morte d'Arthur*, Book VII, chaps. v–vii; *Historia Meriadoci and De ortu Walwanii*, ed. J. D. Bruce (Baltimore and Göttingen, 1913), pp. 20–25, 85–88; Ulrich von Zatzikhoven, *Lanzelet*, trans. K. G. T. Webster (New York, 1951), p. 95. There are, of course, other combats at fords in Arthurian romance (cf. Potvin, vss. 11,110 ff., 20,633 ff., 37,105 ff.; H. O. Sommer, *Vulgate Version of the Arthurian Romances* [Washington, 1908–16], iii. 140–2, 197 ff., 203 f., 214; iv. 216 f.; Chrétien de Troyes, *Chevalier de la Charrette*, vss. 714–934); but none of these seem to be dominated by the pattern observable in the romances listed. For comments on the ford combat cf. Cross and Nitze, p. 54, n. 6; *Mod. Phil.*, xii (1915), 604, n. 1; *Didot-Perceval*, ed. W. Roach (Philadelphia, 1941), 70–73; *Celtic Review*, iii. 148; *Historia Meriadoci*, ed. Bruce, pp. lvi–lviii; Loomis, *Arthurian Tradition*, pp. 127–33.

[10] *Zeitschr. f. rom. Phil.* xviii (1893), 246–55; *Eger and Grime*, ed. J. R. Caldwell (Cambridge, Mass., 1933). It should be noted that Béroul (*Tristan*, vss. 1320 f.) mentions 'le Gué Aventuros, et iluec a une aube espine', that the *Merveilles de Rigomer* mentions twice (vss. 7040, 9433) the 'Gués de Blance Espine', and that Chrétien (*Yvain*, vs. 4705) mentions the death of 'li sire de la Noire Espine'. The last mentioned is evidently identical with Laniure, whom Gawain vanquished at a ford, according to Heinrich von dem Türlin's *Diu Crône*, vss. 8853–925. Note also that Perceval's opponent at the ford (*Didot-Perceval*, ed. Roach, p. 196) was son of 'le roine de le Noire Espine'; that Gareth after his victory at the river passage (Malory, Book VII, chap. vi) came to a black 'launde', where there was a black hawthorn; that Arthur's opponent, Gasozein, in *Diu Crône* (vss. 3424 f.) haunts 'den vurt vür Noirespine'; and that the Percy Folio version of *Eger and Grime* twice (vss. 1406, 1457) gives the name 'Loosepine' to the faery lady who healed Eger after his combat beyond the ford and who later married Grime, the victor. The ballad, 'Sir Cawline', which is certainly akin to *Eger and Grime*, as Professor Hibbard (*Mediaeval Romance in England*, p. 317) pointed out, places the eerie combat with the eldritch knight near a thorn tree on the moors. There is much evidence to show that thorn trees near wells were regarded by country folk in Wales and Cornwall as sacred late into the nineteenth century (cf. J. Rhys, *Celtic Folklore*, i. 355, 361 f.; M. A. Courtney, *Cornish Feasts and Folk-lore* (Penzance, 1890), pp. 32 f.). Very apposite is the statement by W. G. Wood-Martin (*Traces of the Elder Faiths of Ireland* (London, 1902), ii. 156): 'When it [the whitethorn] grows alone near the banks of streams, or on forts, it is considered to be the haunt and peculiar abode of the fairies.' Cf. also ibid. ii. 22, 81, 88, 96. This belief in the connexion of a magic thorn tree with springs or fords must surely be responsible for the persistent association of the ford combat with an *espine*.

[11] *Didot-Perceval*, ed. Roach, p. 71.

The Combat at the Ford in the 'Didot Perceval'

represented in Welsh texts, all but two of which antedate the year 1100. Let me summarize:

In the course of his search for the house of his grandfather Bron, Perceval came to a ford beside a beautiful meadow and watered his horse. From a pavilion beyond the water a knight sallied out but, before encountering Perceval, bade a damsel provide the intruder with a shield and lance. At the first shock Perceval hurled his antagonist to the ground and then subdued him with his sword. The strange knight identified himself as Urbain, son of the Queen of the Blackthorn (*le roïne de le Noire Espine*), and told the following history. One tempestuous night Urbain spied a damsel riding on a mule (MS. D, 'a palfrey') at a great speed. He followed and tried to overtake her, but the night was black, and only by the flashes of lightning could he keep her in sight. He followed her into one of the most beautiful castles in the world. There she welcomed him and consented to become his mistress. He was to defend a ford near the invisible castle, and now he was within eight days of completing a year of delight with the damsel and her maidens. But he was vanquished, and it was for Perceval now to defend the ford for a year. Perceval refused. Suddenly there was a great tumult, followed by a smoke and thick darkness. The voice of Urbain's mistress was heard, cursing Perceval and calling on Urbain to flee or he would lose her love. The unfortunate knight tried to ride off but was held back by Perceval. A flock of large black birds swooped upon Perceval and tried to peck out his eyes, and Urbain, inspired with new courage, attacked him. Things were going badly until he struck down one of the black birds. She turned at once into a lovely woman and was carried off dead by the other birds. Pressed for an explanation, Urbain revealed that the birds were his mistress and her maids and that the noise and the tumult were caused by the destruction of her magic castle. The slain bird was his mistress' sister, but all was well since she was now in Avalon. With Perceval's permission Urbain departed, leaving his horse, and soon after he was spirited away amid great rejoicing, and the horse too disappeared. 'Et quant Percevaus le vit si le tint a grant mervelle.'[12]

It is no wonder that Professor Roach recognized the primitive nature of this tale or that Nutt remarked: 'This incident stands out pre-eminent in the Didot-Perceval for its wild and fantastic character. It is a genuine Celtic *Märchen*, with much of the weird charm still clinging to it that is the birthright of the Celtic folk-tale.'[13] Miss Weston, however, was the only

[12] Ibid., pp. 195–202.
[13] A. Nutt, *Studies on the Legend of the Holy Grail* (London, 1888), p. 129.

scholar to make a definite connexion with Celtic tradition. Let me quote:

> The distinctive feature of our story is the appearance of the lady and her maidens under the form of birds. . . . So far as I have been able to discover, this power of assuming bird form appears to be somewhat closely connected with Avalon. In the *Vita Merlini*, Geoffrey, speaking of the 'Insula Pomorum quae fortunata vocatur' (i.e. Avalon), and the nine sisters who bear rule there, says of the chief of them, Morgen,
>
> > Ars quoque nota sibi qua scit mutare figuram
> > Et resecare novis quasi Daedalus aera pennis.
>
> In the *Prophecies of Merlin* we find Morgain sending her messengers in the form of birds to convey the Dame d'Avalon to her presence.[14] Here the dead Bird-maiden is carried to Avalon; the connexion can hardly be fortuitous.
>
> A parallel to the role here played by the maidens is found in Owen's army of ravens in *The Dream of Rhonabwy*. So far as the action is concerned the parallel is extremely close. Owen's birds 'with one sweep descend upon the heads of the men—and they seized some by the heads, and others by the eyes, and some by the ears, and others by the arms, and carried them up into the air, and in the air there was a mighty tumult with the flapping of the wings of the triumphant ravens.' Here, Perceval 'vit entor lui si grant plenté d'oisiaus que tous li airs entor lui en fu couvers, et estoient plus noir qu'onques rien qu'eüst veüe, et li voloient parmi le hiaume les uels esracier de le teste'. In *D.* [the Didot MS.] the birds are 'grans, corsuz, et plus neirs que errement'. All this corresponds closely with the ravens of the Mabinogi.[15]

Thus far Miss Weston. We can go farther and link up the tradition of the metamorphosis of Morgen and her sisters into birds with the tradition of Owain's ravens. According to several texts, Morgain was the daughter of a King Avallo or a certain Avalloc, and she was the mother of Yvain by Urien.[16] She therefore has her counterpart in the Welsh Modron, who, according to a triad, was the daughter of Avallach and the mother of Owain by Urien.[17] Putting together the evidence, we discover who Owain's ravens,

---

[14] *Les Prophecies de Merlin*, ed. L. A. Paton (New York and London, 1926), i. 416. According to Hartmann von Aue (*Erek*, ed. M. Haupt (Leipzig, 1871), vss. 5177 f.), Famurgan, the *gotinne*, could fly through the air.

[15] J. L. Weston, *Legend of Sir Perceval* (London, 1906–9), ii. 207 f.

[16] *Romanic Review*, xxix (1938), 176 f.

[17] J. Loth, *Mabinogion*² (Paris, 1913), ii. 284. Prof. Thomas Jones assures me that this triad is old and authentic.

who battled so fiercely with the knights of Arthur, were: they were his mother, Modron, and her sisters, the daughters of Avallach, in bird form. The statement in the *Didot Perceval* that the wounded Bird-maiden was carried off, not to the isle of Avalloc, but to Avalon ('or ces eures est ele en Avalon') is due to the common misinterpretation by the French of the Welsh *ynys Avallach* (i.e. the isle of Modron's father, Avallach) as *isle d'Avalon*, a place-name.[18] The truly Celtic nature of this transformation of Morgain and her sisters into bellicose black birds was confirmed by another reference of Miss Weston's to the ferocious and vindictive Irish goddess, the Morrígan, who took many shapes, including that of a crow.[19] That there were marked points of resemblance between Morgain and the Morrígan was demonstrated by Miss Paton and Zenker,[20] and it is therefore most significant that in the *Cattle-raid of Cooley* the Morrígan, like a female Proteus, assumed many shapes when she attacked Cúchulainn during his combat with Loch at a ford and was wounded severely by him.[21] Being healed by magic, she flew away in the form of a crow and lighted on a whitethorn bush, which thereafter was called the Whitethorn of the Crow.[22] Thus Irish traditions of the Morrígan; Welsh traditions of Modron, her son Owain, and his ravens; and the French tradition of Perceval's combat at the ford with Urbain and his black birds—Morgain and her sisters—are intimately related.

The antiquity of this material can be judged by the fact that the saga of the *Cattle-raid* is assigned by the best Irish scholars to the eighth century.[23] And though the *Dream of Rhonabwy* was composed as late as the thirteenth century,[24] Nutt was right in asserting that

[18] On the original meaning of Avallach and its relation to Avalon cf. *Romanic Review*, xxix. 176 f.; *PMLA*, lvi (1941), 920; J. Rhys, *Studies in the Arthurian Legend* (Oxford, 1891), pp. 335 f. Rhys's suggestion that Avallach was 'a dark divinity' forms a part of his classification of the Celtic gods, which is accepted, I believe, by no one.

[19] Weston, op. cit., ii. 208. On the Celtic battle-goddesses and their transformation into crows, cf. *Rev. Celt.*, i (1870–2), 32–57; *PMLA*, lvi (1941), 5 f., 12.

[20] L. A. Paton, *Fairy Mythology of Arthurian Romance* (Boston, 1903), pp. 11 f., 21–24, 148–66; *Zts. f. franz. Sprache u. Lit.*, xlviii (1925–6), 82–92; cf. Cross in *Mod. Phil.*, xii. 605, n. 4.

[21] R. Thurneysen, *Die irische Helden- und Königsage* (Halle, 1921), pp. 169–74.

[22] Ibid., p. 176 (bottom), n. 1: 'Nach ihrem Hohn fliegt sie als Krähe auf den Weißdorn über Grellach Dolair, der daher Sge na h-Enche ar Murthemni heißt.'

[23] Ibid., p. 112. The detail of the crow on the whitethorn belongs, however, to the third version, which was not written down until the thirteenth or fourteenth century (ibid., p. 147).

[24] J. Gwenogvryn Evans, *White Book Mabinogion* (Pwllheli, 1907), p. xxv.

'the distinguishing feature of the story, the raven army of Owen, is surely very old'.[25]

We have another Welsh story of Urien, Modron, and their son Owain in a text written down about the year 1556.[26] It is thus translated by T. Gwynn Jones:

> In Denbighshire there is a parish called Llanferrys, and Rhyd y Gyfarthfa (the Ford of the Barking) is there, and in olden times the dogs of the country would come there to bark, and no one would venture to go to see what was there until Urien Rheged came. And when he came to the ford, he saw nought but a woman washing. And then the dogs stopped barking, and Urien took hold of the woman, and had possession of her. Then she said, 'The blessing of God upon the feet that brought thee here.' 'Wherefore?' he asked. 'Because,' she said, 'it is my destiny to wash here until I have a son by a Christian, and I am the daughter of the King of Annwn. Do thou come here at the end of a year, and thou shalt have the son.' And so he went and got a son and a daughter, none other than Owain ab Urien and Morfudd, daughter of Urien.[27]

In spite of the lateness of the record, there can be no doubt of the antiquity of this material also. It harmonizes with the triad which lists among the three blessed births of the Isle of Britain 'Owein, son of Urien and Morvudd, his sister, at the same time in the womb of Modron daughter of Avallach'.[28] It parallels three Irish traditions of the Morrígan, all of which antedate the year 908:[29] she came in the form of a beautiful young woman to a ford, announced herself as the daughter of King Buan, and offered Cúchulainn her love; she was a washer at a ford; she appeared to the god Dagda as a woman washing at a ford and mated with him there.[30] The Welsh tale must be in essence very old and serves to explain why Urbain's mistress should be represented as dwelling with her lover in an invisible palace beside a ford.

---

[25] C. Guest, *Mabinogion*, ed. A. Nutt (London, 1904), p. 346.
[26] Text in J. G. Evans, *Report on Manuscripts in the Welsh Language* (1898), i. 911; trans. in *Aberystwyth Studies*, iv (1922), 105.
[27] T. Gwynn Jones, *Welsh Folklore and Folk-custom* (London, 1930), p. 107.
[28] Loth, op. cit., ii. 284.
[29] Kuno Meyer in *Fianaigecht* (Dublin, 1910), pp. xviii f., dates *Reicne Fothaid Canainne* in the late eighth or early ninth century. The *Táin Bó Cualnge* ('Cattle-raid of Cooley'), we have seen, goes back to the eighth century. The *Second Battle of Mag Tured* is dated before 908 (*Zeitschr. f. celt. Phil.*, xviii. 80, 89).
[30] Thurneysen, pp. 169 f.; Meyer, p. 17; T. P. Cross and C. H. Slover, *Ancient Irish Tales* (New York, 1936), p. 38. On Irish traditions of meeting a supernatural woman at a ford cf. Cross in *Mod. Phil.*, xii. 604-8.

The association of Modron with a river-crossing is perhaps older than any other feature of her story, for Celtic mythologists are agreed that her name is derived from that of the goddess Matrona, who was widely worshipped from Cisalpine Gaul to the Rhine Valley and who gave her name to the Marne and other rivers in Gaul.[31] Matrona's character as a water-divinity seems to have descended to Modron and even to Morgain, whom Étienne de Rouen in the *Draco Normannicus* (1167-9) called *nympha perennis*.[32] The original divinity of Modron was also recognized in curious ways. In the tale translated above, she called herself 'daughter of the King of Annwn', the land of the Welsh gods. Her Arthurian counterpart, Morgain, was referred to by medieval writers not only as *la Fée* but also as *dea, déesse, goddes, gotinne*, and *Margan dwywes o annwfyn* ('goddess from Annwn').[33] Apparently, however, Modron's heathen origin was so notorious in Christian Wales that her name was frequently suppressed, even though stories about her continued to circulate and to be firmly believed.[34] As a character *under her own name* she never plays a part, so far as I know, in Welsh story, though she is, of course, mentioned in *Kulhwch* as the mother of Mabon, who was taken from her when three nights old.[35] The story of her union with Urien in the sixteenth-century manuscript permits no doubt as to her identity but leaves her anonymous.

An even more remarkable suppression is, I believe, to be detected in the first of the *Four Branches of the Mabinogi*, that treasury of Brythonic myth and folk-lore, dating probably from the eleventh century. I believe it is possible to identify Modron with the nameless wife of Arawn, king of Annwn, whose palace lay not far from

[31] Hastings, *Encyclopaedia of Religion and Ethics*, iii. 292; *Celtic Review*, iii (1906), 48; J. Rhys, *Lectures on the Origin and Growth of Religion as Illustrated by Celtic Heathendom*² (London, 1892), p. 29; T. Gwynn Jones, *Welsh Folklore*, p. 17; *Cymmrodor*, xlii (1930), 140. On the Matronae cf. *infra*, pp. 127-9.

[32] E. K. Chambers, *Arthur of Britain* (London, 1927), p. 265.

[33] Ibid., p. 272; W. J. A. Jonckbloet, *Roman van Lancelot* ('s Gravenhage, 1849), II. lxix; *Gawain and the Green Knight*, ed. J. R. R. Tolkien and E. V. Gordon (Oxford, 1925), vs. 2452; Hartmann von Aue, *Erek*, vs. 5161; Ifor Williams, *Pedeir Keinc y Mabinogi* (Cardiff, 1930), p. 100. The form 'Margan' has probably been influenced by the name of the famous Glamorganshire abbey, Margan (Giraldus Cambrensis, *Opera*, vi. 67).

[34] Rhys, in his *Lectures on the Origin*, p. 423 n., shows that the famous fairy lady of Little Van Lake was probably Modron. On the Welsh lake ladies and their relation to Modron, cf. *infra*, pp. 120-4.

[35] Loth, op. cit., i. 312, 323-8, 343. On the story of Mabon's imprisonment cf. *Cymmrodor*, xlii (1930), 129-47. Mabon, son of Modron, is also mentioned as Uther Pendragon's man in the Black Book of Carmarthen (Chambers, p. 64).

the River Cuch, the northern boundary between the counties of Carmarthen and Pembroke. One reason for suspecting that this Otherworld queen was no other than Modron is the fact that her husband Arawn was the leader of the Wild Hunt in *Pwyll*,[36] as he was still in recent times, according to Welsh folk-belief,[37] whereas Adam de la Halle informs us that Morgue la Fée (Modron's counterpart) adopted as her lover Hellekin, the leader of the *chasse furieuse*.[38] If we may equate Hellekin with Arawn, then we may equate Arawn's wife with Modron. A more cogent argument for this equation lies in the fact that Arawn's nameless wife is linked to a situation strongly reminiscent of that which the *Didot Perceval* attaches to Urbain's mistress, the fay of Avalon. We infer from the mabinogi[39] that Arawn had been unsuccessful in mortal combat at a ford with Hafgan, another king of Annwn. He met Pwyll, prince of Dyfed, in Glyn Cuch, persuaded him to fight Hafgan a year later at the ford, and in return transformed Pwyll into his own shape and sent him to his palace near by, to dwell there for the intervening year with the privilege of sleeping each night with his most beautiful queen. Pwyll spent the year with all delights and diversions, except that he denied himself the favours of the queen. At the year's end he encountered Hafgan at the ford and slew him. He then met Arawn, resumed his own form, and returned to his dominions. I have shown in the preceding chapter that this is a partially euhemerized version of the annual conflict between summer and winter, which has left other clear traces in Welsh legend and folk ritual and has even influenced *Gawain and the Green Knight*.[40] For us the important point is the resemblance of this episode to the adventure of the Perilous Ford. In both *Pwyll* and the *Didot Perceval* we have a faery palace near a river; in both we have a mortal (Pwyll, Urbain) dwelling with a fay in the palace; in both stress is laid on the obligation of the

---

[36] Loth, op. cit., i. 84 f.

[37] M. Trevelyan, *Folklore and Folk-stories of Wales* (London, 1909), pp. 48, 53; *Journ. Engl. and Germ. Phil.* xlii. 174–6. On the Wild Hunt cf. also *Mod. Phil.*, xxxviii (1941), 289, n. 2, 299 f.; *Kölner Anglistische Arbeiten*, iv (1929), 61–66; *Yale Romanic Studies*, xxii (1943), 21–28; Stith Thompson, *Motif-index of Folk-literature*, E501.

[38] A. Rambeau, *Die dem Trouvère Adam de la Hale zugeschriebenen Dramen* ('Ausgaben u. Abhandlungen aus d. Gebiete d. romanischen Philologie', vol. lviii (1886)), pp. 91 f. M. Gustave Cohen identified Morgue and her two companion fays of Adam's play with the Matres of Gaulish mythology (*Roman Courtois au XIIe Siècle* (Paris, 1938), p. 64).

[39] Loth, op. cit., i. 84–92.

[40] *Journ. Engl. and Germ. Phil.*, xlii. 170–81.

mortal to engage in combat at a ford; in both the term of office is a year. In view of the already accumulated evidence for the Celticity of Perceval's adventure with Urbain and his mistress, one can hardly ascribe these parallels to accident. Urbain's mistress being Morgain, her counterpart in *Pwyll* must be Modron.

If it be objected that Pwyll met the Otherworld queen under circumstances quite different from those under which Urbain met his faery mistress, and therefore the parallel breaks down, it is only necessary to turn on to the next episode in the mabinogi to find the correspondence we need. Let me summarize:[41]

Pwyll, sitting on the Mound of Arberth, saw a damsel riding by, and after twice sending a squire in vain to summon her, he pursued her himself on his swiftest horse and urged it to its limit of speed.[42] Being unable to overtake her, he implored her to wait for him, and she readily complied. He perceived that no woman could compare with her for beauty, and when she declared her love for him, he agreed to marry her at the end of the year.

Compare this with Urbain's account of his meeting with the fay, as it is given in the Didot manuscript:[43] 'Then I saw riding ahead of me one of the fairest damsels that ever was, and she was moving fast on a palfrey. As soon as I saw her, I started after and followed her.' (The Modena manuscript adds: 'and I strained hard to reach her'.) When Urbain followed her into the castle, she showed him every hospitality and readily consented to become his mistress. Though some of the parallels between Pwyll's and Urbain's adventures may be commonplace, not every mortal lover meets his faery lady riding a horse so swift that he cannot overtake her and then discovers that she is more than willing to reciprocate his sudden passion. It seems fairly obvious that the chief difference between the story of Urbain and his love and the story of Pwyll and Arawn's wife is due to the absorption of another romance of Pwyll's, his pursuit and wooing of Rhiannon.

There is, perhaps, another reason for the blending of the two Welsh legends besides the fact that Pwyll was the mortal hero of both adventures. Whereas the faery lady in one is identifiable with Modron and is descended from the famed Celtic goddess Matrŏna, meaning 'the Great Mother', the other faery lady is called Rhiannon,

[41] Loth, op. cit., i. 92–98.
[42] On faery horses which cannot be overtaken cf. Cross and Slover, op. cit., p. 101.
[43] Ed. Roach, p. 197.

a name which Celtic scholars derive phonologically from a hypothetical Rigantona, meaning 'the Great Queen'.[44] Both names therefore originated as divine titles and were perhaps applied to the same divinity.[45] Be that as it may, there were strong tendencies toward syncretism in the mythology of the Celts, as Professor Robinson and others have discerned.[46] Circumstances would therefore favour what is common enough in any case—the exchange of attributes and legends between one goddess or fay and another. Moreover, it is worth noting that the name Rhiannon contains the same Celtic root as does the second element in the name of Modron's Irish counterpart, the Morrígan.[47] There was surely a basic kinship between these Celtic goddesses.

Whereas the *Dream of Rhonabwy*, the tale of Urien, and *Pwyll* offer significant analogies to the *Didot Perceval* account of Urbain and his mistress and the encounter at the ford, the mabinogi of *Manawydan*, probably of the same date as *Pwyll*, offers two other curious parallels. When the faery castle of Urbain's mistress was destroyed, we read: 'Perceval heard so great a tumult that it seemed to him as if all the forest sank into an abyss. From this noise, which was so great, a smoke issued and a darkness so great that one could not see the other.'[48] Later Urbain explained: 'Now know that the noise which ye heard and the great tumult was my damsel's castle which she cast down.' Compare this with a passage in *Manawydan*, describing the enchantment that overtook the land of Dyfed (South Wales): 'A peal of thunder, and with the magnitude of the peal, lo, a fall of mist, so that no one of them could see the other. After the mist, lo, every place filled with light. When they looked where they were wont before to see flocks, herds, and dwellings, nothing could they see, no house, beast, smoke, fire, man, or dwelling.'[49] Though in the *Perceval* it is a magic castle which is destroyed and in the mabinogi it is the material buildings which vanish, yet the accompanying circumstances are the same: a roar and a cloud so thick that no person can see another.

A second remarkable parallel occurs at the end of *Manawydan*.

[44] *Cymmrodor*, xlii. 140.
[45] This was the contention of Prof. Gruffydd in the article cited in the preceding note.
[46] Hastings, iv. 409.
[47] On derivation of Morrígan cf. Paton, *Fairy Mythology*, pp. 158 f.
[48] Ed. Roach, p. 199.
[49] *Mabinogion*, trans. G. and T. Jones, Everyman's Lib., p. 43.

It will be remembered that the mistress of Perceval's enemy transformed herself and her sisters into birds and attacked him, that he wounded one of them, and thus forced Urbain to reveal who these creatures were. In the mabinogi we have a strangely similar story.[50] Manawydan's wheat crop had been devoured on successive nights, and, determined to discover the perpetrators, he watched until midnight. He perceived an army of mice and, rushing in among them, he succeeded in capturing one. The next day he went to the Mound of Arberth, whence he had witnessed the sudden desolation of Dyfed, and there proceeded to hang the mouse. He was interrupted successively by a clerk, a priest, and a bishop, who turned out to be three forms of his enemy Llwyd. In vain Llwyd pleaded for the life of the mouse; but, when Manawydan proved adamant, Llwyd confessed that the captured mouse was his own wife and the others were the ladies of her court.[51] He promised to remove the enchantments from Dyfed, the mouse was set at liberty, and when Llwyd struck her with a wand, she turned into the most beautiful of women. It is hardly necessary to point out that, except for the substitution of mice for blackbirds and the consequent change in the form which their hostility took, the Welsh and the French texts tell much the same tale. The hero is involved in a conflict with an enemy; the wife or mistress of that enemy and her ladies transform themselves and make war on the hero; he strikes one of them down; she reverts to human shape; the enemy yields and discloses that this belligerent female is his own wife or his mistress' sister.

The Perilous Ford adventure in the *Didot Perceval* reveals itself on examination as a mosaic of plots and motifs which in different combinations are found in the *Four Branches of the Mabinogi* and in other Welsh tales which, though recorded centuries later, give internal evidence of their antiquity. The world is the world of Brythonic paganism, in which mortals mate with river-nymphs, the summer spirit and the winter demon fight an annual battle at a ford, crows and mice are but malevolent supernatural forces in disguise.

[50] Ibid., pp 49–54. There is a remarkable analogue (though with different denouement) in a modern tale from Westmeath (cf. Rhys, *Celtic folklore*, i. 124).

[51] It is a curious fact that the hounds of Annwn in modern folk tradition were frequently called the 'Hounds of the mothers' (*Cŵn mamau*) and sometimes appeared as mice (T. Gwynn Jones, *Welsh Folklore*, p. 203). Giraldus Cambrensis reports that Ynys Lenach, now called Puffin Island, was inhabited by hermits, and any dissension among them was followed by a plague of mice. *Itinerary*, ii, ch. 7.

To find this world mirrored in the *Four Branches* is, of course, no new discovery. Matthew Arnold, to mention no earlier critic, published in 1867 his *Study of Celtic Literature*, declaring that the characters of the *Mabinogion* 'are no mediaeval personages; they belong to an older, pagan, mythological world'. It is surprising, however, to find that even in the distorting mirror of thirteenth-century French romance the magic and the wonder are still vividly discernible.

Clearly, then, the oft-repeated pattern of the combat at the ford was no invention of Chrétien's; clearly, it was a heritage from Welsh mythology; clearly, the repetition of the motif by the French romancers was due, not to a lack of inventive power, but to that universally recognized characteristic of the medieval mind—reverence for tradition.

CHAPTER VIII

Morgain la Fée and the Celtic Goddesses

> Heavens defend me from that Welsh fairy!
> *Merry Wives of Windsor*

> ... or Lady of the Mere
> Sole sitting by the shores of old romance.
> WORDSWORTH, *Poems on the Naming of Places*, IV

THOUGH neither Shakespeare nor Wordsworth had the famous queen of faerye, Morgain, in mind, the quotations may well illustrate the diversity of attitudes, from extreme repugnance to charmed wonder, which the medieval romancers exhibit in their descriptions of her person and their delineation of her character. Morgain may be the most beautiful of nine sister fays, or an ugly crone. She may be Arthur's tender nurse in the island valley of Avilion, or his treacherous foe. She may be a virgin, or a Venus of lust. Mark Twain's Connecticut Yankee, who had made her personal acquaintance, declared: 'I have seen a good many kinds of women in my time, but she laid it over them all for variety.' She enthralled the fancy of the Middle Ages, and has lived on to our day not only in literature but also in folk-lore. As the Fata Morgana, she still evokes the mirages in the Straits of Messina.

Manifestly a creature of tradition rather than invention, she must have had a long and complicated history—a history which has yet to be written. In the following pages I attempt a sketch of her genesis and evolution which seems justified by the evidence. Nothing could be more astonishingly elaborate, and, if true, more significant for the understanding of Arthurian romance. The mysteries of her complex character become clear, and much besides that is most perplexing in the *Matière de Bretagne*.

The fay makes her first appearance in literature as Morgen in a well-known passage in Geoffrey of Monmouth's *Vita Merlini* (*c.* 1150).[1] She is the fairest and the chief of nine enchantresses, skilled

---

[1] Geoffrey of Monmouth, *Vita Merlini, University of Illinois Studies in Language and Literature* (Urbana, 1925), vs. 920. For a study of Morgain cf. L. A. Paton, *Studies in the Fairy Mythology of Arthurian Romance*, Radcliffe College Monographs (Boston, 1903).

in flying swiftly through the air and in the art of healing. They dwell on an island of amazing fertility, which we easily recognize as the Isle of Avalon, for hither Arthur was brought to be healed after the battle of Camblan. This passage might seem the logical starting-point for our inquiry, but though I shall refer to it now and then, I prefer to take up first the second appearance of Morgain in literature, a less familiar passage in the *Roman de Troie*, which Benoit de Ste-Maure composed about 1160. In the excellent edition by Constans, vss. 8023-33, we are introduced to the steed of Hector of Troy.[2]

Hector mounted on Galatee, which Orva the fay had presented to him, for she loved him much and held him very dear, but he would not have her lie with him. Because of the humiliation which she felt over this she hated him as much as she could. It was the very handsomest horse on which any mortal man ever mounted, and the best, the swiftest, the boldest, and the biggest; so fine a creature was never born.

First, let it be noted that no one has been able to point out a fay named Orva, Orna, Oua, Orains, Ornains, Orueins, Oruain, or Ornais—some of the variants supplied by the manuscripts. Though these readings are supported by eleven manuscripts in all, they would seem to have little authority. One manuscript gives Panthesilee. This name derives some support from the fact that about 15,000 lines later the Amazon queen is said to have fallen in love with Hector, though she had never seen him, and to have grieved over his death. But since Panthesilee is the reading of only one manuscript, and since nothing is said later of the queen's giving Hector a steed or of her hatred for him, 'Orva la fee' cannot be a corruption of Panthesilee.

More promising are the readings of the name furnished by six manuscripts: Morgain, Morguein, Morgan, Morganz. It may or may not be significant, but the manuscripts which support these forms, DM[1]P[2]KRE, belong to different families according to Constans's classification.[3] Now we know that Morgain la Fée had already appeared in Geoffrey of Monmouth's *Vita Merlini*. Is there any reason to believe that Benoit de Ste-Maure actually had in mind the somewhat notorious lady of the *Matière de Bretagne*?

There is evidence that he knew that cycle of story. He mentions

---

[2] Benoit de Ste-Maure, *Roman de Troie*, SATF (Paris, 1904), i. 434 f.
[3] Ibid. vi (1912), 105.

Morgain la Fée and the Celtic Goddesses

lais de bretons in vs. 23599. When faced with the task of giving names to the thirty bastard sons of Priam, he drew on Wace for at least four: Cador de Lis, Gilor d'Acluz, Cassibilan, Duglas.[4] It is noteworthy that within a space of forty-eight lines Wace gives Cador, Alclut (later variant, Acluz), and Gillamurus, which might easily have become Gillor through omission of the sign for *m*.[5] Cassibilan is easily identifiable as the Cassibelan who plays a considerable part in the earlier part of the *Brut*. It is curious that though apparently Benoit recognizes Acluz as a place-name, he transforms the River Duglas[6] into a Trojan prince. It is also odd that Dinas d'Aron, mentioned immediately after Cassibilan (vs. 8008), is also a place-name converted into a man's name. In Chrétien's *Conte del Graal* there is clear allusion to Dinasdaron as a place in Wales, where Arthur held court, and in certain manuscripts of the first continuation we read of two noble cities, 'l'une en Gales, Disnadaron, ensi l'apelent li Breton'.[7] Of course, it is chronologically impossible that Benoit should have found the name in the *Conte del Graal*, and we cannot specify with exactitude where he did find it. But it is significant that the Bretons are cited as authority for the word; that Dinas, meaning 'fortress', is an element in some Welsh place-names; and that Dinas Brân, as we have seen, was referred to in the thirteenth century as a 'ville' lying on the marches of *Gales*.[8] Constans was therefore right in assigning Dinas d'Aron to an *origine bretonne*.[9] Other hints of Arthurian influence on Benoit's list of the bastard sons of Priam are the appearance of Dodinel in one manuscript,[10] the addition of 'de Lis' to Cador's name, and the inclusion of a

---

[4] Vss. 8007, 8121, 8123, 8125. For Constans's discussion of these names cf. vol. vi, p. 245. Note also the substitution of Logres for the classic Locris.

[5] Wace, *Brut*, ed. Leroux de Lincy (Rouen, 1838), ii, vss. 9642–90. The form Acluz occurs in vs. 9500 as a variant. It is noteworthy, also, that though the passage was not translated by Wace, Geoffrey names among those who fell in Arthur's last battle Gillarus, Cador Limenich, and Cassibelanus. Cf. *Historia Regum Britanniae*, ed. A. Griscom (New York, 1929), p. 501.

[6] Wace, op. cit. ii, vs. 9282.

[7] H. Newstead, *Bran the Blessed in Arthurian Romance* (New York, 1939), p. 97, n. 41. Cf. also *Historia Meriadoci and De Ortu Walwanii*, ed. J. D. Bruce (Baltimore, 1913), p. xlvi; H. O. Sommer, *Vulgate Version of the Arthurian Romances*, iv (Washington, 1911), p. 85.

[8] Cf. *supra*, pp. 42 f.

[9] *Troie*, vi. 245.

[10] In vs. 7994 MS. A gives Dodinel as the name of the first royal bastard, while MSS. HM¹ give Odiniax, A² gives Odiniels. The Arthurian name Dodinel (cf. *Medieval Studies in Memory of G. Schoepperle Loomis* (New York, 1927), pp. 166–70) appears as Odiniaus in Potvin, *Perceval le Gallois* (Mons, 1866–71), iv, vs. 23857. Probably, then, MS. A of *Troie* gives the correct reading.

certain Brun le Gimel.[11] It is at least noteworthy that a certain Bran de Lis and other members of the de Lis family play a considerable role in the *Conte del Graal*.[12] Certainly Benoit knew not only Wace but also something of the Breton *contes*, and did not scruple to borrow names from these sources.

Therefore, it is very much to the point that he introduced Morgain la Fée sixteen lines after Dinasdaron and about a hundred lines before Gillor d'Acluz, Duglas, and Cador de Lis.

The fact that a majority of the manuscripts omit the initial of Morgain's name and give such forms as Orain, Ornain, Oruein, Oruain, need not surprise us. For some reason Morgain was as much given to dropping the letter as certain ladies are given to dropping their handkerchiefs. Bruce showed that Urganda and Argante parallel the Oruain and Oruein of the *Troie* in this omission.[13] He might also have pointed out that, whereas the wife of Urien in the *Huth Merlin* is Morgain la Fée, in the *Historia Meriadoci* the wife of Urien is Oruen.[14] This, let us observe, is almost the same result as the omission of the initial produced in one manuscript of *Troie*—Oruein.

The balance of probability lies, then, in favour of the reading Moruain, or Morgain, rather than Panthesilee or Orva, Oua, Orains, &c. But can we go farther and produce positive support for Morgain la Fée? Are there traditions that she was rebuffed by one on whom she had cast her affections, or that she gave a marvellously swift and powerful horse to a lover? Though we do not find in any single source both these traditions attached to Morgain, yet separately they occur more than once.

In the *Vulgate Lancelot* the hero twice spurned the proffered love of Morgain. On one occasion[15] he was lured to her castle by a damsel and was incarcerated. Morgain 'loved him as much as a woman could love a man because of his beauty. She grieved sorely because he would not love her *par amour*, for she had often besought him, but he would not hear of it.' At another time[16] three enchantresses—Morgain, the Queen of Sorestan, and Sebille—placed a

---

[11] Brun le Grimel is mentioned in vs. 8118.
[12] J. L. Weston, *Legend of Sir Perceval* (London, 1906), i. 7, 302–7.
[13] *Mod. Lang. Notes*, xxvi (1911), 65 ff.; *Rev. Engl. St.*, x (1934), 4.
[14] *Historia Meriadoci*, pp. 12 f.; *Huth Merlin*, ed. G. Paris, J. Ulrich, SATF (Paris, 1886), i. 201 f.
[15] Sommer, op. cit. v. 215–18.
[16] Ibid. v. 91–93. On Morgain as one of three fays cf. *infra*, pp. 118, 127–9.

spell on Lancelot while he was asleep and had him conveyed in a horse litter to a castle and there imprisoned. Morgain claimed him for herself because she was of higher lineage, saying, 'for this reason he would hold me dearer and love me more than you'. The three appeared before him the next morning and offered him his freedom on condition that he would take one of them for his love. He angrily rejected them all. With the aid of a damsel he was able to escape and attend a tournament.

Another variation on the same theme may be recognized in Morgain's earlier imprisonment of Lancelot.[17] She so dealt with him while he was asleep that he could not rise, and had him conveyed in a horse litter and placed in a vault. There she endeavoured to obtain from him a ring which Guinevere had given him as the symbol of her love, but he rejected the proposal. Morgain allowed him to depart in order to be at the Dolorous Tower. *En route* her damsel, by her instructions, tried to seduce him but in vain. Still another reflection of the theme appears in the tale of Alixandre l'Orphelin, which in some ways parallels the history of Lancelot.[18] Morgain drugged the young knight, whom she addressed as *biaus douz amis*, and had him conveyed in a litter to her castle. A damsel warned him that her mistress kept him for no other cause but only to satisfy her lust. Alixandre declared that he would rather castrate himself than lie with so ugly and old a thing as Morgain was. With the damsel's aid Alixandre was delivered and undertook feats of arms. It is clear that we are dealing with a persistent tradition that Morgain's amorous designs on an imprisoned knight were spurned by him. This theme is usually attached to Lancelot, and is combined once with the motif that Morgain permitted him to depart on condition that he would return, and once with the motif that he was eager to attend a tournament. It is, therefore, not irrelevant that on two other occasions in Arthurian romance Lancelot was the prisoner of a lady, who took an amorous interest in him without success, who permitted him to leave her castle to attend a tournament on condition that he return, and who, *nota bene*, provided him with a horse.

In Chrétien's *Chevalier de la Charrette*[19] Lancelot was held in

[17] Ibid. iv. 123–8.
[18] *Alixandre l'Orphelin*, ed. C. E. Pickford (Manchester, 1951), pp. 26–28. On Alixandre cf. L. A. Paton, op. cit., pp. 55–59; *Les Prophecies de Merlin*, ed. Paton (New York, 1926), i. 375–421.
[19] Chrétien de Troyes, *Karrenritter*, ed. W. Foerster (Halle, 1899), vss. 5445–521.

prison by the wife of Meleagant's seneschal. He mourned because he could not attend a tournament. The lady offered to let him attend if he would grant her his love and return to prison. He refused her love, but she freed him on his promise to return, and gave him a horse, which was wondrously handsome, strong, and bold. In the *Vulgate Lancelot*[20] the Lady of Malehot held Lancelot in prison. He asked permission to attend an assembly of arms, and she granted it on condition he would return. She gave him a horse. On his return, having heard of his prowess, she fell in love with him, but he made no response to her overtures. A year later she again allowed him to go to the assembly, promising him a *cheval boin*.

What is evidently the same formula, though with significant variations, is attached to another hero. In *Il Bel Gherardino*, an Italian *cantare* of about 1350, which, though localized in the Mediterranean area, contains much authentic Arthurian material, the hero was imprisoned by the Soldan of Alexandria.[21] Note that this is a southern land. The Soldan's wife fell in love with Gherardino, and threatened to cry out if he would not accede to her desires. He reluctantly did so. When a tournament was proclaimed, Gherardino asked leave to attend it. The queen was ready to consent if he would return to her, but when he refused to promise, she agreed to liberate him if he would slay her aged husband in the tournament. She then gave him three suits of armour and three horses, 'piu begli intorno a cinquecento miglia'. On the third day in white arms he spurred his *buon destriero* against the Soldan, overthrew him, and cut off his head.

Though the lady's name is missing in these three stories, they belong to a type consistently associated with Morgain, and in them we find the motif of rejected love combined with the gift of an excellent horse, as in *Troie*. We are clearly on the right scent.

The singularity of the horse is stressed in other forms of the basic tradition. There are several instances of ladies who give horses of wonderful speed and strength to their lovers or protégés. In some of these Lancelot is still the recipient of the animal; in several the giver is a fay; in two it is possible to identify the giver as Morgain. Despite the absence of the despised love motif, we are still dealing with the same tradition.

[20] Sommer, *Vulgate Version*, iii. 213f., 225–8, 231.
[21] *Fiore di Leggende*, ed. E. Levi, *Scrittori d'Italia* (Bari, 1914), pp. 21–28.

In Chrétien's *Chevalier de la Charrette*[22] Lancelot was delivered from a tower by the sister of Meleagant, prince of 'the realm from which no stranger returns'. In return he promised always to be hers. When he asked leave to depart for his combat with Meleagant, she addressed him as 'biaus douz amis chiers', and gave him 'un merveilleus cheval, ... le meillor qu'onques veist nus'. Later Lancelot refers to her as 'une moie amie'. The combat took place at a sycamore beside a spring, in a glade where the grass was at all seasons new. This was evidently a land of eternal summer. Meleagant was astounded at the sight of Lancelot, was defeated and beheaded.

In the *Historia Meriadoci*[23] a damsel, abducted by Gundebald, king of the land whence no one returns, gave to Meriadoc a steed of marvellous beauty and strength, whose points are described in realistic detail. She instructed him to use it against Gundebald. Meriadoc, riding the horse, approached by a causeway the beautiful gardens where Gundebald had his palace. Gundebald was astounded at the sight of Meriadoc, fought, and was slain. Meriadoc became the *ami* of the damsel. Evidently a common tradition lies behind these two tales of a lady who gives her lover the marvellous steed which enables him to overcome the lord of the land whence no one returns.

Another form of the tradition appears in Ulrich von Zatzikhoven's *Lanzelet*.[24] The Lady of the Sea, a faery queen, gave her foster-son

---

[22] Vss. 660–728, 6887–7109. Note that Melvas and Maheloas, both identical with Meleagant, were kings of a summer country. Loomis, *Arthurian Tradition*, pp. 214–19.

[23] Ed. J. D. Bruce, pp. 42–46. Cf. description of Grey of Macha, *Bricriu's Feast*, ed. G. Henderson (London, 1899), p. 61.

[24] Ulrich von Zatzikhoven, *Lanzelet*, trans. K. G. T. Webster (New York, 1951), pp. 27–87. A remarkable parallel with an episode in the Welsh *Peredur* has hitherto been overlooked. In *Lanzelet*, the hero was taken by a faery queen to a castle of gold, bright as a star, on an island Paradise. She and her maidens trained him in noble customs and manners; marvellous creatures of the sea taught him how to deal and parry blows. On his departure the fay gave him a horse and arms. In *Peredur* the hero overcame one of the nine sorceresses of Kaer Loyw. This place was mistakenly identified with Gloucester, Latin Gloecestria, much as *Ynis Witrin* (Isle of Glass) was mistakenly identified with Glastonbury, and *Gwlad yr Haf* (Land of Summer) with Somersetshire. Cf. Loomis, *Celtic Myth*, p. 190; *PMLA*, lvi (1941), 926; J. Rhys, *Studies in Arthurian Legend* (Oxford, 1891), pp. 241, 346, n. 1; W. St. Clair Baddeley, *Place-Names of Gloucestershire* (Gloucester, 1913), pp. 70–72. But Kaer Loyw actually means Shining Fortress, the adjective *gloyw* being lenated according to rule after a feminine noun. The sorceress of the shining fortress foresaw Peredur's future, and promised to give him a horse and arms and to train him in horsemanship and the use of weapons. He went with her to the palace of the sorceresses and remained with them for a while. When he departed, he chose a horse and arms. Loth, *Mabinogion* (Paris, 1913), ii. 75 f.; J. G. Evans, *White Book Mabinogion* (Pwllheli, 1907),

Lanzelet white arms and 'a passing good horse that was fleet and strong'. She instructed him to fight with Iweret, her great foe. He sailed over the sea, and on landing had difficulty at first in controlling his spirited horse. After some adventures he found Iweret dwelling in a castle beyond a blooming valley in a wood that was green both summer and winter. The fight took place at a linden beside a spring, and Lanzelet slew Iweret. Closely connected with this tale is the gift of a fay, La Dame du Lac, to her foster-son Lancelot in the *Vulgate Lancelot*.[25] She bestowed on him white arms and a large, strong, swift horse, which was likewise white. Though the relation between Lancelot and the water fay in these two tales is not that of lover and mistress, the German version proves that the gift of the marvellous horse is still connected with the fight in a land of perpetual summer, as in Lancelot's encounter with Meleagant.

We meet the tradition again in the Breton lais. Graelent's faery mistress sent him 'un destrier tot blanc'. There was none fairer or swifter under the sky.[26] The steed plays a considerable part in the poem, but not in combat. The English *Sir Launfal*, which parallels *Graelent* in many ways, makes much of the white steed. The faery lady promised her lover Launfal her steed Blaunchard, and a squire brought it, 'whyt as flour'.[27] Later we learn incidentally that

p. 70. Not only is the parallel between Lanzelet's and Peredur's training by fays in shining fortresses sufficiently striking, but it becomes even more so when it is recognized that in both cases the fay is demonstrably Morgain. Conclusive evidence for this identification of Lanzelet's foster-mother will be given in the next page or two. Here I merely point out the similarity between her island Paradise and that of Morgen as described by Geoffrey of Monmouth (*Vita Merlini*, ed. Parry, vss. 908–17). The sorceress who trained Peredur betrays her identity with Morgen, first, by the fact that she was one of nine, and secondly, by her knowledge of the future. According to Geoffrey, Morgen was one of nine enchantresses and taught her sisters *mathematicam*, which in this context can only mean astrology and the art of forecasting the future. In *Peredur*, therefore, we have an instance of Morgain's gift of a horse to a hero. Here, too, we have the traditional feud between the enchantress and the hero (cf. J. G. Evans, *White Book Mabinogion*, p. 89), though the motivation is entirely different. Both Lanzelet's and Peredur's training have undoubted analogues in Cúchulainn's training by Scáthach. Cf. Rhys, *Studies in the Arthurian Legend*, pp. 81 f.; Rhys in *Anthropological Essays Presented to E. B. Tylor* (Oxford, 1907), pp. 285 ff.; Mary Williams, *Essai sur la Composition de Peredur* (Paris, 1909), pp. 117–19; E. Windisch, *Das keltische Britannien bis zu Kaiser Arthur* (Leipzig, 1912), pp. 137 f.

[25] Sommer, *Vulgate Version*, iii. 118. La Dame du Lac is named Ninienue (ibid. iii. 374), but has inherited much from Morgain.

[26] *Lays of Desiré, Graelent, and Melion*, ed. E. M. Grimes (New York, 1928), p. 88, vss. 354, 373 f.

[27] *Middle English Metrical Romances*, ed. W. H. French, C. B. Hale (New York, 1930), pp. 356–8. On white horses of fays, cf. Loth, *Mabinogion*, i. 93–96; *Romanic*

Launfal's arms also were white.[28] A tournament was held for love of Launfal and Blaunchard, and through the 'stedes dent' many a knight was borne to ground.[29] A giant, Sir Valentyne, sent a challenge for his leman's sake. Launfal sailed over sea to Lombardy, a southern land, and once more the white horse enabled him to win the victory and to kill Valentyne. At the end of the poem Launfal rode away on Blaunchard with his mistress to her home in the isle of Olyroun.[30] This isle is, of course, Oléron, off the French coast. But three other versions of the same story—Marie de France's *Lanval*, which gives Avalon;[31] the Rawlinson manuscript *Sir Landeval*, which gives Amylyone;[32] the Percy Folio *Sir Lambewell*, which gives Amilion[33]—show what the original name of the island was. Indeed, Kittredge proved that Olyroun was simply a substitution for Avalon.[34] The famous faery isle was therefore the home of Launfal's mistress, and both *Sir Landeval* and *Sir Lambewell* assure us that she was the daughter of its king.

The gift by a fay of a wonderful steed to her lover or protégé was evidently a stock motif, employed very early by the Arthurian *conteurs* and the composers of Breton lais, since from them Chrétien and Marie de France must have derived it.[35] Benoit, who knew

Review, xxvi, 318, vs. 99; Malory, *Morte d'Arthur*, Bk. III, ch. 5; M. W. Latham, *Elizabethan Fairies* (New York, 1930), p. 97; T. P. Cross, C. H. Slover, *Ancient Irish Tales* (New York, 1936), p. 440.

[28] Vs. 742.   [29] pp. 360-2.

[30] p. 379. With Launfal's becoming guardian of a faery realm (vss. 1024-32). cf. Lancelot in King Pelles's Isle of Joy and King Orcan in his island. *Mod. Lang. Rev.*, xxiv (1929), 425-7; Sommer, *Vulgate Version*, i. 273-6; v. 403-6.

[31] Marie de France, *Lais*, ed. Warnke, ed. 3 (Halle, 1925), p. 112.

[32] *American Journal of Philology*, x (1889), p. 32, vs. 530. Cf. the form Auylyon given by Malory, Bk. VII, ch. 27; Bk. XXI, ch. 5.

[33] *Percy Folio Manuscript*, ed. J. W. Hales, F. J. Furnivall (London, 1867), i. 164.

[34] *American Journal of Philology*, x. 13 f. The name, Triamour, which the fay bears in *Launfal*, finds no support from the other versions, and is therefore the poet's arbitrary addition, not her real name.

[35] It is noteworthy that in four Italian *cantari* of the *trecento* which show marked resemblances to the *Lanval–Graelent* pattern, this motif appears. Gherardino becomes the lover of La Fata Bianca in her faery palace, and when he departs she gives him a magic glove and he finds destriers ready caparisoned for him and his squire. *Fiore di Leggende*, ed. E. Levi, pp. 10-14. The daughter of Morgain la Fée, la Pulzella Gaia, under similar circumstances gives to Galvano a magic ring, and the first wish he makes is for 'un destriero poderoso e bello'. Ibid., pp. 35 f. Gismirante meets a fay in a forest, who offers him her love, and though he rejects her, she gives him a destrier saying: ' "Questo è di si fatta fama, porteratti in tre giorni sanza inganni là dove il tuo non anderebbe in dieci anni." ' Ibid., p. 176. Bruto di Brettagna meets a fay in a forest, who tells him that he may boast of her as the most beautiful of mistresses, and gives him a destrier, saying: ' "Tu ha caval che

lais de bretons, could well have known it. It is of no small significance, therefore, that two of the fays who gave marvellous white steeds can be identified with Morgain. Launfal's mistress, we have seen, was originally the King of Avalon's daughter, and Launfal went to dwell with her in that 'jolyf ile' for ever. Needless to say, Avalon was the traditional abode of Morgain. Lanzelet's foster-mother, the Lady of the Sea, dwelt in an island paradise like Avalon, and possessed a faery pavilion which healed all the ills of him who entered it,[36] thus reminding us of Morgain's healing arts.[37] Moreover, she was the mother of Mabuz.[38] This gives her away completely, since Mabunz is a regular Anglo-Norman nominative formed from French Mabon and would be represented in manuscript by Mabūz; in the Welsh *Kulhwch and Olwen* Mabon's mother is repeatedly called Modron; and a Welsh triad represents her as the daughter of Avallach and the mother of Owein by Urien.[39] Now Morgain la Fée, as we learn from various sources, was the daughter of Avallo or Avalloc, and the mother of Yvain by Urien.[40] Mabuz's mother, who gave Lanzelet the singularly mettlesome horse, was therefore Morgain.[41] And the king of Avalon's daughter, who gave Launfal her powerful Blaunchard, was really the daughter of King Avallo, Morgen.

It is noteworthy that while in the English lai of *Sir Launfal* we have the amorous fay, originally Morgain, who offers herself to the

corre come vento e meneratti dove tu vogl' ire." ' Ibid., pp. 202–4. On these cantari cf. E. Levi, *I Cantari Leggendari del Popolo Italiano, Giornale Storico della Letteratura Italiana*, Supplemento 16 (1914), pp. 26–45, 92–113. As Levi showed (p. 105), Bruto's meeting with the fay and the gift of the horse are based on Andreas Capellanus's *De Amore* (ed. A. Pages, Castellon de la Plana, 1929, p. 153): 'Sic tandem ei osculum porrexit amoris et equum illi, super quo residebat, exhibuit atque subiunxit: "Hic equus ad omnia te optata loca perducet." '

[36] Ulrich von Zatzikhoven, op. cit., pp. 89 f.
[37] Paton, *Fairy Mythology*, index *sub* 'Morgain, balm of'; also pp. 38, 46.
[38] Ulrich von Zatzikhoven, op. cit., p. 74.
[39] J. Loth, *Mabinogion*, ii. 284.
[40] *Romanic Rev.* xxix (1938), 176 f. Besides the evidence from Welsh Avallach, three Latin texts indicate that the island took its name from a person. Guillaume de Rennes in his *Gesta Regum Britanniae* (*c.* 1235) speaks of the wounded Arthur as going to the 'aulam Regis Avallonis'. Paton, *Fairy Mythology*, p. 46. An interpolation in William of Malmesbury's *De Antiquitate Glastoniensis Ecclesiae* gives two explanations of *insula Avalloniae*, 'insula pomorum' or 'de quodam Avalloc'. E. K. Chambers, *Arthur of Britain* (London, 1927), p. 266. Giraldus Cambrensis in the *Speculum Ecclesiae* (*c.* 1216) also gives the two explanations, from 'aval Britannice, quod pomum sonat, . . . vel a (A)vallone quodam, territorii illius quondam dominatore'. Ibid., p. 273.
[41] Note that la Pulzella Gaia was daughter of Morgana. Cf. *supra*, p. 113, n. 35.

hero and presents him with a marvellous steed, the fay is not rebuffed as we should expect. But it is equally noteworthy that there is another amorous lady in the poem who is rebuffed and hates Launfal in consequence. That lady is, of course, Guinevere. Launfal spurns her overtures because he is faithful to Morgain, just as Lancelot spurns the advances of Morgain, over and over again, because he is faithful to Guinevere. It becomes obvious that the basic element in the story of Launfal is simply the jealous rivalry of Guinevere and Morgain so prominent in the Lancelot romances, except that the roles of the ladies are reversed. This fact and the suppression of Morgain's name in the English lai has prevented us from recognizing at once that here are all the elements of Benoit's allusion: Morgain la Fée, who presented to the hero a mount which was 'the very handsomest horse, . . . the boldest and the biggest'; there is also the lady who 'loved him much and held him very dear, but he would not have her lie with him. Because of the humiliation which she felt over this she hated him as much as she could.'

What induced Benoit to transfer this tradition from Launfal or Lancelot to Hector? The answer is provided by Rusticien de Pise, who wrote of Morgain as wishing to avenge herself on the Arthurian knight Hector for the shame he spoke to her.[42] Evidently, then, Benoit did not invent the story but merely transferred it from 'Estor li fiz au roi Ares', as Chrétien calls him (who seems to have shared Lancelot's loathing for Morgain), to his own hero—much to the modern reader's amazement.

Why did Benoit name the gift-horse after the Greek sea-nymph Galatea, whose name he might have found in the *Metamorphoses*? Again we find our answer in another Arthurian romance. *Escanor* tells how the fay Esclarmonde, who is plainly modelled after Morgain, bestowed on her lover, Escanor le Bel, the most famous steed of the *Matière de Bretagne*, Gringalet.[43] Evidently Benoit knew this story as told of Morgain and Estor, and having classicized Estor by making him Hector, he classicized his horse by naming it Galatee, suggested by the last two syllables of Gringalet.

This introduction of the fay of Avalon into the *Roman de Troie* about 1160 was anticipated by the introduction of allusions to *tot l'or d'Avalon* in the *Couronnement Louis* about 1130, and by the possibly

---

[42] E. Löseth, *Tristan en Prose* (Paris, 1891), p. 430.
[43] Loomis, *Arthurian Tradition*, pp. 157 f.

earlier absorption into the *Pèlerinage Charlemagne* of a group of Arthurian motifs.[44] In the last instance Professor Laura Hibbard Loomis and the late T. P. Cross have proved that the motifs can be traced back to Ireland.[45] Cross has also shown that *Launfal* and its analogue, *Graelent*, are deeply indebted to Ireland.[46] Without repeating in its fullness his study of the water fay in these lais, let me recall certain parallels with Irish goddesses which shed light on the nature and antecedents of Morgain.

Remarkable are the resemblances between Launfal's mistress and Macha.[47] Macha's watery origin is suggested by the fact that she is daughter of Strangeness, son of Ocean.[48] Like the fay of Avalon, she offers herself to a human lover and is accepted. As with Launfal, his wealth at once increases. As with Launfal, she imposes on him a taboo 'not to speak of her in the assembly'. He breaks the taboo and boasts of her swiftness, as Launfal boasts of his mistress's beauty. Even more astonishing are the similarities between the steeds of the fays and the Grey of Macha, Cúchulainn's horse. This steed came out of a lake, as presumably did the white steed of the Dame du Lac which she gave to Lancelot. The name, Grey of Macha, 'implies that he had been sent from Macha's fairy abode as a gift to her mortal protégé'. It was seemingly her own horse, just as Blaunchard was referred to by the fay as 'my stede lel'. The Grey of Macha fought beside his dying master. 'Fifty fell by his teeth and thirty by each of his hoofs.'[49] Launfal in the midst of a tournament alighted from Blaunchard.[50]

> Of hys stede he dede hym ly3t
> And bare hym doun yn the dale . . .
> Than my3te me se scheldes ryve,
> Speres tobreste and todryve,

---

[44] *Romanic Rev.*, xxxii (1941), 19–22.   [45] *Mod. Phil.*, xxv (1928), 331 ff.
[46] *Mod. Phil.*, xii (1915), 585 ff. By an incredible oversight this article and Cross's study of *Yonec* in *Revue Celtique*, xxxi (1910), 413 ff., are not mentioned by Bruce in his discussion of the origin of the Breton lais in *Evolution of Arthurian Romance*, i. 52–66, nor by Warnke in *Die Lais der Marie de France*, ed. 3 (Halle, 1925), pp. cxxx ff., clv ff., nor by Prof. J. Harris in his edition of *Gugemar, Lanval, and Yonec* (New York, 1930).
[47] *Mod. Phil.*, xii. 605 f., 608, 624–6.
[48] Note that in *Launfal*, vss. 280 f., the fay's father was 'kyng of fayrye of Occient', apparently a substitution for Ocean, and that in *Landeval* she was the king's daughter of Amylione, 'That ys an ile of the fayré, In occian full faire to see'.
[49] T. P. Cross, C. H. Slover, *Ancient Irish Tales*, p. 388. Cf. *Bricriu's Feast*, ed. Henderson, p. 89.
[50] *Middle English Metrical Romances*, ed. French and Hale, pp. 361 f., vss. 476 ff.

> Behynde and ek before;
> Thoru3 Launfal and hys stedes dent
> Many a kny3t, verement,
> To ground was ibore.

When Cúchulainn was about to go forth to his death, the Grey would not let himself be harnessed to the chariot by anyone, but 'came and let his big round tears of blood fall' on his master's feet.[51] Likewise, Graelent's steed, the gift of his faery mistress, when parted from his master, made great dole, 'and was not at peace either by night or by day. . . . They wished to catch and hold him, but no one could ever seize him.'[52]

Despite the difference in colour, the Grey of Macha and the white faery horse are remarkably alike. Both are the steeds of fays; both are given to mortal favourites; both fight beside their dismounted masters; both refuse to be controlled by any others; both mourn at separation. It may be well to see what more we can discover about Macha.

A gloss in a fourteenth-century manuscript runs:[53] 'Machae, a scald-crow; or she is the third Morrigan.' This gloss is significant because it indicates that Macha was equated with a crow; that she was one of a trio of similar figures;[54] that she appeared also under the name of Morrígan.[55] This uncanny divinity, as Miss Paton recognized,[56] offers some striking resemblances to Morgain la Fée. In the *Cattle Raid of Cooley*,[57] the earliest redaction of which goes back to the eighth century at least, we find the Morrígan meeting Cúchulainn at a ford[58] in the form of a young woman in a mantle of many colours. She declares herself to be the daughter of King Buan. 'For the record of thy deeds have I loved thee, and all my valuables

---

[51] Cross, Slover, op. cit., pp. 333 f.
[52] *Desiré, Graelent, and Melion*, ed. Grimes, p. 101.
[53] *Mod. Phil.*, xii. 605.
[54] On triads of Celtic goddesses cf. J. A. MacCulloch, *Religion of the Ancient Celts* (Edinburgh, 1911), pp. 71–73.
[55] On the meaning of this name cf. Paton, *Fairy Mythology*, p. 159; C. Donahue, *PMLA*, lvi (1941), 6. In a ninth-century gloss 'lamia, monstrum in femine figura', is explained by the word *morrigain*. On the medieval concept of *lamiae* cf. Johannis de Alta Silva, *Dolopathos*, ed. H. Oesterley (Strassburg, 1873), pp. 70 f. and *infra*, p. 129.
[56] Paton, *Fairy Mythology*, pp. 148–66.
[57] E. Hull, *Cuchullin Saga* (London, 1898), pp. 164–9.
[58] In *Bricriu's Feast*, ed. Henderson (London, 1899), p. 44, Ath na Morrigna, the Morrígan's Ford, is mentioned. For other Irish goddesses who appear at fords cf. *Mod. Phil.*, xii. 607.

and cattle I bring with me.' Cúchulainn, however, rejects her offer. She threatens him with vengeance. When he engages in single combat with Loch at a ford, she transforms herself into various shapes to hamper him. He wounds her, but she is healed. One version relates that she flies away in the form of a crow and lights on a hawthorn tree.[59] In the saga with the somewhat mysterious title of *Táin Bó Regamna*[60] Cúchulainn meets, according to the Egerton manuscript, the Morrígan, according to the Book of Leinster, the Bodb (i.e. crow). She is a red woman, clad in red, riding a chariot near a ford. When she taunts him, Cúchulainn springs at her; she vanishes, only to reappear as a black bird on a bough. She threatens him with her vengeance just as in the *Cattle Raid of Cooley*.

Thus we conclude that Macha, alias the Morrígan, was one of a group of three goddesses; was wont to assume the shape of a crow; appeared to Cúchulainn twice near a ford; offered him her love, only to be rejected; conceived a hatred for him; attacked him in various forms while he was engaged in combat at a ford near a hawthorn; was wounded and recovered.

In these respects, as well as in those already noted, Macha or the Morrígan resembles Morgain. Morgain appeared as one of a trio of fays, not only to Lancelot as we have observed, but also to Renouart, Floriant, and the burghers of Arras.[61] Morgain made amorous overtures to various knights and conceived a violent hatred for those who spurned her. She and her sisters could transform themselves into birds.[62] In the *Didot Perceval* we recognize Morgain in a nameless fay whose home was in Avalon.[63] She declared her love to a knight, the son of the Queen of the Black

---

[59] Thurneysen, op. cit., p. 176, n. 1 (lower).

[60] Ibid., pp. 309 f. Trans. A. H. Leahy, *Heroic Romances of Ireland* (London, 1906), ii. 132-40.

[61] Morgain is one of three fays in *Bataille Loquifer*, *Floriant et Florete*, and Adam de la Halle's *Jeu de la feuillée*. Paton, *Fairy Mythology*, pp. 49 f., 190, 253. For medieval belief in a trio of fays cf. ibid., p. 193, n. 1; Robert Mannyng of Brunne, *Handlyng Synne*, ed. F. J. Furnivall, E.E.T.S. (London, 1901), Part I, p. 21; J. A. MacCulloch, *Medieval Faith and Fable* (1932), pp. 22, 38-40; E. Faral, *Recherches sur les sources latines* (Paris, 1913), p. 309; H. L. D. Ward, *Catalogue of Romances* (London, 1883), i. 817; E. K. Chambers, *Medieval Stage* (Oxford 1903), ii. 306; Le Roux de Lincy, *Livre des Légendes* (Paris, 1836), pp. 257 f.

[62] Geoffrey of Monmouth, *Vita Merlini*, ed. Parry, vss. 922 f.; Hartmann v. Aue, *Erek*[2], ed. M. Haupt (Leipzig, 1871), vss. 5177 f., 5185 f.; Paton, *Fairy Mythology*, p. 50; *Prophecies de Merlin*, ed. L. A. Paton (New York, 1925), i. 416.

[63] *Didot-Perceval*, ed. W. Roach (Philadelphia, 1941), pp. 197-202.

Morgain la Fée and the Celtic Goddesses

Thorn, and dwelt with him in a palace beside a ford which in analogous stories is called 'le Gué de l'Espine'.[64] She and her sisters in the form of black birds attacked Perceval as he was fighting her lover at the ford. Her sister was killed, but was spirited away to Avalon to be revived.

Between them Macha and her *alter ego*, the Morrígan, account, then, for much in the legend of Morgain la Fée, including the gift of the marvellous horse to her lover, and the scorned passion transmuted into hate, which we found in the *Roman de Troie*.

It is certain that the Irish elements in the *Matière de Bretagne* did not pass directly from Ireland to France, but were transmitted through Wales.[65] Moreover, we have already had occasion to note that Morgain had a Welsh counterpart, Modron, who, like her, was the mother of Owein (Yvain) by a mortal father, Urien, King of Rheged. Does Modron turn out to be an intermediate figure between Macha and the Morrígan on the one hand and Morgain and the anonymous fays of Avalon on the other?

The oldest Welsh texts tell little of Modron, except that *Kulhwch* (c. 1100) informs us that she was also the mother of Mabon, and that he was stolen from her side when he was three days old. But very significant matter is preserved in a Welsh manuscript of about 1556.[66] Urien met on the bank of a ford in Denbighshire a woman washing. He had his will of her, whereupon she blessed him and proclaimed herself the daughter of the King of Annwn (the elysian abode of the gods). She promised that if he would return at the end of a year he would have their child, and she then presented him with twins, Owein and Morfydd. Since these are the names of the twins whom Modron bore to Urien,[67] the identity of the fay of the ford is certain. The name Modron, all authorities agree, is derived from a Celtic river-goddess, Matrŏna.[68] Matrŏna meant the Great Mother, and this is not unconnected with the fact that in recent

---

[64] Cf. *supra*, p. 94, n. 10.
[65] Cf. *supra*, pp. 34 f.
[66] *Aberystwyth Studies*, iv (1922), 105–9. *Hist. MSS. Commission, Report on MSS. in Welsh Language*, ed. J. G. Evans (1898), i. 911. It is doubtless this story which is reflected in the tradition that Urien had a son Yvain li Avoutre, 'the Bastard'. Cf. *Perlesvaus*, ed. W. A. Nitze and others (Chicago, 1932–7), ii. 210.
[67] Loth, *Mabinogion*, ii. 284.
[68] T. Gwynn Jones, *Welsh Folklore and Folk-Custom* (1930), p. 17; Hastings, *Encyclopaedia of Religion and Ethics*, iii. 292; *Cymmrodor*, xlii (1930), 140 f.; *Celtic Review*, iii (1906), 48; MacCulloch, *Religion of the Ancient Celts*, pp. 123, 183; J. Rhys, *Lectures on the Origin*, ed. 2 (London, 1892), pp. 28 f.

times the Welsh called the female fairies *Y Mamau*, 'the Mothers',[69] as in Brittany they are called 'nos Bonnes Mères les Fées'.[70] It is probably, therefore, no coincidence that above the ford in the parish of Llanferres where Urien met Modron rises a mountain called Moel Famau, 'the Hill of the Mothers'.[71]

Despite the paucity of our information about Modron she betrays a resemblance to Macha in bearing twins, a boy and a girl, to a human lover.[72] She reveals her kinship to the Morrígan by her appearance at a ford, by her announcement that she is the daughter of a king, and by the marked similarity between her mating with Urien and the Morrígan's mating with the Dagda. According to the *Second Battle of Moytura*,[73] a mythological text of the ninth century, the Dagda met a woman washing at the river Unius in Connaught and united with her; she was the Morrígan. Thus in striking ways Modron discloses her relationship to Macha and the Morrígan; and Modron, as we know, was the Welsh counterpart of Morgain. We are therefore confirmed in the belief that Modron is in some way an intermediate figure between the Irish goddesses and the Arthurian fay.

Though little record of Modron under her own name is left in Welsh literature, we have some compensation in the many folk-tales of a usually nameless fay who seems to have inherited the Modron tradition.[74] These tales were current as early as the twelfth century, since Walter Map gives a version in *De Nugis Curialium*. Attached to many pools and lakes throughout Wales, they follow one general pattern of the taboo type, already familiar through our study of Launfal and Graelent. A beautiful maiden who dwelt beneath the waters of a lake appeared several times to a youth and was finally persuaded to marry him. She gave warning, however,

[69] Hastings, *Encyclopaedia*, iv. 410; E. Hull, op. cit., p. 49; *Celtic Review*, iii. 29.
[70] W. Y. E. Wentz, *Fairy-Faith in Celtic Countries* (Oxford, 1911), p. 203.
[71] About 14 miles in a straight line from Moel Famau is the town of Ruabon, originally *Rhiw Vabon*, the hill of Mabon, Modron's son. Cf. W. J. Gruffydd, *Math Vab Mathonwy* (Cardiff, 1928), p. 179, n. 41. On other connexions of Denbighshire with mythology cf. *supra*, pp. 42–51.
[72] Thurneysen, op. cit., p. 362.
[73] *Rev. Celt.*, xii (1891), 85; *Anthropos*, xxvi (1931), 448. Both translators, Stokes and Lehmacher, assume that the Morrígan was washing herself, but 'og nige' does not necessarily mean this, and the analogy with the Welsh tale suggests that she was washing something else.
[74] J. Rhys, *Celtic Folklore* (Oxford, 1901), i. 2–130. Some force seems to have operated to suppress Modron's name, both in the *Four Branches of the Mabinogi* and in popular tradition.

that if ever he should strike her thrice she would leave him. She brought with her many cattle and horses from the lake, and the youth prospered. When at last he broke the taboo, she returned to the lake with all her cattle. The general similarity to the Breton lais is patent, and certain versions contain other significant parallels. In the most famous version, that of the Llyn y Fan Fach in Carmarthenshire, the lake damsel is given in marriage to the youth by 'a hoary-headed man of noble mien and extraordinary stature, but having otherwise all the force and strength of youth'.[75] He, also, rises from the waters. In several versions he is identified as her father and as a king.[76] One remembers how in other tales the water fay announces to the mortal whom she desires that she is the daughter of King Buan or the King of Annwn. The Llyn y Fan Fach version tells how, after the fay's departure to the lake, she returned to give her eldest son a bag full of medical prescriptions, and once pointed out to her sons healing plants and herbs in a dingle, ever since called Pant-y-Meddygon, 'The Dingle of the Physicians'.[77] Here seems to be preserved the well-known skill of Morgain, who according to Geoffrey of Monmouth was more skilled in the healing art than her sisters, and had learned what useful properties all the herbs contained.[78] Another version of the story relates that the mortal lover obtained his mistress only when he was able to pick her out from her two sisters. Again one is reminded of Morgain and the two other fays presenting themselves to Lancelot for his choice.[79] According to a version connected with Cwellyn Lake near Caernarvon, the fay bore to her husband a son and a daughter, who were the handsomest children in the whole country.[80] It is perhaps not irrelevant to recall that Modron bore a son and a daughter to Urien,

---

[75] Rhys, *Celtic Folklore*, i. 7. Cf. *Perlesvaus*, ed. Nitze, i, ll. 2415–17, ll. 9957–8.

[76] Rhys, *Celtic Folklore*, i. 8, 92, 127. When the fay called her cattle to return with her to the lake, she said: 'Dewch i gyd i lys y brenin!' 'Come all to the palace of the king!' Ibid., i. 24 n., 26, 29. One of the lakes to which the legend clung was called Llyn Alfach (ibid., i. 25), and it is possible that Alfach is a corruption of Avallach, the name of Modron's father.

[77] Ibid., p. 11. The healing power of the water-fays seems to be a persistent tradition. Possibly Milton records the folklore of the Welsh border when he represents Sabrina, nymph of the Severn, as visiting the herds along the twilight meadows, helping all urchin blasts, and healing with precious vialed liquors the ill-luck signs. *Comus*, vss. 842–7. Cf. E. Hull, *Folklore of the British Isles* (London, 1928), p. 68; C. S. Burne, *Shropshire Folklore* (London, 1883–6), pp. 412–34.

[78] *Vita Merlini*, ed. Parry, vss. 918–21. Cf. supra, p. 105, n. 1, and Hartmann v. Aue, *Erek*, ed. M. Haupt (Leipzig, 1871), vss. 5213–15.

[79] Rhys, *Celtic Folklore*, i. 17.   [80] Ibid., p. 46.

and that the daughter's name was a synonym for beauty with the Welsh poets.[81] Nor is it perhaps mere accident that in the Cwellyn Lake version, as in many others, the return of the fay to her lake is connected with the attempt to put a bridle on a spirited steed.[82] She and her husband 'went out together to catch a horse in the field, and as the animal was somewhat wild and untamed they had no easy work before them'. Unfortunately, when the young man threw the bridle at the horse, it struck his wife and she disappeared. Two versions speak of the fay as swifter of foot than her husband.[83] This incident of the bridle seems to represent an effort to combine the tradition of the lake-steed which none but its master could harness, such as the Grey of Macha; the swift-footed fay, such as Macha herself;[84] and the popular superstition that a fairy could not endure contact with iron. Rhys, moreover, points out that in one version the fay's displeasure seems to be caused not by the breaking of a taboo but by her husband's taking a human wife.[85] As she called her cattle to come 'to the palace of the king', her father, she added: 'Back, thou wife of the House up Hill: never shalt thou milk my cows.' Rhys comments: 'This seems to suggest that the quarrel was about another woman, and that by the time when the fairy came to call her livestock into the lake she had been replaced by another woman who came from the Ty-fry, or the House up Hill.' We are reminded of the marked element of female rivalry in the tales of Morgain la Fée. Even if one concedes the possibility that some of these connexions between the modern Welsh folk-tale of the Lady of the Lake and the legends of Morgain, Launfal's mistress, Modron, and Macha are fortuitous, they cannot all be; there are too many of them. Legends of Modron survived orally in Wales to the end of the nineteenth century.[86]

Late into the nineteenth century thousands of people gathered at Llyn y Fan Fach the first Sunday in August, apparently with some expectation of seeing the fairy. Hartland, among his interesting comments on the legend, remarked:[87] 'I have little doubt that

[81] J. Loth, *Mabinogion*, i. 284, n. 4; ii. 284.
[82] Rhys, *Celtic Folklore*, i. 46. Cf. ibid., pp. 61, 88. The bridle motif is as old as the 12th century. Ibid., pp. 71 f.   [83] Ibid., pp. 54, 61.
[84] Thurneysen, op. cit., p. 362.   [85] Rhys, *Celtic Folklore*, i. 26 f.
[86] Rhys in *Lectures on the Origin*, p. 423, n. 1, pointed out that the fay of Llyn y Fan Fach was probably Modron, since her eldest son was Rhiwallon son of Urien, and Urien was the lover of Modron. But it is difficult to identify Urien with a young farmer.
[87] E. S. Hartland, *Science of Fairy Tales* (London, 1891), p. 330.

in this superstition we have the relic of a religious festival in honour of an archaic divinity whose abode was in the lake.'

Though in these Welsh folk-tales, as in the Breton lais, the water fay is a beautiful and sympathetic figure, there are other Welsh traditions which represent her as a hideous and fearsome hag. In this dual nature she betrays her kinship to Morgain and the Morrígan.[88] Morgain was both the enemy of Arthur and his nurse in Avalon. She appears, as we have seen, as the most beautiful of fays and as a 'laide chose', so that the author of the *Huth Merlin* felt obliged to account for the discrepancy.[89] Likewise, the Morrígan is at times Cúchulainn's watchful protectress; at others she is his enemy, seeking to destroy him.[90] She appears to him at a ford, once as a beautiful young woman, once as a red woman with red eyebrows.[91] So, in Welsh folk-lore, we may recognize Modron not only as the lovely fay of the lake who brings her husband wealth and beautiful children but also as a fearful hag, haunting pools and foreboding death and doom. This sinister aspect is already to be inferred from the Denbighshire folk-tale of 1556, which depicts her washing at a ford.[92] Irish literature makes it quite clear that 'the Washer at the Ford' is the water-goddess in the role of one forecasting the death of those who see her.[93] Sometimes she is fair to look on, but a description of her in the *Triumphs of Turlough* (c. 1350) presents her as deformed and ugly to the last degree.[94] She was washing a cairn of heads, arms, and legs, and a load of spoils on the shore of Loch Rask. She declared herself to be one of the Tuatha Dé Danann, and apprised Turlough that these were the limbs and the heads of his army. We should not be surprised to find Modron surviving in Welsh folk-lore as the Gwrach-y-Rhibyn, a hideous hag, who sometimes appeared beside a piece of water, splashing it with her hands, or who dipped herself up and down in a pool.[95] She was black of hair and eyes, and was dressed in black. The crow nature

---

[88] Cf. Paton, *Fairy Mythology*, pp. 7 f., 145–8.
[89] Ibid., p. 151.
[90] Ibid., pp. 22, 34.
[91] Cf. *supra*, p. 117, n. 57; p. 118, n. 60.
[92] Cf. *supra*, p. 98.
[93] The Morrígan is described as washing spoils in a text dated c. 900. K. Meyer, *Fianaigecht* (Dublin, 1910), pp. 7, 17. On Washer at the Ford cf. G. Schoepperle in *Journ. of Engl. and Germ. Phil.*, xviii (1919), 1–7; *Aberystwyth Studies*, iv. 108 f.; *Mod. Phil.* xii. 604, n. 3; W. Sikes, *British Goblins* (London, 1880), pp. 216–19; P. Sébillot, *Folklore de France* (Paris, 1905), ii. 351–5, 423–31.
[94] *Triumphs of Turlough*, ed. Magrath and O'Grady, ii (1929), 93.
[95] M. Trevelyan, *Folklore and Folk-stories of Wales* (London, 1909), pp. 65–67; Sikes, op. cit., p. 216.

comes out, as with the Morrígan and Macha, for she had batlike wings and would claw and peck a man, 'just as an eagle might have done'. One cannot forget the fay in the *Didot Perceval*, who is so clearly identifiable with Morgain, who dwelt in a palace beside a ford, and who attacked Perceval in the form of a black bird.[96]

There can, I think, be no doubt that Modron was as imposing and as ubiquitous a figure in Welsh legends of the Middle Ages as were her counterparts, the Morrígan and Morgain, in Irish saga and Arthurian romance.

What of the three names, so tantalizingly similar and yet so bafflingly impossible to derive, one from another, by any phonetic or common-sense agency? Miss Paton once sagely remarked:[97] 'We may as well acknowledge the fact that no fay nor mortal was ever more elusive or erratic in career than is a proper name in mediaeval literature, and that with the multitudinous opportunities for a misunderstanding in an oral or a misspelling in a written source, theories as to its domestication on foreign soil according to strict phonological conventions "gang aft agley".' But even though it were possible that Modron is a wildly erratic deformation of Morrígan, the possibility is ruled out by the certainty that Modron is derived from the Celtic deity Matrŏna. It is particularly odd that if the Welsh transferred the traditions of the Morrígan to Modron, the Bretons, when they took over the Modron tradition, should have reverted to a form so reminiscent of the Morrígan.

A partial explanation of these shifts may be found in a scrap of folk-lore from western Wales, which shows that late in the nineteenth century people talked of a water-sprite named Morgan, and naughty boys were warned that they would be carried off by Morgan into the lake of Glasfryn near Llangybi, Caernarvonshire.[98] Though the gender of this sprite seems to have been male, the original sex may be indicated by the coat of arms of the owners of Glasfryn, which represents a mermaid,[99] and by the fact that in Brittany also, though Morgan is a man's name, there were in the nineteenth century widespread traditions of water-nymphs called

---

[96] Cf. *supra*, pp. 95–97.

[97] *Fairy Mythology*, p. 152. For erratic development of proper names cf. Loomis, *Arthurian Tradition*, pp. 54 f.; J. S. P. Tatlock, *Scene of the Franklin's Tale Visited* (Chaucer Soc., 1914), p. 68; *Zeits. f. Deutsches Altertum*, lii. 97–107; R. W. Chambers, *Widsith* (Cambridge, 1912), p. 160.

[98] Rhys, *Celtic Folklore*, i. 372 f.

[99] Ibid., p. 368.

Morgan or Mari Morgan, which suggest affinity to the legend of Glasfryn.[100] Let me quote one legend from Île Molène.[101]

> The Morgan is a fairy eternally young, a virgin seductress,[102] whose passion, never satisfied, drives her to despair. Her place of abode is beneath the sea; there she possesses marvellous palaces where gold and diamonds glimmer. Accompanied by other fairies, of whom she is in some respects the queen, she rises to the surface of the waters in the splendour of her unveiled beauty. . . . By moonlight, she moans as she combs her fair hair with a comb of fine gold, and she sings in a harmonious voice a plaintive melody whose charm is irresistible. The sailor who listens to it feels himself drawn toward her, without power to break the charm which drags him onward to his destruction; the bark is broken upon the reefs; the man is in the sea, and the Morgan utters a cry of joy. But the arms of the fairy clasp only a corpse; for at her touch men die, and it is this which causes the despair of the amorous and inviolate Morgan.

Other traditions, however, relate that when sailors yield to the seductions of Mari Morgan, they go to live with her in her palace beneath the waves, where, rich and content, they live long and beget on her many children.[103] This Breton Lorelei and the sprite of Glasfryn lake seem to be related, since both are given to drawing human beings down to their watery homes, and both bear the oddly masculine name Morgan. Indeed, the Provençal poem, *Jaufré*, tells how the hero was pushed into a spring by a damsel who leapt in after him, and clasped him to her, and the two descended to her lovely land. The damsel was 'la fada del Gibel', that is, Morgain.[104] In the Île d'Ouessant the female fay is called Morganes, feminine of Morgan, and is more benevolent than sinister.[105] One tale relates how a Morganes, surprised as she spread out her treasure on the shore, gave some of it, wrapped in sheets, to two girls and imposed on them a taboo. One of them broke it and her portion was transformed into horse-dung; the other obeyed the fay and found precious stones and gold enough to make her and her family rich.

---

[100] Sébillot, *Folklore de France*, ii. 35–38, 121, 132 f. On the Breton Morgans cf. *Comparative Literature*, ii (1950), 294–8; *Annales de Bretagne*, lvi (1949), 210–15.
[101] W. Y. E. Wentz, *Fairy-Faith in Celtic Countries* (Oxford, 1911), pp. 200 f.
[102] Note that in *Gesta Regum Britanniae* Morgan is called *regia virgo*. Paton, *Fairy Mythology*, p. 46.
[103] Sébillot, op. cit. ii. 36.
[104] *Jaufré*, ed. C. Brunel, SATF, ii (1943), vss. 8378–430, 8743–50, 10637–54; Loomis, *Arthurian Tradition*, p. 306; *Annales de Bretagne*, lvi. 211 f.
[105] Sébillot, op. cit. ii. 36 f.

Here we find once more the tradition of the gift of wealth, accompanied by a taboo, which we have already seen attached to Macha, the lake damsels of Welsh folk-lore, and the mistresses of Launfal and Graelent. Though the evidence which connects Macha, the Morgan of Glasfryn lake, the Morgans of the Breton coast, and Morgain la Fée is far from complete, there seems to be enough to make the relationship probable. If we assume that the Welsh water-sprite Morgan received her masculine name originally because it approximated that of the Morrígan, then we have a continuous chain of Morgans between Ireland and France, between the Morrígan and Morgain. There remains only the difficulty of linking Modron up with this chain. How can this be done? The following scheme seems to bring all the facts into harmonious relationship.

The Morrígan and Modron were primarily, it would seem, the Goidelic and Brythonic developments from an ancient Celtic divinity of the waters, and possessed a common heritage of legend. During the Dark Ages, when Irish legends flooded into Wales,[106] particularly along the west coast, the stories of the Morrígan merged to a considerable extent with the cognate tales of Modron. As a result, the same stories which were told of Modron were also told of a water fay who went by the familiar man's name of Morgan, substituted for the Morrígan. This Morgan survived in the folklore of western Caernarvonshire and Cardiganshire late into the nineteenth century. In other parts of Wales Modron's name was forgotten entirely; either she became the anonymous and fascinating faery of many a mountain tarn, or, as a mourning ominous figure, in black, birdlike shape, haunting pools, she was called Gwrach y Rhibyn. But, long before, this compound figure of the Morrígan and Modron had passed with the Arthurian legend and with her father Avallach, her husband Urien, and her sons Mabon and Owein, to Brittany. The name Modron left some slight imprints in Arthurian nomenclature, for it seems the probable original of Moronoe, who is Morgen's sister in the *Vita Merlini*, and of Marrion, Morgain's sister in the *Bataille Loquifer*.[107] But it was the Welsh name Morgan, substituted for the Morrígan, which was generally accepted by the Bretons because of its previous familiarity in their

---

[106] C. O'Rahilly, *Ireland and Wales* (London, 1924), pp. 92 ff.; *Transactions of Honourable Soc. of Cymmrodorion*, 1912–13, pp. 63–80; W. J. Gruffydd, *Math Vab Mathonwy* (Cardiff, 1928); *Mod. Phil.* xxxiii (1936), 228 f

[107] Paton, *Fairy Mythology*, pp. 39, 50.

Morgain la Fée and the Celtic Goddesses

nomenclature. Fragments of the tradition lingered on well into the nineteenth century along the Breton coast, linked to the sea-nymphs, the Morgans. But the great mass of tales which had belonged to the Morrígan and Modron was spread in the twelfth century throughout the French-speaking world by the Breton *conteurs* as the legend of Morgain la Fée. And even after the legend had found its way into other lands and languages, there were authors who still recognized her divinity, referring to her as *dea, goddes, dwywes,* and *gotinne*.[108] One manuscript of the *Vulgate Lancelot* attempts a rationalistic explanation.[109]

It was true that Morgain, the sister of King Arthur, knew much of enchantment and spells, surpassing all women; and by reason of the great devotion that she gave to them she left and forsook the company of folk and spent day and night in the great deep forests and [beside the] fountains, so that many folk, of whom there were numerous fools throughout the land, said that she was not a woman but they called her Morgain the goddess (*déesse*).

Of course, it is no new discovery that the fays of medieval romance and of modern European folk-lore are descended from the goddesses of the pre-Christian era; the word 'fay' itself is derived from Latin *fata*. Grimm and Maury elaborated the theory at length.[110] MacCulloch and Professor Robinson have recognized the particular importance of the Celtic Matres or Matrŏnae for faery mythology,[111] and M. Gustave Cohen has divined their relationship to Morgain.[112]

La fée Morgue du *Jeu de la Feuillée*... n'en est pas moins à mon sens une des *matres et fatae* de la mythologie celtique, qui paraissent sur les monuments funéraires de la Gaule par groupe de trois (comme aussi dans le *Jeu* d'Adam le Bossu).

This hypothesis is now confirmed up to the hilt by the demonstration that Morgain inherited the family relationships and the role of Modron, who in turn derived her name from the Celtic

---

[108] Cf. *supra*, p. 99.

[109] *Roman van Lancelot*, ed. W. J. A. Jonckbloet ('s Gravenhage, 1849), ii, p. lxix. Cf. the remarks about the fondness of the fay Niniane and the goddess Diane for hunting in the *Huth Merlin*, ed. Paris and Ulrich, ii. 119, 145.

[110] J. Grimm, *Deutsche Mythologie*, ed. 4 (Berlin, 1875–8), i. 332 ff.; A. Maury, *Croyances et Légendes du Moyen Âge* (Paris, 1896), pp. 1–67.

[111] MacCulloch, *Religion of Ancient Celts*, pp. 45 f.; Hastings, *Encyclopaedia*, iv. 410.

[112] G. Cohen, *Roman Courtois au XII Siècle* (Paris, 1938), p. 64. Cf. MacCulloch, *Medieval Faith and Fable*, p. 38.

goddess Matrŏna. For the authorities are agreed that the Matrŏnae and the Matres of the Gallic inscriptions are indistinguishable.[113] Moreover, the authorities agree that the cult of the Matres and Matrŏnae blended with that of the other goddesses. Windisch asserted:[114] 'Mit den Matres sind ähnliche Gottheiten combiniert worden'; and Professor Robinson speaks of 'the difficulty, if not the impossibility, of keeping the worship of the Matres and Matrŏnae distinct from all other cults'.[115]

Here, then, is the explanation of Morgain's multiple personality, her infinite variety. She has acquired not only the attributes and activities of Macha, the Morrígan, and Matrŏna, but also the mythic heritage of other Celtic deities. She is a female pantheon in miniature.

She was a sort of naiad or nereid, haunting springs, rivers, fords, lakes, and seas, or dwelling beneath their surfaces; she was a foster-mother of heroes, who took them in their infancy, trained them for high adventure, and watched over them in peril; she showered wealth on her favourites; she sometimes appeared in a group of three fays; she foretold the future; she was both a beneficent and a sinister power; she lay in wait for mortals, offering them her love; she possessed a very swift and powerful horse.

Now let us observe how these aspects and functions of Morgain correspond to those of the goddesses of Gaul and Britain, the Matrŏnae and their kindred divinities. Matrŏna herself gave her name to the rivers Marne, Maronne, and Maronna,[116] and therefore presided over flowing waters. She would be close kin to Ritona, the goddess of the ford (Welsh *ryd*), who gave her name to the River Rieu (dép. Gard).[117] Naturally, too, Matrŏna would be confused with the Celtic *nymphae* of the springs, whose worship is attested by inscriptions.[118] A divine mother, as her name implied,

---

[113] M. Ihm, *Der Mütter- oder Matronenkultus und seine Denkmäler, Jahrbücher des Vereins von Alterthumsfreunden im Rheinlande*, lxxxiii (1887), 11; Maury, op. cit., p. 7; J. Rhys, *Lectures on the Origin*, p. 100.

[114] E. Windisch, *Das keltische Britannien bis zu Kaiser Arthur* (Leipzig, 1902), p. 103.

[115] Hastings, *Encyclopaedia*, iv. 409.

[116] A. Holder, *Altceltischer Sprachschatz* (Leipzig, 1904), ii. 470 ff.; *Celtic Review*, iii (1906), 48; Hastings, *Encyclopaedia*, iii. 292. On cult of rivers in Gaul and Britain cf. Sébillot, op. cit. ii. 373 ff.; E. Hull, *Folklore of the British Isles*, pp. 54–59.

[117] Holder, op. cit. ii. 1194; Hull, op. cit., p. 55.

[118] Windisch, op. cit., p. 102. On well-worship cf. Hull, op. cit., pp. 68, 106–17; MacCulloch, *Religion of Ancient Celts*, pp. 181 ff.; Rhys, *Celtic Folklore*, i. 354 ff.

she would be equated with the Matres, who were frequently represented holding an infant or its swaddling clothes in their laps.[119] Like them she was the bestower of wealth and held fruit as a symbol.[120] Like them she was regularly worshipped in groups of three.[121] In Britain the Matres were identified with the Parcae, who likewise formed a trinity, foretold the future, and were regarded as both *benignae* and *invidiosae* or *malae*.[122] In Britain there was found an inscription to *lamiis tribus*,[123] and the *lamiae* were conceived as 'ladies of the fayry, whyche dooe allure yong men to company carnally with theym'.[124] Most significant, in view of Morgain's persistent association with a supernatural horse, is the popularity in Gaul and Britain of the goddess Epona, who was born of a mare and was regularly represented in sculpture as mounted on a steed.[125] Since Epona often was shown with a cornucopia and a platter of plenty, she would tend to merge with Matrŏna.

From ancient Gaul Morgain seems to have derived still other features of her tradition. Pomponius Mela (*c.* A.D. 45) reported that in the island of Sena there dwelt nine priestesses, able to transform themselves into animal shapes, to heal the incurable, and to foretell the future.[126] Here then we find a traditional source for the nine enchantresses who appear in *Peredur* and Geoffrey's *Vita Merlini*,[127] for the island of the sea where Morgain and her attendant fays had their dwelling, for their powers of metamorphosis and of healing, and for their knowledge of events to come.

---

[119] E. Espérandieu, *Recueil Général des Bas-reliefs, Statues, et Bustes de la Gaule Romaine* (Paris, 1907–38), iii, figs. 1741, 1742, 1815, 1816, 1819, 1831, 2081. Cf. vol. x, Index, for other examples. On the Matres cf. especially Ihm, op. cit.; *Archaeologia Aeliana*, xv (1892), 314 ff.; Hastings, *Encyclopaedia*, iv. 406 ff.

[120] Espérandieu, op. cit. viii, figs. 6307, 6356, 6358, 6401, 6412, 6559, 6560.

[121] Cf. *supra*, p. 117, n. 54.   [122] Ihm, op. cit., pp. 66, 69.

[123] E. Hübner, *Inscriptiones Britanniae Latinae* (Berin, 1873), No. 507; *Revue Celtique*, xii (1891), 128.

[124] M. W. Latham, *Elizabethan Fairies*, p. 53.

[125] Espérandieu, op. cit. iii, figs. 2117, 2124, 2127, 2335. Cf. vol. x, Index, for other examples. Cf. also the classical encyclopaedias of Roscher and Pauly–Wissowa on Epona. It is likely that she had some influence on the fay Rhiannon in *Pwyll*, who not only rode on a supernatural horse but was also, as a punishment, compelled to stand by the horse-block and carry strangers on her back. Cf. W. J. Gruffydd, *Rhiannon* (Cardiff, 1953), pp. 103–5.

[126] Paton, *Fairy Mythology*, pp. 43 f. *PMLA*, lvi. 907 f.

[127] Cf. *supra*, p. 111, n. 24. For other Celtic examples of nine fays cf. Wood-Martin, *Elder Faiths of Ireland* (London, 1903), i. 135; *Medieval Studies in Memory of G. Schoepperle Loomis* (New York, 1927), p. 275; W. Stokes, E. Windisch, *Irische Texte*, Ser. IV, vol. i, p. 164.

Though the theory that Morgain owed much to the Irish legends of Macha and the Morrígan is surely correct, it seems equally certain, in view of the fay's demonstrated descent through Modron from Matrŏna, that she also inherited a great part of the syncretic tradition of the goddesses of Gaul and Britain. The divergent lines of Goidelic and Brythonic mythology seem to have converged to produce the composite legend of Morgain la Déesse.

This chapter contains but a small part of what might be written on the subject. But it will suffice, I hope, to outline the history of the great queen of faerye from the reign of Caligula (A.D. 37–41), to which the earliest inscriptions to the Matres are assigned,[128] down to the twentieth century.[129]

[128] *Archaeologia Aeliana*, xv. 318.
[129] Useful studies of the fays of romance are in W. Hertz, *Spielmannsbuch*, ed. 2 (Stuttgart, 1900), pp. 59 ff., and in J. Bolte, L. Mackensen, *Handwörterbuch des deutschen Märchens*, ii. 74 ff. Prof. Philippson has an excellent article on the Matrŏnae in the *Germanic Rev.*, xix (1944), 81 ff.

CHAPTER IX

'*The Spoils of Annwn*'

An Early Welsh Poem

IN *Breuddwyd Rhonabwy* we read: 'Behold, bards came and recited a song before Arthur, and no man understood that song . . . save that it was in Arthur's praise.' These words fittingly describe a poem (No. XXX) in the thirteenth-century *Book of Taliesin*, entitled *Preiddeu Annwn*,[1] which would seem to mean 'The Spoils (i.e. plunder) of the Other World'. Sharon Turner, who was the first to offer a translation, frankly confessed that the Welsh scholars of his day did not profess to understand above one-half of any of the Taliesin poems.[2] He asserted—not without reason—that in the particular verses under discussion 'all connexion of thought seems to have been studiously avoided';[3] and in conclusion he exclaimed, 'Could Lycophron or the Sybils, or any ancient oracle, be more elaborately incomprehensible?'[4]

This obscurity is due in part to the antiquity of the language. No one would maintain that it goes back to the middle of the sixth century, when according to Nennius (*c.* 826) there flourished a historic bard Taliesin.[5] But Sir Ifor Williams, whose kindness I cannot sufficiently acknowledge, wrote me (28 November 1939): 'The poem is definitely pre-Norman. You can compare the language and technique with those of *Armes Prydein*, *c.* 900. How much earlier, I cannot say yet.' A second cause of obscurity is the corruption of the text, which inevitably occurred when a thirteenth-century scribe undertook to copy a manuscript centuries older. A third and potent source of perplexity lies in the highly allusive nature of much bardic composition, which assumed familiarity with oral (and perhaps written) traditions now in large measure lost. As Anwyl once expressed it, the *Book of Taliesin*, 'in its incoherent and fragmentary

---
[1] *Facsimile and Text of the Book of Taliesin*, ed. J. G. Evans (Llanbedrog, 1910), p. 54, l. 16–p. 56, l. 13.
[2] S. Turner, *History of the Anglo-Saxons*, ed. 5 (London, 1828), iii. 617.
[3] Ibid., p. 634.   [4] Ibid., p. 636.
[5] Nennius, *Historia Brittonum*, ed. F. Lot (Paris, 1934), pp. 130, 201. On Taliesin cf. *Cymmrodor*, xxviii (1918).

allusions, contains in almost inextricable confusion much of the débris of early Welsh legends'.[6]

The cryptic nature of *Preiddeu Annwn* has led to two wholly fantastic efforts at translation and interpretation, by Edward Davies and J. Gwenogvryn Evans.[7] It has also led more cautious scholars to avoid any attempt at exegesis. Indeed, in the present state of our knowledge it does not seem possible to offer any satisfactory translation of the last three of the seven stanzas, or to hazard any remarks as to their content except that stanzas 5 and 6 allude to the same calamitous expedition of Arthur as do the first four, and that stanza 7 is a scornful gibe at the Christian monks and their ignorance of the strange lore on which the bards prided themselves.

The first four stanzas, however, have gradually become clearer, and it is to these alone that the present article is devoted. Rhys made good use of Nennius, of *Kulhwch ac Olwen*, and of another poem in the *Book of Taliesin* (No. XIV) to elucidate some of the allusions;[8] Professor Gruffydd and Sir Ifor Williams have called attention to certain parallels in the *Pedeir Keinc y Mabinogi*.[9] I have already pointed out some connexions with French Arthurian romance,[10] and one of these has been accepted by Professor Nitze in his edition of *Perlesvaus*.[11] Professor Newstead has offered similar comments.[12] I have felt increasingly that a study of the material now available would make the references in the first four stanzas quite intelligible. But I should not have dared to offer a translation to the scrutiny of Celtic linguists, being myself but a novice, if I had not had the previous translations of Stephens,[13] Robert Williams,[14] and Rhys,[15] had not been able to use the first sections of the monumental *Geirfa*

[6] *Zts. f. Celt. Phil.* ii (1899), 127 f.

[7] *Poems of Taliesin*, ed. J. G. Evans (Llanbedrog, 1915), pp. 126-9; E. Davies, *Mythology of the Druids* (London, 1809), pp. 513-26.

[8] J. Rhys, *Lectures on the Origin*, pp. 263. f.; *Studies in the Arthurian Legend* (Oxford, 1891), 300 f., 307 f.; *Celtic Folklore, Welsh and Manx* (Oxford, 1901), ii. 679.

[9] *Pedeir Keinc y Mabinogi*, ed. I. Williams (Cardiff, 1930), p. liii; *Rev. Celt.* xxxiii. 460 f.

[10] R. S. Loomis, *Celtic Myth and Arthurian Romance* (N.Y., 1927), pp. 91 f., 201-4, 211-13, 330; *Speculum*, viii (1933), 428 f. Cf. *supra*, pp. 36-39, 60.

[11] *Perlesvaus*, ed. W. A. Nitze and others, ii (Chicago, 1937), 154 f.

[12] H. Newstead, *Bran the Blessed in Arthurian Romance* (New York, 1939), pp. 21, 25 f., 68, 91, 148, 150.

[13] T. Stephens, *Literature of the Kymry* (Llandovery, 1849), 192-204; (London, 1876), pp. 183-7.

[14] In W. F. Skene, *Four Ancient Books of Wales* (Edinburgh, 1868), i. 264-6.

[15] Malory, *Morte d'Arthur*, ed. J. Rhys, Everyman's Lib. 1. xxii-xxiv.

Barddoniaeth Gynnar Gymraeg, and had not secured the invaluable criticism and advice of five most eminent students of Welsh. These were Professor J. Lloyd-Jones, author of the *Geirfa*, Professor W. J. Gruffydd, author of the brilliant study of *Math Vab Mathonwy*, Sir Ifor Williams, who is publishing the poetry of the *cynfeirdd* under the auspices of the University of Wales Press Board, Professors Fred N. Robinson and Kenneth Jackson. The last mentioned has been particularly helpful with his criticism of this article. Though it must be expressly understood that none of these scholars is responsible for the following tentative translation, I am greatly in their debt for whatever merits it may possess, and I indicate in footnotes the chief divergences in rendering.[16]

PREIDDEU ANNWN

I

Golychaf wledic pendeuic gwlat ri
py ledas y pennaeth dros traeth mundi
bu kyweir karchar gweir ygkaer sidi
trwy ebostol pwyll aphryderi
Neb kyn noc ef nyt aeth idi
yr gadwyn trom las kywirwas ae ketwi
A rac preideu annwfyn tost yt geni
Ac yt urawt parahawt yn bardwedi
Tri lloneit prytwen yd aetham ni idi
nam seith ny dyrreith o gaer sidi

II

Neut wyf glot geinmyn cerd ochlywir
ygkaer pedryuan pedyr ychwelyt
yg kynneir or peir pan leferit
Oanadyl naw morwyn gochyneuit
Neu peir pen annwfyn pwy y vynut
gwrym am yoror amererit
ny beirw bwyt llwfyr ny rytyghit
cledyf lluch lleawc idaw rydyrchit
Ac yn llaw leminawc yd edewit
A rac drws porth vffern llugyrn lloscit
Aphan aetham ni gan arthur trafferth lethrit
namyn seith ny dyrreith o gaer vedwit

[16] The Welsh text may be found in Skene's *Four Ancient Books*, ii. 181 f., or in works cited in notes 1 and 15.

III

Neut wyf glot geinmyn kerd glywanawr
ygkaer pedryfan ynys pybyrdor
echwyd amuchyd kymyscetor
gwin gloyw eu gwirawt rac eu gorgord
Tri lloneit prytwen yd aetham ni arvor
namyn seith ny dyrreith o gaer rigor

IV

Ny obrynafi lawyr llen llywyadur
tra chaer wydyr ny welsynt wrhyt arthur
Tri vgeint canhwr a seui arymur
oed anhawd ymadrawd ae gwylyadur
tri lloneit prytwen yd aeth gan arthur
namyn seith ny dyrreith ogaer golud

THE SPOILS OF ANNWN

I

I worship the Lord, the Sovereign, the King of the Realm (i.e. heaven),[17]
Who[18] hath extended his sway over the world's strand.

Perfect (i.e. richly equipped)[19] was the prison of Gweir in the Faery Fortress (Kaer Siddi),
According to the tale of Pwyll and Pryderi.
No one before him went into it,
Into the heavy blue (i.e. steel) chain which held him, faithful youth,[20]
And before the spoils[21] of Annwn dolefully he chanted.
And till the Judgement our bardic prayer will last.[22]
Three shiploads of Prydwen we went into it;
Save seven none returned from the Faery Fortress (Kaer Siddi).

[17] *pendeuic gwlat ri*: Lloyd-Jones suggests, 'ruler of the kingly domain', or 'sovereign of a country's king'. Williams translates, 'the Supreme, the King-Ruler'.
[18] Williams and Jackson both note that *py* must be a scribal error for *ry*.
[19] *kyweir*: cf. discussion *infra*. Williams translates 'ready'.
[20] *kywirwas ae ketwi*. Lloyd-Jones suggests as alternative, 'it was a faithful youth that it guarded'.
[21] *preideu*. Williams prefers 'herds of cattle', refers to its use in this sense in his *Pedeir Keinc*, p. 231, and suggests that Gweir had been turned into a cowherd.
[22] *parahawt yn bardwedi*. Williams and Lloyd-Jones agree that *wedi* represents *gweddi*, 'prayer'.

II

I am illustrious if song be heard.[23]
In the Four-Cornered Fortress (Kaer Pedryvan), four-sided,[24]
My[25] first utterance,[26] it is from[27] the cauldron that it was spoken.
By the breath of nine maidens it (i.e. the cauldron) was kindled.
Even the Chief of Annwn's cauldron, what is its nature?
Dark blue (i.e. enamel)[28] and pearls are round its rim.
It will not boil the food of a coward; it has not been destined.[29]
The sword of Llwch Lleawc[30] was . . . [31] to it,
And in the hand of Lleminawc it was left.[32]
And before the gateway of hell lamps were burning,
And when we went with Arthur,—glorious hardship,—[33]
Save seven none returned from the Fortress of Carousal (Kaer Veddwit).[34]

[23] *cerd ochlywir*. Lloyd-Jones writes: 'Though this may stand for *cerdd o chlywir*, it is much more likely that *ochlywir* is connected with *gochlywet*.... The rhyme is -it, and one should perhaps read *cerdd gochlywit*, "song was heard".'
[24] *pedyr ychwelyt*. Both Lloyd-Jones and Williams refer to a passage in the *Red Book of Hergest, pedryfan dwfyn pedrychwelit*. Williams translates this as 'four-cornered is the world, four-sided'. Lloyd-Jones sees in *pedyrychwelyt* a verbal form, 3rd sing. pres. ind. or imperative or impf. or aor. impersonal, and suggests translating, 'it was borne'.
[25] *yg*. All authorities think it probable that *yg* is the common contraction for *vyg*, 'my'.   [26] *kynneir*. Lloyd-Jones suggests 'praise'.
[27] Williams prefers translating 'of'.
[28] *gwrym*. Williams and Jackson believe that the word is *gwrm* or *gwrwm*, a noun meaning 'dark blue'; Williams suggests a reference to enamel work. Gruffydd sees no objection to *gwrym*, meaning 'ridge'. Lloyd-Jones holds both meanings possible.
[29] *ny rytyghit*. Lloyd-Jones suggests the alternative translation 'it would not be forsworn'. Jackson and Gruffydd favour the translation given. Williams suggests that the -*t*- is an infixed pronoun, the verb is *ynghit* (from *wnc*, 'near'), and the *ry*- expresses possibility. The meaning would then be, 'he cannot approach it'.
[30] *lluch lleawc*. Lloyd-Jones and Williams take these to be two adjectives, 'shining, flashing', and 'destructive, death-dealing', and ignore the connexions pointed out in the commentary below. Gruffydd says: 'We seem to have here (1) *lleu lleawc* (vide *Kulhwch ac Olwen*), (2) *llew (llaw) lleminawc*.'
[31] *idaw rydyrchit*. Lloyd-Jones and Williams agree that 'was lifted to it' is impossible. The former suggests, 'appears to him', the latter, 'was sought from it'. Neither seems very plausible.
[32] *yn llaw leminawc yd edewit*. Williams compares *llaw lleminawc* with Irish *lugleimnech*, 'making short jumps', and translates the whole passage, 'at a quick pace he departs from it'.
[33] *trafferth lethrit*. Gruffydd prefers 'mighty in prowess'; Williams, 'famed was the disaster'; Lloyd-Jones suggests, besides the translation given, 'glorious in difficulty'.
[34] *vedwit*. Lloyd-Jones writes: '"Carousal" is as good a suggestion as any other that might be offered, although *meddwdawd* and *meddweint* are the usual forms.' Williams refers to a little-known saint, Meddwid. Baring-Gould and Fisher, *Lives of the British Saints*, iii. 458. Cf. discussion below.

III

I am illustrious; song is heard.[35]
In the Four-Cornered Fortress (Kaer Pedryvan), the isle of the strong door,[36]
Noonday and jet-blackness are mingled.[37]
Bright wine was their liquor before their retinue.[38]
Three shiploads of Prydwen we went on the sea;
Save seven none returned from Kaer Rigor.

IV

I, lord of letters, do not reward mean folk.[39]
Beyond the Fortress of Glass (Kaer Wydyr) they had not seen the prowess of Arthur.
Three score hundred men stood on the wall.
It was difficult to converse with their sentinel.
Three shiploads of Prydwen went with Arthur;
Save seven none returned from the Fortress of Frustration (Kaer Goludd).[40]

---

[35] *kerd glywanawr*. Williams writes: 'Read *clywanor* to rhyme. Cf. *Canu Aneirin*, ll. 298-299, "song is heard".' Lloyd-Jones offers three possibilities, 'song is the ruler of honour', 'song in praise of a leader', 'a song that will be heard'.

[36] *ynys pybyrdor*. Gruffydd suggests that this is in apposition to the subject of *wyf*, and means 'the mighty lord of the isle'. Lloyd-Jones suggests that it is in apposition to *kaer pedryfan*, and means 'stout defence of the isle'. Cf. discussion below.

[37] *echwyd amuchyd*. Lloyd-Jones and Jackson admit the translation given. Lloyd-Jones prefers, 'by noon and by night there will be mixed bright wine . . .'. Williams denies that *echwyd* riming with *muchyd* can be *echŵydd*, 'mid-day'; thinks that *dwfyr*, 'water', has been omitted after *pybyrdor*; suggests the translation, 'fresh (or drinking) water is mixed with jet', a reference to their hardships on the voyage. 'Then comes the contrast: but before their hosts they were wont to drink sparkling or clear wine.' To this interpretation one might object that probably not the voyagers but the dwellers in the *kaer* drank the wine supplied by the spring. Cf. discussion below.

[38] *gorgord* should be emended to *gosgor*.

[39] *Ny obrynafi lawyr llen llywyadur*. Williams and Lloyd-Jones interpret *lawyr* as a compound of *llaw* and *gwyr*, 'mean men, common folk'. Williams substitutes *llyadur* for *llywyadur*, and translates the line, 'I set no value on book-reading folk'. It marks 'the contempt of the bard for the *llaw-wyr*, . . . who read their mss., but know nothing of Arthur's feats in Faeryland'. Jackson questions translating *obrynafi* as 'I set value on'.

[40] *golud*. Cf. discussion below. Williams writes: 'After *caer* soft mutation occurs so that the original must be taken to be *Coludd*. I know of no instance of *coludd* with any other meaning than "entrails, bowels". . . . Cf. the use of *perfedd* for "middle" and "bowels". Caer Goludd, the Middle Fort, or the Fortress in the Middle of the Earth, the Mediterranean Fort!'

The Title. As Morris-Jones pointed out,[41] the title of the poem is inserted in a later hand than that of the text, but was probably traditional. It does fit the poem, for *preiddeu*, the plural of *preidd*, means 'spoils, plunder', and the poem, as we shall see, is concerned with a raid by Arthur and his warriors upon Annwn, to carry off a cauldron and perhaps other treasures as well.

Annwn. This word, which is given its earlier spelling *Annwfyn* in the first stanza, certainly meant originally the pagan Other World, the land of faerye. But as in many other mythologies, the location of the Other World was among the Celts a matter of conflicting traditions. Irish confusion on the subject is notorious. The home of Manannán, the sea-god, which is called Tír Tairngire, is in *Echtra Chormaic*[42] conceived as a palace, surrounded by a magic mist, but set above ground in the Irish landscape and approachable on foot; but in *Acallám na Senórach*[43] it lies on an island over seas. In *Serglige Conculaind*[44] Manannán's wife and sister-in-law, Fand and Líban, though they dwell in an island elysium in an abode resembling Manannán's palace, nevertheless are called folk of the *síd*, that is, of the old prehistoric burial-mounds. In *Echtra Conlai*[45] the hero is wooed by a goddess from Mag Mell, an island elysium, but she and her people are said to dwell in a *síd*. Still another localization of the Other World is found in *Fled Bricrend*,[46] where it is clear from the converging evidence that Cúroí is an embodiment of the sun and storm, and that his fortress, revolving as fast as a mill-stone after his departure by night, is the sky, revolving round the pole, with its myriad stars. This very concept occurs in an Anglo-Saxon astronomy:[47] 'The heaven locketh up in its bosom all the world, and it turneth ever about us, swifter than any mill-wheel. . . . It is all round and solid and painted with stars.' The *Veda*, too, knows the sky as a revolving dome.[48] And the regular departure of Cúroí

[41] *Cymmrodor*, xxviii. 238.
[42] W. Stokes, E. Windisch, *Irische Texte*, iii (1891), 211–16; T. P. Cross, C. H. Slover, *Ancient Irish Tales* (New York, 1936), pp. 504 f.
[43] S. H. O'Grady, *Silva Gadelica* (London, 1892), ii. 199 f.; Stokes, Windisch, op. cit. iv (1900), 107 f.
[44] Stokes, Windisch, op. cit. i (1880), 214, l. 20; 215, ll. 6, 11; 217, l. 6; 218, l. 26; 219, l. 17; especially 227, and translation of same in *Serglige Con Culaind*, ed. M. Dillon (Columbus, Ohio, 1941), p. 48.
[45] Cross, Slover, pp. 488–90; *Zts. f. celt. Phil.* xvii (1927), 195–205.
[46] R. S. Loomis, *Celtic Myth*, pp. 49 f.; *PMLA*, xlvii (1932), 320–3.
[47] Cockayne, *Leechdoms, Wortcunning, and Starcraft in Early England* (Rolls Series), iii. 233.
[48] J. Hertel, *Die Himmelstore im Veda und im Awesta* (Leipzig, 1924), pp. 41, 44.

at nightfall on an eastern journey is paralleled in a modern Breton folk-tale, in which a man whose role corresponds exactly to that of the sun in other tales of the same group, is said to depart from his home at the end of the world every night and return every morning.[49] But Cúroí's fortress is also realistically identified with a prehistoric *cathair* on a southern spur of Slíab Mis.[50] The Other World is also pictured in some Irish stories as a beautiful plain beneath the surface of a lake or spring.[51] Under Christian influences, as in *Imrám Curaig Maíledúin*, the elysian isle was sometimes converted into the island abode of a hermit or a community of monks, miraculously furnished with food and drink.[52] The most common characteristics of these happy dwellings are the immortality of the inhabitants, the abundance and miraculous provision of food and drink, and the richness of the vessels of plenty.

Welsh conceptions of Annwn were very similar.[53] There is the same uncertainty as to its situation, but also the same emphasis on the beauty of its immortal denizens and the plentiful provision for their appetites and thirst. Annwn as described in *Pwyll* seems to be a palace within easy walking or riding distance of Glyn Cuch, which divided Pembroke from Carmarthenshire. It was not, apparently, visible at all times, but, like the magic *kaer* in *Manawydan*,[54] like the castle of the Fisher King in Chrétien de Troyes's *Conte del Graal*,[55] suddenly appeared in the midst of a terrestrial landscape. The essentials of the description of Annwn in *Pwyll* are as follows:[56]

> To the court (*llys*) he (Pwyll) went; and in the court he saw sleeping-houses and halls and chambers and the most fairly adorned buildings that man had ever seen. . . . And the hall was richly equipped (*gyweir-*

---

[49] *Revue des Traditions Populaires*, x (1895), 571. Cf. ibid. xvi. 119 f.; F. M. Luzel, *Contes populaires de Basse-Bretagne* (1887), i. 6, 17, 33, 58; *Rev. Celt.* ii (1873-75), 289 ff.

[50] *Ulster Journal of Archaeology*, 1860, p. 111; *Royal Soc. of Antiquaries of Ireland, Journal*, xxix. 5; xl. 288; xli. 46.

[51] For example in O'Grady, *Silva Gadelica*, ii. 290 f., and P. W. Joyce, *Old Celtic Romances* (Dublin, 1920), pp. 252 ff.

[52] Joyce, op. cit., pp. 143 f., 157 f., 164 ff.; A. O'Kelleher, G. Schoepperle, *Life of Colum Cille* (Chicago, 1918), pp. 389 ff. See specially A. C. L. Brown in *Mod. Phil.* xiv (1916), 67 ff.

[53] *Pedeir Keinc*, ed. I. Williams, pp. 99–101. *Folklore*, xviii (1907), 146–51.

[54] *Pedeir Keinc*, p. 55 f.; J. Loth, *Mabinogion* (Paris, 1913), i. 159 f.

[55] Chrétien de Troyes, *Conte del Graal*, ed. A. Hilka (Halle, 1932), p. 136.

[56] *Pedeir Keinc*, p. 4. Loth, *Mabinogion*, i. 87.

wyt). Here he beheld household and troops and the fairest troop and the best arrayed (*cyweiraf*) that anyone had ever seen, coming in, and the queen with them, the fairest woman that anyone had ever seen, and a golden gown on her of shimmering silk. And thereupon they went to wash themselves and they went to the tables. . . . And they consumed food and drink and sang and caroused. Of all the courts of the earth that he had seen, that was the court with least stint of food and drink and golden vessels and royal treasures (*teyrn dlysseu*).

A similar picture is given in the sixteenth-century *Buchedd Collen Sant*.[57] The saint, being summoned to speak with Gwynn ap Nudd, *brenin Annwn a'r tylwyth teg* (King of Annwn and the faery folk), on the top of Glastonbury Tor, ascended the hill, and saw what he had surely never seen there before:

the fairest castle he had ever beheld, and around it the best-appointed retinues (*gosgorddion*) and a multitude of minstrels and every kind of music of voice and string, and steeds with youths on their backs, the comeliest in the world, and maidens of noble mien, sprightly, light of foot, light of dress, and in the bloom of youth, and every magnificence becoming the court of a puissant sovereign. . . . And Collen went into the castle, and when he came, the king was sitting in a golden chair. And he welcomed Collen honourably and asked him to eat, and he would get, besides what he saw on the table before him, the most luxurious of every dainty and delicacy that the mind could desire concerning them, and would get of every drink and osey to satisfy him that his heart could wish.

Collen perceived that the gaily clad servitors were devils, refused Gwynn's hospitality, sprinkled holy water on their heads, and the castle vanished, leaving nothing but the green tussocks.

Annwn is here regarded, on the one hand, as the faery castle, usually invisible to mortals, but occasionally made visible in a familiar terrestrial setting, much as in *Pwyll*. It is somewhat surprising to find it set on top of a hill.[58] As for the King of the Other World, the Welsh, like the Irish, knew many: in *Pwyll* there are

---

[57] Two MS. texts survive and are printed in *Y Greal* (London, 1805), pp. 339–41, and in Baring-Gould and Fisher, *Lives of the British Saints* (London, 1913), iv. 377. The translation is made from the former. A recent edition is in *Rhyddiaith Gymraeg. Y Gyfrol Gyntaf* (Cardiff, 1954), pp. 36–41. For a somewhat similar story cf. *Minor Poems of the Vernon MS.*, ed. F. J. Furnivall, pt. II, E.E.T.S., vol. cxvii (1901), 484 ff.; A. B. Van Os, *Religious Visions* (1932), p. 173.

[58] Cf., however, the faery castle in *Thomas of Erceldoune*, ed. J. A. H. Murray (London, 1875), pp. 12 f.

Arawn and Hafgan, and here is another, Gwynn ap Nudd.[59] Gwynn has important connexions with Celtic paganism since his father is generally regarded as the Welsh counterpart of the Irish Nuada, king of the Tuatha Dé Danann,[60] and both Nudd and Nuada derive their names from Nodons, one of whose temples was located at Lydney on the Severn.[61] The Christian missionaries and monks were not inclined to question the existence or the power of the gods; like Milton in *Paradise Lost*, they merely converted the pagan pantheon into the devils of hell.[62] Thus Gwynn ap Nudd and his attendant sprites appear in *Buchedd Collen* as demons, and his faery palace vanishes under a sprinkle of holy water. Likewise in *Kulhwch* the devils of Annwn are mentioned, and Gwynn, their chief.[63] And in the very poem we are studying *uffern* (< Latin *infernum*) is employed as the equivalent of Annwn.

But while on the one hand the old conception of Annwn as a faery palace, occasionally visible in a natural landscape setting, is reflected in *Pwyll* and *Buchedd Collen*, another ancient conception seems to have placed it beneath the earth. A poem in the *Book of Taliesin* (No. VII) contains the phrase, *yn annwfyn sis elvyd, yn awyr uch elvyd*, meaning 'in Annwn below the earth, in the air above the earth'. And Dafydd ap Gwilym speaks of the fox's dwelling *hyd annwn* (toward Annwn).[64] But this subterranean world was far from being a land of shades, a Hades. Two Welshmen, Walter Map and Giraldus Cambrensis, writing towards the end of the twelfth century in Latin, have described this lower realm as a fair, though somewhat dim, land, inhabited by high-minded dwarfs and abounding in treasure.[65]

In our poem, however, another localization is clearly indicated, for it is by sea in the ship Prydwen that Arthur and his men made their raid on Annwn. And a passage from poem XIV in the *Book of*

---

[59] On Gwynn cf. Guest, *Mabinogion* (1849), ii. 323 ff.; *Black Book of Carmarthen*, ed. J. G. Evans (Pwllheli, 1906), pp. x–xv.
[60] *Proceedings of the Roy. Irish Acad.* xxxiv (1917–19), C, 145 ff.
[61] Ibid., p. 147.
[62] Very clearly the elements of the equation appear in Fiacc's *Hymn* (c. 800), which asserts that the Irish used to worship the peoples of the *síd* (*tuatha síde*), and in the conclusion to *Serglige Conculaind* (A version, eleventh century), where we read that the power of the demons was great before the advent of the Faith and they were called the folk of the *síd* (*aes síde*). Stokes, Windisch, *Irische Texte*, i (1880), p. 14, l. 41; p. 227; *Serglige Con Culaind*, ed. Dillon, p. 48.
[63] Loth, *Mabinogion*, i. 314 n., 315; J. G. Evans, *White Book Mabinogion*, col. 484.
[64] *Pedeir Keinc*, ed. Williams, p. 100.
[65] The passages are quoted above in the chapter 'King Arthur and the Antipodes'.

'The Spoils of Annwn': an Early Welsh Poem 141

Taliesin, shortly to be discussed, confirms this notion of Annwn as a seagirt isle, informing us that 'around its corners are ocean's currents'.

Thus it is possible to assert with assurance that the ancient Welsh conceived of Annwn, abode of the former divinities, as a palace which appeared and then disappeared in a familiar landscape setting, or as a delightful subterranean region, or as an elysian isle. When Christian clerics identified the King of Annwn with the devil, then of course Annwn had to be hell, though it still retained the illusion of beauty. Always the inhabitants were noted for their hospitality; the place abounded in treasure, particularly in costly vessels for the service of the table.

There seems to be no warrant in medieval Welsh literature for the view that Annwn in any of its forms was a land of the dead.[66] The only trait which reminds one specifically of Hades is Collen's refusal to eat the food of Annwn, but Hartland has shown that this motif is equally applicable to fairyland;[67] it proves nothing. Since it is not uncommon to find scholars of repute speaking generally of the Celtic Other World as a Hades, a *Totenreich*, or a *terre des morts*, it may be well to examine the evidence both chronologically and geographically. It is true that the evidence of Caesar and Procopius proves that in their times Gauls and Britons entertained ideas of a land and a lord of the dead. Probably, too, the Irish at one time thought of their barrows as abodes of the ancestral spirits. But these facts prove nothing as to the period of the early texts, roughly from A.D. 800 to 1200. Neither, on the other hand, do modern folk-beliefs recorded in Ireland, Wales, or Cornwall, to the effect that inebriate peasants have recognized their departed friends and kinsfolk among the fairies. Deeply rooted as are the superstitions of primitive folk and modern peasantry, they do change radically or become obsolete. For example, the Anglo-Saxons even before their conversion to Christianity seem to have lost all their eschatological beliefs.[68] The significant fact is that from the Dark and early Middle

---

[66] Two efforts to interpret the Celtic Other World as a land of the dead are those of A. C. L. Brown in *The Origin of the Grail Legend* (Cambridge, Mass., 1943), and A. H. Krappe in *Rev. Celt.* xlviii (1931), 94. Neither seems to offer satisfactory proof from texts of the period and the peoples in question. The latter admits, moreover, on pp. 108 f. that there are no dead, *jamais des morts*, in his land of the dead, and that is a fatal admission.

[67] E. S. Hartland, *Science of Folklore*, pp. 40–44.

[68] Cf. the famous story of King Edwin's council in 627 (Bede, *Ecclesiastical History*, Bk. II, ch. 13) and the Anglo-Saxon elegies of *The Ruin* and *The Wanderer*.

Ages, besides the Welsh accounts of Annwn, we possess a fairly bulky Irish literature dealing with the visits of heroes to the Other World, and in nearly all the dead are conspicuous by their absence. So far as I am aware, only one of the supernatural isles, Tech Duinn, is identified as the place whither many of the Irish go after death.[69] It is noteworthy that the references to it are very few and that, as Father Lehmacher observes,[70] 'Donn, der Gälen Stammvater und Totenherrscher, tritt nie in Gesellschaft der übrigen Götter auf'. The *imrama* like those of Tadg and Maeldúin, which do introduce recognizable human beings into the Otherworld Isles, evidently do so in the effort to harmonize with Christian beliefs and speculations and with the unquestioned fact that some of the remoter islands, such as the Skelligs and the Blaskets, afforded a refuge from the world to religious solitaries or communities. It is with justice that Nutt, Eleanor Hull, Kuno Meyer, MacCulloch, Dom Gougaud, Professors Hibbard and Nitze[71] have protested against the casual assumption that every Celtic faery-land was a *Totenreich*. Even Le Braz admitted that only two texts (one of them referring to Tech Duinn) out of the copious prose epic of Ireland favoured this view, and declared, 'Par ailleurs, toutes les fois que des êtres venus de l'autre monde apparaissent dans l'épopée irlandaise, ces êtres sont des fées, et non des morts.'[72]

In the main the Irish of the period in question were quite clear on the subject: the people of the *síd* were not mortals. Nowhere is the point made more emphatically than in *Acallám na Senórach* of the twelfth century.[73] A woman from the cave of Crúachan, daughter of Bodb Derg and grand-daughter of the Dagda, approached St. Patrick and the Fenian hero Caeilte. St. Patrick exclaimed, 'It is a wonder to us how we see you two: the girl young and invested with all comeliness; but thou, Caeilte, a withered ancient, bent in

---

[69] K. Meyer in *Sitzungsberichte der Preußischen Akademie der Wissenschaften*, 1919, pp. 537 ff. Cf. also on Donn, *Proceedings of Roy. Irish Acad.* xxxiv, C. 163–5.
[70] *Anthropos*, xxvi (1931), 438.
[71] *Folklore*, xviii (1907), 121 ff., 445 ff.; Hastings, *Mythology of All Races*, iii (Boston, 1918), 123; Hastings, *Encyclopaedia of Religion and Ethics* (1909), ii. 689–96; J. A. MacCulloch, *Religion of the Ancient Celts* (Edinburgh, 1911), pp. 370–6; L. Gougaud, *Les Chrétientés Celtiques* (Paris, 1911), p. 25; *Romanic Rev.* iv (1913), 178 ff.; T. P. Cross, W. A. Nitze, *Lancelot and Guenevere* (Chicago, 1930), p. 71; K. Meyer, loc. cit., p. 545.
[72] A. Le Braz, *La Légende de la Mort*, ed. 3 (Paris, 1912), I, pp. xxiii–xxv.
[73] S. H. O'Grady, *Silva Gadelica*, ii. 202 f.; Stokes, Windisch, *Irische Texte*, iv (1900), 111.

the back and dingily grown grey.' Caeilte replied: 'Which is no wonder at all, for no people of one generation or of one time are we: for she is of the Tuatha Dé Danann, who are unfading and whose duration is perennial; I am of the sons of Milesius, that are perishable and fade away.' This point is of the highest significance. With the few exceptions already noted, the inhabitants of the Irish and Welsh Other World are the 'ever-living ones', survivors of the pagan pantheon, like Manannán or Lug or Gwynn ap Nudd, or their wives and kinswomen like Fand or the Sovereignty of Erin or Arawn's wife. Unless I am much mistaken, in only one instance is it said that human beings at death go to the *síd*;[74] and even here the text makes it plain that these princes go to dwell among the immortals, not as mortals in the ordinary course of events, but as kinsmen of the immortals, allied to them by marriage. For the three sons of King Lugaid Menn had been wedded in the *síd* of the Tuatha Dé Danann to three faery women, daughters of Midir, and though they returned to reign in the world, 'in virtue of marriage alliance they came back again to the Tuatha Dé Danann, and from that time forth have remained there'.[75] It is evidently for the same reason—partaking of the divine nature through marriage—that the mortals, Connla, Laegaire mac Crimthann, and Nera, were permitted to dwell for ever in the *síd*.[76] These were certainly exceptional cases. For the most part the human visitors to the divine abodes— Conn, Art, Cormac, Laeg, Cúchulainn, Maeldúin, Finn, Collen, Arthur and seven of his warriors, &c.—return. Neither in their going nor in their returning is there any suggestion that they have passed through an experience like death. And—another most significant point—it is never said of one of these that when eventually he did die he went back to the land which he had visited earlier.

The Celtic Other World depicted in the Irish literature up to

---

[74] O'Grady, op. cit. ii. 111; Stokes, Windisch, op. cit. iii. 11–13. Cf. p. 13, 'dochuatar ar cúla chúm Tuaithe dé Danann tréna cleamhnus'.

[75] The idea is exquisitely expressed in the *Odyssey*, iv, ll. 561 ff. '"But it is not thy destiny, O Menelaus, child of Zeus, to die in horse-pasturing Argos. The immortal gods will send thee to the Elysian plain and the verge of the world, where fair-haired Rhadamanthus dwells, where life is easiest for man. No snow falls there, nor any violent storm, nor rain at any time; but Ocean ever sends forth the clear, shrill blast of the West wind to refresh mankind; *because thou hast Helen to wife and they count thee to be son-in-law to Zeus*."' Cf. Prof. Coulter in *Trans. Am. Philological Assoc.* lvi (1925), 53.

[76] Cross, Slover, *Ancient Irish Tales*, pp. 488–90, 248–53; O'Grady, *Silva Gadelica*, ii. 290 f.

1200 offers but the slenderest support for the notion that it is a land of the dead; medieval Welsh literature offers none whatsoever. Kings might visit it, heroes might wage warfare within its borders, and raids might be made on its treasures. But with the exception of Tech Duinn and certain islands in comparatively late and deeply Christianized texts, the Other World of the insular Celts contains no mortals among its inhabitants. Those who go there do not pass through any experience suggestive of death. For the most part they return. And in only one instance is it ever suggested that at the end of their earthly life they go back to the *síd*. To call a blissful region where only the immortals—the ancient divinities and their kinsfolk—reside a Hades, and its king a Celtic Pluto, merely because of a passage in the sixth-century Procopius, or because it is sometimes localized under ground, or because of some general analogies with classical traditions, is a gross misnomer. One does not call Ireland the land of snakes.

In Arthurian legend, to be sure, there is some evidence that the Other World has become identified with a *Totenreich*. In *Perlesvaus* a brother of the Fisher King is called 'le Roi du Chastel Mortel';[77] in *Lanzelet* there is a Schatel le Mort;[78] in *Diu Crône* the Grail King declares that he and his folk are dead.[79] The reason for the localizing of Arthur's court in the recesses of Mount Etna may have been due to the infernal reputation of that volcano.[80] But there is a strong presumption that all these traditions had passed to the Continent through the Bretons,[81] and the Bretons, unlike the Welsh, had in the twelfth century, as well as in the nineteenth, a vigorous belief in a king and a people of the dead.[82] The phrases which Chrétien applied to the land of Goirre, however—'le reaume . . . don nus estranges ne retorne', 'la terre . . . don n'ist ne sers ne jantis hon', 'le reaume don nus n'eschappe'—do not admit, as Professor Newstead has shown,[83] any such explanation. For one thing, similar phrases emphasizing the perils of the adventure are attached to half the uncanny castles of Arthurian romance. In Chrétien's earliest romance, *Erec*, the hero is warned that from the castle of Brandigan

---

[77] *Perlesvaus*, ed. Nitze and others, i, ll. 38, 1081, 1646, &c.
[78] Ulrich von Zatzikhoven, *Lanzelet*, trans. K. G. T. Webster, pp. 73–76, 192.
[79] Heinrich von dem Türlin, *Crône*, ed. Scholl (Stuttgart, 1852), ll. 29532–4.
[80] J. A. MacCulloch, *Medieval Faith and Fable* (London, 1932), pp. 98–100.
[81] Cf. *infra*, pp. 183–5.
[82] *Mod. Lang. Notes*, li (1936), 28–30; Le Braz, op. cit., 3rd ed., I, p. xxxii.
[83] H. Newstead, *Bran the Blessed in Arthurian Romance*, p. 137, n. 7.

'ne revint nus qui l'avanture i alast querre', and again 'nus n'an peut eschaper vis'.[84] Of the castle of Brandus des Illes in the *Vulgate Lancelot* we read that 'nus cheualiers errans ni venist quil ni morust ou quil ne fust emprisones'.[85] Of the castle of Corbenic in the *Estoire del Saint Graal* also we learn that 'si i vint puis maint chevalier qui i voloit demorer, mais sans faille nus ni demoura que al matin ne fust troves mors'.[86] Unless one is prepared to accept the view that most of the perilous castles entered by knights of the Round Table were really *Totenländer* and that their antagonists were *Totenherrscher*, one must realize that the clauses quoted are merely variants of a formula emphasizing the perils of the adventure. They are found already in *Kulhwch* with reference to the *kaers* of the giants Yspaddaden and Gwrnach: 'No one has come hither to seek that and has gone away with his life'; 'no guest has returned thence with his life.'[87] This must be the proper interpretation to put on the phrases which Chrétien used of Goirre because not only do Lancelot, Ke, Gauvain, and Guenievre return, but also all the captives of Logres as well. Since Goirre is in fact a land from which everybody comes back alive and happy, it is hardly a land of the dead. And even though the raid on Annwn alluded to in our poem was attended with heavy casualties, seven at least returned in triumph with the cauldron. There is no suggestion here or elsewhere that the souls of those who had died remained in Annwn. Though Breton influence on Arthurian romance is responsible for several more or less explicit identifications of the Other World with the abode of the departed, Welsh literature of the period is completely free from the notion.

The Opening Lines. That the first two lines are an invocation of the Christian Deity is obvious from the analogous opening of poem XIV in the *Book of Taliesin*: 'I will praise the Lord, the ruler of every kindred';[88] and from the conclusion of the *Preiddeu Annwn* itself, 'I will pray to the Lord, the great Supreme, that I be not wretched. Christ be my portion!'[89] As Rhys noted:[90] 'The poem opens with the usual tribute to Christianity which not infrequently begins and ends the Welsh poems most replete with heathen lore.'

---

[84] Ed. W. Foerster (Halle, 1890), ll. 5436 f., 5463.
[85] H. O. Sommer, *Vulgate Version of the Arthurian Romances*, iii (Washington, 1910), 143, ll. 35 f.
[86] Ibid. i. 289, ll. 24 f. For other examples cf. *PMLA*, xlviii (1933), 1007 ff.
[87] J. G. Evans, *White Book Mabinogion*, cols. 473, 486; Loth, *Mabinogion*, i. 291, 318 f.   [88] W. F. Skene, *Four Ancient Books of Wales*, i. 274.
[89] Ibid., p. 266.   [90] Rhys, *Lectures on the Origin*, p. 248.

The Imprisonment of Gweir. Who Gweir was, why he was imprisoned, why he chanted—these are among the most obscure features of the poem, but even on them it may be possible to get some light. The prison of Gweir is said to be *kyweir*, a word which may be translated as 'ready', 'prepared', 'perfect'. It should be noted that twice this word or its verbal form appears in the description of Annwn in *Pwyll*, quoted above, *cyweirwyt* and *cyweiraf*. It also occurs in an almost identical line in the Taliesin poem No. XIV,[91] describing the chair of the poet in Kaer Siddi, which we shall see presently, was simply another name for Annwn. 'Ys kyweir vyg kadeir ygkaer sidi.' Evidently *kyweir* was considered a peculiarly appropriate adjective for the description of the Other World. It can hardly mean simply 'ready' or 'prepared'; this would imply preparation for some special occasion, of which there is no hint. Wiliems in 1632 defined the word as *ornatus*.[92] It must mean here 'adorned', and refer to the constantly stressed beauty and wealth of Annwn.

Annwn, we have discovered, was sometimes regarded as an island, and was localized off the west coast of Britain. I am inclined, therefore, to accept Rhys's suggestion:[93] 'It is not improbable that the legend about Gweir located his prison on Lundy, as the Welsh name of that island appears to have been Ynys Wair, "Gwair's Isle".' This seems all the more plausible since another tradition about Annwn, we shall discover, seems to have placed it on the island of Grassholm, and still another on the island of Bardsey. These would be the three outstanding lonely islands off the western coasts of North Wales, South Wales, and Cornwall.

Since we learn that Gweir 'dolefully chanted', it is probably to this sorrow of Gwair son of Gwestyl that Llywarch ap Llywelyn refers in 1216 and Einion Wan a few years later.[94] Incidentally it should be noted that neither the name Gwestyl applied to Gweir's father in these poems nor that of Gweiryoedd in the following triad have much authority, since it was not uncommon to invent alliterating patronymics freely.[95]

---

[91] *Facsimile and Text of Book of Taliesin*, ed. Evans, p. 34, l. 8.
[92] T. Wiliems, *Dictionarium Duplex* (London, 1632). Cf. Lloyd-Jones, *Geirfa Barddoniaeth Gynnar Cymraeg*, Rhan 3, p. 271.
[93] Rhys, *Celtic Folklore*, ii. 679.
[94] E. Anwyl, *Poetry of the Gogynfeirdd* (Denbigh, 1909), pp. 96, 121; C. Guest, *Mabinogion*, Everyman's Lib., p. 350.
[95] Gwalchmai and Gwalhavet, names invented or substituted by the Welsh for the French Arthurian names of Galvain and Galahot (?), seem to have been provided

A triad in the fourteenth-century *Red Book of Hergest* furnishes information regarding the imprisonment of Gweir.[96] 'The three supreme prisoners of the isle of Britain: Llŷr Lledyeith, Mabon ab Modron, Gweir son of Gweiryoedd.' Of these three imprisonments the only one on which we possess any early information in Welsh is that of Mabon in *Kulhwch*. The text dates from about 1100,[97] but the figure of Mabon is far older, since he derives his name from the Apollo Maponos of Romano-British inscriptions.[98] According to the story,[99] Kei and Gwrhyr, mounted on a salmon, arrive before the walls of Kaer Loyw, and hear lamentations within.

Gwrhyr said, 'What man is it who wails in this house of stone?' 'Alas, man, he who is here has reason to wail. Mabon son of Modron is here in prison; and no one was ever confined so cruelly in a prison as I, neither the prison of Lludd Llaw Ereint nor the prison of Greit son of Eri.'

Having learned that only by combat can Mabon be freed, Kei and Gwrhyr return to Arthur. The king gathers an army, and while he is attacking the *kaer*, Kei and Bedwyr mount the salmon's back, Kei breaches the wall and carries Mabon out to safety.

From this brief résumé it would appear that though the story of the imprisonment of Mabon is clearly not identical with that of Gweir, it does betray some resemblances. While Mabon is not Gweir, both seem to have bewailed their captivity. While Kaer Loyw (Gloucester) is not Kaer Siddi, yet both are approached by water. While Arthur and his host are not said to have reached Kaer Loyw in his ship Prydwen, yet in the very next adventure recounted in *Kulhwch* after the deliverance of Mabon, we read that 'Arthur sent a part of his army by sea on Prytwen, his ship'.[100] Evidently we are dealing with kindred traditions. Features of the one are likely to turn up in the other. Still not much is to be learned directly from Welsh literature about the imprisonment of Gweir. We shall find in a later stage of this study, however, that French Arthurian

arbitrarily with a patronymic Gwyar. Cf. Evans, *White Book Mabinogion*, col. 469. Rhys's surmises in regard to these names (*Studies in Arthurian Legend*, pp. 166–9) seem baseless, since Galahad is demonstrably a Biblical substitution (A. Pauphilet, *Études sur la Queste del S. Graal* (Paris, 1921), p. 136) and Galvain has no original connexion with Gwalchmai. Cf. *PMLA*, liv (1939), 656 ff.

[96] Loth, *Mabinogion*², ii. 267. [97] Ibid. i. 40.
[98] Rhys, *Lectures on the Origin*, pp. 27 f.
[99] Evans, *White Book Mabinogion*, cols. 492 f.
[100] Evans, *White Book*, col. 493.

romance solves some of the riddles presented by the poem, including that of the unhappy Gweir.

Kaer Siddi, the Faery Fortress. We may assert with confidence that Kaer Siddi is a name for Annwn, for it was characteristic of the medieval Celts to give several names to the Other World. Among the Irish it was Mag Mell or Tír na nÓg or Tír na mBeo or Tír Tairngire.

Rhys, abandoning an earlier guess as to the meaning of *sidi*, gave in 1901 an interpretation which has been accepted by Morris-Jones, Professor Gruffydd and Sir Ifor Williams,[101] and may be regarded as established. It seems probable that the genitive singular or plural of the Irish word *síd*, namely *síde*, meaning literally 'of the faery mound (or mounds),' was used so frequently to modify a noun that it came to have adjectival force and was practically equivalent to the adjective 'faery'. Thus *ben síde, suan síde, ceol síde*, meaning literally 'woman, sleep, music of the faery mound' have come to mean simply 'faery woman, sleep, music'. Since there is no trace of the meaning 'faery mounds' in the description of Annwn, it is probably in the secondary adjectival sense that the Irish word *síde* was taken over by the Welsh and applied to the fortress of Annwn. Compare the later Irish compound forms *sídhlios, síodhbhrugh*, meaning 'faery court, faery mansion'.

A second reference to Kaer Siddi is in poem No. XIV of the *Book of Taliesin*.[102] The bard is supposed to be speaking in his own person, and begins and ends, as in *Preiddeu Annwn*, with the conventional pious prologue and epilogue. He alludes to his singing before the sons of Llŷr at Aber Henvelen[103] and before Urien; to the cauldron of Ceridwen and the liberation of Elphin; to his own presence at the battle of Goddeu; and then to his accompanying Brân to Ireland and the slaying of Morddwyd Tyllon—subjects treated in the mabinogi of *Branwen, Hanes Taliesin*, and poem No. VIII of the *Book of Taliesin*. Just before the pious epilogue comes this:[104]

> Perfect (*kyweir*) is my seat in Kaer Siddi.
> Nor plague nor age harms him who dwells therein.

[101] Rhys, *Celtic Folklore*, ii. 678; *Cymmrodor*, xxviii. 238; *Enc. Brit.*, ed. 11, v. 642. Rhys and others, as Prof. Jackson points out to me, were mistaken in thinking the noun *síd* by itself meant a 'fairy'.
[102] *Facsimile and Text of Book of Taliesin*, ed. Evans, p. 34, l. 8. For a poor translation of whole poem cf. Skene, *Four Ancient Books*, i. 274.
[103] *Cymmrodor*, xxviii. 197.
[104] For renderings of these lines cf. ibid., p. 236; Rhys, *Arthurian Legend*, p. 301; Rhys, *Celtic Folklore*, ii. 678.

Manawyd and Pryderi know it.
Three organs around the fire play before it.
And around its corners are ocean's currents,
And the fruitful (i.e. wonder-working) spring is above it.
Sweeter than white wine is the drink in it.

The reading and interpretation of the fourth line are uncertain, but the rest is tolerably clear. Taliesin occupies the bardic chair amidst the riches of Kaer Siddi, the faery fortress of the ancient gods. Manawyd, more familiar as Manawydan, the old sea-god, and his stepson Pryderi are also there. All are immune from disease and old age. The fortress is set on an island in the midst of the ocean. The spring 'above it' perhaps alludes to an entrance to the underworld through a spring, such as that by which Diarmaid entered *Tír fá Thuinn* in the *Gilla Decair*.

This blissful abode of Manawyd or Manawydan vab Llŷr vividly recalls traditions concerning the dwelling of his Irish counterpart, Manannán mac Lir, identified in Cormac's *Glossary* (*c.* 900) as, by reputation at least, a god of the sea.[105] Manannán's palace, like Annwn, though sometimes conceived as a sudden apparition of splendour in the midst of the landscape, apparently accessible by foot, is also imagined as an island in the ocean.[106] Before it is a shining spring, from which the hosts drank.[107] At the Feast of Goibniu, ordained by Manannán, those who partook escaped age and decay.[108] Evidently the Irish and Welsh traditions of the sea-god's abode were closely akin.

Annwn Localized on the Island of Gwales. The description of Kaer Siddi as the island abode of Taliesin, Pryderi, and Manawyd, where disease and old age are unknown, makes possible a most illuminating connexion. According to the mabinogi of *Branwen* these very three and four others, by the orders of Brân, son of Llŷr, journeyed first to Harlech on the west coast of Wales, abode there feasting and revelling for seven years, and then proceeded to Gwales in Pembrokeshire to revel for eighty years more.[109]

And there was for them there a fair and royal place above the ocean, and a large hall was there, and they entered the hall. . . . And that night

---

[105] *Cormac's Glossary*, ed. J. O'Donovan (1868), p. 114; R. S. Loomis, *Celtic Myth*, p. 187. [106] Cf. *supra*, p. 137, nn. 42, 43.
[107] Cross, Slover, *Ancient Irish Tales*, p. 505.
[108] *Zts. f. Celt. Phil.* xviii (1929), 193. On Goibniu's Feast cf. *Atlantis* (London), iii (1862), 389 n.; Stokes, Windisch, *Irische Texte*, iv. 177, 189, 327.
[109] *Pedeir Keinc*, ed. I. Williams, p. 46 f. Loth, *Mabinogion*², i. 148 f.

they were plentifully supplied and joyful. And of all the sorrow that they had seen before their eyes and of all that each of them had gotten himself, naught came to mind to them, either of that or of any mourning in the world. And there they spent the four-score years, so that they never knew having a more joyful or pleasant time than that. Nor did any of them know of the other that he was older by that time (*yn [byn yn] hynny o amser*) than when they came there.

Rhys, Loth, Henry Owen, and Sir Ifor Williams are agreed that the question, 'what was Gwales?' is best answered by a quotation from George Owen's *Description of Pembrokeshire* (date 1603):[110] 'ffarre of in the sea standeth the Iland Gresholme so called of Mr. Saxton, but of the neighbours Walleyes, a small Iland viii^t miles from the maine, and for the Remotenes thereof and small proffettes yt yeldeth, is seldome frequented.' This island, now usually called Grassholm, is the westernmost point of Wales. In the *Pembroke County Guardian* of 1896 a Captain John Evans was reported to have said that passing Grassholm Island he was surprised to see two or three feet below water a beautiful green meadow, and he had heard old people say that there was a floating island off there that sometimes rose to the surface and then sank so that no one saw it again for years.[111] According to Howells's *Cambrian Superstitions* (date 1831)[112] 'the Milford Haven folk could see the green Fairy Islands distinctly lying out a short distance from land; and the general belief was that they were densely populated with fairies'.

Evidently the tradition that there was a faery isle in the neighbourhood of Grassholm took a long time in dying. And in the eleventh century Grassholm itself must have been identified with the island Annwn, just as we have seen that Lundy off the Cornish coast, known to the Welsh as Ynys Wair, probably represents an attempt to localize Annwn as the island of Gweir's imprisonment.

There is another rationalistic effort in this story besides the identification of Annwn with Grassholm. We are told that the company of seven revellers, including Taliesin, Manawydan, and

---

[110] Rhys, *Arthurian Legend*, pp. 269, 394; Loth, op. cit. i. 145, n. 2; *Pedeir Keinc*, p. 214; G. Owen, *Description of Pembrokeshire*, ed. H. Owen (London, 1892), p. 112.

[111] Rhys, *Celtic Folklore*, i. 171 f. A variant of this island tradition is that of the submerged country. Ibid. i. 382–ii. 419.

[112] Quoted ibid. i. 161. Cf. also Wirt Sikes, *British Goblins* (London, 1880), pp. 9 f.; Rhys, *Arthurian Legend*, pp. 269–71.

Pryderi, took with them to Harlech and Grassholm the severed head of their leader Brân vab Llŷr and feasted in its presence.[113]

No more distressed were they to be in the company of the head then than when Blessed Brân had been alive with them. And by reason of the four-score years it was called the Hospitality of the Noble Head (*Ysbydawt Urdaul Benn*).[114]

First, it should be noted that Brân himself earlier in the story had been accustomed to preside at sumptuous feasts, and that one occasion when the hosts went to Ireland to avenge Branwen was called the Hospitality of Brân, *Yspadawt Vran*. This suggests that the Hospitality of the Noble Head and the Hospitality of Brân were equivalent expressions, that Brân himself was the 'Noble Head', since the word *penn* meant not only 'head' but also 'chief', and might cause an inventive *cyvarwydd* to fabricate the story of Brân's decapitation. This suspicion is reinforced by the fact that Brân's decapitation and the presence of his head at the ambrosial feasts in Gwales seem rather pointless, and by the fact that the Head of Annwn's cauldron is specifically mentioned later in our poem where *pen annwfyn* is clearly a title of the owner of a miraculous vessel. Another strong support for this view is the allusion of Taliesin in poem XIV[115] to his singing 'at the hospitality (*yn yspydawt*) over joyless (*aflawen*)[116] liquor (*gwirawt*), before the sons of Llŷr at Ebyr Henvelen [probably the Bristol Channel]'.[117] These lines clearly refer to the *Ysbydawt Urdaul Benn*, which ended only when the revellers looked out of the door towards Aber Henvelen; and they show that not only one son of Llŷr, Manawydan, was present, but also the other, namely Brân, was present in person—not merely his severed head. The point seems clinched by Dafydd ap Gwilym's reference to the Head of Annwn's cauldron of rebirth,[118] and that must mean Brân's cauldron, described in *Branwen*. A reasonable conclusion from all this, corroborated by much evidence

---

[113] *Pedeir Keinc*, pp. 46. f.; Loth, op. cit. i. 149.

[114] *Pedeir Keinc*, p. 47; Loth, op. cit. i. 150. Though Williams questions (*Pedeir Keinc*, pp. 220–2) the translation of both *ysbydawt* and *urdaul*, with all deference to his authority I cannot share his scepticism. Cf. Loth, i. 390.

[115] Cf. p. 148, n. 103.

[116] This startling adjective probably refers to the tradition found in *Peredur*, Wolfram's *Parzival*, and *Sone de Nausay* where the Grail castle is the scene of lamentation. *Rev. Celt.* xlvii (1930), 40.

[117] *Bull. Board of Celt. Studies*, viii (1937), 302; *Pedeir Keinc*, pp. 215 f.

[118] *Cymmrodor*, xxviii. 197.

assembled elsewhere,[119] is that the redactor of the traditions found in *Branwen*, puzzled by the proverbial but ambiguous phrase 'ysbydawt Urdaul Benn' and by the presence of the 'Penn' at the joyous revels on Grassholm made the blunder of taking *penn* in its physiological sense and had to concoct a preliminary story of Brân's decapitation and an appended tale of the disposal of Brân's head in the White Hill at London to accord with his misinterpretation.

We have already observed the diversity of traditions regarding the localization of Annwn, and the multiplicity of its kings— Gwynn, Arawn, Hafgan. It is therefore no surprise to find that evidence points pretty clearly toward Brân vab Llŷr as another 'Penn Annwfyn', and it can hardly be coincidence that like his brother, Manawydan vab Llŷr, Brân should be regarded by Celtic mythologists as a Welsh counterpart of Manannán mac Lir, and should be presiding over similar ageless feasts in an island of the sea.

We are thus, by comparing various sources, able to round out the picture presented by the first few lines of our poem. Annwn, the paradise of the Welsh divinities, is imagined as a western isle, perhaps identified with Grassholm in the Irish sea. There was the faery fortress; there sometimes sat the bard Taliesin himself, in his bardic chair, and there too were the god Manawydan, his brother Brân, his stepson Pryderi, and others. It was a place where there was perpetual banquet and where none knew age and decay. But there was also a prisoner, Gweir, loaded with chains, whose keening must have introduced a note of sorrow into this elysian abode.

'*The Story of Pwyll and Pryderi.*' The fourth line of the poem runs: 'Trwy ebostol Pwyll a Phryderi.' Many renderings have been given of this line since the crucial word (*ebostol*) is obscure. *Ebostol* should derive from Latin *apostolus* and would then mean 'messenger, apostle'. But, as Sir Ifor Williams has shown,[120] there has probably been some confusion with *epistola*, and there is evidence that in certain connexions *ebostol* meant a prose lesson read during mass. Hence, he believes, it came to have the more general sense of a prose narrative to be read—in short, a story, a synonym of *ystorya*, *cyvarwyddyd*. In this context *trwy* would have the well-authenticated

---

[119] *Rev. Celt.* xlvii. 39 ff. The idea that Brân's head protected the island against plague from over the sea finds analogues elsewhere. Cf. Loomis, *Arthurian Tradition*, p. 350, n. 29; *Folklore Record*, v (1882), 14.

[120] *Pedeir Keinc*, pp. lii f.; Malory, *Morte d'Arthur*, Everyman's Lib., I, p. xxii, n. 2.

'The Spoils of Annwn': an Early Welsh Poem

meaning of 'according to', and the whole line would signify: 'according to the story of Pwyll and Pryderi'.

We have, of course, in the first of the *Four Branches of the Mabinogi*, namely, *Pwyll Pendeuic Dyvet*, a story of Pwyll and Pryderi. We learn how Pwyll, Prince of Dyfed (south-western Wales), visited Annwn, and thus acquired the title of Penn Annwn, and how he begat Gwri, later called Pryderi, and how the boy grew to manhood and succeeded to the throne of Dyfed. Pryderi is, moreover, as Professor Gruffydd has made plain, the connecting figure in the three other 'branches'. Evidently the *Four Branches* might be called 'ebostol Pwyll a Phryderi'. But scholars are generally agreed, and the studies of Professor Gruffydd have abundantly demonstrated,[121] that the traditions embodied in them are not unique forms; they are not even standard forms but grotesquely garbled versions. There is every reason to suppose that there were many other and less distorted versions, and one of them may have combined the story of Gweir's captivity with that of Arthur's raid on Annwn. This tale, then, would have been the 'ebostol Pwyll a Phryderi'.

The Expedition of Arthur. Six of the seven stanzas composing the poem end with a sort of refrain, which informs us that Arthur led an attack on Annwn, accompanied by three shiploads of warriors, in his ship Prydwen, and that all were lost or killed except seven survivors, who probably included Taliesin (or otherwise he would not have been alive to compose the poem) and Arthur himself. As Rhys long since pointed out,[122] there is a more euhemerized version of this legend in *Kulhwch ac Olwen*, probably set down in its present form within a decade or two of 1100. The youthful hero, Kulhwch, invoked the aid of Arthur and his warriors, including Taliesin *penn beirdd*[123] (the chief of bards), in winning Olwen as his bride. In order to obtain her he had to procure certain magic objects, among them the cauldron of Diwrnach the Irishman, steward of Odgar, king of Ireland. Arthur, after obtaining many of these objects, sent a messenger from Cornwall to Odgar demanding the vessel. Odgar in turn demanded it of Diwrnach, but in vain, and the messenger returned empty-handed to Arthur.[124]

[121] W. J. Gruffydd, *Math Vab Mathonwy* (Cardiff, 1928). *Transactions of Honourable Soc. of Cymmrodorion*, 1912–13, pp. 4 ff.
[122] J. Rhys, *Lectures on the Origin*, pp. 263 f.; *Studies in the Arthurian Legend*, p. 10; Malory, *Morte d'Arthur*, Everyman's Lib., I, p. xxv.
[123] Evans, *White Book Mabinogion*, col. 462.
[124] Ibid., col. 498 f.; Loth, *Mabinogion*², i. 334 f.

Arthur set out and a light host with him and went on Prydwen his ship, and came to Ireland. And they set out for the house of Diwrnach the Irishman. The hosts of Odgar observed their number. And after they had eaten and drunk their fill Arthur asked for the cauldron. He [Diwrnach] said that if he would have given it to anyone, he would have given it at the word of Odgar, king of Ireland. When it was refused them, Bedwyr arose and seized the cauldron and placed it on the back of Hygwydd, Arthur's servant.... Llenlleawc the Irishman grasped Kaledvwlch and brandished it, and slew Diwrnach the Irishman and all his host. The armies of Ireland came and fought with them. After putting the armies wholly to flight, Arthur and his men embarked in their presence in the ship, and the cauldron with them full of the treasure of Ireland.

Here, as in *Preiddeu Annwn*, we have a raid by Arthur and his men in his ship Prydwen, and the identity of the two traditions is confirmed by the appearance, in the next stanza of our poem, of a cauldron, object of the raid, and of a certain Llwch Lleawc, who brandished a sword. But the euhemerist has converted the faery isle into Ireland, the magic cauldron, soon to be discussed, into a receptacle for treasure, the Head of Annwn into the King of Ireland's steward. The disastrous losses sustained by Arthur have been converted into a victory.

Kaer Pedryvan, the Four-Cornered Fortress. This title of Annwn, which must mean 'Four-Cornered' or 'Four-Towered', will be discussed in connexion with stanza 4.

The Nine Maidens. Though the third line of the second stanza is very doubtful, the fourth is clearly to be translated: 'By the breath of nine maidens it [i.e. the cauldron] was kindled.' Now it is significant that Taliesin, Arthur, and nine maidens are brought together on an Otherworld island in Geoffrey of Monmouth's account of Arthur's passing to Avalon in *Vita Merlini* (c. 1150).[125] Taliesin, in his character of one who understands all the secrets of Nature, gives an account of the universe and finally describes the *Insula Pomorum*, a name which attempts to translate the Welsh *Ynys Avallach* or Isle of Avalon. Here Nature provides all things abundantly, and life is prolonged beyond a hundred years. Here dwell nine sisters, of whom the chief and most beautiful, Morgen, is skilled not only in the arts of healing but also in those of shape-shifting and travelling through the air, and she has taught mathematics (i.e. astrology) to her sisters. Taliesin goes on to declare that after the battle of

---

[125] Ed. J. J. Parry (Urbana, 1925), ll. 908–40. On date cf. E. Faral, *Légende Arthurienne*, prem. partie (Paris, 1929), ii. 36.

'The Spoils of Annwn': an Early Welsh Poem

Camlan 'we' brought thither the wounded Arthur, and there left him reposing on a golden bed in the charge of Morgen.

That the isle of Avalon was one form of the Celtic paradise has long been recognized, and there is a curious corroboration of this in a manuscript which speaks of *Margan dwywes o annwfyn*, 'Margan, goddess from Annwn', who concealed Arthur in Ynys Avallach to heal him of his wounds.[126] The antiquity of this Celtic tradition concerning the nine supernatural women is proved by the oft-quoted statement of Pomponius Mela (*c.* A.D. 45).[127] Speaking of the island Sena off the Breton coast, he says:

> Gallici numinis oraculo insignis est: cuius antistites, perpetua virginitate sanctae, numero novem esse traduntur. Galli Senas vocant, putantque ingeniis singularibus praeditas, maria ac ventos concitare carminibus, seque in quae velint animalia vertere, sanare, quae apud alios insanabilia sunt, scire ventura et praedicare: sed non nisi deditas navigantibus, et in id tantum, ut se consulerent profectis.

The knowledge which Geoffrey displays of Morgan and of her association with Avalon I have shown to be based on Welsh tradition, transmitted through the Bretons;[128] the same may be safely predicated of his knowledge of the coming of Arthur and Taliesin to an island paradise, where men live to be over a hundred, and where nine maidens of mysterious powers dwell, for all these features are found in the *Book of Taliesin*. Though it is true that Geoffrey is following his characteristic method of combining Celtic with scholarly Latin tradition, as in many other instances,[129] and has here drawn some of his descriptive phrases from Isidore and Solinus,[130] yet he surely did not find the nine maidens, any more than he found their chief Morgen, in Pomponius Mela. Mela, Geoffrey, and our Welsh poem are drawing on a common tradition. It is, in fact, Mela, rather than Geoffrey, who makes it possible to

---

[126] *Pedeir Keinc*, ed. I. Williams, p. 100. It should be clearly understood that Margan is not the original Welsh name of the *dwywes o Annwfyn*, but was introduced by the Bretons. So unfamiliar was Morgan in Wales that the redactor of *Geraint*, finding this name in his French original, plus the mysterious Breton word *Tud*, took her to be a male physician. Cf. *Rev. Celt.* xiii (1892), 496 f.; *Romania*, xxviii (1899), 322 ff. For other hypotheses about Morgan Tud cf. L. A. Paton, *Studies in the Fairy Mythology of Arthurian Romance* (Boston, 1903), pp. 259 ff.; Loth, *Contributions à l'Étude des Romans de la Table Ronde* (Paris, 1912), p. 51.

[127] On this passage, cf. T. D. Kendrick, *The Druids* (London, 1927), pp. 139 f.; L. A. Paton, *Fairy Mythology*, pp. 43 f.; *Rev. Celt.* x (1889), 352; Rhys, *Celtic Folklore*, i. 330 f.; (Lady) F. S. Wilde, *Ancient Legends, Mystic Charms, and Superstitions of Ireland* (London, 1888), p. 114.   [128] Cf. supra, pp. 124–7.

[129] *Mod. Phil.* xxxviii (1941), 302 ff.   [130] F. Lot in *Romania*, xlv (1918–19), 1 ff.

understand the cryptic lines in *Preiddeu Annwn*; the maidens were prophetesses, and in this role they 'kindled' the cauldron from which issued the poetic utterances.

It is pertinent further to remark that in the *Hanes Taliesin*, published and translated by Lady Guest, the bard obtains his prophetic and poetic gifts through the virtue of three drops of liquor from a boiling cauldron, the cauldron of Inspiration and Science, prepared by a witch woman, Caridwen.[131] Though the text comes from the sixteenth century, it is generally conceded that it contains some ancient traditions, and since in poem No. XVI of the *Book of Taliesin* Ceridwen mentions her cauldron, and in poem No. XV three *awen* (inspirations) are said to come from a cauldron,[132] we may regard the concept of a cauldron of poetic afflatus, tended by one or more supernatural women, as an authentic ancient feature.

The Cauldron of the Head of Annwn. Though the first reference to the cauldron characterizes it as a vessel of bardic inspiration, the later references point to other and seemingly inconsistent functions. Here again we are dealing with conflicting concepts. Though a cauldron might be used to boil a potent brew of herbs that would induce a poetic frenzy, its more common employment among the Celts was doubtless to produce an 'Irish stew' for daily sustenance and for festal occasions. Cauldrons occupied a conspicuous and honoured place in the palaces of Irish kings.[133] Their counterparts in the palaces of the gods had magic properties. There was the Cauldron of the Dagda, chief of the Túatha Dé Danann; 'no company ever went from it unthankful'.[134] Evidently this was a cauldron of plenty. There was the *coire aisic*, 'Cauldron of Restitution', which Cormac mac Airt established at Tara and which was so called because it returned to each his proper food.[135] It was filled with meat of swine and beeves, and an incantation of lords, poets, and wizards was sung over it. Each person was then brought before it and whatever meat he took out on his fork would be appropriate

---

[131] H. M. and N. K. Chadwick, *Growth of Literature* (Cambridge, 1932), i. 103 f., 263, 461.

[132] Ibid.

[133] Cross, Slover, *Ancient Irish Tales*, pp. 199, 328, 353; *Banquet of Dun na n-Gedh*, ed. J. O'Donovan, p. 51.

[134] Cross, Slover, op. cit., p. 28. Cf. V. Hull in *Zeits. f. celt. Phil.* xviii. 86. On Celtic cauldrons cf. A. C. L. Brown, in *Kittredge Anniv. Papers*, pp. 235 ff.

[135] Stokes, Windisch, *Irische Texte*, iii. 205 f.; *Banquet of Dun na n-Gedh*, p. 51. On elaborate etiquette of meat-portions cf. *Transactions of Roy. Irish Acad.*, xviii, Antiquities, pp. 200–11.

to his rank, 'to wit, a thigh to a king and to a poet, a chine for a literary sage, a shin-bone for young lords', and so forth. There was also the Cauldron of Truth, filled with hot water, which served in ordeals.[136] Accused persons dipped their hands in it, and the innocent suffered no harm. Evidently the purposes and associations of these magic cauldrons were varied, and it need not surprise us, therefore, that the Cauldron of the Head of Annwn possessed more uses than that of inspiring poetry.

It is obvious that since the Cauldron of the Head of Annwn would not boil the food of a coward, it was a testing talisman. It is evidently the same as the cauldron listed among the Thirteen Royal Treasures (*Brenhin Dlyseu*) of the Isle of Britain. Though the latter is first mentioned in a manuscript dated about 1460,[137] it is most fully described in a late sixteenth-century list:[138]

> The cauldron of Tyrnoc the Giant; if one put into it meat for a cowardly man, it would never boil enough, and if one put [in meat] for a brave man, it would boil enough in haste, and then distinction was obtained between the brave and the cowardly.

Several points are to be noted in connexion with this discriminating cauldron which link it indirectly with the cauldron of the Head of Annwn. Its properties are strikingly reminiscent of those attributed to the 'Cup of Truth' of the Irish sea-god Manannán. This vessel would break in pieces in the presence of a liar but would put itself together again if three truths were told.[139] And like the cauldron of Tyrnoc it served as a testing talisman; it was 'used to distinguish between truth and falsehood with the Gael'. Since Manannán's cup and the cauldron of the Head of Annwn, probably Brân or Manawyd, both possessed this power of discrimination, it is worth noting that both vessels are associated with divinities of the sea, who were sons of Ler or Llŷr, and who instituted banquets where the feasters knew neither old age nor disease.[140]

---

[136] Stokes, Windisch, iii. 210.

[137] MS. Peniarth 51, Nat. Lib. Wales, Aberystwyth, p. 170. 'pair dyrnwch.'

[138] MS. Peniarth 77, p. 214. 'Pair Tyrnoc (*written above*: dyrnawg) cawr, o rhoid ynddo gic i wr llwrf, digon byth nis berwai, ac o rhoid i wr dewr digon a verwai ar vrys, ag yno y caid gwahan rhwng y dewr ar llwrf.'

[139] Cross, Slover, op. cit., pp. 506 f.; Stokes, Windisch, iii. 211 ff. *Romanische Forschungen*, xlv (1931), 72.

[140] According to *Branwen*, Brân son of Llŷr possessed a cauldron which restored to life the bodies of the slain which were cast into it. Surely it is a somewhat repellent notion to cast corpses into a cooking-vessel, and nowhere else, if I am not mistaken,

The lists of the Thirteen Treasures, which include the cauldron of Tyrnoc, give variant readings of the name—*Dyrnwch, Dyrnog*—which suggest that it is identical with that of Diwrnach, seneschal of the king of Ireland. This suggestion is confirmed by the fact that Tyrnoc's cauldron is distinguished by the same faculty as the cauldron of the Head of Annwn, whereas Diwrnach's cauldron is the centre of the same story of Arthur's raid as is the cauldron of the Head of Annwn. Furthermore, Diwrnach's cauldron is listed among the objects of Kulhwch's—and consequently of Arthur's—quest together with the *mwys* of Gwyddno Garanhir, which miraculously multiplied the food of one man into enough for a hundred; and these two objects appear together among the Thirteen Treasures. Altogether the indications are that, whoever this Tyrnoc the Giant was, his cauldron not only possessed this power of discrimination but was also the object of a raid by Arthur's men, and to all intents and purposes was identical with the cauldron of the Head of Annwn.

The Thirteen Treasures of the Isle of Britain. The list of the Thirteen Royal Treasures (*Brenhin Dlyseu*) of the Isle of Britain, though it cannot be found in a manuscript earlier than 1460, is surely composed of elements much older.[141] The *mwys* (platter?)[142] of Gwyddno

---

though the references to cauldrons in medieval Irish and Welsh literature are numerous, is one of them used for this purpose. And it is not difficult, I believe, to see how this gruesome idea arose. That the feasts of Brân, like Manannán's Feast of Age, preserved those who partook from sickness, old age, and decay, seems fairly patent, and it seems natural to infer that since cauldrons provided the boiled meat at such banquets, Brân's cauldron was credited with the virtue of preserving youth and of curing wounds. Now perhaps it was the famous classical legend of Medea's cauldron into which she plunged the aged Aeson and restored his youth, or, more probably, the Irish tradition of the resuscitation of slain warriors by immersion in a well or bath (cf. C. O'Rahilly, *Ireland and Wales* (London, 1924), p. 108; A. H. Krappe, *Balor with the Evil Eye* (New York, 1927), pp. 132 ff.), which has led the author of *Branwen* to attach to the reviving cauldron of Brân this unseemly method of healing. Thus, perhaps, the property of preserving and restoring the health of those who partook of its contents, so suitable to the vessel of the Head of Annwn, where there was neither age nor decay, has been transmogrified into the grotesque faculty of restoring life to the corpses cast into it.

[141] Lists of the Thirteen Treasures have been printed in Edward Jones, *Bardic Museum* (London, 1802), pp. 47 ff.; *Y Brython*, 1860, p. 372; C. Guest, *Mabinogion*, Everyman's Lib., pp. 328 f.; *Y Greal* (London, 1805), p. 188.

[142] Rhys (*Arthurian Legend*, p. 313) points out that the Irish cognate *mias* is used in Matt. xiv. 8 for the charger on which John the Baptist's head was placed. Cúroí Mac Dáiri possessed a cauldron, vat (*dabach*), drinking-horn, and platter (*mias*). *Zts. f. celt. Phil.* iii. 39. Thurneysen, *Irische Helden- und Königsage* (Halle, 1921), p. 445.

Garanhir and the cauldron of Tyrnoc are, as we have seen, found likewise in *Kulhwch ac Olwen*, dated about 1100. The platter (*dysgl*) of Rhydderch and the drinking-horn of Brân are, as Professor Newstead has demonstrated elsewhere,[143] identifiable with the platter or *graal* in Chrétien de Troyes's *Conte del Graal* and with the horn in the land of Brandigan in Chrétien's *Erec*, and thus antedate 1180, to say the least. Only one of the Thirteen Treasures, the ring of Luned, is definitely derived from, and is therefore later than *Iarlles y Ffynnawn*,[144] a tale adapted from a French romance,[145] and probably no older than 1180. Moreover, the cauldron, the platter, and the drinking-horn were almost certainly the magic vessels which supplied the famous banquets of the Head of Annwn. They were probably among the *teyrn dlysseu* (royal treasures), which are mentioned in the description of Annwn in *Pwyll*. And since Annwn, its immortal inhabitants, and its appurtenances must have descended from pagan beliefs, the origin of these vessels of plenty must be sought in a period before the evangelization of Britain. They were once, like Manannán's cup of truth and the cauldron of the Dagda, the possessions of the Celtic gods.

Now though the list of the Thirteen Treasures can claim such a glamorous antiquity for some of the objects, the manuscript versions of the sixteenth century betray inevitable alteration. Names have been corrupted: Ceidio becomes Rudio; *Llen Arthur* (the veil of Arthur) becomes *llen aur* (the veil of gold).[146] Euhemerism is potent. Brân, the old sea-god and presumptive lord of Annwn, becomes 'Brân Galed or Gogledd' (Brân the Niggardly from the North)[147]— a local association with Northumbria, derived from Geoffrey of Monmouth, who represents that region as the heritage of Brennius.[148] A Welsh translator equated Brennius with Brân.[149]

The phrase *Brenhin Dlyseu* (royal treasures), used in some of the lists of the Treasures of the Isle of Britain, may have encouraged the

---

[143] H. Newstead, *Bran the Blessed in Arthurian Romance*, pp. 20, 68, 86 ff.
[144] Evans, *White Book Mabinogion*, col. 237.
[145] But not from Chrétien's *Ivain*. Cf. A. C. L. Brown, in *Romanic Rev.* iii. 143 ff.; Loomis in *Mod. Lang. Notes*, xliii (1928), 215; R. Zenker, *Ivainstudien*, Beiheft, *Zts. f. rom. Phil.* lxx (1921).
[146] MS. Peniarth 77, Nat. Library of Wales, pp. 215, 213.
[147] Prof. Thomas Jones in *Mod. Lang. Rev.*, xxxv (1940), 403 f. supports this translation and shows that two conflicting concepts of Brân's nature existed. On *calet* cf. *Cymmrodor*, xxviii. 192.
[148] *Historia*, ed. A. Griscom, p. 276.
[149] Ibid.

euhemeristic process, for many of the talismans have been dissociated from their divine owners and assigned to various renowned kings of British history. A. C. L. Brown observed the same phenomenon in Irish legend:[150] 'The Sagas bear witness that these talismans of the gods had been transferred to the historical or supposedly historical heroes: Cuchulinn, Cormac, Crimthann, Finn, and the like.' The platter (*dysgl*) of plenty and the flaming sword have become the possessions of Rhydderch Hael, king of the Britons of Strathclyde, who fought at the battle of Arderydd near Carlisle about 575.[151] The magic chess-board, which seems to be the original of the chess-board in the Grail castle in *Perlesvaus*, has been assigned to Gwenddoleu ap Ceidio, the British opponent of Rhydderch; the magic whetstone to Tudwal Tudclud, the father of Rhydderch; the horse-collar to Clydno Eiddin, a contemporary of Rhydderch mentioned in the *Gododdin*.[152] Still another treasure, the chariot or chair, has been allotted to Morgan Mwynvawr, king of Glamorgan, who died in 972.[153]

The introduction to the list of the regalia as printed by Edward Jones in 1802 from manuscript sources offers other matters of interest in connexion with *Preiddeu Annwn*. It may be translated:[154]

Here are the Thirteen Treasures of the Royal Treasures of the Isle of Britain. They were kept in Caerleon on Usk, and went with Myrddin ap Morfran to the Glass House in Enlli [Bardsey Island]. But some authors write that Taliesin, chief of bards, obtained them.

First, let us note that we seem to have here an echo of the tradition which connects Taliesin with Annwn (Kaer Siddi) in the two Welsh poems (Nos. XXX and XIV) we have been discussing, in *Vita Merlini* with the Insula Pomorum (Avalon), in *Branwen* with Gwales. In *Preiddeu Annwn* the bard includes himself among those who accompanied Arthur to Annwn; in the other poem he refers to his seat in Kaer Siddi. In *Vita Merlini* he accompanied the wounded Arthur to the joyous isle. In *Branwen* he was one of the ageless feasters on Grassholm. The traditions are not wholly consistent—what Welsh traditions are?—yet they accord in linking Taliesin with

[150] *Mod. Phil.* xxii (1924), 113.
[151] Geoffrey of Monmouth, *Vita Merlini*, ed. Parry, pp. 15-19; Skene, *Four Ancient Books*, i. 66, 174; Nennius, *Historia Brittonum*, ed. Lot, pp. 75 f.
[152] *Canu Aneirin*, ed. I. Williams (Cardiff, 1938), pp. xxxviii, xl, 17, l. 416.
[153] Loth, *Mabinogion*², ii. 311, n. 1.
[154] Jones, *Bardic Museum*, p. 47; Rhys, *Arthurian Legend*, p. 354; *Lectures on the Origin*, p. 155.

Annwn, conceived as a joyous island abode, or with its treasures. It is further to be remarked that in this introduction to the list Annwn seems to be localized on still another island near the Welsh coast, Bardsey. Most interesting is the fact that the treasures are supposed to have been taken to 'the Glass House' in Bardsey, where, according to another version, they are still. As we shall have occasion to observe in connexion with stanza 4, a structure of glass was certainly one of the persistent elements in the Welsh concept of the Other World, appearing in many forms, and this seems to be one of them.

The importance of the list of the Thirteen Treasures of the Isle of Britain should not be minimized by students of Welsh and Arthurian legend merely because our earliest manuscript authority is of the fifteenth century.

Llwch Lleminawc. Concerning this warrior of Arthur's, who brandished a sword in the attack on Annwn, there is a remarkable muddle as to his name. In one line he appears as Llwch Lleawc, in the next as Lleminawc. The corresponding figure in *Kulhwch* is Llenlleawc the Irishman.[155] The same man seems to be listed among Arthur's warriors in *Kulhwch* twice as Llenlleawc, once as Llwch Llawwynnyawc, once as Lloch Llawwynnyawc,[156] and in the *Black Book of Carmarthen* under the more archaic form Lluch Llauynnauc.[157] This is not a unique case: in two versions of one triad we find the same person called Lludd Llurugawc and Llyr Lluyddawc. What are we to make of all this confusion? what of the strange fact that though Llenlleawc was on Arthur's side in the struggle with Diwrnach the Irishman, he was himself Irish, *Gwyddel*? The puzzle may be explained by the fact that the person and the name were borrowed from some foreign people, probably from the Irish since Llenlleawc was of that race and since the Welsh are known to have borrowed a few figures famed in Irish saga and enrolled them among Arthur's warriors, e.g. Manawidan ab Llŷr in the *Black Book of Carmarthen*[158] and Cnychwr mab Nes, Cubert mab Daere, Fercos mab Poch, Lluber Beuthach, Corvil Bervach, and Sgilti in *Kulhwch*.[159]

[155] Cf. *supra*, p. 153, n. 12.
[156] Evans, *White Book Mabinogion*, cols. 461, 464, 466.
[157] Skene, *Four Ancient Books*, ii. 51; Malory, *Morte d'Arthur*, Everyman's Lib. I. xix; J. G. Evans, *Facsimile of Black Book of Carmarthen* (Oxford, 1888), f. 47ᵛ.
[158] Ibid.
[159] *Rev. Celt.*, xli. 489; C. O'Rahilly, *Ireland and Wales*, pp. 114 f. Sgilti Ysgawndroed, 'the Nimble-footed', is of course the swift Fenian hero, Caeilte.

Now it is fairly obvious that the person with whom we are concerned had a nomen Llwch and a cognomen variously given as Lleminawc, Llenlleawc, and Llawwynnawc. Can it be accident that one of the great figures of Irish legend, one who had a powerful influence on the mabinogi of *Math*, as Professor Gruffydd has demonstrated,[160] was Lugh, to whose name, as then pronounced, Llwch was the closest possible approximation, and who had an epithet which is given in *Cath Maige Tured* as Lonnbémnech[161] and in *Oided Chloinne Tuirenn* as Loinnbhéimionach?[162] This cognomen, meaning 'of the mighty blows', though it is not common, evidently is traditional, and the tradition seems to extend back at least to the eleventh century, to which Flower assigned the extant redaction of *Cath Maige Tured*.[163] The Welsh seem to have found Lonnbémnech difficult or meaningless, and made substitutions. One was Llyminawc, which occurs as a proper name in the *Book of Taliesin*, poem XLVII, and which is also an obsolete adjective meaning 'very keen, sharp, or intense', or 'leaping' (Owen's *Dictionary*, 1803), cognate with Irish *leimnech*. Another substitution, Llawwynnawc, meaning 'of the windy (?) hand', may be plausibly attributed to the influence of Lugh's other epithet Lamhfada, 'long-hand'. I, for one, cannot ascribe to coincidence the similarity between the long-handed Lug Lonnbémnech and the strangely handed Llwch Lleminawc. And though direct parallels between the two personages are impossible because no stories of the Welsh warrior remain to us except Lleminawc-Llenlleawc's brandishing of the sword, yet almost every other consideration favours the identification. The legend of Lugh has profoundly influenced the mabinogi of *Math* and left its imprint on *Kulhwch*.[164] It has also furnished some of the most striking features of the opening of the *Queste del Saint Graal*[165] and must have passed through Welsh channels like the other Irish materials of Arthurian romance. Since, moreover, Llwch was evidently prominent among Arthur's warriors in Welsh tradition, it is natural to look for his counterpart in the French texts. Now

---

[160] W. J. Gruffydd, *Math Vab Mathonwy*.
[161] *Rev. Celt.*, xii (1891), 127. It occurs in Brit. Mus., MS. Harley 5280, f. 69a, a MS. of first half of sixteenth century.
[162] E. Hull, *Cuchullin Saga*, pp. lvi f.
[163] R. Flower, *Cat. of Irish MSS. in Brit. Mus.* ii (London, 1926), 319. Prof. Vernam Hull would date it still earlier, *Zts. f. Celt. Phil.* xviii. 80, 89.
[164] Cf. *supra*, n. 160, and C. O'Rahilly, *Ireland and Wales*, pp. 117–19.
[165] Cf. *supra*, pp. 24–26. For influence on Chrétien's *Charrette*, cf. M. F. Speyer in *Romanic Rev.* xxviii (1937), 195 ff.

'The Spoils of Annwn': an Early Welsh Poem

llwch as a common noun means 'lake', and in Llwch Llawwynnawc we have the original of Arthur's great knight, Lancelot of the Lake, the name being evidently assimilated to the French name Lancelin.[166] It is a remarkable corroboration of Lancelot's descent from Lugh or Luch Lamhfada through Lluch Llauynnauc that there are eight parallels between the Arthurian and the Irish hero.[167] We have in the *Huth Merlin* a Lancer, 'chevalier d'Irlande', whose relation to Balaain corresponds closely to that of Lancelot to Malory's hero Beaumains.[168] Moreover, the story of Arthur's war with Lancelot parallels in striking points his wars with Lucius Hiberus and King Loth,[169] in whose names it is hard not to discover latinizations of the Welsh elements Llwch and Gwyddel (= Hibernus)[170] and a development of the variant Welsh form Lloch.[171] The best reading of vs. 1737 in Chrétien's *Erec* confirms this connexion up to the hilt by presenting us with a 'Loz li irois', Loth the Irishman.

To present all the proofs for these onomastic equations would tire the reader and shed little light on *Preiddeu Annwn*. Suffice it to say that two other famous names in Irish saga, Cúchulainn (> Guiglain)[172] and Bláthnat (i.e. 'Little Flower', > Florie)[173] have descended into French romance; that the trisyllabic common noun *bachlach*, consistently applied to the challenger in *Fled Bricrend*, reappears as the name of the challenger to the Beheading Test in *Gawain and the Green Knight*, Bercilak;[174] and that Lugh's epithet Lamhfada also turns up in the name Laquis or Laquin (Lac+

---

[166] Lancelin is recorded in Brittany as early as 1069. Cf. H. Morice, *Mémoires pour Servir de Preuves à l'Histoire Ecclésiastique et Civile de Bretagne* (Paris, 1742–6), i. 432. Zimmer, Lot, and Bruce all recognize the influence of Lancelin. Cf. *Zts. f. Franz. Spr. u. Lit.*, xiii (1891), 43 ff.; *Romania*, xxv. 12; J. D. Bruce, *Evolution of Arthurian Romance* (Baltimore, 1923), i. 193.

[167] Ulrich von Zatzikhoven, *Lanzelet*, trans. Webster, pp. 15–18.

[168] *Merlin*, ed. G. Paris, J. Ulrich (Paris, 1886), i. 223, n. 1, 225 f., 230. On the original identity of Balaain and Beaumains cf. *PMLA*, liv (1939), 656 ff.; Loomis' *Celtic Myth*, pp. 250–2, 348.

[169] Loomis, *Arthurian Tradition*, pp. 188 f. For confusion of Gales and Gaule, cf. Sommer, *Vulgate Version*, i. 293, n. 10. In a MS. of Wace's *Brut* (Bib. Nat., fr. 375, f. 219r) 'Franche' and 'Cambrie' are both equated with Gales.

[170] Though Hiberus seems to be the best authenticated form, the late Prof. Hammer kindly informed me that two MSS., Lincoln Cathedral, No. 98, f. 91v, and Camb. Univ. Lib., Mm. 5. 29, f. 93r, give Hibernius.

[171] Loth, in *Rev. Celt.* xvi (1897), 84; E. T. Griffiths, *Chantari di Lancelotto* (Oxford, 1924), p. 186.

[172] *PMLA*, xlviii (1933), 1018–21.

[173] Loomis, *Celtic Myth*, pp. 7, 11–15, 22, 228. *PMLA*, xlviii. 1005, 1015–21, 1032.

[174] Loomis, *Arthurian Tradition*, pp. 418–20; A. Buchanan in *PMLA*, xlvii (1932), 316 f.; xlviii. 1024–6.

diminutive termination -*in*) de Lampadaiz.[175] For fuller discussion of these matters the reader should consult articles cited in footnotes.

Kaer Veddwit, the Fortress of Carousal. Veddwit, though not elsewhere recorded, probably meant, according to Rhys,[176] 'revelry, carousal', and probably contains the same root as *medd* (mead), *meddwi* (to get drunk). The initial *v* represents mutation of *m* according to the rule that after a noun in the feminine singular a following genitive is lenated when it is equivalent to an adjective.[177] This interpretation is of course borne out by the line in the next stanza, 'Bright wine was their liquor before their retinue', and by the references in *Pwyll, Buchedd Collen*, and *Branwen*, already quoted, to the lavish potations in Annwn and its euhemerized counterpart, Gwales. It accords, moreover, with the Irish island paradise as described in *Imram Maíledúin* and *Tochmarc Étaíne*: in the former we read of the inhabitants,[178] 'beautiful, numerous, wearing richly dight garments, and feasting with golden vessels in their hands', and of their ale music; in the latter saga Midir sings:[179] 'Though choice you deem the ale of Inis Fáil [Ireland], more intoxicating is the ale of Tír Már. . . . Warm streams flow through the land, the choice of mead and wine.' Perhaps the most constant feature of the pagan Other World as conceived by the Celts (and by other peoples) was the quality and the quantity of the beverages.

The Strong Door. The literal meaning of *ynys pybyrdor* is clear, 'the island of the strong (*pybyr*) door', and Stephens and A. C. L. Brown so translated the words.[180] But Brown and Rhys both were tempted by descriptions of revolving castles to think of this door as an active or quick door, a revolving barrier.[181] It seems wiser to seek a less mobile portal, and we find it in the island fortress of the Queen of Maidenland, as described by Ulrich von Zatzikhoven about 1200.[182] The Queen has been identified in the chapter on Morgain la Fée as the celebrated enchantress; her island has properties which equate it with Avalon; and the gate or door (*porte*) of the wall was a hard diamond. Considering the other correspondences with

---

[175] *Romania*, liv (1928), 518; lxiii (1937), 388.
[176] Rhys, *Arthurian Legend*, p. 301.
[177] J. Strachan, *Introduction to Early Welsh* (Manchester, 1909), p. 12.
[178] K. Meyer, A. Nutt, *Voyage of Bran* (London, 1895), i. 169.
[179] *Ériu*, xii (1938), 181.
[180] T. Stephens, *Literature of the Kymry* (1876), p. 185; *Studies and Notes in Phil. and Lit.*, viii (1903), 78.
[181] Ibid., p. 79. Rhys, *Arthurian Legend*, p. 302.
[182] *Lanzelet*, trans. K. G. T. Webster, pp. 28, 160.

Arthurian tradition, we may safely take this door of diamond to be the strong door of our poem.

The Crepuscular Light. As was pointed out in note 37 above, the rendering of *echwyd amuchyd kymyscetor* is far from certain, Sir Ifor Williams believing that *echwyd* cannot be the word for 'noonday'. Other experts admit the possibility, however, and if *muchyd* meaning 'jet' can be interpreted as 'jet-blackness', then the line would refer to the mingling of strong light and deep darkness in a sort of twilight. This dim illumination is characteristic of the subterranean Other World of the dwarfs as described by Giraldus and Walter Map in passages quoted in the chapter on King Arthur and the Antipodes.[183] Giraldus describes a 'terram pulcherrimam . . . obscuram tamen et aperto solari lumine non illustratam'. Map tells how King Herla passed through a dark tunnel 'in lumine quod non videbatur solis aut lune sed lampadarum multarum' to the homes of the pygmies. Of course, to no one who has followed the discussion thus far will it seem an objection that the island paradise and the subterranean lamp-lighted region are not easy for us to reconcile imaginatively. Nothing is more manifest than that the Celts blended such incongruous pictures, not only without effort but even with delight.

Kaer Rigor. In *PMLA*, lvi. 917-25, I offered two alternative emendations of Rigor either one of which seemed to make sense and to accord with Welsh tradition, namely, *Kaer Rigorr*, the Fortress of the King Dwarf, and *Kaer Rigorn*, the Fortress of the Royal Horn. But all the authorities assure me that both are excluded by the prevailing rhyme in *-ôr*, and I can only defer to their judgement. Sir Ifor Williams proposed that *Rigor* is the mutated form of *Grigor*, 'Gregory', but, though there is a village on the Dingle Peninsula called Castle Gregory, it meets none of the requirements.

The Fortress of Glass and the Silent Sentinel. As Rhys pointed out over fifty years ago, stanza IV has a clear analogue in the tradition recorded by the South-Welsh priest Nennius in his *Historia Britonum* (*c.* 826). Telling the story of the colonization of Ireland, he relates:[184]

Postea venerunt tres filii militis Hispaniae cum triginta ciulis [ships] apud illos et cum triginta conjugibus in unaquaque ciula, et manserunt ibi per spatium unius anni. Et postea conspiciunt turrim vitream in medio mare, et homines conspiciebant super turrim et quaerebant

---
[183] Cf. *supra*, pp. 65 f., 73.
[184] Ed. F. Lot, *Bibl. de l'École des Hautes Études*, vol. cclxxiii (Paris, 1934), p. 156.

loqui ad illos et numquam respondebant. Et ipsi uno anno ad oppugnationem turris properaverunt cum omnibus ciulis suis et cum omnibus mulieribus, excepta una ciula quae confracta est naufragio, in qua erant viri triginta totidemque mulieres. Et aliae naves navigaverunt ad expugnandam turrim, et dum omnes descenderant litore quod erat circa turrim, operuit illos mare et demersi sunt et non evasit unus ex illis. Et de familia illius ciulae quae relicta est propter fractionem, tota Hibernia impleta est usque ad hodiernam diem.

We have to do in these lines with a very ancient tradition concerning a raid by warriors in ships upon an island fortress of glass, the watchmen who would not reply, and the fatal ending of the attack for all but one shipload. It is obviously the same story as that referred to in *Preiddeu Annwn*. In the *Historia Britonum* the tradition is fitted into the legendary colonization of Ireland, and the sole survivors of the attack on the glass tower are equated with the ancestors of the Irish, the so-called 'Milesians'.[185] In *Preiddeu Annwn* the same tradition is identified with Arthur's famous attack on Annwn. Though we have already been obliged to surmise the origin of much of the material in the poem in pagan times, here is something more: conclusive evidence that one tradition at least goes well back to the year 800.

This tradition of a fortress or palace of glass[186] on an island seems to be very well known to the Welsh and even to the Arthurian romancers who used Welsh material transmitted by Breton *conteurs*. Kaer Wydyr is probably the Ty Wydyr, or 'Glass House', on the isle of Bardsey, to which, as we have seen, Taliesin or Merddin went taking the Thirteen Treasures of the Isle of Britain. This Otherworld abode is probably to be identified with the Ynis Gutrin, Insula Vitrea, mentioned by Caradoc of Lancarvan in his *Vita Gildae* about 1125,[187] and by a false etymology identified with Glastigberi, modern Glastonbury. Its original mythical nature is clearly preserved by Chrétien de Troyes in *Erec*,[188] when he refers to Maheloas as 'the lord of the Isle of Glass; in that isle one hears no thunder, nor does lightning fall there nor tempest [rage]; no toad

---

[185] Cf. *Perlesvaus*, ed. Nitze, ii. 152 f.
[186] On various medieval traditions of buildings of glass cf. references furnished by Patch in *PMLA*, xxxiii (1918), 610 n.; by L. A. Paton, *Studies in Fairy Mythology*, p. 40 n. 2; by J. D. Bruce, *Evolution of Arthurian Romance*, i. 200, n. 14.
[187] *Perlesvaus*, ed. Nitze, ii. 58. Cymmrodorion Record Series, ii (London, 1901), p. 410. On date cf. Tatlock in *Speculum*, xiii (1938), 139–52.
[188] Ed. W. Foerster (1890), ll. 1946 ff.

or serpent abides there, and it is neither too hot nor wintry'. And since Maheloas is generally conceded to be identical with Meleagant in Chrétien's *Chevalier de la Charrette*, the land of Goirre, of which Meleagant is lord (together with his father) and which can be approached only by bridges over or under water, is doubtless also the Isle de Voirre, disguised by the scribal substitution of *g* for *v*. A striking confirmation of this hypothesis is the fact that the fifteenth-century prose version of *Erec* makes precisely this same substitution and gives *isle de guerre* instead of *isle de voirre*.[189]

The motif of the silent inhabitants of the Other World island occurs not only in *Perlesvaus*, as we shall presently see, but also in *Imram Brain* and *Historia Meriadoci*, in both of which it is combined with that of mocking laughter.[190]

Kaer Goludd, the Fortress of Frustration. The meaning of *golud* is among the most doubtful points in the translation. Though Rhys suggested that it represented the modern *golud* (riches),[191] and that meaning would fit in pat with the constant emphasis on the wealth of Annwn, yet Professor Lloyd-Jones offers strong objection on the ground that the final consonant must have been the voiced spirant dental represented in modern Welsh by *dd* to rime with *-ur*, whereas the Middle Welsh form of the word for 'riches', *golut*, would not rime with *-ur*. He adds:

If *goludd* fails to show initial mutation, there is the noun and verb *goludd*, 'frustration, hindrance, delay'. . . . I am not suggesting that this explains *kaer goludd*, but from the point of view of form and rhyme it is far better than *golut (golud)*, which seems to me impossible on these grounds.

Though the interpretation of *goludd* as 'frustration' must be regarded with due caution, nevertheless it does make some sense. Kaer Siddi is the fortress where all but the stoutest of heroes are frustrated in their efforts to carry off its treasures. Kaer Wydyr, we have seen, is the tower of glass where all the besiegers were swallowed by the sea, and may be identified, as we shall see later, with the island in *Historia Meriadoci* called the 'terra de qua nemo revertitur' because all who approached it were swallowed up by

---

[189] Ibid., p. 264, l. 36.
[190] *Perlesvaus*, ed. Nitze, ii. 275; Cross, Slover, *Ancient Irish Tales*, pp. 594 f.; *Historia Meriadoci*, ed. J. D. Bruce (Baltimore, 1913), pp. xxxiii, 31; A. C. L. Brown in *Romanic Rev.* iii (1912), 159.
[191] Rhys, *Arthurian Legend*, p. 301.

the surrounding marsh, and with the water-girdled land of Goirre, in Chrétien's *Chevalier de la Charrette*, 'don nus estranges ne retorne'. Despite all legitimate doubts as to the meaning of *goludd*, Annwn might aptly be named the Fortress of Frustration.

The Isle of the Ageless Elders in 'Perlesvaus'. A startlingly clear reflection of many of the Otherworld features alluded to in *Preiddeu Annwn* and in Taliesin poem XIV is to be seen in an island described in the French romance of *Perlesvaus* (1200–30).[192] The features in question may be enumerated as follows: (1) A fortress on an island. (2) A four-cornered fortress (Kaer Pedryvan). (3) A prisoner who 'dolefully chanted'. (4) Inhabitants who drank wine before their retinue. (5) A warrior in a glass fortress with whom it was hard to converse. (6) Ageless inhabitants. (7) A spring.

The French text relates the following adventure of the hero Perlesvaus, who is of course more familiar under the name Perceval.[193]

> The ship sped on by day and by night as it pleased God, till they saw a castle on an island of the sea.... They approached the castle and heard four horns sound at the four corners of the walls.... They issued from the ship, and entered the castle on the sea side, and there were the fairest halls and the fairest houses that anyone ever saw. He looks beneath a very fair tree, ... and sees the fairest fountain, ... and it was all surrounded by rich pillars of gold.... Above [emend *desouz* to *desor*] this fountain two men were sitting, whiter of hair and of beard than is new-fallen snow, and they seemed young of visage. As soon as they see Perlesvaus, they rise to meet him. They bow and adore the shield which he bore at his neck.... 'Sir', say they, 'marvel not at what we do, for we knew well the knight who bore the shield before you [Joseph of Arimathea]. We saw him many times before God was crucified.'... Perlesvaus looks beyond the fountain and sees in a very fair place a cask (*tonel*) made as if it were all of glass, and it was so large that there was within a knight all armed. He looks into it and sees that he is fully alive, but the knight would not reply at all.... They lead him into a great hall.... 'Sir', say the two masters to Perlesvaus, 'this rich house which you see is a royal hall.'... He looks around and sees the richest tables of gold and ivory that he had ever seen. One of the masters sounds a bell thrice, and thirty-three men came into the hall, ... and they all seemed to be thirty-two years old.... Then they went to wash at a rich laver of gold, and then went to sit at the tables.

[192] On date cf. *Perlesvaus*, ed. Nitze, ii. 73–89; *Romanic Rev.* xxxvii (1937), 351 f. For previous discussions of these resemblances cf. Loomis, *Celtic Myth*, pp. 201–4; *Speculum*, viii (1933), 428 f.; *Perlesvaus*, ed. Nitze, ii. 151–5.
[193] *Perlesvaus*, i, ll. 9543–603.

The masters caused Perlesvaus to sit at the highest table by himself. In that place they were served in a right glorious and holy manner.... Perlesvaus looks above him and sees a golden chain descending, loaded with right sweet precious stones, and a crown was in the middle. The chain descended with great precision, and it was held by nothing save the will of Our Lord. As soon as the masters saw it lowered, they opened a great wide pit in the midst of the hall, ... There issued from it the loudest and the most dolorous cries that anyone ever heard.

Here in this one scene from a French romance most of the seven features of Annwn just enumerated are easily recognizable. The prisoner who 'dolefully chanted' must be one of those whose dolorous cries were heard issuing from the pit. The warrior in a glass tower with whom it was hard to converse must be the knight in the glass cask who would not reply to Perlesvaus's efforts at conversation; for nothing could be easier than the confusion of *torele* (little tower) and *tonel* (cask). The longevity of the inhabitants is attested by the youthful faces of the white-haired masters and by the fact that they were living before the Crucifixion.

Further to clinch the matter we discover in the mabinogi of *Manawydan* a description of a magic *kaer* (tentatively identified by Anwyl with Kaer Siddi),[194] which appeared suddenly where none had been seen before and which, though it shows little correspondence to *Preiddeu Annwn*, curiously rounds out the Welsh features in the island castle of *Perlesvaus*. For Pryderi, entering, found it empty of living thing, but 'he saw as it were about the middle of the floor of the castle a well, and marble work around it, and on the edge of the well a golden bowl above a slab of marble, and chains ascending to the sky, and he could see no end to them'.[195] Though there may be some doubt about the identity of this marble-bordered spring with the fairest fountain, surrounded by rich pillars of gold, or of the golden bowl with the laver of gold, yet there can be little doubt that the strange chains with no visible support, descending from the sky, found in both stories, represent a common tradition. And if there be any doubt of its Celticity, let us turn to a legend of the clerics of St. Columba.[196] They arrived at an island

---

[194] *Zts. f. Celt. Phil.* ii (1899), 130.

[195] Evans, *White Book Mabinogion*, col. 70. The inferior Red Book text adds that the chains were attached to the bowl.

[196] M. O'Donnell, *Life of Columcille*, ed. A. O'Kelleher, G. Schoepperle (Urbana, Ill., 1918), p. 399. The cowl was still preserved at Kilmacrenan in Donegal in O'Donnell's day. Ibid., p. xl, n. 3; p. 403.

with a fair house in the middle and were courteously welcomed. 'Whilst they were there, a beautiful golden cowl was let down upon the floor of that royal hall. And not one of the folk of the house took it up.... They were richly served and had great cheer that night, and they were given well-brewed ale, so that they were drunken and merry.' The golden cowl has taken the place of the golden crown, but the bibulous behaviour of these clerics makes it certain that once more we are really dealing with the pagan Other World, some such island as that seen by Máeldúin, whose inhabitants, we remember, wearing 'richly dight' garments, feasted with golden vessels in their hands and trolled out their ale-songs across the waters.

The passage in *Perlesvaus* is thus proved to contain, not only the seven features of the Welsh Other World mentioned in *Preiddeu Annwn*, but also the chains descending from above and probably the golden bowl of the enchanted castle in *Manawydan*. The antiquity of some of these elements may be guessed when we realize that the feature of the warrior in the *tonel* of glass can be traced back to Nennius, A.D. 826 at latest.

The pagan atmosphere has been sanctified with conscience and taste, just as the pagan Irish *imrama*, A. C. L. Brown has shown, were elaborately ecclesiasticized.[197] None the less, the visit of Perlesvaus to the island of the ageless elders offers, strangely enough, one of the fullest and most vivid pictures of the Welsh Other World we possess, and enables us to understand and visualize some of the obscurer phrases in *Preiddeu Annwn*.

Gweir and Gohars. The continuation of the story in *Perlesvaus* gives us our best and surest clues as to the presence of Gweir in Kaer Siddi. Immediately after the reference to the dolorous cries issuing from the pit uncovered in the hall of the ageless elders, we read:[198]

Perlesvaus hears this dole and marvels much what it can mean.... The masters cover again the pit, which was right hideous to behold, and the voices piteous which issued from it. The worthy men rose from the tables when they had eaten, and rendered thanks right sweetly to Our Lord. [They then explain to Perlesvaus the chain, the crown, and the cries emanating from the prisoners in the pit.] 'You shall wear the crown on your head as soon as you return, and shall sit in the chair, and you shall be king of an island which is near and right abundant in

---

[197] *Mod. Phil.*, xiv (1916), 385 ff.
[198] *Perlesvaus*, ed. Nitze, i, ll. 9605–34.

all good things. . . . But beware, when you will be king, that the isle is well provided, for if you do not take heed, you shall be placed in the Isle of Poverty, whence proceeded the cries you heard a while ago in this hall. . . . For those who have been kings of the Plenteous Isle and who have not behaved well are among those folk in the isle destitute of all wealth whom you heard.'

We thus learn that the lamentations heard by Perlesvaus are those of former rulers of a plenteous isle near by who have been unworthy of their office, and negligent in seeing that the land was abundant in good things. Since Gweir, the wailing prisoner in Kaer Siddi, is presumably one of the prisoners whose cries are heard in the hall of the elders, we may tentatively infer that Gweir's captivity was due to his misrule of a plenteous island near by. At the same time, we cannot help observing that, whereas it would seem from the earlier passage that the prisoners were confined in a pit beneath the hall, yet the passage just quoted implies that they were in a third island, which was destitute of all wealth. Evidently the author is struggling with a confused tradition as to the whereabouts of the prisoner kings.

Nevertheless, despite a certain confusion, the author within a few pages introduces us to a Gohars, king of a plenteous isle near by, who for his sins is seized by Perlesvaus and chained securely on a rocky islet, and left there to mourn his fate. Since Gohars represents almost exactly what the French would have made of Gweir (the *h* being silent and the *s* being simply the nominative termination), this coincidence in names can hardly be fortuitous. After Perlesvaus had left the isle of the ageless elders and found adventure in two other islands, he sailed to an isle of plenty.[199] He learned that the king was an evil ruler, and that the land of plenty belonged to him. Perlesvaus made him captive, brought him to a solitary rock in the sea, which may legitimately be called an isle destitute of all wealth; there Gohars was heavily chained, like Gweir, and left 'in great dole on the rock, and never after did he drink or eat there'.[200] Of course, it may be said that the prison of Gweir was *kyweir*, which seems to mean 'perfect, richly equipped', and the prison of Gohars was just the opposite; but we have already called attention to the confusion in *Perlesvaus* as to where the wicked kings of the plenteous isle were confined. One tradition seems to have placed them in the pit in the very midst of the richest and

[199] Ibid., l. 9763.   [200] Ibid., ll. 9809 f.

fairest hall that Perlesvaus had ever seen, adorned with silken hangings. And it is this tradition which is reflected in *Preiddeu Annwn*. There seems to be no adequate reason for denying the identity of Gweir and Gohars or for doubting the traditional basis for the implication that his imprisonment was a punishment for his failure to keep a rich land well supplied with good things.

Welsh literature furnishes a striking corroboration of this view. We have already observed that in the mabinogi of *Manawydan* Pryderi entered an enchanted *kaer*, saw there the rich fountain, the golden bowl, and the chain descending from the sky, which Perlesvaus also saw in the isle of the ageless elders. We must now proceed to observe that in this *kaer* Pryderi became a prisoner, just as it was threatened that Perlesvaus might become a prisoner if he failed, as king of a plenteous land, to keep it supplied with good things. It is, therefore, somewhat startling to observe that before Pryderi's imprisonment he, as prince of Dyfed, had ruled his realm prosperously and was beloved by his people, and that as he and his mother and stepfather made the circuit of the land, 'they had never seen a country better inhabited than it, nor a better hunting ground, nor one more abundant in honey and fish'.[201] Shortly afterward Pryderi, after a feast at his capital at Arberth, rashly took his seat on the *gorsedd* of Arberth,[202] a sort of throne-like mound, which had the property that anyone who sat on it received wounds or saw a wonder.[203] No sooner had he done so than there was a roar and a mist, and when the mist had cleared, they looked in the direction where they had seen the flocks and the cattle and the dwellings, and all had disappeared. The palace, though standing, was empty of people, and in the mead-cellar and the kitchen there was desolation.

I venture to assert that one could not find a clearer picture than this in *Manawydan* of a *terre plenteurose* which has ceased to be *bien garnie* through the rash act of its ruler. It cannot be mere coincidence that Pryderi is later made captive in an enchanted *kaer* which betrays on the one hand its identity with the Welsh Annwn, and on the other its identity with the castle in *Perlesvaus* where were heard the cries of those kings of a plenteous isle who had allowed it to sink into poverty.

Of course, on certain points the surviving Welsh traditions do

[201] *Pedeir Keinc*, ed. I. Williams, pp. 27, 51.
[202] Ibid., p. 51. [203] Ibid., p. 9.

'The Spoils of Annwn': an Early Welsh Poem 173

not harmonize with those found in *Perlesvaus*; in *Manawydan*, for example, the faëry *kaer* appears, and then vanishes, on the mainland of Dyfed, whereas its counterpart in the French romance is on an island; several circumstances of Pryderi's captivity do not correspond to those of Gohars's. But the former difference is precisely what we have learned to expect in the accounts of Annwn, and the latter differences are the inevitable result of the highly contaminated state of the *Four Branches*. And there remains another striking parallel between the story of Pryderi in *Manawydan* and that of Perceval in Arthurian romance which proves their common origin. For Pryderi's rash act of sitting on the *gorsedd* of Arberth after a royal feast, and the consequent roar, mist, and the desolating enchantment of Dyfed remind us of an episode in the *Didot Perceval*.[204] The youthful Perceval came to the royal festival of Pentecost, and boldly asked to sit in the siege perilous of the Round Table. No sooner had he done so than the seat cried with such anguish that it seemed as if all the world would fall into the abyss; and from the cry which the earth uttered, there issued a great darkness so that they could not see more than a league. A voice then announced that the enchantments of Britain had begun, and that the Fisher King, Bron, had fallen into a great malady. From other French romances we know that this malady of the Fisher King was directly associated with the wasting of the land.[205] Likewise, from the romances we learn that the Fisher King was Perceval's uncle,[206] while the Welsh text informs us that Pryderi's mother wedded Manawydan and thus became the sister-in-law of Brân.[207] It is evident that the French romances of Perceval and the Fisher King represent cognate[208] traditions with those found in *Manawydan*, *Branwen*, and *Preiddeu Annwn*. And it is equally obvious that Perceval has inherited the role of Pryderi, while the Fisher King has inherited that of Brân.

Moreover, Professor Gruffydd long since, with his brilliant intuition, perceived that *in a sense* Pryderi and Gweir were identical figures and much the same story of the captivity of one in Annwn was likely to be told of the other.[209] This partial identity of the

[204] Ed. Roach, pp. 143–50.
[205] Loomis, *Arthurian Tradition*, pp. 389–91.
[206] *Peredur*, Wolfram's *Parzival*, *Perlesvaus*, Manessier.
[207] *Pedeir Keinc*, p. 50.
[208] I say 'cognate' because manifestly the Welsh texts are somewhat remote from the oral traditions from which they and the Breton *conteurs* ultimately drew.
[209] *Revue Celt.* xxxiii (1912), 452 ff.

two did not prevent their co-existing side by side as separate characters. Thus arose one source of confusion. Another source of complication was the fact that both Pryderi and Gweir were, on the one hand, youthful heroes with whom the reader was supposed to sympathize, and, on the other, princes responsible for the desolation of their lands, and therefore subject to severe condemnation. Thus it came about that Perceval in the *Didot Perceval* and elsewhere is subjected to severe condemnation, even though he is the romantic hero;[210] thus it happened that Gohars became a villain. Still further confusion arose from the fact that Gweir's name seems to have been used interchangeably with Gwri and Gware and Gwrvan; so that whereas in *Kulhwch* Llwch Llawwynnawc has two sons named Gweir, his French counterpart Loth has sons named Guirres, Gaheres, and (by metathesis) Agravain.

'Sone de Nausay' and the 'Historia Meriadoci'. Quite as remarkable, though not as complete as in *Perlesvaus*, are the connexions between the island palace of Annwn as conceived by the Welsh and three island palaces—two described in *Sone de Nausay*,[211] a French poem of the latter part of the thirteenth century, and one in the *Historia Meriadoci*, a Latin prose romance of the second quarter of the same century. The first island in *Sone* is called Galoche, and, as Bruce detected,[212] the name is simply a corruption of the feminine adjectival form *galesche* (Welsh). On it is a castle with four towers, presumably at the four corners, and a central tower. Three streams issuing from rocks meet at the castle. As in *Perlesvaus* the island is inhabited by a religious community, who welcome the hero and provide a lavish feast. 'They had an abundance to eat; so much was brought them that it might prove a hardship to those who served them with food.' Much is made of the relics preserved in this island: (1) the *greal* (platter); (2) the bleeding *fiers* (spear-head); (3) the *cors* (body) of the long-lived Fisher King, ruler of Lorgres (England), who, from a malady in his reins, found his only diversion in fishing from a boat; (4) the sword of the same king.

---

[210] On inconsistency of characterization in the Matter of Britain cf. Newstead, *Bran the Blessed in Arthurian Romance*, p. 149 and n. 10; T. Jones in *Mod. Lang. Rev.* xxxv. 403 f.; A. B. Hopkins, *Influence of Wace on the Arthurian Romances of Crestien de Troies* (1913), pp. 80–102.

[211] Loomis, *Celtic Myth*, pp. 206 ff.; *Sone de Nausay*, ed. M. Goldschmidt (Stuttgart, 1899), ll. 4339 ff., 17017 ff. See above, pp. 53 ff.

[212] Bruce, *Evolution of Arthurian Romance*, i. 350, n. 16.

In view of the certainty that *Perlesvaus* has derived much from Wales, it is impossible to resist the impression that we have here another Celtic survival. For not only are there correspondences with *Perlesvaus*, but there are also features, absent from *Perlesvaus*, but clearly related to Welsh tradition. The island is recognized as Welsh; it contains springs; it contains a four-cornered castle; it is the scene of lavish feasting. Moreover, three of the four relics seem identifiable with three of the Thirteen Treasures. The Grail can be identified on many counts with the Platter of Rhydderch, which produced whatever food one desired.[213] The *cors* of the Fisher King has been confused with the horn of Brân,[214] which produced whatever drink one desired, for *cors* is the nominative of the French word for horn as well as for body, and the Fisher King in the *Didot Perceval* was named Bron, and because of a mysterious malady found his only relaxation in fishing from a boat. Since, then, two of the relics preserved in the palace of the 'isle Galoche' are recognizable among the Thirteen Treasures preserved in the Glass House on a Welsh island, we may with some assurance identify also, though proof is missing, the sword preserved in the 'isle Galoche' with the sword of Rhydderch.

The romance of *Sone* tells how, much later, the hero returns to Galoche and then proceeds for his wedding to another very beautiful island. Here too there are a spring and four towers. It is connected with the land only by a causeway and a sword-bridge, at which when Meleagant was lord many lost their heads. The island is square in shape, and Sone and his bride barely escape with their lives from a storm which overwhelms it with great waves. This second island in *Sone* has complex relationships. It is, of course, related to the first island in *Sone*, to the island in *Perlesvaus*, and seems to contain reminiscences of the spring, the four corners, and the Glass Fortress of Annwn. The sword-bridge and the lordship of Meleagant show obvious kinship with the land of Goirre described in Chrétien de Troyes's *Chevalier de la Charrette*. It is possible also that the great storm which overwhelmed the second island fortress in *Sone* is derived from the ancient tradition reported by Nennius concerning the rising of the sea when the attackers landed from

---

[213] *Rev. Celt.*, xlvii (1930), 56; *Romanische Forschungen*, xlv (1931), 70; *Speculum*, viii. 430.
[214] Newstead, op. cit., pp. 86–95.

their ships on the isle of the glass tower, and the drowning of them all.

This second island in *Sone*, which seems therefore to possess traditional value, displays further connexions, as Bruce made clear,[215] with the island of Gundebaldus described in the Latin Arthurian romance, *Historia Meriadoci*.[216] Both are square, both have four towers, both are approached by a causeway. Moreover, while this island in *Sone* corresponds to Chrétien's water-girdled land of Goirre as to the sword-bridge and its former lord Meleagant, the similar island in *Historia Meriadoci* likewise recalls Goirre but in an independent way. The island of Gundebaldus is called 'terra de qua nemo revertitur', and the realm of Goirre, as everyone knows, is one 'don nus estranges ne retorne'. Gundebaldus has carried off a damsel, whom the hero undertakes to deliver; so Meleagant has carried off the queen, whom the hero undertakes to deliver. Moreover, the island of Gundebaldus is surrounded by marshes, and the *insula vitrea* of Melvas in *Vita Gildae* is likewise.

It is impossible to explain all these correspondences between *Perlesvaus, Sone, Historia Meriadoci, Le Chevalier de la Charrette,* and *Vita Gildae* as due to late literary borrowings. The relationships are too complex. Can one seriously believe that the author of *Sone,* the latest of these romances, sat down with copies of all these other texts and made a patchwork of them; that of his own initiative he called the first island Galoche, brought to it the Grail, the *cors* of the Fisher King, and the sword—relics so reminiscent of three of the Thirteen Treasures preserved in the Glass House on the isle of Bardsey; and that, recognizing the identity of the *tonel de voirre* in *Perlesvaus,* the realm of Goirre in the *Charrette,* and the *insula vitrea* in *Vita Gildae* with the *turris vitrea* of Nennius, he caused those who landed on the second island to be wellnigh overwhelmed by the waves of the sea? This is not credible. Even Bruce, who cannot be accused of partiality to lost Arthurian traditions, declared that in his opinion the analogies between this second island in *Sone* and the island in *Historia Meriadoci* are due to a common tradition. Even more necessary is it to assume a common tradition, and a very intricate one, to account for the interrelationships of the French, Latin, and Welsh texts we have been considering—a tradition in which many Welsh conceptions of an Otherworld island have been superimposed upon each other.

[215] *Historia Meriadoci*, ed. J. D. Bruce, p. xxxiv.   [216] Ibid., pp. 43 f.

'The Spoils of Annwn': an Early Welsh Poem

The *Preiddeu Annwn* can be understood only as a mosaic of Welsh bardic lore about the Other World. The poet imagines Annwn, now as a faery fortress on an island (which others identified with Lundy, Grassholm, Bardsey, or Ireland); now as a dim subterranean land, lighted by lamps; now as hell. It may be called the Faery Fortress, the Four-Cornered Fortress, the Fortress of Carousal, the Fortress of Frustration (?), or the Glass Fortress. There is a strong suggestion that Brân the Blessed was the Chief of Annwn. Probably Pwyll, Manawydan, and Pryderi were in his retinue of immortal revellers. The distinctive features of the place were a spring of white wine; luxurious arrangements for quaffing it; a cauldron (part cooking-vessel, part testing-talisman, part cauldron of inspiration) tended by nine maidens, corresponding to Morgen and her eight sisters of the Isle of Apples; a glass tower, 6,000 warriors on its walls, and a sentinel who would not answer the curious or communicative visitor. With this conglomerate vision of Annwn the poet associated two stories. One is that of Gweir, enchained in the midst of elysian plenty and loudly bewailing his lot: this punishment he brought on himself by bringing famine or desolation on the land of which he was king. The other story is that of Arthur's expedition, with three shiploads of his ship Prydwen, to win the cauldron. Llwch Lleminawc plied his sword to good advantage and seized the booty, but seven only, including of course Taliesin, Llwch, and Arthur, returned from this disastrous victory.

This poem was attributed to Taliesin, partly because he was considered a contemporary of Arthur, partly because he was regarded, like Arthur, as semi-divine and thus was familiar with Annwn and possessed a bardic chair there, but mainly because he was the great forerunner and patron of the poets who perpetuated the traditions of heathendom.[217] These poets made concessions, adaptations, omissions, but they could hardly hide the fact that Manannán and Mag Mell, Gwynn ap Nudd and Kaer Siddi, were survivals of the old pre-Christian world. And so, though priests and monks might thunder curses, the Welsh bards and *cyvarwyddiaid* continued to sing and tell tales, and found in the laity patronage and protection. For them Taliesin was *penn beirdd* (chief of bards); his poems were their inspired patterns and their justification.

---

[217] On heathenism in bardic poetry cf. H. M. and N. K. Chadwick, *Growth of Literature*, i. 469–71; Morris-Jones in *Cymmrodor*, xxviii. 238–48. On heathenism in custom and saga cf. Loomis, *Celtic Myth*, pp. 39–51, 184–7.

Even when the actual verses of Taliesin became obsolete in language or were forgotten, new ones were composed to take their place. Thus, it would seem, originated the bulk of the poems in the *Book of Taliesin*; and thus *Preiddeu Annwn* came to be written.

CHAPTER X

The Arthurian Legend before 1139

IN *Speculum*, xiv (1939), 357 f., the late Professor Tatlock made the following statements:

The plain fact is that, with no possibility of disproving that it existed, there is no evidence for a largely developed Arthur-saga anywhere whatever before Geoffrey. There is none in the occurrence in various lands of Arturus, Artusius, &c., as a man's name; none in the Arthurian relief at Modena; none in Geoffrey's *Historia*; none in the writings of his contemporaries or predecessors. Of what has been considered such evidence in writers shortly after him some certainly and the rest probably reflect the immense interest and fresh invention stimulated by the *Historia* itself. Outside Nennius, the *Annales Cambriae*, and the saints' lives, nearly all the evidence for the vogue of Arthur before Geoffrey relates merely to the Briton hope in Wales and Brittany for his messianic return; which no more proves an active cycle of stories about him than American popular observances about Santa Claus prove the familiarity of stories about him.

Any pronouncement by Tatlock in the field of medieval studies deserves respect. But so do the contrary views on these points of Rajna, Kingsley Porter, Gaston Paris, Gardner, Foerster, and Bédier, not to mention any living scholars. The final appeal, as always, must be not to authority but to facts and logic. Since the points challenged by Tatlock are those to which I have called attention on two occasions,[1] it would seem as if the onus of supporting them fell upon my shoulders. I should like to pay tribute to the scholarly sportsmanship displayed by my opponent, who graciously elucidated his position on certain matters and supplied me with references on one of his most telling points.

In one of these communications he expressed his view of Geoffrey's relation to the cycle.

Before Geoffrey, Arthur was relatively obscure, somewhat absurd or vague, and without a cycle of stories. Geoffrey made him an important, imposing, and attractive figure; not such, however, as to lend himself

[1] *Speculum*, iii (1928), 24 ff.; xiii (1938), 221 ff.

much to romance on the basis of what Geoffrey gives. To Arthur, I should think, were attracted tales already existing about others, not or little connected with him, and sheer invention.

The issues are clear: Was there anywhere in the world before 1139, the date when Geoffrey's *Historia* was still a complete novelty to Henry of Huntingdon, the English historian,[2] and could not yet have had any influence on the popular imagination, a cycle of stories about a heroic Arthur? And does the cycle of stories which admittedly existed shortly after 1139 owe its attachment to Arthur to the influence of Geoffrey of Monmouth?

Let us first take up those evidences for a cycle of stories before 1139. For two of them Tatlock himself supplied us with an early dating. We omit from consideration the references to Arthur in the *Gododdin* (dated by Sir Ifor Williams *c.* 600),[3] in Nennius (*c.* 800),[4] in the *Annales Cambriae* (*c.* 955),[5] in the *Chronicle of Mont St. Michel* (*c.* 1056),[6] in the *Liber Floridus* (*c.* 1120)[7]—references some of which suggest the existence of stories but do not prove it—and those Welsh saints' lives which assign to Arthur an absurd or ignominious role and which certainly have no connexion with the later romantic tales. With these exclusions, eleven references remain:

1. THE TESTIMONY OF HERMAN OF LAON. The canons of Laon, sent to raise funds for the rebuilding of their cathedral, on their way from Exeter to Bodmin were shown the seat and the oven 'illius famosi secundum fabulas Britannorum regis Arthuri'.[8] The journey of the canons of Laon took place, as everyone concedes, in 1113. And though M. Faral raised a doubt as to the authenticity of Herman's account,[9] Tatlock himself vindicated its authenticity and early dating.[10] 'It is entirely clear that, with his own work on the history of the Laon church and its bishop Bartholomew, Herman has incorporated, with revisions, two reports from the canons who had made

---

[2] E. K. Chambers, *Arthur of Britain* (London, 1927), pp. 44 f., 251.

[3] *Canu Aneirin*, ed. I. Williams (Cardiff, 1939), introd. 'Gododdin', vss. 1241 f. Prof. Kenneth Jackson kindly brought this to my attention.

[4] *Nennius et l'Historia Brittonum*, ed. F. Lot (Paris, 1934), pp. 68–71, 109, 194–6, 216.

[5] *Mabinogion*, ed. J. Loth (Paris, 1913), ii. 372.

[6] R. H. Fletcher, *Arthurian Material in the Chronicles* (Boston, 1906), p. 34.

[7] E. Faral, *Légende Arthurienne*, première partie (Paris, 1929), i. 256. Cf. R. S. and L. H. Loomis, *Arthurian Legends in Medieval Art* (New York, 1938), p. 15.

[8] Faral, op. cit., i. 226 n.   [9] Ibid., pp. 228–33.

[10] *Speculum*, viii (1933), 454–65.

The Arthurian Legend before 1139

the two journeys written more than thirty years earlier.'[11] 'It seems impossible to doubt that, twenty years or so before Geoffrey of Monmouth wrote his *Historia*, they found Cornishmen holding their country to be Arthur's, pointing to his chair and oven, and heartily believing him still alive.'[12] Moreover, we cannot doubt that by the same evidence King Arthur was already famous as the central figure of certain *fabulae Britannorum* by 1113.

The precise meaning of *Britannorum*, however, demands attention. For these are obviously to be distinguished, as Gröber noted, from those *Britones* who, a few lines farther down, Herman states are wont 'jurgari cum Francis pro rege Arturo'.[13] The *Britones*, as the fact that they quarrel with the French of the Continent suggests, and as further evidence adduced in the following pages demonstrates, were the contemporary inhabitants of Brittany.[14] The *Britanni*, therefore, are clearly identified as insular Celts. It was they who pointed out the seat and oven of Arthur and asserted that theirs was the land of Arthur; it was they whose tales, as told in French, the canons had heard. The passage does not inform us how far these tales had spread, nor does it give any clue as to their content. Some indication, however, as to the content of these tales of the southwest is offered by the fact that the proper names (Gorlois, Briťael, Ridcaradoch, Modredus) and the region connected with Arthur's begetting and his last fatal battle, as recounted by Geoffrey of Monmouth, are Cornish.[15] It is possible to ascribe the first three

---

[11] Ibid., p. 455.   [12] Ibid., p. 465.

[13] Faral, op. cit., i. 226 n. Gröber made this distinction in *Zts. f. rom. Phil.*, xx (1896), 426. F. Lot by ignoring this distinction as applied to Brythonic peoples of the twelfth century produced a hopeless confusion. Cf. *Romania*, xxiv (1895), 499 ff.

[14] For evidence cf. Zimmer in *Göttingische Gelehrte Anzeigen*, 1890, pp. 793–805; Brugger in *Zts. f. franz. Spr. u. Lit.*, xx[1] (1898), 79 ff.; xliv[2] (1922), 78 ff.; Chrétien de Troyes, *Karrenritter*, ed. W. Foerster (Halle, 1899), pp. cxi–cxxiii; R. S. Loomis, in *Mod. Phil.*, xxxiii (1936), 232–7. Even Lot repeatedly admits that generally in the twelfth century the words *bretons* and *Britones* as applied to contemporaries meant the Continental Bretons. Cf. *Romania*, xxiv (1895), 500, 505; xxviii (1899), 7. Curiously enough, he argues that Warinus Brito, to whom Henry of Huntingdon wrote in 1139 (E. K. Chambers, op. cit., p. 251), could not have been a Breton since Henry refers to him as a compatriot; as a historian, Lot must have known that the king of England had many subjects of Breton extraction living in England. Cf. *Romania*, xxiv. 499.

[15] *Romania*, xxviii (1899), 342; xxx (1901), 11; J. Loth, *Contributions à l'Étude des Romans de la Table Ronde* (Paris, 1912), pp. 63 f.; A. E. Hutson, *British Personal Names in 'Historia Regum Britanniae'* (U. of Calif. Pub. in English, v, 1940), pp. 60, 67 f., 93.

names to Geoffrey's artful effort to render his nomenclature plausible,[16] but not the last, for Modred had no connexion with Cornwall except that he died there. It is therefore highly probable that all four Cornish name-forms were derived simply and naturally from Cornish stories, remains of the *fabulae Britannorum*, certified by Herman of Laon as existing in 1113.

2. THE 'VITA GILDAE' BY CARADOC OF LANCARVAN. Whereas most of the early Welsh saints' lives which introduce Arthur are hostile to the hero,[17] Caradoc seems to be more sympathetic with the popular view.[18] It is natural, therefore, to find him giving us two stories of Arthur which are a part of the great secular tradition. He tells of a feud between the king and a brother of Gildas, Hueil, and this very same feud is the subject of an allusion in *Kulhwch and Olwen*.[19] He also tells the story of Guinevere's abduction in a form clearly cognate with Chrétien's famous romance.[20] The hagiographic pattern and monkish bias have influenced the secular tale in Caradoc's version, but it is universally recognized that his Melvas is Chrétien's Meleagant.[21] It has been also recognized that Chrétien's description of Maheloas's *isle de voirre* in *Erec*, an elysian isle where there is never any storm or winter, is anticipated by Caradoc's making Melvas king of an *aestiva regio* and of Glastonbury, interpreted as the Saxon equivalent of Welsh Ynisgutrin, Latin *insula vitrea*.[22] The manifold and deep-rooted connexion of the theme of Guinevere's abduction with early Celtic tradition have been the subject of numerous studies, of which one may name in particular those of Gaston Paris, Miss Schoepperle, and the late T. P. Cross.[23] Evidently Caradoc of Lancarvan displays familiarity with current secular Arthurian fiction. The crucial question is: when did he compose the *Vita Gildae*?

Tatlock has again given us the most carefully reasoned and documented discussion of the date,[24] and his conclusion is: 'though it cannot be positively proved, there is every reason to believe his

[16] Hutson, loc. cit., p. 90 ff.
[17] Faral, op. cit., i. 236–44.
[18] E. K. Chambers, *Arthur of Britain*, pp. 262–4.
[19] *Mabinogion*, ed. J. Loth (1913), i. 273.
[20] G. Schoepperle, *Tristan and Isolt* (New York, 1913), ii. 528–36; T. P. Cross, W. A. Nitze, *Lancelot and Guenevere* (Chicago, 1930), pp. 3–21, 47 n. 2, 55.
[21] J. D. Bruce, *Evolution of Arthurian Romance* (Baltimore, 1923), i, 201.
[22] Ibid., p. 200; *Perlesvaus*, ed. W. A. Nitze and others, ii (Chicago, 1937), 58.
[23] *Romania*, x (1882), 491 ff.; xii (1884), 512 ff. See also *supra*, n. 20.
[24] *Speculum*, xiii (1938), 139–52; xiv (1939), 350–3.

Vita Gildae to have been written before, perhaps long before, Geoffrey's *Historia*, and no reason for a date after this.'[25] Tatlock shows that Caradoc in all probability left Lancarvan as a young man in 1086;[26] therefore, he must have been in the neighbourhood of seventy in 1136, and not likely to compose his only work after that date.[27] Moreover, Geoffrey's condescending relinquishment of the task of carrying on the history of the Welsh kings to Caradoc[28] must have been inspired by something Caradoc had written. And it is perhaps significant that though William of Malmesbury and the later Glastonbury propagandists oddly neglected the Glastonbury material provided by the *Vita Gildae*, William did, as Tatlock pointed out,[29] insert in the third version of his *Gesta Regum* (1135–40) the statement that Gildas spent many years at Glastonbury, and William was possibly the author of the statement in the *De Antiquitate* that Gildas died and was buried there. It looks as if both Geoffrey and William knew the *Vita Gildae* as a recent work, but held it in small regard. A plausible date for the book would be the early thirties; an almost certain *terminus ad quem* 1136. Already, then, on Tatlock's own showing, certain matters referred to in *Kulhwch and Olwen* and the main theme of Chrétien's *Chevalier de la Charrette* were in existence.

3. WILLIAM OF MALMESBURY'S 'GESTA REGUM ANGLORUM'. Here there is no question of date, for all agree that the first edition was completed in 1125. The question is one of interpretation. William says: 'Hic est Artur de quo Britonum nugae hodieque delirant, dignus plane quem non fallaces somniarent fabulae.'[30] *Nuga*, as we see from Walter Map's use of the word in his title *De Nugis Curialium*, is a tale which, whether true or false, made little pretence to edification. M. Faral, with whom Tatlock seems to agree, asserted that the only *nugae* to which William referred consisted of the Breton hope of Arthur's return.[31] We have already observed and shall observe that other romantic tales of Arthur were in circulation. A. C. L. Brown's interpretation of the passage is to be preferred.[32]

---

[25] Ibid., xiv. 353.   [26] Ibid., xiii. 145.   [27] Ibid. xiv. 353.
[28] Geoffrey of Monmouth, *Historia Regum Britanniae*, ed. A. Griscom (New York, 1929), p. 536.
[29] *Speculum*, xiv. 352 n. Cf. William of Malmesbury, *Gesta Regum Anglorum*, ed. W. Stubbs, i (London, 1887), 24.
[30] Wm. of Malmesbury, op. cit. i. 11.
[31] Faral, op. cit. i. 250, 260.   [32] *Speculum*, ii (1927), 449.

There is, moreover, the highly important word *Britonum* to be dealt with. Zimmer and Dr. Brugger assembled ample evidence to show that, while *Britones* as applied to men of Arthur's time meant the insular Britons, its reference in the twelfth century was uniformly to their Continental descendants in Brittany, and even Lot admitted this as a general rule, though he vainly tried to prove certain exceptions.[33] It is sufficient to point out that in this instance the evidence is overwhelming. First, we have the testimony of Geoffrey of Monmouth and Giraldus Cambrensis as to contemporary usage. Geoffrey declares that after the time of Cadwallader his countrymen 'iam non uocabantur britones set gualenses'.[34] Giraldus is equally explicit: 'Usque in hodiernum, barbara nuncupatione et homines Wallenses et terra Wallia vocitatur.'[35] Secondly, William of Malmesbury's own practice conforms to this rule. Referring to the tenth century, he says: 'Britones omnes, quos nos Walenses dicimus.'[36] But he calls a count of Brittany simple 'comes Britonum Conanus',[37] and refers to contemporary Bretons as 'Britones transmarini' or simply 'Britones'.[38] Thirdly, when William records the discovery of Gawain's grave in Wales, he calls Arthur's nephew Walwen,[39] a form utterly unknown in Welsh, equally remote from Gwalchmai, which the Welsh substituted for French Galvain,[40] and from Gwallt-A(d)vwyn, which is more and more clearly indicated as the Welsh source of Galvain.[41] William used a form which was certainly not Welsh and which is very close to the Walwanus and Gwalwanus of the early Cambridge manuscript of the *Historia Regum Britanniae* used by Griscom as his basic text,[42] and startlingly close to the Walwanus recorded near Padua in 1136.[43] That both of these

[33] Cf. *supra*, p. 181, n. 14. Lot contends (*Romania*, xxiv (1895), 500) that the *nugae Britonum* of William of Malmesbury must refer to the insular Celts because it would be *bien singulier* if an Englishman needed to learn Arthurian legends from Bretons of Armorica when the Welsh and Cornish were so much nearer. However, there is nothing strange about the situation if one realizes that England received an influx of Bretons after 1066 and that they were French-speakers, whereas the Welsh and the Cornish still had to acquire the language. Evidently the Breton *conteurs* had already made progress in adapting their tales to French tastes when they arrived and rapidly acquired such a reputation as entertainers that even in England they never had any real competition from the Welsh and Cornish *cyfarwyddiaid*.
[34] Geoffrey of Monmouth, op. cit., p. 535.
[35] Giraldus Cambrensis, *Opera*, ed. Dimock, vi (London, 1868), 179.
[36] William of Malmesbury, op. cit. i. 135.
[37] Ibid. i. 211.   [38] Ibid. ii. 478.   [39] Ibid., p. 342.
[40] Loomis, *Arthurian Tradition*, pp. 147 f.   [41] Ibid., pp. 149-54.
[42] Geoffrey of Monmouth, op. cit., pp. 31-33, 444, 474 f., 490-2.
[43] *Romania*, xvii (1888), 361 f.

The Arthurian Legend before 1139

were Continental forms of the name Gawain will be shown later. Fourthly, the probability that William had heard Breton stories is supported by Bédier's statement that after the battle of Hastings 'toute la civilisation normande se trouva brusquement transplantée telle quelle dans les châteaux d'Outre-Manche, et les jongleurs armoricains y suivirent leurs patrons: jongleurs armoricains, mais plus qu'à demi romanisés, mais vivant au service de seigneurs français, et contant pour leur plaire'.[44] The *Britones* whose *nugae* on the subject of Arthur and Gawain were familiar to William of Malmesbury were certainly professional Breton *conteurs*. We can legitimately infer that these tales, when William wrote in 1125, were also known in Brittany.

4. GEOFFREY OF MONMOUTH'S TESTIMONY. In the *Prophetia Merlini* composed in 1134 or 1135 Geoffrey has a brief passage concerning an *aper Cornubiae*, which everyone recognizes as Arthur.[45] 'In ore populorum celebrabitur et actus eius cibus[46] erit narrantibus.' No modern scholar doubts what has long been suspected, that the *Prophetia Merlini*, in so far as it is not mere rigmarole or an expression of the fond hopes of the Brythonic peoples, is an ex-post-facto prophecy. Does not the Fool in *Lear* exclaim: 'This prophecie Merlin shall make, for I live before his time'? Therefore, before the publication of Geoffrey's *Historia* Arthur's name was on the lips of peoples, and—more important—furnished a livelihood to story-tellers. M. Faral and Tatlock both asserted that there was as yet no cycle of stories attached to him, only the tradition of his messianic return.[47] If this be so, how was it possible for professional reciters to make a living repeating every few minutes the idea 'qu'Arthur n'était point mort et devait un jour revenir parmi les Bretons', interspersed with brief topographic remarks on Arthur's chair and oven and Gawain's grave? These were the only legends of Arthur that the secular story-tellers had to tell in 1135 according

[44] Thomas, *Tristan*, ed. J. Bédier, ii (Paris, 1905), 126 f. Cf. Zimmer in *Göttingische gelehrte Anzeigen*, 1890, pp. 788–91. Zimmer is mistaken in his remarks about Alain Fergant.

[45] Geoffrey of Monmouth, op. cit., p. 385 (Bk. VII, ch. 3). Cf. E. K. Chambers, *Arthur of Britain*, p. 25; E. Faral, *Légende Arthurienne*, première partie, ii. 54.

[46] That *cibus* in this context meant 'food', not 'material', is proved by a passage in *Annales Monastici*, Rolls Series, i. 485: 'histrionibus potest dari cibus, quia pauperes sunt'; and by another passage in *Mon. Hist. Germ. SS.* vi, p. 687': 'infinitam multitudinem histrionum et joculatorum sine cibo et muneribus vacuam et merentem abire permisit.'

[47] Faral, op. cit. i. 260; *Speculum*, xiv (1939), 358.

to M. Faral and Tatlock, and yet they made a living by it. *Credat Judaeus Apella.*

Again, in the first sentences of his *Historia*, published between 1136 and 1139, Geoffrey states that the deeds of Arthur and many other kings of the Britons were pleasantly rehearsed from memory by word of mouth *a multis populis*.[48] Tatlock, though not disputing the fact alleged by Geoffrey, answered a query of mine concerning the 'many peoples' by the interpretation, 'I should suppose Celts'. Bruce and Rajna supposed quite otherwise.[49] Which supposition is correct? I think no one will deny that only three Celtic peoples had any traditions of Arthur: Welsh, Cornish, and Bretons. Would Tatlock have asserted in any other context than this that *multi* meant three? Here was a point on which Geoffrey could not afford to draw the long bow. He numbered among his readers too many clerics, ill informed doubtless as to the days of Brutus, Bladud, and Belinus, but sufficiently aware of what was going on in contemporary Europe. He might lie as he pleased about a book which Archdeacon Walter had brought out of Brittany,[50] for no one could force him to produce the book. But he could not afford to say that tales of Arthur were current among many peoples if only Celts had heard such tales. When he said *a multis populis* he could not have ventured far beyond the truth and he could not have meant three. The acts of Arthur and the other kings—there are plenty of other kings in Welsh and French romance—were, on Geoffrey's own testimony, known outside the Brythonic group of peoples.

5. THE TESTIMONY OF AILRED OF RIEVAULX. In his *Speculum Caritatis*, written in 1141–2, Ailred tells of a novice in the Yorkshire monastery of Rievaulx who reproached himself because, though in his past secular life he had been frequently moved to tears by 'fabulis quae vulgo de nescio quo finguntur Arcturo', by 'fabulis et mendaciis', it was almost a miracle if he could extract a tear at a pious reading or discourse.[51] These *fabulae et mendaciae de nescio quo Arcturo* are certainly not the narratives of Geoffrey's *Historia*. If in

---

[48] Geoffrey of Monmouth, op. cit., p. 219.
[49] J. D. Bruce, *Evolution of Arthurian Romance*, i. 20; *Studi Medievali*, N.S., ii (1929), 215.
[50] That Geoffrey meant Brittany by *ex Britannia* is proved by his use of *Gualiis*, surely Wales, in this very passage, and by his own definition in Bk. V, ch. xii: 'Armoricum regnum quod nunc Britannia dicitur.'
[51] Migne, *Patrologia Latina*, cxcv, col. 565. Trans. G. G. Coulton, *Five Centuries of Religion* (Cambridge, 1923), i. 359. On date cf. *Bulletin of John Rylands Library*, vi (1921–2), 454 f., 478.

The Arthurian Legend before 1139

1139 Henry of Huntingdon, a historian by vocation, did not detect at once Geoffrey's fraud, a callow novice is hardly to be credited with the discovery two years later. Nor would the Arthur so fully introduced to us in the pseudo-history have been referred to as *nescio quis Arcturus*. Moreover, so far as I know, the narrative of Geoffrey never moved anyone to weeping, whereas we know from the testimony of Peter of Blois that the tales of the minstrels about Arthur, Gawain, and Tristan did.[52]

How then did Tatlock interpret this confession? He wrote:

> As to Ailred of Rievaulx (aside from what seems to me the improbability of pre-Geoffrey Arthurian tradition in NE. Yorkshire), he knew Walter Espec, who certainly before 1147 had a copy of the *Historia Regum Britanniae* (Gaimar). If the anecdote of the novice is 'straight goods', I'd attribute it to tale-telling due to the captivating Geoffrey, who had a vogue in SE. Yorkshire only a year or so later (Alfred of Beverley).

First, as to the improbability of pre-Geoffrey Arthurian tradition in northern Yorkshire, we have already noted William of Malmesbury's attestation in 1125 of Breton tales about Arthur; we have already noted Bédier's conviction that Breton *conteurs* came with their Norman masters into England after the Conquest. Now when Ailred wrote, northern Yorkshire had contained for something like seventy-five years a Breton court. Ever since 1069 the greatest fief in the North Riding, the honour of Richmond, had been in the hands of a Breton family, founded by Alan Rufus, second cousin of the duke of Brittany.[53] Stephen, who was both earl of Richmond and count of Penthièvre from 1093 to 1137, inherited extensive lands in Brittany, spending much of his time there, and many tenants of the 'honour' were of Breton origin.[54] In the entourage of these counts of Richmond and Brittany we encounter such Breton names as Conan, the count's chaplain, Ruald, the constable, Guiomar, the steward.[55] Alan III, the earl at the time Ailred was writing, calls himself 'Alanus comes Anglie et indigena comesque

---

[52] E. K. Chambers, *Arthur of Britain*, p. 267.
[53] *Victoria History of County of York, North Riding*, ed. W. Page, i (London, 1914), 2 f.; P. Jeulin, 'Un grand "Honneur" anglais', *Annales de Bretagne*, xlii (1935), 265 ff.
[54] C. T. Clay, *Early Yorkshire Charters*, IV (1935), p. ix.
[55] Ibid. iv. 11, 15, 16. On these names cf. J. Loth, *Contributions à l'Étude des Romans de la Table Ronde* (Paris, 1912), p. 98; *Zts. f. franz. Spr. u. Lit.*, xlix. 202 ff.

Britannie'.[56] If there was one place in all England where on grounds of antecedent probability one could assume that Breton *conteurs* told their enthralling tales of the Arthurian cycle in French, it would be in the North Riding of Yorkshire. And Richmond was only about thirty miles away from Rievaulx.

Secondly, let us see whether Geffrei Gaimar, writing about 1147, offers any better explanation of these *fabulae et mendaciae de nescio quo Arcturo*. He merely tells us that he used in the composition of his *Estorie des Engles*, along with various other works, a manuscript identifiable with the *Historia Regum Britanniae*, which a Lady Fitz-Gilbert of Scampton, Lincs., had borrowed from her husband, who had borrowed it from Walter Espec, who had in turn asked for the copy and received it from Robert of Gloucester, one of the dedicatees.[57] There can be no doubt that Ailred knew Walter Espec, pious founder of Rievaulx Abbey.[58] But putting two and two together does not help us much in this instance, for Espec's Latin book and the tales which Ailred's novice at Rievaulx had known before 1141 could have had little connexion. If Ailred had read Geoffrey of Monmouth's *Historia*, would he have permitted, even in the mouth of a novice, the allusion to Arthur as *nescio quis Arcturus*? Moreover, as Tatlock should have been the first to recognize, it is a pure assumption that Espec's book even existed in 1141. It is hardly cricket to postulate that copies of the *Historia* were in existence in any year convenient for one's theories, and at the same time rigorously challenge the existence of any oral tradition before the date at which it is certified. But the most serious objection to the belief that the novice had heard widespread tales of Arthur inspired by Espec's manuscript is the fact that Geoffrey wrote in Latin. Giraldus Cambrensis makes it clear that even in his more cultivated day works in Latin appealed to only a very select few of the nobility; that in order to get any recognition it was necessary to have the work translated into French.[59] Espec himself probably had his *Historia* orally translated for him by his chaplain or other cleric. On the basis of generally admitted facts, it is hard to believe that anybody, except a few clerics, had actually read Espec's

---

[56] Clay, op. cit. iv. 29.

[57] Chambers, op. cit., pp. 260 f.; *Mod. Lang. Rev.*, xxv (1930), 75.

[58] Ailred describes Espec's appearance in *Relatio de Standardo*. Cf. *Chronicles of the Reigns of Stephen, Henry II, and Richard I*, ed. R. Howlett, iii (London, 1886), 183.

[59] Giraldus Cambrensis, *Opera*, ed. Dimock, v (London, 1867), 410 f.

manuscript before it was lent to the FitzGilberts, and hardly anyone else knew the contents except a few noble friends of Espec. One Latin manuscript in lay hands was not likely to extend its influence very far in the troublesome reign of Stephen. It had to await peace and a French translation. Bédier's theory of the propagation of the *chansons de geste* offers no parallel. There were powerful reasons why the clergy of St. Denis, Vézelay, and St. Guilhem should explore their Latin chronicles and charters, and encourage lay minstrels to compose poems in honour of Charlemagne, Girard de Roussillon, and Guillaume d'Orange. It is quite the opposite with the clergy or the nobility of Yorkshire: they had, so far as we can judge, no particular motive to compose or to cause others to compose moving tales of Arthur just because they had been reading Geoffrey of Monmouth. Only one exception occurs to me. The Breton earls of Richmond would have had a motive, but they did not need the spur of Geoffrey's book. They already had their *nugae Britonum*.

Thirdly, there is the assertion of Alfred of Beverley, writing in south-eastern Yorkshire about 1149. This, though it proves nothing as to conditions eight years earlier (no one was more insistent than Tatlock that we cannot accept the existence of anything until the year when it is first attested), does *seem* to prove that in 1149 stories based on Geoffrey were widespread.

Ferebantur tunc temporis per ora multorum narrationes de historia Britonum, notamque rusticitatis incurrebat qui talium narrationum scientiam non habebat. . . . Quaesivi historiam, et ea vix inventa, lectioni eius intentissime studium adhibui.[60]

Since *historiam* in the latter sentence certainly means Geoffrey's book, must not *historia* in the first sentence refer to the same? This interpretation is logical but not satisfactory. If Geoffrey's Latin work was so accessible and so commonly read that all who considered themselves more than boors knew the stories, at least by hearsay, how did it come about that a Latin-reading cleric interested in history, Alfred of Beverley, was among the last to hear about it? This seems as probable as that Tatlock should have been led to look into M. Faral's *La Légende Arthurienne* only after everybody else at the University of California was talking about it.

A more cautious interpretation of the passage would seem to be

[60] Chambers, op. cit., p. 260.

this. The 'narrationes de historia Britonum', told by many and familiar to all cultivated persons, must be the 'fallaces fabulae' known to William of Malmesbury, the *gesta* of Arthur and many others which according to Geoffrey 'a multis populis quasi inscripta iocunde et memoriter praedicarentur', the 'fabulae de nescio quo Arcturo' which had so often moved Ailred's novice. These we know enjoyed a great vogue; these we know were circulated 'per ora multorum'. If Alfred of Beverley refers to them as 'narrationes de historia Britonum', the explanation is not far to seek. With these *fabulae* were now mingled assertions that they were not to be taken for mere lies, because there was to be seen at Espec's castle of Helmsley or elsewhere a sober chronicle which corroborated some of the facts. Alfred, therefore, speaks respectfully of the tales and tries to find the sober chronicle, which turns out to be the *Historia Regum Britanniae*. This in my opinion seems a more reasonable interpretation of the passage than the supposition that, while all the knowledgeable folk in Yorkshire had been captivated by Geoffrey, presumably either because there were manuscripts in every castle and monastery library or because some of their friends possessed a remarkable faculty of emotional recitation of the tales, Alfred, the one man in Yorkshire who had ambitions to write of ancient British history, remained in ignorance of the great literary sensation.

Not only, therefore, does a knowledge of the *Historia* on the part of Gaimar and Alfred between 1147 and 1150 postdate by a few years the testimony of Ailred of Rievaulx to the existence of *fabulae* about Arthur as a most powerful form of secular fiction, but evidently the *Historia* does not account for their genesis. The fact that Ailred knew Espec and that Espec possessed a Geoffrey manuscript is an irrelevant coincidence. Neither Ailred nor his novice is likely to have referred to stories culled from the *Historia* as *mendaciae*, as *fabulae de nescio quo Arcturo*; moreover, as I shall emphasize more fully later, when we do get written *fabulae* and *mendaciae* about Arthur in England, in the *lais* of Biquet and Marie de France and the *Tristan* of Thomas, the narrative plot owes nothing to Geoffrey or Wace.[61] Taken in conjunction with the other early evidence which we have reviewed, Ailred's witness must be interpreted as a reference to the emotional power of the Breton *conteurs* at the time that Geoffrey was writing his work or very shortly after.

On the basis, then, of the five witnesses thus far examined whose

[61] M. Pelan, *L'Influence du Brut de Wace* (Paris, 1931), pp. 96 f., 123 f.

The Arthurian Legend before 1139

evidence concerns Arthurian tradition before or about 1139, we come to certain conclusions: the stories were sufficiently numerous, varied, and fascinating to furnish a livelihood to professional reciters; they were often too fantastic to be regarded as sober history; one at least of them shows affinities with *Kulhwch and Olwen* and Chrétien's *Chevalier de la Charrette*; they were already told by many peoples including those of the Continent; Breton *conteurs* seem to have been the main agency for their dissemination outside Wales and Cornwall.

Let us now turn to the remaining six witnesses. The dates of five of them are more open to question than the dates of the five already cited, but all seem to refer with great probability, if not certainty, to conditions prevailing before 1139. Do they or do they not harmonize with and corroborate the evidence already produced?

6. 'KULHWCH AND OLWEN'. Here beyond dispute is an elaborate piece of fiction, which not only proves the existence in Wales of romantic stories of Arthur, but also reveals significant analogies to the pre-Geoffrey traditions already examined and to later French and English romances. It displays acquaintance, as has been noted, with the feud of Arthur and Hueil related by Caradoc of Lancarvan.[62] It knows of the abduction of another king's wife by Gwynn ap Nudd,[63] who by one tradition had his palace on Glastonbury Tor;[64] the assembling of an army by the outraged husband; a battle; and the settlement of the dispute by the intervention of a third party— a story which reveals a marked parallelism (though the names are different) to the story of Guinevere's abduction as told by Caradoc. It contains certain commonplaces of the later romances:[65] the youthful hero sets out for Arthur's court; Kai takes a churlish attitude and receives Arthur's rebuke; the youth rides on horseback into the hall and demands a boon, which Arthur grants. Moreover, as in Chrétien's *Ivain*, he meets a giant herdsman;[66] as in *The Carl of Carlisle*, he arrives at a giant's castle and hurls spears at the giant, who is the father of his *amie* and destined wife.[67] *Kulhwch* also contains the full story of the Twrch Trwyth, a boar, son of a prince,[68]

---

[62] *Mabinogion*, ed. J. Loth (1913), i. 273.
[63] Ibid. i. 331 f.   [64] Cf. *supra*, p. 139.
[65] *Mabinogion*, ed. J. Loth (1913), i. 248-58.
[66] Ibid., p. 289; R. S. Loomis, *Celtic Myth*, pp. 118-22; R. Zenker, *Ivainstudien* (*Beihefte zur Zts. f. rom. Phil.*, lxx, Halle, 1921), pp. 238-49.
[67] *Mabinogion*, ed. Loth, i. 299; Loomis, *Celtic Myth*, p. 100.
[68] *Mabinogion*, ed. Loth, i. 310, 336; *Perlesvaus*, ed. W. A. Nitze and others, ii (Chicago, 1937), 142 f.; J. Rhys, *Celtic Folklore, Welsh and Manx* (Oxford, 1901), ii. 509-37.

mentioned as the *porcus Troit* in the *additamenta* to Nennius, and also in the continuation of the *Conte del Graal* as Tortain, a boar, son of a magician.[69] Singer has pointed out that the eyelids of Yspaddaden have counterparts in *Rigomer*.[70] Here, then, is a Welsh romance which displays unmistakable connexions with the oldest (Nennius's *mirabilia*) as well as the latest (*Carl of Carlisle*) traditional Arthurian literature. The only question is the date of *Kulhwch*.

On this matter, of course, the only competent authority is the testimony of Celtists, and the overwhelming weight of that authority is in favour of a date before the *Historia Regum Britanniae*. Thurneysen, recognized everywhere as among the greatest of Celtic scholars, assigns *Kulhwch* to the first quarter of the twelfth century.[71] M. Vendryes, editor of the *Revue Celtique*, suggests the end of the eleventh.[72] Gwenogvryn Evans, cataloguer of Welsh manuscripts for the Royal Historical Commission and acknowledged expert in palaeography, testifies: 'The Winning of Olwen is the oldest in language [of the Mabinogion]. . . . The name of Arthur, it is argued, does not occur in the Four Branches, therefore they are older than Geoffrey. The name of Arthur does occur in Kulhwch, therefore it is later than Geoffrey, or at least Arthurian incidents have been grafted on older tales. It is a workable theory; it is clear, concise, and plausible. But for all that the linguistic test of the respective texts of the White Book challenges it.'[73] The matter was most fully argued by Joseph Loth on linguistic grounds, and he came to the conclusion, maintained to the end of his life, that *Kulhwch* belonged to the late eleventh or early twelfth century.[74] The most recent scholarship is represented by Professor Idris Foster, who in 1940 gave the date of the extant recension as about 1100.[75] The unanimous verdict of those most entitled to an opinion is that *Kulhwch and Olwen* was written down, as we have it, before 1139.

[69] F. Lot, *Nennius et l'Historia Brittonum* (Paris, 1934), p. 217. For form of name cf. *Perlesvaus*, ed. Nitze, ii. 143; *Romania*, xxviii (1899), 217 n., 578.

[70] S. Singer, *Germanisch-romanisches Mittelalter* (Zürich, 1935), pp. 178 f.; *Mabinogion*, trans. T. P. Ellis, J. Lloyd (Oxford, 1929), i. 197; *Merveilles de Rigomer*, ed. Foerster, Breuer (Dresden, 1908), i, vs. 3543 ff.

[71] *Zeitschrift für celtische Philologie*, xii (1918), 283; xx (1936), 133. I regret to say, however, that I do not find Thurneysen's argument acceptable.

[72] *Rev. Celt.* xlviii (1931), 411.

[73] *White Book Mabinogion*, ed. J. G. Evans (Pwllheli, 1907), p. xiv.

[74] Loth, *Contributions à l'Étude des Romans de la Table Ronde*, pp. 42–45; *Moyen Age*, xli (1931), 309.

[75] *Essays and Studies Presented to Prof. Eoin MacNeill*, ed. J. Ryan (Dublin), pp. 28 f.

7. BLEHERIS, THE WELSH 'CONTEUR'. Though the transmission of Arthurian tales to the Anglo-Normans and French has been shown to have been the work of Bretons,[76] nevertheless there is an astonishing amount of evidence to indicate that the most famous of the early Arthurian *conteurs* on the Continent was a Welshman by birth.[77] The fullest record of his activity is provided by the second continuator of the *Conte del Graal*, formerly identified with Wauchier de Denain, who, in telling the adventures of Gawain and a certain dwarf knight, cites as his authority Bleheris, 'who was born and reared in Wales, . . . and who told it to the count of Poitiers, who loved the story and held it more than any other firmly in memory'.[78] The authenticity of this reference is borne out by several facts. The description of the dwarf knight which immediately follows corresponds to the popular Welsh conception of dwarfs as recorded by Giraldus Cambrensis.[79] The reputation of Bleheris as an Arthurian authority is proved by the fact that the first continuator of the *Conte del Graal* cites him also,[80] that Thomas in his *Tristan* (*c.* 1170) refers to Breri (admittedly the same person) as one 'who knew the acts and tales of all the kings, of all the counts who have been in Britain'.[81] In what is perhaps an interpolation in the *Elucidation* prefixed to the *Conte del Graal* Maistre Blihis (the form, as Dr. Brugger maintains,[82] is a corruption due to the omission of the overstroke signifying *-er-*) is invoked as authority for saying that the secrets of the Grail must not be revealed.[83] The same little poem introduces a knight Blihos Bliheris,[84] who, though he certainly was

---

[76] Loomis, *Arthurian Tradition*, pp. 15–22, 27–32; Brugger, *Zts. f. franz. Spr. u. Lit.*, xx¹ (1898), 79 ff.; Christian von Troyes, *Karrenritter* (Halle, 1899), pp. cxi–cxvii.

[77] The most important articles on Bleheris are: J. L. Weston, *Romania*, xxxiv (1905), 100 ff.; Brugger, *Zts. f. franz. Spr. u. Lit.*, xlvii (1924), 162 ff.; R. S. Loomis, *Mod. Lang. Notes*, xxxix (1924), 319 ff.; J. Van Dam, *Neophilologus*, xv (1929), 30–34. There is nothing in what we know of Bleheris which would suggest that he wrote poems, and the hypothesis which would identify the *fabulator* or *conteur* with a Welsh noble, Bleddri ap Cadivor, ignores the social chasm which existed between the professional entertainers and their patrons. Cf. Mary Williams, in *Études Celtiques*, iv (1937), 219 ff. For contemptuous attitude of poets to the *conteurs* cf. Loomis, *Arthurian Tradition*, p. 22, n. 50.

[78] J. L. Weston, *Legend of Sir Perceval*, i (London, 1906), 288.

[79] L. A. Paton, *Studies in the Fairy Mythology of Arthurian Romance*, pp. 127–9. Cf. *supra*, p. 66.   [80] *Romania*, xxiii (1904), 338; Weston, op. cit. i. 241.

[81] Thomas, *Tristan*, ed. J. Bédier, i. 337; ii. 95–99.

[82] *Zts. f. franz. Spr. u. Lit.*, xlvii. 163, n. 2.

[83] *Elucidation*, ed. A. W. Thompson (New York, 1931), p. 86.

[84] Ibid., p. 91. Cf. also p. 81.

not in any literal sense identical with the *conteur* Bleheris, nevertheless must have acquired by association of names the outstanding professional attribute of the Welshman, for 'he knew such excellent tales that no one could tire of listening to his words'. About 1194 Giraldus in his *Descriptio Cambriae* attaches the responsibility for a jest about fishing coracles to 'famosus ille fabulator Bledhericus, qui tempora nostra paulo praevenit'.[85] Thus there is ample testimony that a renowned professional story-teller of Welsh birth existed, and that French and Anglo-Norman poets knew his reputation and invoked him as authority for stories of Tristram, Gawain, and the Grail. That he really did visit a count of Poitiers, as the second continuator asserts, is confirmed by the fact that the earliest references to Tristram as a famous lover come in the 1150's from two troubadours, Cercamon and Bernard de Ventadour, both intimately associated with the court of Poitou.[86] If we realize that Bleheris must have given his enthralling recitals in French, and that his stories were versions already acclimated on the Continent, probably improved versions of the stock-in-trade of Breton *conteurs*,[87] his career as sketched by the second continuator accords with all the pertinent facts.

But once more there is the question of date; when did the visit to the count of Poitou take place? Giraldus says that Bledhericus 'tempora nostra paulo praevenit.'[88] Though Lot once introduced as his candidate for identification with Bledhericus a certain Bishop Bleddri who died 172 years before the publication of the *Descriptio Cambriae*,[89] we can be sure that Giraldus did not mean any such interval by the word *paulo*. He used a similar phrase in the *Itinerarium Cambriae*, written about 1191: 'Parum autem ante haec nostra tempora';[90] and here we can define his meaning, for he refers to an amazing experience which happened at the age of twelve to a priest, who told the story as an old man to Giraldus's uncle, David, who held the see of St. David's from 1148 to 1176.[91] If the priest was sixty-two years old when he told the story, and he told it in the first year of David's episcopacy, then we should have the year 1098 as the upper limit for the meaning of 'parum ante haec nostra

---

[85] Giraldus Cambrensis, *Opera*, vi (London, 1868), 202.
[86] *Zts. f. Rom. Phil.*, xli (1921), 223 ff.; *Mod. Phil.*, xix (1922), 287 ff.
[87] *Mod. Lang. Notes*, xxxix (1924), 326 f.; *Romania*, liii (1927), 96–99; *Zts. f. franz. Spr. u. Lit.*, xlvii (1924), 169 n.
[88] Cf. *supra*, n. 85.
[89] *Romania*, li (1925), 406.
[90] Giraldus Cambrensis, op. cit. vi. 75.
[91] Ibid., p. 104, n. 1.

tempora'; if he were fifty-two years old and he told it in the last year of David's episcopacy, then we should have 1136 as the lower limit. We shall probably not be far wrong, then, if we conclude that Bleheris flourished between 1100 and 1140.

There remains the identification of the count of Poitiers. Lot, in the same article in which he suggested the possibility that Bleheris might have been a bishop who died in 1022, made a case for the identification of the count of Poitiers with the celebrated troubadour, William VII, who held the title of count of Poitou and duke of Aquitaine from 1086 to 1127. The significant point is that, a century after his death, about the time when the second continuator coupled Bleheris with the *conte de Poitiers*, a Provençal referred to the renowned troubadour simply as *lo coms de Peitieus*.[92] To be sure, it is possible that William VIII, who ruled Poitou and Aquitaine for ten years after his father's death in 1127, may have been the count who enjoyed Bleheris' recital—a view held at first by Miss Weston and by Ezio Levi and to which I once subscribed. Yet he achieved no such fame and notoriety as William VII, is less likely to have been referred to simply as *le conte de Poitiers*, and though the troubadour Cercamon wrote an elegy for him, unlike his father he seems to have shown little interest in the *gai saber*. Though the troubadour count seems the more probable patron of Bleheris, yet either he or his son would fit within the chronological limits suggested by Giraldus's reference to Bledhericus. All this converging testimony, therefore, would make it practically certain that the Welsh *fabulator* was reciting his tales of Tristram and Gawain at the court of Poitou before 1137.[93]

---

[92] A. Richard, *Histoire des Comtes de Poitou* (Paris, 1903), i. 502.

[93] Dr. Brugger once argued (*Zts. f. franz. Spr. u. Lit.*, xxxi[2] (1907), 153–8) that the count of Poitiers must have been Henry of Anjou after he married Eleanor of Poitou in 1152 and before he became king of England in 1154. There are several objections to this view. For one thing Brugger mistakenly dated the *Descriptio Cambriae* between 1210 and 1220, and so arrived at a date some fifteen to twenty-five years too late. Secondly, the actual limits of the time when Henry was count of Poitou before he ascended the English throne were 18 May 1152 and 17 August 1153, when his eldest son William was made duke of Aquitaine and presumably count of Poitou (Richard, op. cit. ii. 110, 115). It would be strange that the second continuator of the *Conte del Graal* writing some fifty years later should have referred to Henry by such a title. Thirdly, Bernard de Ventadour, who did know Henry after his marriage to Eleanor of Poitou, never refers to him as count of Poitiers but as the duke of Normandy or the king of England. Their son Richard was called *li cuens de Poitiers* from 1169 till he became king (ibid., p. 150, n. 1), but since Giraldus was twenty-two years old when Richard acquired the title, this

8. THE 'COURONNEMENT LOUIS'. As Warren pointed out many years ago,[94] signs of the circulation of Arthurian legend on the Continent are found in this, one of the earliest of the *chansons de geste*, dated by Ernest Langlois about 1130.[95] Twice in this patriotic French epic, composed in the Île de France, occurs the phrase *tot l'or d'Avalon*, both times in *laisse* xliii, which affords strong linguistic evidence of antiquity.[96] There can be little doubt that Avalon is the elysian isle of Arthurian fable, for no other place of the name had any special repute for riches. But nothing in Geoffrey's *Historia* or Wace describes an abundance of gold in Avalon. In Geoffrey's *Vita Merlini* (date *c.* 1150) Arthur's bed in the Isle of Apples is golden, but Avalon is not mentioned.[97] It is then highly improbable, first, that the *Couronnement* is later in date than the *Vita Merlini*; secondly, that in any case it derived from Geoffrey the gold of Avalon. Curiously enough, it is another *chanson de geste*, the *Bataille Loquifer*, composed by Graindor de Brie, which gives us our first elaborate picture of the gold of Avalon.

> The chief tower was so contrived that there was no stone that was not set in gold. . . . The roof was cast in gold; on a pommel the eagle of gold was fixed.[98]

Freymond proved that the *Bataille Loquifer* in its account of Arthur in the Other World betrays some knowledge of the Welsh traditions of the Cath Palug.[99] The Welsh conception of the Other World in the twelfth century emphasized the store of gold.[100] It cannot be regarded, therefore, as mere coincidence that two French poems should know of the gold of Avalon, one of them as early as 1130. Both must have been acquainted with a genuine tradition of Welsh origin, communicated to the French world by Breton *conteurs*.[101]

identification cannot be reconciled with the fact that Bleheris made his visit to the count a little before Giraldus's time.   [94] *Mod. Lang. Notes*, xiv (1899), 48.

[95] *Couronnement Louis*, ed. E. Langlois (1920), p. vii; ed. of 1888, p. clxx.

[96] *Speculum*, iii (1928), 24, n. 1.

[97] Geoffrey of Monmouth, *Vita Merlini*, ed. J. J. Parry (*University of Illinois Studies in Language and Literature*, 1925), p. 85.

[98] Le Roux de Lincy, *Livre des Légendes* (Paris, 1836), p. 250.

[99] *Beiträge zur romanischen Philologie, Festgabe für G. Gröber* (Halle, 1899), pp. 311 ff.

[100] *Mabinogion*, ed. Loth, 1913, i. 87: 'C'était bien de toutes les cours qu'il avait vues au monde, la mieux pourvue . . . de vaisselle d'or et de bijoux royaux.' Giraldus Cambrensis, op. cit. vi. 76: '. . . auri quo abundabat regio . . . .'

[101] The Breton transmission is determined, not only by considerations already presented, but also by the fact that the form Avalon never occurs in Welsh texts. Cf. *Romanic Rev.*, xxix (1938), 176 f.; *Mod. Phil.*, xxxiii. 234 f.

9. THE 'PÈLERINAGE CHARLEMAGNE'. This again is regarded on linguistic grounds as one of the oldest of the *chansons de geste*, but unfortunately opinions differ as to the date, and while Voretzsch puts it shortly after 1109,[102] others would place it in the second quarter of the century.[103] It is not possible, then, to assert with confidence that the poem antedates the publication of the *Historia Regum Britanniae*. But even if it were composed as late as 1145, it would be difficult to reconcile its existence with any vogue for Arthurian romance established by Geoffrey of Monmouth. For this burlesque epic has been demonstrated by a succession of scholars to be full of Irish and Arthurian motifs, and this state of affairs, as I shall presently show, implies an elaborate Arthurian *conte* as a source for almost everything but the visit to Jerusalem and the acquisition of relics. Now since the *Historia* was still little known to English clerics in 1139 and 1141 and, of course, could not have reached the French laity till later, it is next to impossible that it could have stimulated the production of an Arthurian romance in time to stimulate in turn a Carolingian adaptation by 1145.

The peculiarity of the *Pèlerinage* is that, though it contains no Arthurian allusion like the *Couronnement* and no obvious borrowing from the Round Table cycle like the *Bataille Loquifer*, it has long been recognized as showing marked affinities to Irish literature on the one hand and to Arthurian romance on the other. Of course, the visit to Jerusalem and the obtaining of the relics form a separate element with its own tradition, linked to the fair of Lendit.[104] But Thurneysen first detected reminiscences of old Celtic story-telling, and Webster, Reinhard, Cross, and Laura Hibbard Loomis have pointed out Irish parallels.[105] Their cogency was recognized by Bédier.[106] Child, Gaston Paris, Huet, Kittredge, and Webster have pointed out several Arthurian analogues.[107] These are to be found

---

[102] C. Voretzsch, *Introduction to the Study of Old French Literature*, trans. Du Mont (New York, 1931), p. 176.

[103] J. Coulet, *Études sur l'Ancien Poème Français du Voyage de Charlemagne* (Montpellier, 1907), p. 69; Bédier, Hazard, *Histoire de la Littérature Française Illustrée* (Paris, 1923), i. 9.

[104] J. Bédier, *Légendes Épiques*, ed. 3, iv (Paris, 1929), 137 ff.

[105] R. Thurneysen, *Keltoromanisches* (Halle, 1884), pp. 18–21; *Englische Studien*, xxxvi (1906), 337 ff.; *Mod. Phil.*, xxv (1928), 331 ff.; *Univ. of Michigan Publications in Lang. and Lit.*, viii (1932), 27 ff. [106] Bédier, op. cit. iv. 154 n.

[107] F. J. Child, *English and Scottish Popular Ballads* (1882–98), i. 274 ff.; *Hist. Litt. de la France*, xxx. 110 f.; *Romania*, xli (1912), 531 ff.; *Studies and Notes in Philology and Literature*, viii (Boston, 1903), 212 f.; *Englische Studien*, xxxvi (1906), 337 ff.

in *Hunbaut, Rigomer, Arthur and Gorlagon, De Ortu Walwanii, Diu Crône, King Arthur and King Cornwall, Meraugis de Portlesguez*, the Prose *Lancelot, Artus de la Petite Bretagne*, and the *Avowing of Arthur*.[108] The fact that the *Pèlerinage* contains several noteworthy Irish features should alone suggest that its main plot is based on an Arthurian *conte* transferred to Charlemagne, and this suspicion is corroborated by the fact that parallels are found in ten Arthurian stories. It is clinched by the fact that not one of these ten parallels contains the slightest trace of the Carolingian and ecclesiastical character of the *Pèlerinage*—not one hint of Charlemagne, of Jerusalem or Constantinople, of relics or celestial intervention. Probably no story-tellers stole from each other more freely than those of the Middle Ages, but they were seldom experts in removing the tell-tale marks of origin. That all ten Arthurian romancers should have been particularly cautious and particularly expert in this regard is a preposterous supposition. And yet, if we reject it, we are left with only one other hypothesis to account for the Celtic and Arthurian relations of the *Pèlerinage*; namely, that the *chanson* itself, apart from the story of the relics, is a *rifacimento* of an early Arthurian *conte*. To this theory there can be no objection except that it postulates knowledge of Arthurian *contes* in the neighbourhood of Paris before the date of the *Pèlerinage*, and that, we have seen, is no objection at all.

10. THE MODENA ARCHIVOLT. The late Professor Gerould and I have already discussed at length in the pages of *Speculum* the problem of dating this assuredly Arthurian sculpture over the north doorway of Modena cathedral in the Po valley;[109] and I should not go into the matter again if it were not that Tatlock's statement quoted at the beginning of this article did not show that arguments from architectural history, military costume, and horse furniture had no validity for him. In a private communication he kindly made his position clear. 'I have no new evidence worth mentioning as to the date of

---

[108] *Hunbaut*, ed. Stürzinger and Breuer (Dresden, 1914), pp. 2–5; *Mervelles de Rigomer*, ed. W. Foerster (Dresden, 1908), i. 470–82; *Studies and Notes in Philology and Literature*, viii. 150 f.; Heinrich von dem Türlin, *Diu Crône*, ed. G. H. F. Scholl (Stuttgart, 1852), vss. 3356 ff.; *Historia Meriadoci and De Ortu Walwanii*, ed. J. D. Bruce (Baltimore, 1913), pp. 86 f.; Child, op. cit. i. 283 ff.; Raoul de Houdenc, *Meraugis de Portlesguez*, ed. M. Friedwagner (Halle, 1897), pp. 70 f.; H. O. Sommer, *Vulgate Version of Arthurian Romances*, iv (Washington, 1911), 266 f.; *Arthur of Little Britain*, trans. Berners (London, 1814), pp. 139 f.; W. H. French, C. B. Hale, *Middle English Metrical Romances* (New York, 1930), pp. 611 f.

[109] *Speculum*, x (1935), 355 ff.; xiii (1938), 221 ff.

The Arthurian Legend before 1139

the Modena sculpture, whether early or late twelfth century. My feeling is that the latter date has rather the best of it, and I of course feel, as some others I realize don't, a strong *a priori* probability in its favour. I also feel that to date a work of art within a generation or two on the kind of evidence adduced in this case is risky business.'

I think it is not unfair to Tatlock to say that on this matter he had no cogent evidence; he had only feelings, particularly a very significant feeling as to *a priori* probabilities in favour of a late dating, to which I shall return later. Meanwhile, to such impressionism I wish to oppose three substantial arguments, arguments which cannot be dismissed as 'risky business'. These are: (*a*) the opinions of unbiased art experts; (*b*) a chronological sequence of Italian sculptures of unquestioned date, by which the uninitiated can judge with their own eyes where the Modena archivolt belongs; (*c*) the evidence of names carved on the sculpture.

In presenting the opinions of art experts I deliberately omit those, even the most distinguished, who are prominently involved in the controversy over the priority of Lombard sculpture. I cite only those who cannot be accused of *parti pris*, and therefore omit the direct testimony of Kingsley Porter as the chief champion of an early date.[110] Venturi, whose *Storia dell'Arte Italiana* has long been a classic work, declared: 'La porta della Pescheria dovette esistere già nel tempio costruito da Lanfranco e inaugurato il 30 di aprile 1106.'[111] Von Vitzthum, formerly professor at Göttingen, author of *Die Malerei und Plastik des Mittelalters*, assigned the archivolt to the contemporaries of Wiligelmus, early in the twelfth century.[112] Important is the statement of Camille Martin, author of the sumptuous volume, *L'Art roman en Italie*: 'L'unité de la construction prouve en tout cas que les travaux furent achevés en grande partie au commencement du XIIe siècle',[113] and he refers specifically to the Porta della Pescheria as already existing in 1106. This, be it noted, is an admission from a French expert. Professor Frankl, formerly of Halle, recognized as one of the greatest authorities on the architectural history of the Middle Ages, has already been quoted in my previous article as placing the sculptural activity on the façade and the north portal in the first twenty years of the twelfth

---

[110] A. K. Porter, *Lombard Architecture* (New Haven, 1917), iii. 16.
[111] A. Venturi, *Storia dell'Arte Italiana*, iii (Milan, 1904), 160.
[112] G. von Vitzthum, *Die Malerei und Plastik des Mittelalters* (1924), pp. 80 f.
[113] C. Martin, *L'Art roman en Italie* (Paris, 1912), i. 8 f.

century.[114] Professor Panofsky of the Institute for Advanced Study and Dr. Saxl of the Warburg Institute in a joint article wrote as follows: 'Thus as early as about 1100 we are struck by the remarkable relationship between the two opposite regions of Italy (as witness the sculptures of Bari and Modena).'[115] The reference is obvious to the connexion between the two archivolts at Bari and Modena, discussed in my previous article.[116] Professors Toesca and Robb both attribute the work of Wiligelmus on the façade of Modena cathedral to the first years of the twelfth century, and recognize that the archivolt is the work of early disciples.[117] Professor Morey of Princeton graciously permits me to quote from a letter of his of 7 December 1927. 'I have thought that Porter was right and Mâle was wrong on the date of the Modena Sculptures, and I am glad to see you bring a convincing evidence in support of the early date.' Finally, it is most significant that Mrs. Krautheimer-Hess, who wrote an elaborate and impressive dissertation at Marburg, dating the early Modena sculptures about 1150, has since written to my colleague, Professor Schapiro (12 August 1929): 'Daß meine Datierung der Porta della Pescheria um die Mitte des Jahrhunderts um 20–30 Jahre zu spät angenommen ist, war mir selbst schon seit einiger Zeit klar. Zum mindesten, soweit es die Archivolte betrifft.'

So far as I am aware, no art historian in the United States, Italy, England, or Germany has placed the early Modena sculptures, including the Arthurian relief, later than 1130. Only M. Mâle and M. Deschamps among all the experts in medieval art are still committed to the view that the work of Wiligelmus and his associates at Modena belongs to the second half of the twelfth century.[118] The reason for this attitude on the part of French scholars is obvious. A flourishing school of sculpture in Lombardy early in the twelfth century would upset some sacred dogmas of French archaeology. An examination of the arguments of Mâle and Deschamps reveals nothing substantial.[119] When, therefore, Tatlock

[114] *Jahrbuch für Kunstwissenschaft*, 1927, pp. 46 f.
[115] *Metropolitan Museum Studies*, iv (1932–33), 260 f.
[116] *Speculum*, xiii. 222 f. Cf. M. Wackernagel, *Die Plastik des XI und XII Jahrhunderts in Apulien* (Leipzig, 1911), p. 118.
[117] P. Toesca, *Storia dell'Arte Italiana, Medio Evo*, i (Turin, 1927), 755, 761; *Art Bulletin*, xii (1930), 374.
[118] E. Mâle, *L'Art Religieux du Douzième Siècle* (Paris, 1922), p. 269 n.; *Monuments et Mémoires, Fondation Piot*, xxviii (1927), 69 ff.
[119] *Nuovi Studi Medievali*, ii (1925–6), 105; *Speculum*, iii (1928), 26 f.; *Gazette des*

FIGURE A. Pontida, 1095–1100

FIGURE B. Bari, 1098

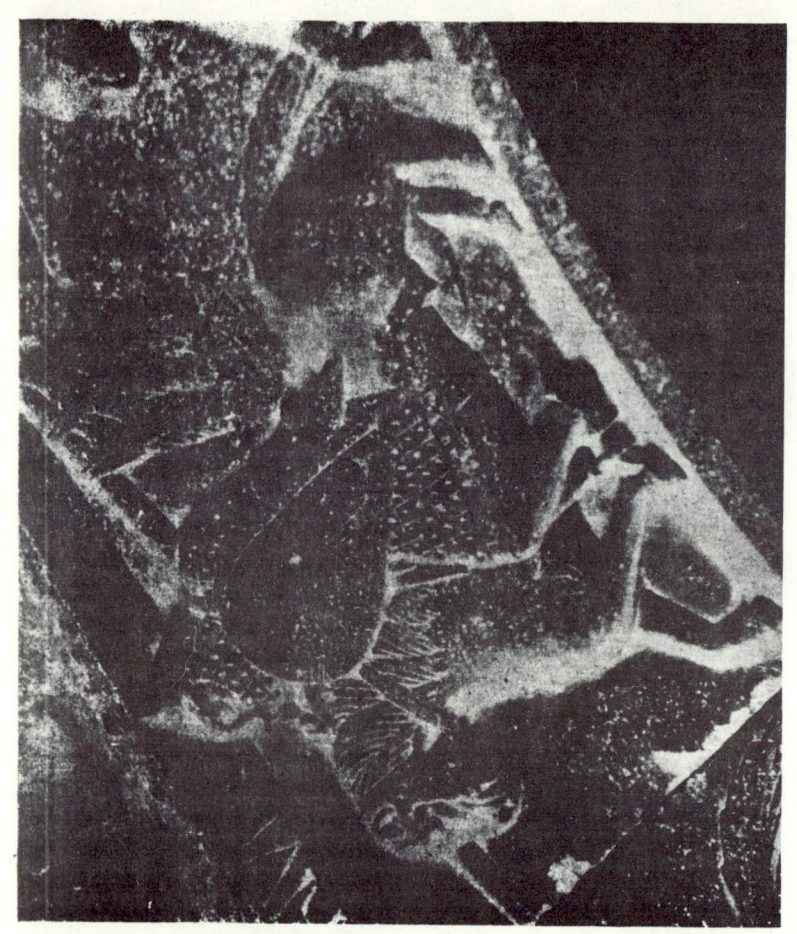

FIGURE C. Modena

FIGURE D. Ferrara, 1135–41

FIGURE E. Parma, 1178

204

FIGURE F. Modena

expressed his feeling in favour of a late date for the Arthurian archivolt, he was opposing his feeling to the great preponderance of expert opinion in the field of medieval art.

But expert testimony is not the final court of appeal; there are always the facts. And luckily there are some questions in art history which even the man without technical training can answer on the evidence of his eyes. This, I think, is one of them. Accordingly the reader will find here reproduced four Italian sculptures dated with something like certainty at intervals between 1095 and 1178, and beside them two details from the Modena archivolt. A comparison should suffice to show whether that relief belongs near 1100, where the majority of art experts would put it, or near 1180, where M. Faral would put it.

The first dated monument (Fig. A) is a sculpture from Pontida, near Bergamo. Porter dated it shortly after 1095 since it formed part of the tomb of San Alberto, who died in that year.[120] Certain features seem characteristic of this date in Italian sculpture: the crude modelling of the horse; the treatment of the tail as a switch of simple, slightly curved strands; the rider's collar with its opening at the neck; the rider's foot hanging down almost to the horse's hoofs. These, then, are features observable in work done in the last lustrum of the eleventh century.

The next monument (Fig. B) is the episcopal throne in the church of San Niccola, Bari, dated by an inscription on it and by historic record in the year 1098.[121] Note, first, the heavy, squat figures of the supporters; and, secondly, the indication of drapery folds on the middle supporter by simple incised lines. These also are features observable in sculpture of the end of the eleventh century.

Skipping some forty years, let us examine a famous relief of St. George over the main doorway of Ferrara cathedral, generally accepted by art experts as work done within a few years before or after 1135 (Fig. D).[122] Sculpture has evidently undergone a marked development since the Pontida horseman was carved forty years

---

Beaux Arts, per. 5, xviii (1928), 116 ff. The arguments of Lefebvre des Noettes and Prof. Leonardo Olschki, since they are not those of art experts, I do not consider here, but have refuted them in *Speculum*, xiii (1938), 224–8, and *Studi Medievali*, N.S., ix (1936), 1 ff.

[120] Porter, *Lombard Architecture*, iii. 295 f.

[121] A. K. Porter, *Romanesque Sculpture of the Pilgrimage Roads* (Boston, 1923), i. 66; *Burlington Magazine*, xliii. 63.

[122] Porter, *Lombard Arhitecture*, ii. 408, 421 f.; *Art Bulletin*, xii (1930), 394–8.

before. The modelling of the horse is more realistic, less wooden. The tail, instead of being a simple group of parallel strands, curls exuberantly; the rider's foot no longer dangles on a level with the fetlocks, but is where it should be; the folds of the rider's skirt and those of the figures below in the arcade are nowhere rendered by mere incised lines as on the Bari throne. The technique of 1135 is patently different from that of 1095–1100.

From the year 1178 we have another Lombard sculpture (Fig. E), which, though it does not offer any analogy in subject with those we have examined, does give us another *point d'appui* and shows figures of draped women to compare with the figure of Winlogee on the Modena archivolt. This sculpture is the Deposition in the Tomb, by Benedetto Antelami at Parma. Its universally accepted date is 1178.[123] Here are no longer the squat figures of the Bari throne, but women of more normal and graceful proportions. The drapery displays a highly stylized, rhythmical treatment of the folds. Eighty years have evidently produced great changes in north Italian sculpture.

Now, with this development in technique in mind, let us turn to some details of the Modena archivolt, and see whether they belong with the Pontida horseman of *c.* 1095 and the Bari throne-supporter of 1098; or with the Ferrara St. George of *c.* 1135; or with the Parma Deposition of 1178. First, note in this mounted figure (Fig. C) the modelling of the horse, the carving of the tail, the position of the rider's foot. Do these belong with the sculpture of 1095 or that of 1135? Next (Fig. F), in this detail of the fortress, note the collar of the man labelled Mardoc, the incised lines indicating folds—features which have met us in the sculptures of 1095 and 1098. Note also the heavy, huddled figure of the woman on the left and her draperies. Can they be contemporaneous with the women of the Deposition of 1178? As between the date 1099–1106, urged by Porter with the support of many facts, and the date about 1180, which M. Faral proposed without the production, so far, of an atom of evidence, there can be little doubt which is closer to the truth. The *terminus ad quem* 1106 may be questioned; but it cannot be postponed very far.

The testimony of art historians, the evidence of the sculptural style, both overwhelmingly confirm the early dating. The argument from the proper names, Galvagin*us* and Isdern*us*, which I first put

[123] Porter, *Lombard Architecture*, iii. 161.

The Arthurian Legend before 1139

forward in 1927, I will not repeat.[124] I merely point out that these name-forms are closer to the Welsh than those employed by Geoffrey and the romancers who follow him, and that I have recently brought additional evidence to prove the derivation of Galvagin*us* from Gwallt-A(d)vwyn.[125] Are we seriously asked to believe that a sculptor of the second half of the twelfth century in Lombardy was dissatisfied with what he was getting in the way of Celtic names from Geoffrey and Wace, and by dint of inquiry was able to ferret out something more archaic? This, so far as I can see, is the only explanation for the name-forms compatible with the belief that the Modena relief owes its existence to the vogue created by Geoffrey and Wace. It seems far more natural to explain these signs of archaism by the date of the sculpture.

The subject of the Modena archivolt has been acknowledged by Foerster and M. Mâle to show kinship with a certain episode in the *Prose Lancelot*,[126] and by Cross and Professor Nitze to be a form of the abduction of Guinevere.[127] It was evidently a highly composite story. The names Winlogee and Artus show that it was brought to Italy by a Breton speaking French, for Winlogee is patently a development of Breton Winlowen,[128] and Artus is a characteristic French development of Arthur.[129] That we should find a highly composite tale at this early date will surprise no one who has read *Kulhwch and Olwen* or has meditated on Kittredge's dictum:

> The fact that we can detect so much rationalizing in the French Arthurian material, and that too in very early texts—in Chrétien for example—shows that these texts come late in the history of the story which each tells. They stand, in a sense, at the end rather than at the beginning of a long course of development.[130]

That the story carved at Modena should be transmitted by Bretons speaking French will surprise no one who has examined the evidence

---

[124] *Medieval Studies in Memory of Gertrude Schoepperle Loomis* (New York, 1927), p. 214; *Studi Medievali*, N.S., ix (1936), 1 ff.; *Speculum*, xiii (1938), 228. The *s* in Isdernus was probably silent, since in the first half of the twelfth century the same woman appears in the records as Gilla and Gisla. Cf. *Romania*, xvii (1888), 362.

[125] Cf. *supra*, p. 184, n. 41. The form Galvaginus has probably been influenced by the name Galginus, recorded in Italy as early as 1032. Cf. *Documenti di Storia Italiana*, iv (Florence, 1870), 302.

[126] *Zts. f. Rom. Phil.*, xxii (1898), 243 ff.; Mâle, op. cit., p. 269.

[127] T. P. Cross, W. A. Nitze, *Lancelot and Guenevere* (Chicago, 1930), p. 23.

[128] *Medieval Studies in Memory of Gertrude Schoepperle Loomis*, p. 222.

[129] *Göttingische Gelehrte Anzeigen*, 1890, p. 832 n.

[130] G. L. Kittredge, *Study of Gawain and the Green Knight*, p. 241.

for the Breton *conteurs* as intermediaries between Welsh and French Arthurian tradition. That it should be a variant of the abduction of Guinevere will surprise no one who has been convinced by Tatlock's dating of the *Vita Gildae*. That it should have found its way to the Lombard plain will surprise no one who has examined the evidence for Arthurian proper names in northern Italy presently to be discussed. The Modena archivolt is not an anomalous or impossible freak; it is in perfect harmony with the rest of the facts.

11. THE NAMES ARTUSIUS AND WALWANUS RECORDED IN NORTHERN ITALY. In 1888 Rajna called attention to the fact that an Artusius appears in a document of 1114 as that of a brother of Ugo, count of Padua, and that another Artusius de Rovaro of the Trevisan march signs a document of 1122.[131] Both, as the circumstances indicate, must have been born and christened before 1092. I was the first to point out that another Artusius is recorded in 1125 as a benefactor of Modena cathedral.[132] The same name, with unimportant variations such as Artusus or Arthusius, keeps cropping up throughout the twelfth century. In 1136 near Padua a certain long-lived Walwanus is recorded for the first time.[133] In 1139 he appears as Walquanus, in 1141 as Walwanus and Valvanus, in 1143 as Walwanus;[134] in 1145 or 1146 as Walwanus he is mentioned together with Count Ugo of Padua, brother of the now defunct Artusius.[135] In 1149 the name appears as Gualguagnus,[136] and finally we learn that in 1181 Dominus Walwanus had been dead over two years.[137] Rajna calculated that this Walwanus must have been christened in the first or second decade of the century.

Rajna concluded that these names proved the popularity of Arthur and Gawain in aristocratic circles before and right after the year 1100, and the fact that these names did not exist in Italy before such a popularity was conceivable strengthened his point. His thesis was accepted generally. Zimmer in 1890 quoted witnesses

---

[131] *Romania*, xvii (1888), 167, 356.
[132] *Regesta Chartarum Italiae*, xvi (1931), 295.
[133] *Romania*, xvii. 362; *Codice Diplomatico Padovano dall' Anno 1101 alla Pace di Costanza*, part 1, ed. A. Gloria (Venice, 1879), p. 236.
[134] *Codice Dipl. Pad.*, &c., pp. 282, 294-6, 309.
[135] Ibid., p. 346.
[136] Ibid., p. 380.
[137] *Romania*, xvii. 363.

The Arthurian Legend before 1139

to the participation of Bretons in the eleventh-century Norman conquests in Italy, and commented on the name-forms:

> Die sogenannte französische Lautform der Namen Artus (aus Arturs), Galvan (Walwan) in Italien beruht dann nicht darauf daß 'la Francia', sondern 'il suo linguaggio' den Vermittler spielte; es ist die Lautform der französisch redenden Bretonen, die natürlich dieselbe war in Italien wie in Nordfrankreich und England.[138]

Unfortunately Rajna did not sufficiently emphasize the identity of these Latinized forms with unquestionable forms of the names of Arthur and Gawain. Artusius seems to have been the regular Italian Latinization of Arthur when the source was French. In an Italian *exemplum* we find Artusius de Britagna;[139] in a library catalogue of the Visconti dated 1426 we read: 'Liber unus in Gallico Regis Artusij'; 'Liber unus in gallico tractans de morte Regis Artusij'.[140] The form Walwanus of the 1136 document (as well as of four others) is exactly that habitually used in one of the best manuscripts of Geoffrey of Monmouth;[141] it differs by only a weakened vowel from the Walwen employed by William of Malmesbury in 1125.[142] A variant of the name, Galvanus, which appears in a Paduan document of 1144,[143] became the regularly established Latinization of Gawain in Italy,[144] just as Galvano became the most common vernacular form.

It is against Rajna's interpretation of these facts that Tatlock delivered his most elaborate attack, and he took the trouble to give

---

[138] *Göttingische Gelehrte Anzeigen*, 1890, pp. 830–2, n. Cf. *Romania*, xvii (1888), 169: 'Artusius e Artusus, accordandosi coll' Artus della tradizione francese.'

[139] Kittredge, op. cit., p. 96.

[140] G. d'Adda, *Indagini Storiche, Artistiche e Bibliografiche sulla Libreria Visconteo-Sforzesca del Castello di Pavia*, parte prima (Milan, 1875), nos. 863, 916.

[141] Geoffrey of Monmouth, *Historia*, ed. Griscom, pp. 444, 474 f. This form has probably been influenced in France by the name Galans, Latinized as Walandus, which appears in the twelfth century and later as that of the traditional Germanic smith Wayland. Cf. P. Maurus, 'Die Wielandsage in der Literatur', *Münchener Beiträge zur Romanischen und Englischen Philologie*, xxv (1902), 32 ff. It is the same Germanic name which appears along with others of the same origin in Lombardy as Walano or Walando as early as 999, and as Gualandus in 1122. Cf. A. Gloria, *Codice Diplomatico Padovano dal Secolo Sesto a Tutto l' Undecimo* (Venice, 1877), pp. 112, 297; *Codice Diplomatico Padovano dall' Anno 1101 alla Pace di Costanza*, part 1, pp. 50, 108. Prof. Dino Bigongiari kindly refers me to W. Bruckner, *Die Sprache der Langobarden* (Strassburg, 1895), p. 320, *sub* 'Guelantus'.

[142] Cf. *supra*, p. 184, n. 39.

[143] Gloria, *Codice Dipl. Pad. dall' Anno 1101 alla Pace di Costanza*, p. 327.

[144] Cf. *supra*, n. 139.

me his references in full. So far as I can see, however, he has not seriously damaged the position. His method was to assemble from Italian records earlier than 1100 names more or less resembling those of Artusius and Galvanus or Walwanus. If these appear before there is any likelihood that the *matière de Bretagne* could have reached Italy, then, he contended, the significance of such names as evidence of the spread of the legend would be reduced.

What are the most striking examples brought forward by Tatlock? He cited an Artusinus from a document of 998.[145] Checking the reference, we find the document beginning: 'Exemplum instrumenti, cujus tenor talis est', and ending: 'Et ego Artusinus notarius exemplavi.' In other words, Artusinus was simply the name of a notary who copied, *when we do not know*, a document of 998. It is not until the twelfth century that we find Artusinus as a recognized diminutive of Artusius.[146] There is nothing to give us pause here; nor is there in an alleged Artusinus of 1097. When we consult the text, we find that it cannot be an original document or a faithful copy but is full of gross blunders. We read: 'promittimus at vobis Baroncellu & Artusinu germanus fratre tuus & at vestros eredis masculini . . . promittimus et obligamus at vobi Baroncellu et Arduinu & at vestri eredibus . . . at vobis Baroncellu & at Alcuini & at vestris eredis masculini.'[147] From this dog-Latin we can conclude merely that the name of Baroncellu's brother in the original document of 1097 began with *A* and ended in *-inus*, and that a copyist in some later century made three guesses, one being Artusinus.

There is, therefore, no authentic record of an Artusinus until the grandson of the Artusius of 1114, who appears in a document of 1148 as 'Artuso filius Manfredi', reappears in documents of 1162 as Artusinus or Arthusinus.[148] The latter forms, therefore, are certainly diminutives of Artus. It is interesting to note that the name was continued in the family, and that Manfred, who was both the son and the father of an Artus, was regarded as the richest man in the Trevisan march.

Though Tatlock was mistaken in adducing two Artusini before 1100, he had better authority for a *fundus Arturianus* near Rome

[145] G. B. Mittarelli, A. Costadoni, *Annales Camaldulenses*, i (Venice, 1755), Appendix, col. 147 f.
[146] *Romania*, xvii (1888), 359 f.
[147] Mittarelli, Costadoni, op. cit. iii, Appendix, col. 136.
[148] Cf. *supra*, n. 146.

The Arthurian Legend before 1139

recorded as early as 792 and another *fundus Arturianus* near Ravenna in 973.[149] These, however, had nothing to do with the hero of the French-speaking Bretons. Arturianus is simply an adjective derived from the common Roman name Artorius, with weakened vowel; and these *fundi Arturiani* were simply estates of some Artorius.

As for early occurrences of the name Walwanus or Galvanus, there is an alleged Galvanus in a charter of 1036,[150] who seems embarrassing until we look at the text. It is not the original but a seventeenth-century copy, which Gaddoni printed with the warning comment: 'Zaccaria hoc diploma transcripsit ex antiquo exemplari in archivo monasterii, amanuensis inscitia, ut ait, depravato.' Zaccaria called attention particularly to the corruption of proper names: Berardus for Gerardus, Quoradum for Gerardum, Chadalocus for Cadalous. The authority for the name Galvanus in 1036 could hardly be worse.

The name-forms which bear closest resemblance to those adduced by Rajna and which at first sight seem to prove that the names were known in northern Italy well before any Breton *conteurs* could have introduced the Arthurian legend, turn out on inspection either to be direct derivatives of the Roman name Artorius (which Artusius and Artusinus cannot be), or to lack authentic record before 1100.

Tatlock was not content with producing names from early Italian records which closely resemble Rajna's forms, but he also cited a Gauginus of 874 and 882, and a Galginus of 1032,[151] decidedly remote from Walwanus, Walquanus, Gualguagnus, Galvanus. The argument seems to be that if a proper name comes into vogue shortly after the appearance of a possible literary or traditional source for that name, that literary or traditional source cannot or need not be the responsible cause if vaguely similar names had already been familiar. Let us see where this reasoning would lead us if applied to a later age and a later vogue. It is generally assumed that the name Oscar became popular in the British Isles and Scandinavia because the vogue of Macpherson's Ossian had introduced the reading public of Europe to Oscar, the son of Ossian. Here we have a close parallel to the appearance of Artusius and Walwanus as proper names in northern Italy about the time that the Modena sculpture

---

[149] *Regesta Chartarum Italiae*, iii. 6, 8, 325; *Regesta di Farfa*, ii. 129; iii. 2; v. 305.
[150] S. Gaddoni, G. Zaccherini, *Chartularium Imolense* (Imola, 1912), ii. 286.
[151] *Regesta Chartarum Italiae*, i (Rome, 1907), 3; *Documenti di Storia Italiana*, iv (Florence, 1870), 302.

shows that Breton *conteurs* had ranged thus far afield. But according to Tatlock's implied argument the connexion between the name Oscar and the Ossianic craze may be denied, since long before 1760 a name vaguely similar to Oscar had been known to the reading public of Europe. There was a name Osric, which recalls Oscar just as clearly as Galginus recalls Galvanus. It appears in the *Anglo-Saxon Chronicle* as early as 634 and as late as 860. It occurs in such widely read works as Bede's *Ecclesiastical History* and Geoffrey of Monmouth's magnum opus, and turns up as that of a minor character in Shakespeare's *Hamlet*. Only a sort of metathesis is necessary to explain the conversion of Osric into Oscar. Even more sensational is the fact that in Anglo-Saxon records of the tenth century, as one may see in Searle's *Onomasticon Anglo-saxonicum*, page 373, the name Osgar appears several times, and what could be nearer to Oscar? Thus we are led by Tatlock's logic to the conclusion that the Ossianic craze had nothing to do with the christening of many Oscars after 1760 because the names Osric and Osgar had appeared long before in English nomenclature. I am not caricaturing Tatlock's logic: I am merely applying it to Oscar. I think no Ossianist will accept it; neither, I hope, will many Arthurians.

The one consideration which might give us pause is the curious fact that these Italian boys were being named after Arthur and Gawain before any similar influence appears in French nomenclature, and it is agreed on all hands that the Bretons must have circulated in France and Norman England before they came down across the Alps. However improbable the priority of the Italians in this regard may seem, nevertheless it should be considered together with the fact that throughout the later medieval centuries the Italians showed a greater fondness for Arthurian names than any other European people. Bernabo Visconti, 'god of delit and scourge of Lumbardye', named his illegitimate children Palamede, Lionello, Ettore, Galeotto, Lancilotto, Sagromoro, Isotta, Ginevra.[152] Rajna adds to this list other names known in Italy: Princivalle, Galeazzo, Galvano, Brandeligi, Erecco, Dinadano, Ivano.[153] Some obscure psychological trait made the Italians more susceptible to the onomastic charms of the Round Table cycle than other peoples,

---

[152] P. Litta, *Famiglie Celebri di Italia* (Milan, 1819–83), I, tav. vii.
[153] *Romania*, xvii (1888), 181–4. Cf. *Giornale Storico della Letteratura Italiana*, v (1885), 129 f.

and this is perhaps sufficient explanation for the fact that in Lombardy and the Trevisan march boys of noble birth were christened Artusius and Walwanus before or shortly after 1100.

It is significant that these are new names; that they begin to appear after the fascination of the Breton tales for the people of the Lombard plain had been recorded in stone at Modena cathedral; that they are attached to men of noble birth, whose fathers would have been most open to the appeal of chivalric story; and that the earliest Artusius and the earliest Walwanus moved in the same aristocratic circle of Padua. Unless there is some stronger objection to Rajna's interpretation of these facts than any yet offered, we cannot dissociate these names from the Artus de Bretania and Galvaginus, who are the most prominent of the knights carved at Modena; from the 'Artur de quo Britonum nugae hodieque delirant', and his nephew Walwen, 'miles virtute nominatissimus', who alone among the figures of the cycle are mentioned by William of Malmesbury in 1125; from the Artusius de Britagna and Galvanus, 'nepos regis Artusii', of the late Italian exemplum.

THERE ARE, THEN, ELEVEN WITNESSES who speak to us in parchment or in stone and tell us that a cycle of romantic stories existed about Arthur and his knights before 1139. Granted that not all are of equal cogency; granted that the date of the *Couronnement Louis* is not fixed beyond peradventure earlier than the publication of Geoffrey's *Historia*, and the *Pèlerinage Charlemagne* may be later, while Ailred's reference is surely later by several years. Yet even the testimony of these three is hard to explain without the presupposition that Arthurian legends had already been in circulation for a few years, and the odds, in my opinion, favour the view that they refer to the same traditions that are certified for 1125 by William of Malmesbury, for 1113 by Herman of Laon, and for even earlier by the Modena sculpture and the proper names in northern Italy. All the conclusions arrived at on the basis of the first five witnesses are confirmed by the latter six. Everything in the history of Arthurian romance fits in with the view that legends, originating in Wales and Cornwall, were through the agency of professional reciters passed on to the bilingual Breton *conteurs*, who before the year 1100 had begun to fascinate audiences wherever French was understood. It was through them and the Welshman Bleheris, who had much the same repertoire, that the vogue of Arthurian romance was established as far as Lombardy well before 1139.

Tatlock was, of course, aware of most, if not all, of the evidence I have adduced, and yet he clung to an interpretation of the facts which at times seems strained, at times stands in flat contradiction to the best expert opinion, at times rests on a corrupt text or a far from cogent logical process. It is obvious that so rational, so cautious a scholar would not have denied the validity of all this evidence unless there were some reason. I think the clue is found in his phrase which I have already quoted, 'the strong *a priori* probability' in favour of a late twelfth-century date for the Modena relief. Naturally I was most curious as to what this presumption against an early Arthurian tradition could be, and I wrote asking what the basis was. Tatlock on 25 August 1939 replied to my query as follows: 'It is partly of course answered in my article *Saints* in *Speculum*.' Then followed the paragraph already quoted on pp. 179–80, which consists of personal inferences and interpretations, not of any basic facts which might justify conclusions. The only direct answer to my question is found in the last sentence of the letter: 'The paucity of anecdote in which he [Arthur] is the chief figure seems to me to support my opinion.'

Tatlock then rested his position really on two points: the evidence of the saints' lives, and the paucity of incident in the romances in which Arthur is the chief actor.

Let us consider the bearing of the Welsh saints' lives on the question of a romantic cycle of tales before Geoffrey. It is, of course, true that except for the *Vita Gildae*, already discussed, and the *Vita Iltuti*,[154] which may be later than Geoffrey's *Historia*, Arthur appears in early Welsh hagiology as a lewd, blustering, somewhat ridiculous *tyrannus*, whose power is contrasted unfavourably with that of the saints. Do these hostile documents, then, give us representative, unbiased examples of Arthurian fiction before Geoffrey? The question almost answers itself. The attitude of the monastic clergy to the heroes of secular story throughout the Middle Ages was likely to be very different from that of the laity, though the militant Christianity of the Carolingian paladins made them acceptable to both parties. Ingeld, Arthur's contemporary, was the hero of a story of revenge, mentioned in *Widsith* and *Beowulf*. For the epic poet he was *glaed sunu Frodan*, the gracious (or glorious) son of Froda.[155] But Alcuin, the monk, in a well-known passage demanded

---

[154] *Speculum*, xiv (1939), 353–6.
[155] *Beowulf*, ed. F. Klaeber, ed. 3 (Boston, 1936), vs. 2025.

indignantly: 'Quid Hinieldus cum Christo? Ille paganus perditus plangit in inferno.'[156] Again, Theodoric the Goth became, as we all know, Dietrich von Bern, central figure of a legend familiar throughout Germany and Scandinavia. But the clergy, because he was an Arian heretic, represented him as the son of a devil, and on the façade of San Zeno at Verona he was carved galloping naked on a horse to his infernal doom. *Petit infera, non rediturus.*[157] He also, like Ingeld, went to hell. Alexander the Great became the centre of a chivalric cycle and one of the Nine Worthies. He was admired not only for his prowess but also for his unparalleled largess. As Marian Whitney wrote: 'All through the Middle Ages we find Alexander cited as the standard of comparison for all others whose virtues are to be celebrated.'[158] But what of the stricter clerical attitude? Moralistic works repeat St. Augustine's anecdote, which makes the great conqueror out to be nothing but a freebooter on a grand scale.[159] They select him as a supreme example of pride, a human Lucifer because he made claims to godhead and attempted to reach the skies in the first flying machine.[160] In the Middle English *Alphabet of Tales* Alexander is a chosen exemplar of *Ambitio* and *Superbia*.[161] Would it be possible to judge of the reputations of Ingeld, Theodoric, and Alexander from clerical testimony alone? That is what Tatlock seemed to do when he maintained on the basis of the saints' lives that Arthur was an obscure and absurd figure among the Welsh before 1139, and hence an even more obscure and absurd figure anywhere else. Is not the argument patently fallacious?

There is the best of reasons for differentiating the verdict of lay minstrels from that of monkish historians and hagiographers; they were often at swords' points. In Wales we have no exception. Let me quote the sentiments of a grey friar expressed in a famous poem by Dafydd ap Gwilym: 'There is nothing in the art of you minstrels but flattery, and useless sounds, and inciting men and women to

[156] W. W. Lawrence, *Beowulf and Epic Tradition* (Cambridge, Mass., 1928), pp. 82, 326.
[157] Porter, *Lombard Architecture*, iii. 531, n. 74.
[158] *Vassar Mediaeval Studies*, ed. C. F. Fiske (New Haven, 1923), pp. 201 f.
[159] John Gower, *Confessio Amantis*, Bk. III, vss. 2363 ff.; *Gesta Romanorum*, trans. C. Swan, tale 146; John of Salisbury, *Polycraticus*, ed. Webb, i. 224; Chaucer, *Works*, ed. F. N. Robinson (1933), p. 871 n.
[160] *Burlington Magazine*, xxxii (1918), 177–85. Cf. Berthold von Regensburg, *Predigten*, ed. F. Pfeiffer (Vienna, 1862), i. 522.
[161] E.E.T.S., O.S., vols. cxxvi, cxxvii (1904–5), tales 49, 737.

sin and falsehood.'[162] So much for the clerical view of the minstrels. Now for the minstrels' view of the monks.

> Monks congregate in a choir like dogs . . .
> Monks congregate like wolves . . .
> They know not when midnight and dawn divide,
> Nor what is the course of the wind nor who agitates it,
> In what place it dies away, on what land it roars.[163]

Considering this poetic exchange of amenities, to expect the monkish writers of saints' lives to represent the darling of the *cyfarwyddiaid* and bards in a flattering light is to expect the Russian propaganda office to reflect the sentiments of Downing Street. What seems to be the main support for Tatlock's conviction that there were no romantic tales of Arthur before Geoffrey—despite all the evidence to the contrary—was simply the evidence of the saints' lives.

Tatlock's other confirmatory point is the paucity of anecdote regarding Arthur himself in the romances, as contrasted with the prominence of Gawain, Lancelot, Tristram, and the rest. In other words, Arthur and his court could not have figured in these stories at first; they came to be localized in Logres, at Camelot or Caerleon, and Arthur was introduced, in the course of transmission and development. So far I am in perfect agreement with Tatlock. It is absolutely certain, for instance, that the Beheading Test and Temptation episodes in the French romances and in *Gawain and the Green Knight* had originally nothing to do with Arthur's court.[164] We know who were originally the chief characters; they were a king of Ulster, his warriors, and a monstrous giant from Munster. It is undoubtedly true that the Round Table cycle attracted to itself many stories, Celtic and otherwise, simply because of the fame of Arthur. But what, apparently, Tatlock took for granted is that Geoffrey's *Historia* alone can account for that fame—an assumption which to my eyes seems a rather glaring example of *petitio principii*. For is not that precisely the point which is in question?

Neither the Welsh saints' lives nor the paucity of anecdotes which assign a chief role to Arthur in the Continental and English romances affords any secure basis for that *a priori* probability by

---

[162] Dafydd ap Gwilym, *Detholion o Gywyddau* (Bangor, 1921), p. 102. Reference kindly supplied by Prof. Kenneth Jackson.
[163] W. F. Skene, *Four Ancient Books of Wales* (Edinburgh, 1868), i. 266; T. Stephens, *Literature of the Cymry* (Llandovery, 1849), p. 194.
[164] *PMLA*, xlviii (1933), 1000 ff.

which Tatlock justified his belief that the traditions of Arthur were scanty, somewhat discreditable, and confined to Celtic territory until Geoffrey exalted him to the throne of western Europe. The plain fact is, then, that ample evidence exists for a widespread, elaborate, fascinating legend of Arthur before the publication of the *Historia*, and that there is no antecedent probability against such a view.

The opposite view, that Geoffrey established the reputation of Arthur and thus made possible the astoundingly rapid development of Arthurian romance, involves very serious difficulties. With the exception of some minor and some dubious matters, the French romancers of the later half of the twelfth century write as if they had never heard of Geoffrey or Wace.[165] As to the fact, Tatlock agreed: 'So far as the romancers ignore Geoffrey of Monmouth, I should attribute it to his irrelevance for them. Their matter is totally different from his. But I think he helped give them an audience or vogue, though he didn't inspire them.' And again, 'Ignoring, hardly marked ignorance of, his work seems to me natural.' It is agreed, then, that Geoffrey's pseudo-history and pseudo-prophecies are totally different from the romances in matter; the early romancers, generally speaking, 'ignore Geoffrey'.

This state of affairs, which seems to me perfectly natural on the assumption that the romancers exploited matter supplied by the pre-Galfridian Celtic tradition, seems to me most unnatural if there was no such tradition and if the one man who furnished the romancers with an audience and a vogue was Geoffrey of Monmouth. If it was the *Historia* which converted the western world to the eminence of the British battle-chief, and if it was knowledge of this fact which led the romancers to compose a whole cycle of tales about his knights of the Table Round, why should they not refer to Geoffrey or Wace as authority rather than to the *conteur* Bleheris? Was it sheer perversity which led them to refer to Wace but once,[166] and to Bleheris, Breri, Blihis, Bliobleheris as an Arthurian authority or a superlative story-teller five times? Why do the figures of Merlin and Modred, so prominent in pseudo-history and so eminently adapted as wizard and villain to effective roles in romance, play no part in the pages of Chrétien or Marie? Mere caprice?

---

[165] Thomas, *Tristan*, ed. Bédier, ii. 101; J. D. Bruce, *Evolution of Arthurian Romance*, i. 37 n.
[166] Bruce, op. cit. i. 37 n.

Surely Tatlock could not maintain that these two personages were not adapted to the purposes of romantic fiction.

Moreover, the nomenclature of the romances is hard to account for if their authors, especially those who were clerics, had been familiar with Geoffrey and Wace, and surely no one was likely to be more familiar than they. Why is it that not one of them ever drew on that part of the long and convenient list of the notables at Arthur's coronation which Geoffrey faked from the Welsh genealogies,[167] or made any use of the non-Celtic names, Holdinus, Borellus, Guitardus, in the same list? Is it 'natural' that, though they introduce Kai, Bedivere, Loth, whose names we have good reason to believe were a part of authentic Welsh tradition,[168] they scrupulously avoid those names which we know could not have been a part of authentic Welsh tradition? To explain this fact, we must attribute to Chrétien and his successors not only a perverse antipathy for borrowing names freely from Geoffrey or Wace, but also a knowledge of Geoffrey's sources and unscrupulous procedures which scholars have only achieved after 700 years.

On the other hand, when Chrétien chooses names for his heroes, he gives us Erec, derived immediately from Breton Guerec;[169] Lancelot, derived from Welsh Llawynnawc or Llenlleawc by contamination with the French name Lancelin;[170] Ivain, son of Urien, derived from Welsh Owain, son of Urien, through Breton Ivan.[171] As for Perceval, it would be possible to assert, though far from easy to prove, that the name is Chrétien's private improvement on Geoffrey's Peredur, yet it is noteworthy that the one other hero of Chrétien's readily identifiable in the *Historia*, namely Ivain, cannot have derived his name from Geoffrey's Iwenus, but from the Breton Ivan.[172] If the romancers exploited Arthur and his knights because Geoffrey had made their names glamorous, why did they reject so large a part of the onomasticon his book supplied, and discriminate on grounds which would have appealed only to a twentieth-century scholar?

[167] R. H. Fletcher, *Arthurian Materials in the Chronicles*, pp. 76 f.; Faral, *Légende Arthurienne*, première partie, ii. 76.

[168] They appear in the *Black Book of Carmarthen* and in *Kulhwch and Olwen*. On the identity of Loth with Llwch cf. *Revue Celtique*, xvi. 84 ff.; E. T. Griffiths, *Chantari di Lancelotto* (Oxford, 1924), p. 186; Romania, liv (1928), 518.

[169] Romania, xxv. 588.   [170] Romania, liv. 517.

[171] H. Morice, *Mémoires pour Servir de Preuves à l'Histoire de Bretagne* (Paris, 1742), i, cols. 457, 469.

[172] *Mod. Phil.*, xxxiii (1936), 233, n. 36.

Furthermore, how can one explain the access which the French romancers evidently had to non-Galfridian Welsh names? There are Meleagant and Maheloas, forms of Welsh Melwas, unknown to Geoffrey; Giflet fils Do, manifestly descended from Gilfaethwy son of Don; Caradoc Briebras; the boar Tortain, which we have noted already as the French counterpart of the Twrch Trwyth; the monster Capalu, which can be hardly anything else than the Cath Palug of the triads. One could extend the list indefinitely.[173] The romancers did not get these Welsh names from Geoffrey or Wace; how did they get them? Did they travel in Wales? Did they send emissaries to Wales? Did they import Welsh manuscripts, where the proper names are indistinguishable without a knowledge of the language from the rest of the text? Or did the initiative come from the Welsh? Were they impelled by the vogue of the *Historia* to attach tales which had previously had nothing to do with Arthur to the new hero? Was this promptly followed by translations of these Welsh tales on a grand scale for the benefit of the French *conteurs*? And did these *conteurs* hasten back to put their newly acquired stock of tales at the disposal of literary men like Chrétien and Andreas Capellanus? And where do the Bretons come in? And why is it that if Yorkshire about 1140 saw a flourishing crop of Arthurian tales, quite independent of any Welsh or Breton influence, inspired solely by Walter Espec's copy of the *Historia*, we have no traces of it? Here are questions on which no upholder of Geoffrey's responsibility for Arthurian romance has thus far shed a ray of light. In vain will one search the publications of Edmund Chambers, M. Faral, Gerould, and Tatlock for any solution to these difficulties.

Until some concrete, plausible hypothesis to account for the phenomena is put forward by the advocates of Geoffrey as the effective cause of Arthurian romance, we may reject the whole scheme of interpretation. It does not fit the facts as does the theory of Welsh traditional development and Breton transmission to the Continent before the year 1100. It involves clear examples of the fallacy of *post hoc ergo propter hoc* and of *petitio principii*. It involves the assumption that the saints' lives are reliable indexes of Arthur's status among the laity. After all, Gaston Paris, Rajna, Bédier, Porter, Zimmer, Foerster, and Miss Weston, not to mention any number of living scholars, were agreed on one thing, however they

---

[173] Ibid., p. 230; *Romania*, lxiii (1937), 383 ff.; H. Newstead, *Bran the Blessed in Arthurian Romance* (New York, 1939); *Mod. Lang. Notes*, xliii (1928), 215 ff.

may have disagreed on others: they recognized the existence of a flourishing Arthurian fiction before Geoffrey of Monmouth. Once this is granted, it is easily demonstrable that this body of fiction furnished far more matter to the *matière de Bretagne* than ever did the *Historia Regum Britanniae*, the *Vita Merlini*, and the *Brut* put together.

GENERAL INDEX

Aber Henvelen, 148, 151
Abergavenny, 13
Acluz, 107
Adam de la Halle (le Bossu), 88, 100, 127
Adeon, 7 f.
Adventures of Cormac, Echtra Chormaic, 31 f., 137
Agravain, 174
Ailred of Rievaulx, 186–90
Alain, king of Norway, 54 f.
Alan Rufus, 187
Alan III, 187
Alclut, 107
Alexandria, soldan of, 110
Alfred of Beverley, 189 f.
Alixandre l'Orphelin, 109
Annales Cambriae, 179 f.
Annwn, 38 f., 81, 83, 98–100, 119, 121, 137-54, 159–61, 164–9, 172 f., 175, 177
Antipodes, 61 ff.
Anwyl, E., 47, 131, 169
Apollo Maponos, 147
Arawn, 79, 81–83, 87, 100, 140, 152
Arberth, 36, 101, 103, 172 f.
Arderydd, 160
Argante, 108
Armes Prydein, 131
Arnold, Matthew, 24, 104
Art, son of Conn, 143
Arthur and Gorlagon, 198
Arthur, 1 f., 11 f., 17, 24–26, 49, 60 ff., 78 f., 82–84, 88, 105 f., 131 ff., 140, 147, 153 f., 159 f., 163, 166, 177, 179–91, 196
Artus de la Petite Bretagne, 198
Atre Périlleux, 85
Augustine, St., 44
Avallach, 72, 88, 96–98, 114, 126, 154 f.
Avalloc, 88, 96 f., 114
Avalon, 61 f., 65, 72, 74, 96 f., 100, 106, 113–16, 118 f., 154 f., 160, 164, 196
Avowing of Arthur, 198

Balin, Balaain, 29–31, 163
Bardsey, 160 f., 166, 176
Bari, 200

Bataille Loquifer, 196 f.
Bath, 1
Baudemaguz, 84
Beaumayns, 14, 163
Becuma, 31
Bede, 5
Bédier, J., 1, 179, 187, 189, 197
Bedwyr, 147, 154
Bel Inconnu, 14 f., 93
Benoit de Ste-Maure, 106 f., 115
Bercilak, 86–89, 163
Bernard de Ventadour, 194
Béroul, 11
Biket, R., 11, 190
Bilis, 64, 74
Birth of Mongan, 80
Black Book of Carmarthen, 161
Blancheflor, 22
Blancheville, 42
Bláthnat, 77 f., 86, 163
Blaunchard, 112, 114, 116
Bleheris, Bledhericus, 67 n. 31, 193–5
Blihis, 193, 217
Boann, 8
Bodb, 8, 118, 142
Bodmin, 180
Book of Aneirin, 51
Book of Leinster, 118
Book of Taliesin, 131, 140 f., 145 f., 148, 155 f., 160, 162
Boron, Robert de, 50, 91 f.
Borrow, G., 51
Bors, Bohors, 25, 30, 34, 47 f., 50
Bran de Lis, 108
Bran Fitz Donwal, 42 f., 45 f., 48 f.
Brân, son of Dyfnwal, 45 f., 49–51, 159, 175
Brân, son of Llŷr, 4, 15, 35, 41, 43 f., 48 f., 51, 53, 56–60, 148 f., 151 f., 157 n. 140, 159, 173, 177
Brandigan, 144, 159
Brandin, L., 42
Brandus des Illes, 145
Brangoire, 48 f.
Branwen, 5, 48, 51, 53, 56–59, 148 f., 151 f., 157 n. 140, 160, 164, 173
Brecon, 82
Brenne, 43
Brennius, 43 f., 59 f., 159

General Index

Brennus, 49, 59
Breri, 193, 217
Bretons, 14, 18, 61, 65, 71, 92, 107, 124-6, 144, 155, 181, 183-9, 193 f., 196
Breuddwyd Rhonabwy, Dream of Rhonabwy, 96 f., 102, 131
Brian, son of Turenn, 29 f.
Bricriu, 143
Bricriu's Feast, Fled Bricrend, 77, 137, 163
Britael, 181
Britanni, 180-2
Britones, 181, 183-5
Brittany, 6, 8, 61, 65, 71 (Britannia Minor), 120, 124, 179, 181, 184, 186 f.
Broceliande, 64
Bro Vrân, 51
Bron, 19, 27, 35, 40 f., 48, 50, 57, 95, 173, 175
Brown, A. C. L., 30, 34, 47, 160, 164, 170, 183
Bruce, J. D., 53, 55, 91 f., 108, 174, 176, 186
Brugger, E., 14, 184, 193
Brugh of Boyne, 8, 30
Brun de Gimel, 108
Brut (Welsh), 5-10, 44 f.
Brutus, 43
Buan, 98, 117, 121
Buchanan, Alice, 77
Buchedd Collen Sant, Life of St. Collen, 9, 139 f., 164
Byron, 1

Cadair Fronwen, 51
Cadiocus, 64
Cadnant, 12
Cador de Lis, 107 f.
Caeilte, 33, 142 f.
Caer, daughter of Ethal, 8 f.
Caer, *see* Kaer
Caer Saint, Caer Aber Saint, Caer Segeint, 2-5, 7, 9 f.
Caerleon, 1-3, 7, 10 f., 13, 160
Caernarvon, 2, 10, 15
Caernarvonshire, 124, 126
Caerwent, 3, 10 f.
Caesar, Julius, 141
Caesarius of Heisterbach, 70
Calan Mei, 81
Caleb Alfassam, 91

Calidon, 5
Caligula, 130
Cambenoyt, 47
Camlan, 106, 155
Caradoc of Lancarvan, 83 f., 166, 182 f., 191
Cardiff, 3
Cardiganshire, 126
Carduino, 14
Carl of Carlisle, 89 f., 191 f.
Carmarthen, 2 f., 7
Carmarthenshire, 100, 121, 138
Cassibelan, Cassibilan, 107
Castellum Puellarum, 16
Castle Gregory, 165
Castrum Arthuri, 17
Catania, 70
Cath Maige Tured, 25, 120, 162
Cath Palug, 196, 219
Cattle-raid of Cooley, 97, 117
Cercamon, 194 f.
Ceridwen, 148, 156
Chambers, E. K., 69, 87
Charlemagne, 189
Charles V, king of France, 90
Charrette, see Chevalier de la Charrette
Chastiel Bran, 42-45, 49 f.
Chester, 2, 42
Chevalier à l'Espée, 89 f.
Chevalier de la Charrette, 84, 93, 109, 111, 144, 167 f., 175 f., 182 f., 191
Child, F. J., 197
Chrétien de Troyes, 9, 13, 17, 22, 32, 50, 60, 64 f., 67, 72-74, 84, 91 f., 107, 109, 111, 113, 115, 138, 144 f., 159, 163, 166-8, 175 f., 182 f., 191
Christ, 22, 30, 54, 58 f., 145
Chronicle of Mont St. Michel, 180
Cnychwr, 161
Coel, 5 f.
Cohen, G., 127
Collen, 139, 143
Colloquy of the Ancients, Accalám na Senórach, 33, 137, 142
Columcille, Columba, 39, 169
Conan, 187
Conn, 27 f., 31 f., 36, 143
Connaught, 120
Connla, 137, 143
Constantine I, 2-4, 6, 18
Constantine II, 2-4, 18
Constantius, Constans, 2, 4 f., 15

General Index

Conte del Graal, 9, 11, 22, 28, 31–33, 91, 93 f., 107 f., 138, 159, 192 f.
Cook, A. B., 87
Corbenic, 19, 34, 41, 47 f., 50, 145
Corlenot, 47
Cormac, Bishop, 149
Cormac, son of Art, 32, 143, 156, 160
Cornwall, 11, 75, 141, 146, 182
Corvil, 161
Couronnement Louis, 115, 196 f.
Creiddylad, 83
Crimthann, 160
Crône, Diu, 79 f., 93, 94, n. 10, 144, 198
Cross, T. P., 116, 182, 197
Cruachan, 142
Cubert, 161
Cuch, 100
Cúchulainn, 34, 77 f., 85–87, 90, 97 f., 116–18, 123, 143, 160, 163
Cunedda, 3
Cúroí, 34, 77 f., 85, 90, 137 f.
Custennyn, 6
Cwellyn Lake, 121 f.
Cwn Annwn, 82
Cyffin, Roger, 51
Cynwyn, 51

Dafydd ap Gwilym, 80 f., 83, 140, 151
Dagda, 8, 33, 98, 120, 156, 159
Daire, 31
Dame du Lac, 112, 116
David, King of Scotland, 16, 50
David II, bishop of St. Davids, 65, 194 f.
Davies, E., 132
Dee, 43, 50 f.
Denbighshire, 51, 98, 119, 123
De Ortu Walwanii, 93, 198
Derbyshire, 67
Deschamps, P., 200
Descriptio Cambriae, 194
Diarmaid, 149
Didot Perceval, 36, 57, 91 ff., 118, 124, 173–5
Dinas Brân, 43, 48–51, 107
Dinasdaron, 107
Dingestow Brut, 5 f., 8 f.
Diwrnach, 153 f., 158, 161
Dodinel, 107
Donn, 142
Donwal, 43
Doon, 16
Draco Normannicus, 61, 64 f., 99

Dream of Maxen, 6–10, 13, 18
Dream of Oengus, 7–9
Dream of Rhonabwy, 96 f., 102, 131
Duglas, 107 f.
Dumbarton, 17
Dunwallo, 43
Dyfed, 36, 79, 100, 102 f., 153, 172 f.
Dynan (Ludlow), 42

Ebyr Henvelen, 151
Echtra Chormaic, 137
Echtra Conlai, 137
Edinburgh, 16
Edward I, 4, 15
Eger and Grime, 85, 94
Einion Wan, 146
Eithne, 30
Elen, 2, 7–10, 13, 18
Elene, 13 f.
Elfildis, 75
Eliodorus, 65, 67–69, 73
Elphin, 148
Elucidation, 193
Enlli, *see* Bardsey
Eochaid Mugmedon, 28
Epona, 129
Erec, 13, 64 f., 84, 159, 163, 166 f., 182
Erging, 6
Ériu, 27
Erris, 33
Escanor, 85, 115
Escanor, 115
Esclarmonde, 115
Espec, Walter, 187–90
Estoire del Saint Graal, 47, 54, 56, 58, 60
Estor, son of Ares, 115
Estorie des Engles, 11, 188
Estrildis, 75
Esyllt, 75
Étienne de Rouen, 61–65, 67, 73 f., 99
Etna, 70 f.
Eudaf, 6 f.
Evans, J. G., 132, 192
Evans, S., 44
Evrain, 12 f.
Ewias, 6
Exeter, 180

Fand, 137, 143
Faral, E., 74, 185, 189
Fata Morgana, 105
Fate of the Children of Turenn, 29–31
Fercos, 161

Fergus, 16 f.
Fergus, son of Dagda, 33
Ffyrdd Elen Luydauc, 8, 13
Figol, 26
Finn, 34, 143, 160
Firth of Forth, 11, 15
Fisher King, 32 f., 35, 39–41, 47 f., 50, 55–57, 59 f., 138, 173–5
FitzGilbert, Lady, 188 f.
Fled Bricrend, 77, 137, 163
Floriant, 118
Florie, 163
Flower, R., 162
Foerster, W., 179
Foster, I. Ll., 192
Fouke Fitz Warin, 42–50
Four Branches of the Mabinogi, 103 f., 173
Frankl, P., 199
Freymond, E., 196
Froissart, 17

Gadeon, 8, n. 32
Gaer, 13
Gaheres, 174
Gaimar, 10, 11, 187–90
Galaad, 22, 25, 26, 30, 36
Galagandreiz, 89
Galaphes, 47
Galatee, 106, 115
Galoche, 55, 57–59, 174–6
Galvagin, 36
Gardner, E. G., 179
Gareth, 94, n. 10
Gasozein, 78–81, 85, 87, 89, 94, n. 10
Gawain, 12, 25, 33, 34, 40, 41, 47, 50, 59, 77 ff., 84 f., 145, 184 f., 187, 193 f., 208–13
Gawain and the Green Knight, 20, 77 f., 100, 163, 216
Gaynor, *see* Guinevere
Geoffrey of Monmouth, 5–7, 10, 16, 43–45, 49 f., 58–60, 63, 74 f., 96, 105 f., 112, n. 24, 121, 129, 154 f., 159 f., 179–207, 213–20
Geomagog, 43 f., 50
Gerould, G. H., 198
Gervase of Tilbury, 50, 64, 67–71, 74
Gesta Regum Britanniae, 63 f., 73
Gherardino, 110
Gibbon, E., 1
Gibel, Gyber, 71, 125
Gildas, 5, 84, 183

Gilla Decair, 149
Gillamurus, 107
Gillor, 107 f.
Ginover, *see* Guinevere
Giraldus Cambrensis, 1, 2, 40, 64 f., 68 f., 73–75, 140, 165, 184, 188, 193–5
Glamorgan, 82
Glasfryn, 124–6
Glastonbury, 83 f., 111, n. 24, 139, 166, 182 f., 191
Gloucester, 111, n. 24, 147
Glyn Cuch, 100, 138
Gododdin, 160, 180
Gogledd, 45, 159
Gohars, 171–4
Gohors, 36
Goirre, 144 f., 167 f., 175 f.
Gomeret, 92, n. 5
Gorlois, 181
Gorsedd Frân, 51
Gougaud, L., 142
Graelent, 112, 116, 120, 126
Graham, A., 16
Graindor de Brie, 196
Grassholm, 146, 150–2, 160, 177
Gratian, 3, 4, 6
Grey of Macha, 116 f., 122
Grimm, J., 82, 127
Gringalet, 115
Griscom, A., 184
Gruffydd, W. J., 1, 34, 38, 59 f., 75, 132, 148, 153, 162, 173
Gualenses, 184
Guest, Charlotte, 156
Guillaume de Rennes, 63 f.
Guillaume le Clerc, 16
Guinevere, 84 f., 88, 93, 109, 115, 145, 182, 191
Guingambresil, 78, 85, 89
Guinglain, 12–14, 163
Guingomar, 65
Guiomar, 187
Guirres, 174
Gundebald, 111, 176
Gurgalain, 40
Gwair, 146. *See* Gweir
Gwales, 56, 59, 149–51, 160, 164
Gwalchmai, 146, n. 95, 184
Gweir, 38, 133 f., 146–8, 152 f., 170–4, 177
Gwenddolau, 40
Gwenddoleu ap Ceidio, 160
Gwlad yr Hav, 84, n. 32

General Index

Gwrach-y-Rhibyn, 123, 126
Gwrhyr, 147
Gwri, 35 f., 41, 174
Gwrnach, 145
Gwrvan, 173
Gwyddno Garanhir, 158
Gwynedd, 92, n. 5
Gwynn ap Nudd, 9, 83–85, 139 f., 143, 152, 177, 191
Gwythyr ap Greidyawl, 83

Haf, 81
Hafgan, Havgan, 79, 81, 87, 90, 100, 140
Harlech, 151
Hartland, E. S., 68, 141
Hector of Troy, 106, 115
Heinrich, G. A., 47
Heinrich von dem Türlin, see *Crône*
Helain the White, 25
Helen, daughter of Eudaf, 6 f.
Helena, mother of Constantine, 2, 4–6, 18
Helie, 11
Helinandus, 40
Hellekin, 88, 100
Henry I, 5, 42, 50
Henry II, 50, 61
Henry IV, emperor, 71
Henry of Huntingdon, 180, 187
Hercules, 75
Herefordshire, 6
Herla, 73, 165
Herman of Laon, 180–2
Hibbard, L. A., 142. See Loomis, L. H.
Historia Meriadoci, 93, 108, 111, 167, 176
Historia Regum Britanniae, 5 f., 45, 59, 179–81, 185–90, 192, 196 f.
Howells, W., 150
Howth, Hill of, 31
Hueil, 182, 191
Huet, G., 197
Hulbert, J. R., 90
Hull, E., 142
Hunbaut, 198
Huth Merlin, 108, 123
Hyde, D., 20
Hygwydd, 154

Iarlles y Fynnawn, 159
Imrám Máiledúin, 138, 164
Insula Pomorum, 75, 96, 177

Insula Vitrea, 166, 176, 182
Irain, 13
Isidore of Seville, 63, 74, 76
Isle de Voirre, 167
Isolt, 75
Itinerarium Cambriae, 65, 73
Ivain, 13, 96, 114, 119, 191, 218
Iweret, 112

Jackson, K. H., 31, 133
Jaufré, 125
Jenkins, T. A., 22
Jeu de la Feuillée, 88, 127
Jones, T. Gwynn, 81, 98
Joseph of Arimathea, 19, 22 f., 31, 41, 54–58, 168

Kaer Goludd, 136, 167
Kaer Loyw, 111, n. 24, 147
Kaer Pedryvan, 135 f., 154, 168
Kaer Rigor, 136, 165
Kaer Siddi, 38, 134, 147–9, 169–71, 177
Kaer Veddwit, 135, 164
Kaer Wydyr, 136, 166 f.
Kei, 147, 191
Kempe, D., 47
Ker, W. P., 88
Keu, 145
King Arthur and King Cornwall, 198
Kittredge, G. L., 77, 88, 113, 197
Kulhwch, 153, 158
Kulhwch and Olwen, 20, 46, 83, 99, 114, 132, 140, 147, 153, 174, 191 f.
Kundry, 28
Kynan Meiriadauc, 6–8
Kynkenadon, 14

La Villemarque, H. de, 23
Lady of the Lake, 17
Laeg, 143
Laegaire mac Crimthann, 143
Lai de l'Espine, 94
Lai du Cor, 11
Lancelot, 21, 25–30, 32 f., 35, 40, 86, 143, 162 f., 218
Lancien, 11
Langlois, E., 196
Lanval, 113
Lanzelet, 112, 114
Lanzelet, 13, 89, 111 f., 144
Laquis, 163
Laudine, 17

Launfal, 112–17, 120, 126
Layamon, 43
Le Braz, A., 142
Lehmacher, G., 142
Levi, E., 195
Lewis, C. S., 89
Lia Fáil, 27, 36
Líban, 137
Libeaus Desconus, 13 f.
Liber Floridus, 180
Life of St. Collen, 9. See *Buchedd*
Lindsay, D., 17
Lionel, 25
Llanbeblig, 4
Llandovery, 13
Llanferres, 120
Llangollen, 43
Llenlleawc, 154, 161 f., 218
Lloch, 161
Lloyd-Jones, J., 133, 167
Lluber, 161
Lludd, 147, 161
Llwch, 49, 76, 135, 161 f., 174, 177
Llwyd, 103
Llyn Brân, 51
Llyn y Fan Fach, 121 f.
Llŷr, 147, 148 f., 151, 157, 161
Llywarch ap Llywelyn, 146
Loch, 118
Loch Rask, 123
Loenois, 15
Logres, 31, 53, 55 f.
Lombardy, 113
London, 6 f., 69
Longinus, Lance of, 30, 54, 58
Loomis, L. H., 116, 197. See Hibbard
Lot, F., 5, 74, 194
Lot, King, 16
Loth, King, 163, 218
Loth, J., 150
Lothian, 15 f.
Luchta, 26
Lucius Hiberus, 75 f., 163
Ludlow, 42
Lugaid Men, 143
Lugh, 21, 25–30, 32 f., 35, 40, 86, 143, 162 f.
Lundy, 146, 177
Luned, 159
Lydney, 140

Mabinogion, 23 f., 35 f., 41, 96, 104
Mabon, 12–14, 51, 99, 114, 119, 147
Mabonagrain, 13
Mabuz, 114
MacCulloch, J. A., 142
Macha, 116–20, 122, 126, 130
Maeldúin, 39, 143, 170
Mag Mell, 137, 148, 177
Maheloas, 84, 166 f., 182
Mâle, E., 200
Malehot, Lady of, 110
Malory, T., 14 f., 17, 24, 30 f., 93, 163
Manannán, 21, 30–32, 35, 137, 143, 149, 152, 157, 159, 177
Manawydan, 36, 38 f., 51, 103, 149–52, 157, 173, 177
Manawydan, 36, 102, 138, 169 f., 172 f.
Manessier, 32
Mannhardt, 87
Map, Walter, 69, 73, 120, 140, 165, 183
Marche, Chastel de la, 48
Mari Morgan, 125
Marie de France, 113, 190
Marne, 99, 128
Marrion, 126
Martin, C., 199
Martin, E., 47
Math Vab Mathonwy, 133, 162
Mathgen, 26
Matilda, Empress, 5
Matres, 127–30
Matrona, 99, 101, 119, 124, 127–30
Matthew of Westminster, 3
Maury, A., 127
Maxen, 6–8, 10
Maxentius, 6
Maximianus, 6 f.
Maximus, 2, 4, 18
Mayo, 33
Meleagant, 54, 84 f., 111, 167, 175 f., 182
Melrose, 16
Melvas, 84, 176, 182, 219
Menai Strait, 2
Meraugis de Portlesguez, 198
Meriadoc, 111
Merlin, 5, 29, 185, 217
Messina, 105
Meyer, K., 142
Mider, 39, 143, 164
Milesius, 143, 166
Milford Haven, 150
Milton, J., 61, 140
Modena, 179, 198–214
Modred, 64, 71, 181 f., 217

General Index

Modron, 13, 88, 96–102, 114, 199–24, 126 f.
Moel Famau, 120
Molène, 125
Mont Dolerous, 16
Moray, 16
Morddwyd Tyllon, 148
Mordrain, 91
Morey, C. R., 200
Morfudd, 98, 119
Morgain la Fée, 62, 72, 76, 88 f., 93, 96 f., 99–101, 105–30, 154 f., 164, 177
Morgan, 124–6
Morgan Mwynvawr, 160
Morois, 16
Moronoe, 126
Morrígan, 97 f., 102, 117–20, 123 f., 126 f., 130
Morris-Jones, J., 38, 137, 148
Mount, St. Michael's, 11
Moytura, 29
Munster, 8, 34
Myrddin, 160, 166

Nabon, 13
Nant yr Ellyllon, 52
Nascien, 91
Nennius, 3–5, 10, 38, 76, 131 f., 165, 175 f., 179 f., 192
Nera, 143
Newstead, H., 53, 93, 144, 159
Nitze, W. A., 22, 34, 45, 47, 86 f., 142
Northumbria, 159
Norway, 54 f., 58 f.
Nuada, 25 f.
Nutt, A., 23, 34, 47, 80, 95, 142

Octavius, 6
Odgar, 153 f.
O'Donnell, M., 39
Ogma, 25
Oléron, 113
Olwen, 153, 192
Orwen, 108
Oswestry, 42 f.
Otranto, 74
Otway, C., 33
Ouessant, 125
Owain, son of Urien, 96–98, 114, 119
Owen, G., 150
Owen, H., 150

Padua, 184
Panofsky, E., 200

Pant-y-Meddygon, 121
Panthesilée, 106
Paris, 198
Parry, J. J., 5
Parzival, 60
Paton, L. A., 97, 124
Patrick, St., 21, 142
Peak Castle, 67
Peblig, St., 10
Pedeir Keinc y Mabinogi, 132
Pèlerinage Charlemagne, 197 f.
Pellam, 29
Pellehan, 91
Pelles, 48
Pembrokeshire, 36, 56, 100, 138, 149
Pennington, W., 32
Penthièvre, 187
Perceval, Perlesvaus, 11, 22 f., 26–28, 31–37, 39, 50, 88, 95–97, 101, 119, 124, 168–74, 218
Perceval's sister, 23, 30, 34
Percy Folio, 113
Peredur, 28, 40, 60, 129
Peredur, 35
Perinis, 11
Perlesvaus, 22, 24, 37, 39, 44–47, 49, 59, 132, 167–76
Peter of Blois, 187
Peverel, Payn, 44, 47, 49 f.
Peverell, William, 67
Pilate, 54
Pisear, 29
Plummer, C., 21
Poitiers, Poitou, count of, 193–5
Pomponius Mela, 75, 129, 155
Porter, A. K., 179, 199
Preiddeu Annwn, 60, 131–78
Procopius, 141, 144, 147
Prophecies of Merlin, 96
Prophetia Merlini, 185
Prophetic Ecstasy of the Phantom, 27
Prose Lancelot, 198
Prose Tristan, 13
Pryderi, 35–39, 133 f., 149, 151–3, 169, 172–4, 177
Prydwen, 134, 136, 140, 153 f., 177
Pwyll, 39, 79, 84, 100 f., 133, 138, 152 f., 177
Pwyll, 79, 84 f., 88, 100–2, 138–40, 146, 164

Queen Mary's Psalter, 46
Queste del Saint Graal, 24, 40, 59

General Index

Radnor, 82
Rajna, P., 179
Red Sea, 61
Reinhard, J. R., 197
Remy, A., 22
Renaud de Beaujeu, 11–15
Rhiannon, 101 f.
Rhyd y Gyfarthfa, 98
Rhydderch, 40, 46, 159 f., 175
Rhys, J., 8, 23, 38, 47, 69, 122, 132, 145 f., 148, 150, 153, 164, 167
Richmond, 187–9
Ridcaradoch, 181
Rieu, 128
Rievaulx, 186, 188
Rigomer, Merveilles de, 192, 198
Rigru, 31
Ritona, 128
Roach, W., 94
Robert of Gloucester, 188
Robinson, F. N., 102, 127 f., 133
Rochat, A., 11, 15
Rodarchus, 5. *See* Rhydderch
Roland of Dinan, 61, 65
Roman de Troie, 106, 108, 110, 115
Rome, 1, 6 f.
Ruald, 187
Rusticien de Pise, 115

Sarn Elen, 2, 13
Saxl, F., 200
Schoepperle, Gertrude, 93, 182
Scott, Walter, 17
Second Battle of Moytura, 25, 120, 162
Segontium, 2–5, 7, 15
Seint, 2, 4, 7, 9, 12
Sena, 129
Serglige Conculaind, 137
Sgilti, 161
Sicily, 70–74
Sinadon, Sinaudon, 11 f., 14, 17
Sir Lambewell, 113
Sir Landeval, 113
Sir Orfeo, 66 n. 30
Slíab Mis, 138
Snaudon, Snauedun, 10 f., 15
Snowdon, 2, 10, 15
Solinus, 75
Sone de Nausay, 53–60, 174–6
Sovereignty of Erin, 28
Spenser, E., 1
Spoils of Annwn, 60
Stirling, 17

Táin Bó Regamna, 118
Taliesin, 131, 148–50, 153–5, 160, 177
Tara, 25, 27, 32, 156
Tatlock, J. S. P., 61–64, 74, 76, 179 ff.
Taylor, A., 82
Tech Duinn, 144
Thomas, author of *Tristan*, 190
Tintagel, 11
Tír Már, 164
Tír na mBeo, 148
Tír na nÓg, 148
Tír Tairngire, 137, 148
Tochmarc Étaíne, 164
Tomen-y-Mur, 13
Tortain, 192
Trimontium, 16
Tristan, 15 f., 187, 194
Triumphs of Turlough, 123
Tudur of Llangollen, 52
Tudwal Tudclud, 160
Turner, S., 131
Twrch Trwyth, 191
Ty Wydyr, 166
Tyrnoc, 157–9

Ulrich v. Zatzikhoven, 89, 111, 164
Urbain, 95, 98, 100–2
Urganda, 108
Urien, 98 f., 108, 114, 119–21, 126

Vendryes, J., 192
Vengeance Raguidel, 13
Venturi, A., 199
Vespasian, 54
Vita Gildae, 83, 176, 182 f.
Vita Merlini, 5, 96, 105 f., 129, 154, 196
Von Vitzthum, G., 199
Vulgate Lancelot, 47, 50, 110, 112, 127, 145, 198

Wace, 44, 64, 107, 196, 217
Wagner, Richard, 34
Walwanus, Walwen, 184
Warren, F. M., 196
Wauchier de Denain, 193
Wayland, 5
Webster, K. G. T., 197
Weinberg, B., 45
Weston, J. L., 53, 94–96
White Book of Rhydderch, 192
Whittington, 42
Wiligelmus, sculptor, 199 f.
William VII of Poitou, 195

General Index

William VIII of Poitou, 195
William of Newburgh, 50
William of Malmesbury, 65, 183–5, 187, 190
William of Worcester, 17
William the Conqueror, 42, 44, 50
William the Lion, 50
Williams, Ifor, 4, 131, 133, 152, 165
Williams, R., 132
Windisch, E., 128

Yeats, W. B., 31
Ynisgutrin, 182
Ynys Avallach, 154 f.
Ynys Wair, 150
Yorkshire, 187–90
Yspaddaden, 145, 192
Yvain, *see* Ivain

Zenker, R., 34, 97
Zimmer, H., 184

INDEX OF SUBJECTS

Abduction of woman, 82–85, 93, 111, 176, 182, 191, 207
Anniversary combat, 77–86, 100, 103
Art, illustrations in, 72–74, 198–204, 209 f.

Beheading test, 78, 89, 92 f.
Birds, fays in form of, 95–97, 105 f., 117–19, 122
Breton hope, 61 f., 179, 183, 185
Brito, meaning of, 181, 184 f.
Bull, 44–46, 50

Cauldron, 29, 39, 135, 148, 151, 153 f., 156–9, 172, 177
Cave, *see* Hollow hill
Chain of gold, 37 f., 169 f.
Chess, 7, 40, 160
Chough, 61
Coins, 3 f.
Cup, 5, 27, 55, 157

Dead, land of, 141–5
Door, strong, 38, 136, 164
Dream-maiden, 7–9
Dwarfs, 64–67, 193

Faery mistress, 95, 98, 100–3, 110–23, 125, 129
Fairies, 52, 120, 150
Fisher King, 35, 41, 48, 50, 53, 55–57, 59, 173–6
Ford combat, 78–80, 83, 85 f., 93–104
Ford, Washer of, 98, 119 f., 123
Fountain, 37 f., 149, 168 f., 172, 174 f., 177

Giant, 44, 47 f., 54, 191
Girdle, 77 f., 89
Glass fortress, tower, or isle, 38, 84, 136, 160 f., 165–9, 175–7, 182
Goat, 72–74
Grail, 19–25, 27 f., 32, 34, 40, 48, 54 f., 58–60, 71, 174–6
Green Knight, 87

Haunted castle, 12–14, 44, 47–49
Head of Brân, 56, 151 f.
Healer, fay as, 62, 114, 121, 129, 154 f.

Hollow hill, 61, 69–73, 137, 142
Holly, 87
Horn, drinking, 31, 40 f., 45–50, 58, 158, 175
Horse, marvellous, 101, 106, 108–17, 122, 129

Initial, omission of, 108
Island castle, 33, 37–39, 55–57, 148 f., 165 f., 168, 173–5
Isle of Maidens, 62, 106, 129, 154–6, 177

Lamentation in Grail Castle, 60, 134, 146 f., 151 n., 170–2, 177
Lance, *see* Spear
Loathly Damsel, 28, 34, 54

Maimed King, 35, 53, 55, 57, 61, 71, 91, 93
Marriage with evil woman, 31, 55, 59
May Day, 81, 83, 86
Mice, fays in form of, 103
Misinterpretation, 38, 40 f., 44–50, 58, 84, 163, 169

Pentangle, 77, 85

Question test, 33 f.

Raven, 51, 61, 96 f.
Revolving castle, 137, 164
Robbery from fairyland, 66, 68 f.
Roman ruins, 1–18
Rome, emperors of, 2–9
Round Table, 11, 17, 24 f.
Ruinous town, 12, 42 f., 51

Saints' lives, 83 f., 166, 169 f., 176, 182 f., 214–16
Seasonal combat, *see* Anniversary combat
Ship, enchanted, 30, 54
Siege Perilous, 26–28, 31, 34, 36, 172 f.
Silent sentinel, 136, 165–9
Spear, Bleeding, 28–30, 32, 34, 54 f., 58, 60, 174
Stone, testing, 25–27

Index of Subjects

Subterranean fairyland, 62–73, 137, 140, 144, 165, 177
Summer, land of, 84, 111 f., 166 f., 182
Summer personified, 79–81
Sun-god, 86, 137
Survival, Arthur's, 61 ff.
Sword, 5, 32–34, 40, 46, 55, 135, 154, 162, 174–6

Taboo, 116, 120–2, 125 f.
Temptation by woman, 80, 85, 89, 108–10, 115, 118, 129
Thirteen seated at table, 59
Thorn, 87, 95, 97, 118 f.
Treasure, buried, 44, 49
Trio of fays, 117 f., 121, 127–9

Variant versions, 50, 57, 59 f., 78

Waking after night in enchanted castle, 32, 34
Waste Land, 26 f., 29, 31, 36, 53, 56 f. 71, 102, 172–4, 177
Water fay, 99, 103 f., 116, 120–8. *See* Ford, Washer of
Wild Hunt, 61, 71 f., 82 f., 88, 100
Winter personified, 81–83, 87 f., 100
Wound, 35, 53, 55–57, 172. *See* Maimed King

Youth, preservation of, 35, 37–39, 59, 148-50, 152, 155, 157, 160, 168 f.

PRINTED IN
GREAT BRITAIN
AT THE
UNIVERSITY PRESS
OXFORD
BY
CHARLES BATEY
PRINTER
TO THE
UNIVERSITY